Reading the Modern European Novel Since 1900

READING THE NOVEL

General Editor: Daniel R. Schwarz

The aim of this series is to provide substantive critical introductions to Reading Novels in the British, Irish, American, and European traditions.

Published

Reading the Modern European Novel Since 1900

A Critical Study of Major Fiction from Proust's *Swann's Way* to Ferrante's Neapolitan Tetralogy

Daniel R. Schwarz

WILEY Blackwell

This edition first published 2018
© 2018 John Wiley & Sons Ltd

The right of Daniel R. Schwarz to be identified as the author of this work has been asserted in accordance with law.

Registered Offices
John Wiley & Sons, Inc., 111 River Street, Hoboken, NJ 07030, USA
John Wiley & Sons Ltd, The Atrium, Southern Gate, Chichester, West Sussex, PO19 8SQ, UK

Editorial Office
9600 Garsington Road, Oxford, OX4 2DQ, UK

For details of our global editorial offices, customer services, and more information about Wiley products visit us at www.wiley.com.

Wiley also publishes its books in a variety of electronic formats and by print-on-demand. Some content that appears in standard print versions of this book may not be available in other formats.

Library of Congress Cataloging-in-Publication Data

Names: Schwarz, Daniel R. author.
Title: Reading the modern European novel since 1900 : a critical study of major fiction from Proust's Swann's way to Ferrante's Neapolitan tetralogy / by Daniel R. Schwarz, Cornell University.
Description: First edition. | Hoboken, NJ : John Wiley & Sons, 2018. | Includes bibliographical references and index. |
Identifiers: LCCN 2017056768 (print) | LCCN 2017059380 (ebook) | ISBN 9781118680667 (pdf) | ISBN 9781118693414 (epub) | ISBN 9781118680681 (cloth)
Subjects: LCSH: European fiction–20th century–History and criticism. | European fiction–21st century–History and criticism.
Classification: LCC PN3503 (ebook) | LCC PN3503 .S33 2018 (print) | DDC 809.3/04–dc23
LC record available at https://lccn.loc.gov/2017056768

Cover image: © Erich Lessing / Art Resource, NY
Cover design by Wiley

Set in 10/12.5pt Minion by SPi Global, Pondicherry, India

10   9   8   7   6   5   4   3   2   1

With love for my wife Marcia Jacobson, with whom I share my life; with appreciation and respect for my Cornell students, who have been teaching me the past fifty years.

Contents

Contents

Acknowledgments

Teaching Cornell students at every level from freshmen to graduate students over the past 50 years has helped me to refine my understanding of how novels work and what they say. Much of the credit for whatever I accomplish as a scholar-critic goes to the intellectual stimulation provided by my students as well as my Cornell colleagues, most notably my close friend Laura Brown.

My wife, Marcia Jacobson, to whom I owe my greatest debt, has read every page of the manuscript at least three times and given me countless valuable insights about the novels I discuss and the words I have written. It is impossible to overstate my debt to her.

My longtime Cornell friend and colleague Brett de Bary helped me understand translation theory and recommended the texts I should read on that subject.

It gives me great pleasure to thank Pauline Shongov, a gifted Cornell Presidential Research Scholar with whom I have worked for five years as she pursued her ambitious dual degree program. She has strongly contributed to the research as well as played an important role in editing, proofreading, and indexing.

I am grateful for the strong support of Wiley-Blackwell, with whom I have had a productive professional relationship for many years. I am grateful for the current leadership of Catriona King and the past leadership of Emma Bennett and Rebecca Harkin, the editorial assistance of Joanna Pyke and Brigitte Lee Messenger, and the supervisory roles of Manish Luthra and Anandan Bommen.

Finally, I wish to acknowledge the continued support of the Cornell English Department leadership and staff, and in particular Roger Gilbert and Vicky Brevetti.

Daniel R. Schwarz
Cornell University
Ithaca, New York
Dec. 15, 2017

Also by Daniel R. Schwarz

How to Succeed in College and Beyond (2016)

Reading the European Novel to 1900 (2014)

Endtimes: Crises and Turmoil at the New York Times (2012; new revised paperback edition 2014)

In Defense of Reading: Teaching Literature in the Twenty-First Century (2008)

Reading the Modern British and Irish Novel 1890–1930 (2005)

Broadway Boogie Woogie: Damon Runyon and the Making of New York City Culture (2003)

Rereading Conrad (2001)

Imagining the Holocaust (1999; revised edition 2000)

Reconfiguring Modernism: Explorations in the Relationship between Modern Art and Modern Literature (1997)

Narrative and Representation in the Poetry of Wallace Stevens: "A Tune Beyond Us, Yet Ourselves" (1993)

The Case for a Humanistic Poetics (1991)

The Transformation of the English Novel, 1890–1930: Studies in Hardy, Conrad, Joyce, Lawrence, Forster, and Woolf (1989; revised edition 1995)

Reading Joyce's "Ulysses" (1987; centenary edition 2004)

The Humanistic Heritage: Critical Theories of the English Novel from James to Hillis Miller (1986; revised edition 1989)

Conrad: The Later Fiction (1982)

Conrad: "Almayer's Folly" to "Under Western Eyes" (1980)

Disraeli's Fiction (1979)

As Editor

Damon Runyon: Guys and Dolls and Other Writings (2008)
The Early Novels of Benjamin Disraeli, 6 volumes (consulting editor, 2004)
Conrad's "The Secret Sharer" (Bedford Case Studies in Contemporary Criticism, 1997)
Joyce's "The Dead" (Bedford Case Studies in Contemporary Criticism, 1994)
Narrative and Culture (with Janice Carlisle, 1994)

Chapter 1

Introduction:
The Novel After 1900

"What we write about fiction is never an objective response to a text; it is always part of a bigger mythmaking – the story we are telling ourselves about ourselves."

Jeanette Winterson[1]

Basic Premises

As with my past books about literature, I am writing this book to share the joy of reading the texts I have chosen. I have chosen works that demand my attention and create a desire – indeed, a need – for me to understand them, sometimes because of their thematic focus, sometimes for their experimental techniques, and usually for a combination of both. All of the works I discuss demonstrate how a particular historical moment shaped the behavior and direction of a nation or significant community, although some of the works are more historically inflected than others. Among my criteria for inclusion in this volume: (1) I revel in rereading and rereading the text; (2) when I am not reading that text, I am thinking about my reading experience; when I awake, the issues generated by the text sometimes displace the more urgent issues of life; (3) I sometimes dream about the text's characters and events; (4) on each rereading and rethinking, I discover new aspects of the text's complexity, subtlety, and originality.

While any inclusive generalizations risk the danger of being reductive, we can say that the novel after 1900 is often experimental in form and challenges our expectations of continuity and consistency. These novels ask the reader to play a significant role in perceiving formal unity and in interpreting idiosyncratic, irrational, and seemingly inexplicable behavior. David Lodge has argued that

Reading the Modern European Novel Since 1900: A Critical Study of Major Fiction from Proust's Swann's Way *to Ferrante's Neapolitan Tetralogy*, First Edition. Daniel R. Schwarz.
© 2018 John Wiley & Sons Ltd. Published 2018 by John Wiley & Sons Ltd.

"The modernist novel is generally characterized by a radical rearrangement of the spatial-temporal unity of the narrative line" (Lodge, "Milan Kundera, and the Idea of the Author in Modern Criticism," 141).[2] What he means is that the narrative of what happened next has given way to radical rearrangements of time and space, unexpected fissures, surprising returns to events in the past, inexplicable accidents, deviations from realism, and radical metaphors. More often than in the past the telling (discourse) of the story is as much or more the author's focal point as the events of the story; hence, in many cases, the telling becomes the center of the reader's experience. What I will be stressing is that readers must respond to the uncanny and unimaginable in both form and content.

What is Modernism?

I am using the term Modernism to refer to the period beginning in the late nineteenth century. Modernism is a response to cultural crisis. By the 1880s we have Nietzsche's *Gay Science* (1882–1887) with his contention that God is Dead as well as Krafft-Ebing's revolutionary texts on sexuality; we also have the beginnings of modern physics in the work of J. J. Thomson. All challenged absolutist theories of truth.

Let us recall that Darwin's *Origin of Species* appeared in 1859 and *Essays and Reviews* (edited by John William Parker) which in 1860 questioned the Bible as revealed history; in the period from 1865 to 1870, Karl Marx began to publish *Das Kapital*, Alfred Nobel invented dynamite, and Freud opened the doors of psychopathology in the 1880s. Otto von Bismarck and Benjamin Disraeli dominated Europe, and colonialism expanded its reach.

In its response to difficult circumstances Modernism is an ideology of *possibility* and *hope*. But paradoxically Modernism is also an ideology of *despair* in its response to excessive faith in industrialism, urbanization, so-called technological progress, and to the Great War of 1914 to 1918 which was believed to be the War to End All Wars.

As we shall see, Modernism goes beyond previous cultures in engaging otherness and questioning Western values. As James Clifford notes, in 1900 "'Culture' referred to a single evolutionary process." He articulates an important aspect of Modernism:

. . . .

The European bourgeois ideal of autonomous individuality was widely believed to be the natural outcome of a long development, a process that, although threatened by various disruptions, was assumed to be the basic, progressive movement of humanity. By the turn of the century, however, evolutionist confidence began

2

to falter, and a new ethnographic conception of culture became possible. The word began to be used in the plural, suggesting a world of separate, distinctive, and equally meaningful ways of life. The ideal of an autonomous, cultivated subject could appear as a local project, not a *telos* for all humankind. (Clifford, *The Predicament of Culture*, 92–93)[3]

. . . .

Modernism contains the aspirations and idealism of nineteenth-century high culture and the prosaic world of nineteenth-century city life; both are colored by an ironic and self-conscious awareness of limitation. Often convictions are framed by an ironic stand indicating an awareness of the difficulty of fulfilling possibility. Prior to modernist questioning, the possibility of a homogeneous European culture existed. As John Elderfield puts it, "history was not always thought to be quite possibly a species of fiction but once comprised a form of order" (Elderfield, *Henri Matisse*, 203).[4]

We must not look for reductive consistency in our narrative of Modernism but for pluralistic and even contradictory explanations. Modernism depends on the interpretive intelligence of a reader's perspective. We need to not only look at assumptions from a modern point of view that is open to destabilizing shibboleths, but we also need to try to understand the world of modern authors and painters from a perspective that takes account of how they intervene, intersect, transform, and qualify the culture of which they are a part.

Modernism emphasizes that we lack a coherent identity and seeks techniques to express this idea. Stressing how each of us is changing every moment, Henri Bergson wrote in *Creative Evolution*:

. . . .

Duration is the continuous progress of the past which gnaws into the future and which swells as it advances. … The piling up of the past upon the past goes on without relaxation. In reality, the past is preserved by itself, automatically. In its entirety, probably, it follows us at every instant; all that we have felt, thought, and willed from our earliest infancy is there, leaning over the present which is about to join it, pressing against the portals of consciousness that would fain leave it outside. (Ellmann and Feidelson, Jr., *The Modern Tradition*, 725)[5]

. . . .

Bergson continues: "What are we in fact, what is our character, if not the condensation of the history we have lived from our birth?" (ibid., 725). Note the parallel to Mikhail Bakhtin's concept that when each of us speaks or writes, our prior systems of language voluntarily and involuntarily manifest themselves in a heteroglossic voice.

We now accept that, given the ever-changing nature of self, each of us has multiple selves and points of view. That shared understanding that we lack one coherent self is a cause of the complex dramatized consciousness of the narrators in Proust's *Swann's Way*, Grass's *The Tin Drum*, Ferrante's Neapolitan tetralogy as well as the multiple narrative perspectives of Pamuk in *My Name is Red* and Kundera in *The Unbearable Lightness of Being*. Is there not a continuity between Oscar Wilde's concept of transcending the self by lying and Henri Bergson's of duration? Both seek to transform the tick-tock of daily life's passing time – what the Greeks called *chronos* – into significant time or *kairos*.

In "Tradition and the Individual Talent," T. S. Eliot affirmed that literary tradition meant writing with an historical sense which

. . . .

compels a man to write not merely with his own generation in his bones, but with a feeling that the whole of the literature of Europe from Homer and within it the literature of his own country has a simultaneous existence and composes a simultaneous order. … No poet, no artist of any art, has his complete meaning alone. His significance, his appreciation is the appreciation of his relation to the dead poets and artists. You cannot value him alone; you must set him, for contrast and comparison, among the dead. I mean this as a principle of aesthetic, not merely historical, criticism. (Eliot, *Selected Essays*, 4)[6]

. . . .

Modernism is inclusive, containing both the aestheticism and complexity of high culture, the straightforwardness and earthiness of working-class culture, and, like its successor Post-Modernism, an ironic awareness of its own self-consciousness. Just as writers like Zola and Grass not only include the urban working class, agrarian workers, and miners but also focus on the lives and aspirations of these people, modernist painters focus on the vernacular in painting – Cézanne's card players, Degas's laundresses, and Picasso's prostitutes, café life, and circus performers. Yet writers such as Pamuk and Kundera also believed in the power of art and in the artist as visionary prophet.

The Role of History in Shaping Fiction

Although I was trained as a formalist focusing on the fictional ontology of literary works, I have become more and more interested in how art, and specifically literature, is a function of culture. The common thread in my work from my early books on Disraeli, Conrad, and Joyce to my studies of New York City between the wars (*Broadway Boogie Woogie: Damon Runyon and the Making of New York City Culture*) and the *New York Times* (*Endtimes? Crises and Turmoil at the*

New York Times) is an effort to balance formal analyses with historical knowledge, expressed by my mantra: "Always the text; always historicize."

Fictional texts are windows not only into the minds of authors but also into the period in which they were written. I have come to think history is always present whether an author is aware of it or not. Thus the historical dimension of a literary text is not always volitional on the part of an author. Certainly *Swann's Way*, once considered the paradigmatic novel of manners with a strong personal inflection, reflects an historical and cultural moment in France and Europe. The same can be said of *Mrs Dalloway* and *To the Lighthouse*, once considered the ultimate hermetic novels of manners, but which on closer inspection make us realize that World War I hovers over both texts.

I begin with two texts published before World War I, *Death in Venice* (1912) and *Swann's Way* (1913). I include one written during World War I, Kafka's *Metamorphosis* (1915), and one written during World War II, Camus's *The Stranger* (1942). Most of my selected novels appeared after World War II: Camus's *The Plague* (1947), Lampedusa's *The Leopard* (1958), Grass's *The Tin Drum* (1959), Bassani's *The Garden of the Finzi-Continis* (1962), Kertész's *Fatelessness* (1975), and a few on the cusp of the twenty-first century – Saramago's *The History of the Siege of Lisbon* (1989), Pamuk's *My Name is Red* (1998) – with Müller's *The Hunger Angel* (2009) and Ferrante's Neapolitan tetralogy (2012–2015) appearing in the twenty-first century.

Certainly several of our novels, notably Saramago's *The History of the Siege of Lisbon*, Pamuk's *My Name is Red*, and Müller's *The Hunger Angel*, have Post-Modernist components. To be sure, many other of our texts also have aspects of the skepticism, irony, resistance to orderly and logical explanations, doubts about the efficacy of language, and structural and thematic discontinuity which we associate with Post-Modernism. This is another way of saying that Modernism not only set the stage for Post-Modernism but also that they have vast similarities and that a dotted rather than a straight line divides them.

The two World Wars and the Holocaust as well as the Cold War between the West and the USSR and the threat of nuclear war loom large in any study of the fiction of this period. My readings will place the texts in the context of what we know about authors' personal experiences and the world to which they are responding. Bassani, Kertész, Grass, and Müller focus on World War II and its effects, with Bassani and Kertész explicitly addressing the Holocaust. We cannot read Camus without knowing about his life in colonial Algeria and his role in the French Resistance. Even novels which seem to focus on remote periods such as Saramago's *The History of the Siege of Lisbon* and Pamuk's *My Name is Red* address major historical transitions and severe cultural clashes, especially between Western Eurocentric and Islamic values.

Not every reader notices the same historical nuances and contexts, in part because we bring different degrees of historical knowledge to our reading, but we cannot ignore the strong historical pressure of twentieth-century European history on events in *The Unbearable Lightness of Being, The Leopard, The Tin Drum, Fatelessness, The Garden of the Finzi-Continis, The Hunger Angel,* and Ferrante's Neapolitan tetralogy, and indeed on most of the novels I discuss in this study.

The problem is when and how much to focus on historical contexts without straying too far from texts. To take an extreme example, the meaning of Holocaust texts such as Elie Wiesel's *Night* or Primo Levi's *Survival in Auschwitz* depends far more on historical knowledge than the poems of Wallace Stevens or the fiction of Proust, although for Proust, knowledge of his biography is more essential than for Stevens. Our knowing something about Joyce's life and Irish history from 1880 to 1922 is far more important in reading *Portrait of an Artist* and *Ulysses* than our knowing about Stevens's life when reading his collected poems, although even there knowledge of his biography and some sense of American history help.

Claire Messud has insightfully described the balance in major fiction between form and ideas:

. . . .

> The novel form, capacious and elastic as it is, nevertheless requires that ideas and emotions – all abstractions, really – be pressed and transformed, passed through the fine sieve of the material world and made manifest in action, conversation, and concrete detail. Fiction is created out of T-shirts and tomato plants, oven fries, chalk dust and rainfall, out of snarky exchanges and subtle glances. Constructing a world out of these apparently random bits – "the nearest thing to life," as George Eliot put it – is a matter of meticulous imagining and careful craft. Making this fictional world come alive is a matter, as Martha Graham put it, of the life force. … [F]iction is like dance (or jazz music) in its tension between freedom and constraint: eventually, choreography must assert control to effectuate a satisfying conclusion. (Messud, "The Dancer & the Dance," 6, 8)[7]

. . . .

What is missing from Messud's observation is the role of history which is much messier to discuss than form but nevertheless essential to our understanding. In this study, I am going to show the relevance of historical contexts to close reading and how close reading, rather than conflicting with historicism, actually complements it. This is not to argue that we should all read similarly; for some readers, historical contexts and biographical knowledge will be less important than for others. How we respond to a literary text is a function of who we are at the time we read and reread.

The inventiveness and originality of the novels I discuss in this volume speak to the importance of both individual imagination and historical context. These novelists understand the role of historical forces as well as the decisions humans need to make to respond to conditions they did not create. Often existential decisions required by specific historical conditions – in the case of Kertész's *Fatelessness* and much of Bassani's Ferrara fiction, the Holocaust – determine an individual's fate. Historiography, albeit fictional, shapes the existential decisions made by characters in Camus's *The Plague* and Lampedusa's *The Leopard*. In these novels, the narrative drama and thematic focus are on how characters respond to events beyond their control. Even in a text which once was thought to barely evoke historical forces like Kafka's *Metamorphosis*, we realize that Gregor is the victim of a capitalistic system where money undermines family and community life. Notwithstanding striking examples in post-1900 Europe of autocracy and its effects, individual lives lived do not conform to the plans and rules of one person and his cohorts. That resistance – in deeds and imagination – is very much part of the fiction I will be discussing.

Another strand of historicism is the interaction between art and literature. Developing strategies presented in depth in my *Reconfiguring Modernism: Explorations in the Relationship between Modern Art and Modern Literature*, I will be discussing influences, parallels, and formal experiments shared by visual artists, especially painters, and novelists. I shall relate Cubism and Futurism, among other movements, to the novels I discuss.

Human Choices

We need to be wary of what Isaiah Berlin calls historical inevitability – in a 1953 lecture of that title – namely the idea that forces rather than humans shape and determine history. This was of course Marx's idea. The alternative that human choices – with all their inconsistencies, obsessions, and irrationality – play an important role need not be restricted to the Great Man or Woman but can take the form of a group of individuals (perhaps anonymous, perhaps known) determining historical direction. In modern times, the 1989 Tiananmen Square uprising was such an event.

As I have mentioned, by the end of the nineteenth century, Darwin, Marx, Freud, and Nietzsche, among many others, were challenging accepted truths about history, nature, and humankind. In response to new ways of thinking, twenty- and twenty-first-century writers often use their fiction to explore and define their own values, psyches, and ideas about the purpose of literature. The result is a polyphonic response in which authors struggle to find meaning in an amoral cosmos and foreground that quest in their narratives. In the novels

I will be discussing, a recurring theme is how do we respond to a world in historical turmoil and bereft of sustaining political and religious certainties in which we can believe? How do we find personal order in such a world? For our authors, as for many of us, the only alternative is existential commitment to a set of values, even while knowing that these values are a tentative arrangement of positions that makes one's own life work rather than moral absolutes.

Thus many of the works I discuss in this volume have a strong autobiographical aspect even while they respond to historical context: Müller's *The Hunger Angel*, Kertész's *Fatelessness*, Bassani's Ferrara stories and novels, Lampedusa's *The Leopard*, Ferrante's Neapolitan tetralogy, and Proust's *Swann's Way*. Indeed, the novels in my study of *Reading the Modern European Novel Since 1900* have far more examples of a strong autobiographical presence than the novels discussed in my earlier *Reading the European Novel to 1900*.

All fiction, indeed all criticism, has an element of autobiography no matter how hard the writers try to efface themselves from texts. But the personal does not mean authors cannot invent characters and events. For authors can and do imagine other genders and ethnicities as well as experiences that they never had and even places they never visited. Yet the protagonists of many of the novels I discuss are often clearly surrogates for the authors. Such is the case of Aschenbach in *Death in Venice*, Gregor in *Metamorphosis*, Georg in *Fatelessness*, the Prince in *The Leopard*, Dr. Rieux in *The Plague*, and Elena in Ferrante's Neapolitan tetralogy. If I may cite an example from a European exile writing in English and well known to most of the aforementioned authors, Conrad's Marlow plays the role of his surrogate in *Heart of Darkness* (1899) and, to a somewhat lesser extent, in *Lord Jim* (1900). Conrad's 1896–1898 letters as well as his Congo Diary show that Marlow is struggling with the same issues – loneliness, anxiety, doubt about the pretenses of imperialism – in *Heart of Darkness* as Conrad struggled with in his life.

A recurring pattern in post-1900 fiction is authors feeling a sense of otherness, that is psychological, political, and/or ethnic separation from the dominant group, usually as a result of historical forces beyond their control. Many of our texts dramatize that marginalization within the narrative about fictional characters. Kertész, Bassani – victims of the Holocaust – and Müller are examples where racial and ethnic reasons are central to estrangement. In Proust, Mann, and Müller, the reasons for marginalization are sexual, while in Kundera they are political and psychological. In Pamuk's *My Name is Red* the miniaturists feel aesthetically and ideologically under siege because their basic assumptions are being challenged by Western realism. Lampedusa's Prince is historically and politically displaced by what he feels is a materialistic order that is replacing the one he knew and which was based on inherited privilege. In a number of our texts, notably those by Kafka and Saramago, economic marginalization within a capitalist economy plays a role.

Saramago's bachelor is psychologically marginalized by shyness and a sense of his inferiority. Kafka's Gregor has become a slave to his office because his family depends on him to pay off debts.

In a world increasingly devoid of certainties, metaphysical or historical or personal, the novel after 1900 also tests the limits of language. A major recurring pattern in these novels is the dramatization of their narrators' and characters' Sisyphean quest to overcome those limits. Or as Müller puts it, "[W]ords have their own truth, and that comes from how they sound. But they aren't the same as the things themselves, there's never a perfect match. ... Even language doesn't reach the deepest places we have inside us" (Müller, "The Art of Fiction No. 225").[8] Nevertheless, the writer must keep trying: "Language is so different from life. How am I supposed to fit the one into the other? How can I bring them together? There's no such thing as one-to-one correspondence" (ibid.). The human choice of language defines the author as well as narrators and characters. As Wittgenstein observed, the limits of one's language are the limits to one's world.

The Complexity of Modernist Texts

As we shall see, reading modernist texts keeps readers off balance and undermines the possibility of monologic responses. Even authorial readings, that is the readings generated by the author's choices, insist on polyphonic readings. Kertész does not permit his reader to become complacent about "knowing" what happens in the camps. Nor will Camus allow us to take a one-dimensional view of human conduct in *The Plague* or *The Stranger*, although he comes closer than many of our writers in subscribing to an ethical if existential code.

Ferrante reminds us that Elena makes mistakes and bad choices; even as Ferrante evokes both her readers' sympathy and empathy for women finding their voices, she does not let them forget that repulsive violence remains a fact of life in Naples. Kafka does not allow readers to impose simple allegories of reading on *Metamorphosis* without pushing them to inquire about what it is to be human and what they would have done if confronted with a transformed loved one, whether by Alzheimer's or physical deterioration.

Authorial readings are supplemented by resistant readings which call attention to what is missing in an author's vision. Thus we see in Mann a tendency to patronize the feelings of the less advantaged. Grass does not seem aware of how he understates the Holocaust. But sometimes readers simply miss the implications of what an author writes. Each generation, indeed each reader, responds to a text differently, and the interpretive history of canonical texts texts shows this. Texts change not only as individual readers change, but also as cultural assumptions change. A paradigmatic example of how readers change is Conrad's *The Secret Sharer* where Leggatt and the Captain have a homosocial relationship that earlier critics didn't notice. When I studied *Swann's Way* in college in the somewhat repressive 1950s much less was made of Swann's sexual proclivities and those of his cohorts than when I teach Proust's texts now.

Principles of Selection

I need to acknowledge that for *Reading the Modern European Novel Since 1900*, I found it more difficult to select novels on which to focus than it was to select the novels for *Reading the European Novel to 1900*, and my choices are more arbitrary. Only a handful (if that) stand out as giants the way *Don Quixote, War and Peace, The Brothers Karamazov*, and *Madame Bovary* do. I have thought deeply about what should be included in this volume and have asked for input from colleagues teaching twentieth- and twenty-first-century literature. In surveying the novels after 1900, I have tried to be more inclusive of different nationalities than in the first volume where I included mostly Russian and French authors with one Spanish author. I include four relatively recent Nobel Prize winners from different countries: Müller (Romania), Saramago (Portugal), Pamuk (Turkey), and Kertész (Hungary) as well as two from an earlier era: Mann (Germany) and Camus (France). Proust and Kafka did not win Nobel prizes, surprising as that might be to our generation of readers.

Since my two volumes are really one, namely the story of the evolution of the European novel, I will on occasion refer back to the novels I discussed in the first volume. The novels I discuss in Volume II are influenced by those in Volume I and are responding to them in what Harold Bloom has called the Anxiety of Influence. Many of the texts in the second volume are in part strong misreadings of novels I discussed in the first. It can be instructive to imagine all our novels in both volumes sitting around a table responding to one another. Indeed, we might think of the novelists in the second volume as taking a class from the writers in the first.

I have tried to include works that I consider masterworks. What makes a literary masterwork? While in some cases I regard my selections as suggestions rather than the results of a full consensus, I am sure future generations will sort out the canonical figures. Yet I am interested in what makes a novel a literary masterwork. Masterworks, whether in literature, the visual arts, or music, demand our attention and create a desire – indeed, a need – to understand them in terms of their value system even while aware that we might not share all their values. Indeed, the novels I am discussing represent radically different value systems, including, in the case of Pamuk and Saramago, non-Western ones.

Translations

As with Volume I, I will be dealing with translations of the original texts and I will be discussing the transformed English text rather than the original. Translations need to be regarded as self-contained ontologies, not versions of something else as if they were workshop copies of original works of art or even second-rate alterations. Translating is at best a kind of artistry, perhaps akin to making tapestries from cartoons.

Adam Gopnik nicely puts it: "Citizens of our language, we act as citizens do, participating, reforming, accepting the rituals and celebrating their alteration, occasionally even voting for new rules and rulers. No words are entirely untranslatable; none are entirely transparent" (Gopnik, "Word Magic," 59).[9] When we read and listen in our own language, we are translating words into our own penumbra of understanding. Or, as David Bellos observes, "despite the endless insistence that the real thing is always lost in translation, we readily translate everything and all the time" (quoted in Gopnik, 59).

Each translator finds his or her own meaning in a text and that shapes the translation just as much as or more than unpacking each work sentence by sentence. Claire Messud observes, "Translation is inevitably to a degree subjective. The quality of a translator will depend, then, not merely on her understanding of the mechanics of a language, or on her facility as a writer of prose, but also on her capacities as a reader of texts, her sense of subtext, of connotation, of allusion – of the invisible textures that give a narrative its density and, ultimately, shape its significance" (Messud, "A New 'L'Etranger,'" 6).[10]

Lydia Davis, who produced a fine translation of *Swann's Way*, has written:

· ·

In translating, then, you are at the same time always solving a problem. It is a word problem, an ingenious, complicated word problem that requires not only a good deal of craft but some art or artfulness in its solution. … You are also thoroughly entering another culture for longer or shorter periods of time. … You not only enter that other culture, but remain to some extent inside it as you return to your own. (Davis, "Eleven Pleasures of Translating," 22–23)[11]

· ·

Davis, one of our best translators, is very much aware of the challenges posed by translation:

· ·

One frustration in translating is the restraint you need to show, having to remain faithful to this text and solve this problem, having to refrain from shifting into your own style or, worse, expressing your own ideas. And there is usually not an exact equivalent of the original, or if there is, it is awkward, or unnatural, and can't be used; translation is, eternally, a compromise. You settle for the best you can do rather than achieving perfection, though there is the occasional perfect solution. Even something so simple as a single word will never find its perfect equivalent; the French *maison*, with all its myriad associations, is really not the same as the English "house," with its own associations. (Ibid., 23–24)

· ·

Conclusion

In the following pages I shall discuss major European novels written after 1900 and I shall be using English translations. I shall bring to this project my lifetime of reading and writing about literature, including some expertise about the form of the novel and the unfolding experience presented by the words on the page. While I acknowledge previous scholarship on each writer, I do not claim to be a world-class authority on either the individual novels or novelists that I discuss.

With each chapter I have included study questions to guide teachers and readers towards what I feel are the most salient issues in my chosen texts. I invite you to join me as I celebrate the experience of reading some of the major works of European literature that were written after 1900.

Notes

1. "A Classic Passes 50," *New York Times* (Jan. 29, 2012).
2. David Lodge, "Milan Kundera, and the Idea of the Author in Modern Criticism," in *Critical Essays on Milan Kundera*, ed. Peter Petro (New York: G. K. Hall, 1999), 137–150; see 141.
3. James Clifford, *The Predicament of Culture: Twentieth-Century Ethnography, Literature, and Art* (Cambridge, MA: Harvard University Press, 1988), 92–93.
4. John Elderfield, *Henri Matisse: A Retrospective* (New York: The Museum of Modern Art, 1992), 203.
5. Richard Ellmann and Charles Feidelson, Jr., *The Modern Tradition: Backgrounds of Modern Literature* (New York: Oxford University Press, 1965), 725.
6. T. S. Eliot, *Selected Essays* (New York: Harcourt, Brace & World, 1960), 4.
7. Claire Messud, "The Dancer & the Dance," *NYR* 63:19 (Dec. 8, 2017) [on Zadie Smith's *Swing Time*], 6, 8; http://www.nybooks.com/articles/2016/12/08/zadie-smith-dancer-and-dance/
8. Herta Müller, "The Art of Fiction No. 225." Interview by Philip Boehm. *Paris Review* (Fall 2014), 210; https://www.theparisreview.org/interviews/6328/herta-muller-the-art-of-fiction-no-225-herta-muller
9. Adam Gopnik, "Word Magic," *The New Yorker* (May 26, 2014), 56–59; see 59; http://www.newyorker.com/magazine/2014/05/26/word-magic
10. Claire Messud, "A New 'L'Etranger,'" *NYR* 61:10 (June 5, 2014), 6.
11. Lydia Davis, "Eleven Pleasures of Translating," *NYR* 63:19 (Dec. 8, 2017), 22–23; http://www.nybooks.com/articles/2016/12/08/eleven-pleasures-of-translating/

Chapter 2

Cultural Crisis: Decadence and Desire in Mann's *Death in Venice* (1912)

"It can never be satisfied, the mind, never."
Stevens, "The Well-Dressed Man with a Beard"

The Author in the Text: Mann and Aschenbach

Describing the process of writing *Death in Venice* (1912), Thomas Mann (1875–1955) recalled,

Originally the tale was to be brief and modest. But things or whatever better word there may be for the conception *organic* have a will of their own, and shape themselves accordingly. … The truth is that every piece of work is a realization, fragmentary but complete in itself, of our individuality; and this kind of realization is the sole and painful way we have of getting the particular experience – no wonder, then, that the process is attended by surprises. (Mann, *A Sketch of My Life*, 43–44)[1]

As I discussed in Chapter 1, the ways our authors use their fiction to define values is an important part of the novel since 1900, and Mann is a notable example. Hence we need not be embarrassed to speak about the relationship between authors and their characters or narrators. Works of fiction often derive from actual experience, even when the triggering events are not so obvious. Many writers and especially modern writers use their fiction to explore and

Reading the Modern European Novel Since 1900: A Critical Study of Major Fiction from Proust's Swann's Way *to Ferrante's Neapolitan Tetralogy*, First Edition. Daniel R. Schwarz.
© 2018 John Wiley & Sons Ltd. Published 2018 by John Wiley & Sons Ltd.

define their own psychic and artistic needs. Using fiction to define one's values and to probe one's psyche becomes a feature of the twentieth- and twenty-first-century novel. Yet even while we are aware of the creative transaction by which life becomes art within authors' imaginations, we need to differentiate between what happens within a text and the actual biography outside the imagined ontology of the text.

For many in the German-speaking world, Mann was the epitome of the "educated burgher," a man of the upper middle class whose comfortable economic status allowed him to acquire not only possessions but also cultural education, refinement, and good taste. Indeed, his works and his interests reflect such a status. Many of his stories and novels – for example, *Buddenbrooks* (1901) – depict an upper-middle-class milieu and the concerns of family life.

Yet Mann rejected identification with bourgeois society. Indeed, he believed that the source of much of his artistic inspiration derived from a realm antithetical to the bourgeois one in which he lived, namely from the realm of the erotic, the sexual, and, in particular, homosexual desire.[2] We do know from Mann's diaries which became public in 1975 that Mann struggled with his own homosexual impulses.

Death in Venice lives on the borderland between Aestheticism and Decadence. It takes its place among texts that open up the subject of homoeroticism with Walter Pater's *Studies in the History of the Renaissance* (1873), Joris-Karl Huysmans's *Against Nature* (1884), and, most blatantly, Oscar Wilde's *Picture of Dorian Gray* (1891). With its discovery of another darker self lurking beneath a respectable exterior, *Death in Venice* also suggests Robert Louis Stevenson's *The Strange Case of Dr. Jekyll and Mr. Hyde* (1886) and Conrad's Kurtz in *Heart of Darkness* (1899).

As Joyce does with Gabriel Conroy in "The Dead" – completed in 1907, only a few years before Mann wrote *Death in Venice* – Mann creates in Aschenbach the man he feared becoming, namely an uninspired artistic icon of a mediocre culture. Mann also creates a narrator who is a surrogate for exploring these fears. The preposition "von" in Gustav von Aschenbach's name indicates that he has been made a member of the nobility for his life of achievement. The narrator renders Aschenbach's consciousness, but never quite stops holding Aschenbach's perspective at an ironic distance.

Leo Carey notes, "*Death in Venice* is one of those works, like [Proust's] *A la recherche du temps perdu*, where the genesis – the process by which life became literature – is almost as fruitful a topic as the finished work itself" (Carey, "Love in Venice," 56).[3] In fact Aschenbach's fame rests on projects – including a novel about Frederick the Great – that Mann abandoned. In May 1911, while on vacation, Mann was fixated on a young Polish boy in Venice at the Hôtel des Bains on the Lido, and much of *Death in Venice* derives from that.[4] As Mann wrote: "[E]verything was given, and really only needed to be fitted in, proving in the most astonishing manner how it could be interpreted within my composition" (quoted in Carey, 56). Mann knew Munich, Aschenbach's home, since it was his home from 1891 until 1933 when he fled Germany after Hitler came to power.

Yet there are limits to the parallel between Aschenbach and Mann, who was a young man when he wrote *Death in Venice*. As Leo Carey observes, "One of the ironies of the work is that, as time went on, Mann, who was in his mid-thirties when he wrote [*Death in Venice*] became more and more like Aschenbach" (Carey, 58). While we know that Mann struggled with homosexual impulses, before we completely equate Mann with Aschenbach, we need to remember that Mann was married and had six children; while attracted to males, we do not know if he had homosexual relationships.[5] Furthermore, Aschenbach is also based on the composer Gustav Mahler, who died in May 1911 shortly before Mann wrote *Death in Venice*. Mahler's facial appearance is one source of Mann's description of Aschenbach's face. Yet notwithstanding the physical resemblance between Aschenbach and Mahler, I believe Mann had a much greater investment in Aschenbach as a way of dealing with artistic and sexual issues in his own life.

In *Death in Venice* Mann creates a series of "what if" assumptions about the relationship between art and life. For example, within the novel he tests the hypothesis that "[A]rt heightens life. She gives deeper joy, she consumes more swiftly. She engraves adventures of the spirit and the mind in the faces of her votaries; let them lead outwardly a life of the most cloistered calm, she will in the end produce in them a fastidiousness, an over-refinement, nervous fever and exhaustion, such as a career of extravagant pleasures can hardly show" (15).[6]

Formally, *Death in Venice* depends on a duet between the omniscient narrator's presentation of Aschenbach and Aschenbach's own perspective. The narrator's ironic analysis holds Aschenbach at a fluctuating distance, even as he sympathetically renders the tale Aschenbach tells himself through indirect discourse. Mann not only presents the cognitive dissonance between the stories Aschenbach tells himself and his actual behavior, but also the inconsistencies between Aschenbach's rationalizations and what is actually occurring as well as the conflict within Aschenbach's mind between the Apollonian values he holds dear and the Dionysian emotions that manifest themselves.

Death in Venice begins in May of an unspecified year in the early twentieth century, a time when "Europe sat upon the anxious seat beneath a menace that hung over its head for months," a menace that found actuality in the assassination of Archduke Franz Ferdinand of Austria in June 1914 in Sarajevo, Bosnia (3).

Mann is also prescient about the breakdown of international order and the onset of World War I. But the immediate crisis was international tension created by the deployment of a German gunship to the Moroccan port of Agadir on July 1, 1911 after a rebellion broke out and the French were threatening to intervene. (My late colleague Edgar Rosenberg, who taught me a great deal about *Death in Venice*, thought that the crisis might refer to a prior Moroccan crisis in 1906 when Germany tried to prevent France from establishing a protectorate in Morocco.)

For Aschenbach writing is a kind of minor triumph befitting the work of a middle-level official; in suggesting that parallel between an author and an official doing the work required of him, Mann not only emphasizes mediocre art as drone work, but also suggests that it serves the political goals of the state. When we meet Aschenbach in Munich, art is service, depending less on imagination and creative energy than upon "sustained concentration, conscientiousness, and tact" that produced "wear and tear" upon his system (3). Toiling to the point of exhaustion, Aschenbach in his own mind has transformed his writing into cultural service as if he held a civil service position within government. He puts in his time each day as if he were punching a clock.

Aschenbach seeks fame rather than truth, and sacrifices inspiration on the altar of pleasing the public whose values echo his own: "[H]is genius was *calculated* to win at once the adhesion of the general public and the admiration, both sympathetic and stimulating, of the connoisseur" (9; emphasis mine). Attributing who Aschenbach is to genetics (although here we might question Mann's science) as well as culture, Mann's narrator tells us that Aschenbach is the descendant of a parental "union of dry, conscientious officialdom and ardent, obscure impulse" (8). In a great image, the narrator quotes an observer who claims that Aschenbach always has held himself like a closed fist (9). Aschenbach's favorite motto is "Durchhalten" or "Hold Fast" and his ambition is simply "to live to a good old age, for it was his conviction that only the artist to whom it has been granted to be fruitful on all stages of our human scene can be truly great, or universal, or worthy of honour" (9–10). While Aschenbach's ambition in Munich is to grow old and maintain his position, the narrator ironically begins tracing the alternative trajectory of Aschenbach's letting go and dying before reaching old age.

Mann regarded Aschenbach as a second- or even third-rate artist, in part because of the limits of the latter's imagination and in part because Aschenbach wore blinders when thinking about historical process and saw history only in terms of his own values and psychic needs. To put it in other terms, Aschenbach lacks what John Keats has called the negative capability to imagine a world beyond himself. At a time when the first years of the twentieth century, especially in Central Europe, were defined by intellectual ferment in art and literature – when the ideas of Nietzsche, Freud, Kandinsky, and Schoenberg were being foregrounded and replacing older concepts of representation – Mann presents Aschenbach as a highly intellectual mannerist for whom artistic technique is more important than powerful emotion.

Aschenbach's art in part is about art and style for the sake of art and style. Aschenbach combines what Peter Schjeldahl, speaking of the mannerist Agnolo Bronzino, calls "the most contrived degree of fantasy, the most candid of appetites" (Schjeldahl, "Then and Now").[7] Like Bronzino, Aschenbach exudes "aristocratic hauteur" and is drawn in his admiration of Greek statues and Tadzio by "erotic glamour" (ibid.).

In the art of Aschenbach, Mann is exploring not only the triumph of the aesthetic as an exercise of willful control, but also the consequences of an ordering form that stifles content, ignores difficult and complex issues, and eschews ambiguity. Not for Aschenbach the messiness of Dostoevsky or Tolstoy. No, Aschenbach has turned art into exacting service, and he needs to flee the bondage to which he has submitted. For him writing has become joyless, "the daily theatre of a rigid, cold, and passionate service" (7). His passion has gone into "scrupulosity" that has "bridled and tempered his sensibilities" (7).

Aschenbach is an aging artist, whose overly fastidious art has become bereft of feeling: "So now, perhaps, feeling thus tyrannized, [the nature and inmost essence of the literary gift] avenged itself by leaving him, refusing from now on to carry and wing his art and taking away with it all the ecstasy he had known in form and expression" (3, 7). Seemingly, having banished disorder, passions, and unruly sentiments, Aschenbach rediscovers these aspects of a repressed Dionysian self in weird, warped, and uncontrollable obsessions, fixations, and unacknowledged needs. Or, put another way, his repressed Dionysian, libidinous self emerges to undermine his Apollonian reason and control.

Mann's narrator uses the Germanic master style – something he does not use in other works – to parody Aschenbach's artistic goals. With their Germanic periods, series of appositions that qualify until they often undermine what precedes, subtle redefinitions of such terms as "passion" and "heroism," and a rhetorical evasion that often fails to locate exactly what is happening, Mann mimes the caution and claustrophobia of Aschenbach's imagination. Yet underneath the seemingly convoluted sentences – sentences which resonate with rich irony even in the English translations I am quoting – are dichotomies: the Apollonian ordered life of Munich and the Dionysian chaotic libidinous world of Venice, work and sloth, service and laxity, boredom and excitement, age and youth, intellect and imagination, commitment to conscience and pursuit of fame. These dichotomies are underlined by the contrast between the jungle imaged by uncontrollable fecundity and the presence of the tiger with the neat routines of German bourgeois life.

Cultural Decadence and Enervation

As Leo Carey nicely puts it, "Aschenbach's story came to embody two kinds of humiliation – that of age in love with youth, and that of an artist whose reputation outweighs his achievement" (Carey, 56).

Now past fifty, Aschenbach, who formerly "could hold out for years under the strain of the same piece of work, with an endurance and a tenacity of purpose like that which had conquered his native province of Silesia," is honored by a culture that values such qualities (10). Lauding "heroism born of weakness" – a heroism paralleling the creative process that leads to his own artistic achievements – Aschenbach speaks to "the spirit of the times" (12). These times are not exactly identified but seem to refer to the period a few years prior to World War I and after the fin de siècle when Decadence and Aestheticism – the world of ivory towers and sacred fonts – were still strongly influential.

Not only did unconventional behavior introduced in the 1890s Decadent period still flourish in the first decade of the twentieth century but homosexuality, in the wake of Oscar Wilde's public behavior and trials, was no longer the hidden subject. Indeed, Frederick the Great, the subject of Aschenbach's prose epic, was reputed to have been gay.

It is worth remembering, too, that Aschenbach – who on the outside is confident, seemingly knowing and disciplined, but on the inside is soft, narcissistic, lacking self-awareness – can be read as a metaphor for Germany and indeed Europe as it is on the threshold of World War I. While in conservative Munich, Aschenbach does not flaunt his emotions or flout community standards. But it is in permissive Venice that his homosexual and pederast impulses overcome repression and he begins to act out those impulses as blatantly as Wilde's Dorian Gray.

Death in Venice stands as an inquiry about what makes great fiction. Mann invites the reader to think about what makes great art and whether greatness is culturally determined. His short novel implies that the dialogue between imagination and formal control – between what and how – is necessary for creating great art. That dialogue informs the paradigm Mann creates in *Death in Venice*, a paradigm that the narrator presents not merely as an alternative to Aschenbach's own creations but also as a judgment.

Mann believed that each generation gets the major artistic spokesman it deserves, and the generation about which he wrote in *Death in Venice* deserves Aschenbach. Its version of heroism is a passive one "which clenches its teeth and stands in modest defiance of the swords and spears that pierce its side" (11). The Christian martyr Saint Sebastian "is the most beautiful symbol if not of art as a whole, yet certainly of the art of which we speak of here" (11). Note that the narrator speaks in the first person plural as if he were very much part of the culture he observes, even as Mann expects the reader to take an ironic perspective.

Within Aschenbach's heroes, as within himself, beneath the unimpressive exterior looms the possibility of a fiery spirit. But in the case of his heroes, and one could say in the case of Aschenbach even in Venice, the ardor within takes a self-flagellating turn into self-sacrifice and enervation.

. . . .

Within that world of Aschenbach's creation were exhibited many phases of the same theme: there was the aristocratic self-command that is eaten out within and for as long as it can conceals its biologic decline from the eyes of the world; the sere and ugly outside, hiding the embers of smouldering fire – and having power to fan them to so pure a flame as to challenge supremacy in the domain of beauty itself; the pallid languors of the flesh, contrasted with the fiery ardours of the spirit within, which can fling a whole proud people down at the foot of the Cross, at the feet of its own sheer self-abnegation; the gracious bearing preserved in the stern, stark service of form; the unreal, precarious existence of the born intrigant with its swiftly enervating alternation of schemes and desires – all these human fates and many more of their like one read in Aschenbach's pages. Reading them, one might doubt the existence of any other kind of heroism than the heroism born of weakness. (11–12)

. . . .

Being honored within one's own culture hardly matters, Mann implies, if the culture itself is mediocre. Aschenbach is recognized as distinguished by a culture steeped in timidity. Aschenbach's conception of heroism lacks the qualities – physical and moral courage, commitment to ideals and to the common good, willingness to fight for the rights of others – that we associate with heroism:

. . . .

Gustav Aschenbach was the poet-spokesman of all those who labour at the edge of exhaustion, of the overburdened, of those who are already worn out but still hold themselves upright; of all our modern moralizers of accomplishment, with stunted growth and scanty resources, who yet contrive by skillful husbanding and prodigious spasms of will to produce, at least for a while, the effect of greatness. There are many such, they are the heroes of the age. And in Aschenbach's pages they saw themselves; he justified, he exalted them, he sang their praise – and they, they were grateful, they heralded his fame. (12)

. . . .

What Mann's narrator describes is heroism manqué for a Europe whose concept of greatness has shrunk. Coming on his father's side from a family of "men who lived their strict, decent, sparing lives in the service of king and state," Aschenbach creates by small acts of will rather than by the idealism and passion that motivated the great European Romantics from Goethe and E. T. A. Hoffmann to Wordsworth and Byron (8). German Romanticism, in particular, valued heroic action, passion, and imagination, and was skeptical of the French Enlightenment's stress on reason and scientific methods requiring careful mustering of empirical evidence. Writing with a view of accolades and recognition, Aschenbach conquers pages like a minor potentate conquers ground, but never examines – as the great Romantics aspire to do – the depths and intricacies of self: "Yes, one might put it that his whole career had been one conscious and overweening ascent to honour, which left in the rear all the misgivings or self-derogation which might have hampered him" (12).

I am stressing that *Death in Venice* needs to be read as a political and historical novel. With noir irony, Mann presents a culture whose values he despises. He defines heroism in terms which are antithetical to the very concept of heroism, and in fact describe a combination of self-sacrifice and adjustment to circumstances. Mann excoriates the German culture of his day which responds to passive figures as heroic as much as his Irish contemporary James Joyce in *Dubliners* (1914) and *Ulysses* (1922) critiques what he felt was an enervated and paralyzed Irish culture.

Mann is not only talking about Aschenbach but also using him as an image of a narcissistic, eviscerated, and enervated European culture. And his vision extends beyond Aschenbach to include the enervated anomie of Munich and by implication, Germany as well as the decadence of Venice, and by implication, Italy. As in Conrad's *Heart of Darkness* (1899), beneath the surface manners and customs, European civilization is revealed as a sham. The lurking tiger represents not only all that civilization pretends to ignore, including basic animal emotions, but also lies, hypocrisy, and everything that sticks its tongue out at human pretensions.

The Death Motif

Death in Venice is about the process of dying, and that process has begun for Aschenbach long before he visits Venice. Mann wants us to recognize that Aschenbach is dying prematurely in his early fifties and has become an old man well before his time.

In several of the novels in this study, illness is a metaphor for moral and spiritual inadequacy. Aschenbach, like Gregor Samsa and the speaker from *Notes from Underground*, is ill. When in Munich Aschenbach first feels the impulse to travel, it comes "upon him with such suddenness and passion as to resemble a seizure, almost a hallucination" (5). His desire to travel is called "the unexpected contagion" (6). The narrator inflects Aschenbach's health issues, his "enervating daily struggle between a proud, tenacious, well-tried will and this growing fatigue" (7).

As in Joyce's *The Dead* and his "Hades" chapter in *Ulysses*, Death is everywhere, pervading the structure and texture of *Death in Venice*. Beginning with Aschenbach's sighting of a mortuary chapel in the cemetery and continuing with the boat – "an ancient hulk belonging to an Italian line, obsolete, dingy, grimed with soot" – that transports him to Italy, the structure and texture are imbued with suggestions of aging, obsolescence, mortality, and death (16). When he arrives in Venice, the gondola is described as "black as nothing else on earth except a coffin. … [W]hat visions of death itself [it calls up], the bier and solemn rites and last soundless voyage! And has anyone remarked that the seat in such a bark, the armchair lacquered in coffin-black and dully black-upholstered, is the softest most luxurious, most relaxing seat in the world?" (21).

We need to note that the narrator engages in hyperbole as if to underline that Aschenbach, for all his supposed temperate nature, actually experiences the world – whether in his writing or in his judgmental or emotional responses to people he meets or in his pursuit of Tadzio – in extreme and reductive ways. Indeed, we see indications of Aschenbach's exaggerated responses in his disgust with old man on the boat and his fear of the physicality of the man he sees at the cemetery. Recused from the world, he cannot put any experience within the normal ken of understanding.

Mann understands that death is often a process of gradual loss of energy, mental capacity, and physical function. Even as the boat voyage to Venice begins, Aschenbach's consciousness is undergoing a transformation that takes the shape of diminished focus and control: "He felt not quite canny, as though the world were suffering a dreamlike distortion of perspective which he might arrest by shutting it all out for a few minutes and then looking at it afresh. But instead he felt a floating sensation" (17–18). Looking disgustedly at the now intoxicated "young-old man" who repulses him, "once more [he had] a dazed sense as though things about him were just slightly losing their ordinary perspective, beginning to show a distortion that might merge into the grotesque" (19).

Death hovers over every episode and informs every passage. Although only in his early fifties, Aschenbach continues losing control and having frequent lapses in focus as if he were an older man. The narrator no sooner describes Aschenbach's looking at the ocean – "[H]e let his eyes swim in the wideness of the sea, his gaze lose focus, blur, and grow vague in the misty immensity of space" – than Tadzio appears (30–31). This episode foreshadows the ending when Aschenbach's death while he is sitting by the sea and watching Tadzio cavort in the ocean.

Juxtaposed to Aschenbach's zeal for control over his art and his own emotional life is the immensity of the ocean which to a rereader becomes associated with death. The narrator stresses how the ocean becomes for Aschenbach an image of the nullification of all that Aschenbach valued: "[The vast ocean is] opposed to his art, and perhaps for that very reason a lure for the unorganized, the immeasurable, the eternal – in short for nothingness. He whose preoccupation is with excellence longs fervently to find rest in perfection; and is not nothingness a form of perfection?" (31).

Aschenbach's Doubles: The Repressed Self Plays Back

Discussing *Crime and Punishment*, R. P. Blackmur remarked that coincidental and fatal encounters are "the artist's way of representing those forces in us not ourselves" (Blackmur, *Eleven Essays in the European Novel*).[8] Such encounters create "our sense of that other self within us that we can neither quite escape nor quite meet up with" (Blackmur, 126). But that other self, I would stress – and, more importantly, so would Mann – is really another version of our self brought out by a confluence of personality and character at a specific time and place. In German *Doppelgänger* means "double walker," and in German culture the doubles are often darkly sinister, even ghostly, and represent evil or misfortune.

These doubles mock Aschenbach and remind us not only of his mortality, but also of the instinctive and sexual aspects of his humanity that he would deny in the spurious existence in which he has been living in Munich. By having Aschenbach see these various mysterious doubles, Mann creates a parallel to Ulysses's physical descent into Hades to meet ghostly figures who have died. To evoke a related classical metaphor, these doubles are like shades crossing over the River Styx – the river that formed the boundary between earth and the underworld – to haunt Aschenbach.

Aschenbach encounters male doubles – or shadow selves – that suggest aspects of himself. These figures fit into three overlapping categories: (1) older men trying to be young, often quite ludicrously, and trying to put their back to the future and live fully in the present; (2) intimidating younger men, who celebrate their physicality and awareness of their bodies; (3) an attractive and seductive adolescent – namely Tadzio – living a decadent Dionysian life seemingly completely opposite from the Apollonian life that Aschenbach had lived, but no less self-immersed and narcissistic than Aschenbach.

Aschenbach's first encounter is with a figure of indeterminate age from the second category. While taking a walk in Munich, Aschenbach sees a man standing in the portico of the cemetery mortuary chapel. To Aschenbach's eyes, he is not a native Bavarian and seems quite threatening; with a rakish appearance and wearing a straw hat, the man has "a bold and domineering, even a ruthless air" (5). The man's intimidating stare causes a transformation within Aschenbach's psyche: "[H]e felt the most surprising consciousness of a widening of inward barriers, a kind of vaulting unrest, a youthfully ardent thirst for distant scenes – a feeling so lively and so new, or at least so long ago outgrown and forgot, that he stood there rooted to the spot, his eyes on the ground and his hands clasped behind him, exploring these sentiments of his, their bearing and scope" (5). Clearly Aschenbach, "hands clasped behind him" as if to signify his rigorous self-control, is challenged and threatened by this libidinous figure who intrudes on his detachment and his enervated ironic perspective.

This figure is the first of various doubles who represent a libidinous, instinctive self that Aschenbach has formerly repressed and brought under control by force of will. Here his tumultuous feelings take the form of a longing to travel, but in a sexualized form of an imagined place antithetical to Munich and to the life he is leading there with its exacting routines: "Desire projected itself visually. ... He beheld a landscape, a tropical marshland, beneath a reeking sky, steaming, monstrous, rank – a kind of primeval wilderness-world of islands, morasses, and alluvial channels. Hairy palm-trunks rose near and far out of lush brakes of fern, out of bottoms of crass vegetation, fat, swollen, thick with incredible bloom. ... Among the knotted joints of a bamboo thicket the eyes of a crouching tiger gleamed – and he felt his heart throb with terror, yet with a longing inexplicable" (5–6). His response here anticipates his orgiastic dream of "the stranger god" not long before his death.

Aschenbach's next encounters are with two doubles who suggest his repressed Dionysian self. The first is an aged, infirm, and dissipated figure who gets on board the steamship that will take Aschenbach to Venice: "A dirty hunchbacked sailor, smirkingly polite, conducted him at once below-ships to a cavernous, lamplit cabin" (16). That man takes us to a dissolute figure of indeterminate age: "There behind a table sat a man with a beard like a goat's; he had his hat on the back of his head, a cigar-stump in the corner of his mouth; he reminded Aschenbach of an old-fashioned circus-director" (16).

The next double is an elderly passenger on the boat; pretending to be part of a group of younger cohorts, he wears a "rakish" Panama hat and a red cravat (17). If we recall that Panama hats are made of straw, we can see that these straw hats, associated with lower-class disreputable males that Aschenbach patronizes, evolve in Aschenbach's mind into a metonymy for that libidinous self that he has been repressing. Aschenbach perceives this passenger as an "old man ... with wrinkles and crow's feet round eyes and mouth" and rouged cheeks pathetically trying to look like the group of young passengers of which he was trying to be a part (17).

Mann's narrator despises this figure as much as Aschenbach, but perhaps is more understanding and sympathetic about how an aging man fights to keep his hold on life and desperately, poignantly, and ultimately pathetically seeks to arrest time. This figure, more than any other, is both a double and a parody of what Aschenbach becomes when he becomes obsessed with Tadzio.

Before they leave the boat, Aschenbach "was forced to endure the importunities of the ghastly young old-man, whose drunken state obscurely urged him to pay the stranger the honour of a formal farewell. ... He drooled, he blinked, he licked the corner of his mouth" (20). Aschenbach is disgusted with this passenger's garish and even decadent behavior; yet the passenger represents the impulsiveness and sexuality that Aschenbach has been denying. The rereader understands that if the old passenger is inebriated, Aschenbach is later intoxicated with obsessive passion. Aschenbach meets another version of an older man trying to be young in the bathing-master at his Lido hotel who is a "barefoot old man in linen trousers and sailor blouse with a straw hat" (29–30).

The rakish figure in the Munich cemetery anticipates – and has much in common with – the Venice street performer who performs in the garden of Aschenbach's hotel. The street performer is a man of indeterminate age who looks unhealthy but has red hair and an "impudent swaggering posture": "He was a man of slight build, with a thin, undernourished face; his shabby felt hat rested on the back of his neck, a great mop of red hair sticking out in front. ... [V]ice sat on [his face], it was furrowed with grimacing, and two deep wrinkles of defiance and self-will, almost of desperation, stood oddly between the red brows" (which the Munich figure also has); he gave off a "suspicious odour ... a strong smell of carbolic" indicating that he was ill, probably with cholera (59–60).

Within the text red becomes the color of decadence and disease. While watching the street performer Aschenbach is drinking "pomegranate-juice and soda-water sparkling ruby-red" (59); Tadzio's "red breast-knot" (32) had fascinated Aschenbach. Thus Mann creates the underlying link between Aschenbach's obsession with Tadzio – an emotional illness – and the physical disease ravaging Venice. Of Tadzio Aschenbach thinks, while in the presence of the street performer: "He is sickly, he will never live to grow up" (62). After obsequiously soliciting money, the performer "threw off his buffoon's mask" and stuck out his (red) tongue "impudently" (62). He knows Venice's secret, namely that the city's officials are hiding the cholera plague so as not to affect the tourist industry. But even after knowing Venice's secret, Aschenbach buys the overripe strawberries which may be the source of what we assume is the cholera that kills him.

Seductive Beauty, Corrupting Pleasure: Venice and Aschenbach's Illicit Love

Venice is equated with corruption and decadence and that is where Aschenbach discovers his attraction for the adolescent boy Tadzio. Mann stresses how Venice has devolved into a playland for visitors from other countries. Venice is the opposite of Munich. Work takes a back seat to pleasure. It is a port between East and West, known for its decadence at the turn of the century and to an extent that is its image now. It attracts tourists but does not have a major industry. Only in Venice can Aschenbach relax: "Aschenbach was not pleasure-loving. Always, wherever and whenever it was the order of the day to be merry, to refrain from labor and make glad the heart, he would soon be conscious of the imperative summons – and especially was this so in his youth – back to the high fatigues, the sacred and fasting service that consumed his days. This spot and this alone had power to beguile him, to relax his resolution, to make him glad" (41).

Anticipating Tadzio's seduction of Aschenbach, for the boy plays a role in enticing the older man, Mann ironically depicts Venice as a narcissistic, corrupt, and immoral seductress: "Yes, this was Venice, this the fair frailty that fawned and that betrayed, half fairy-tale, half snare; the city in whose stagnating air the art of painting once put forth so lusty a growth, and where musicians were moved to accords so weirdly lulling and lascivious. Our adventurer felt his senses wooed by this voluptuousness of sight and sound, tasted his secret knowledge that the city sickened and hid its sickness for love of gain, and bent an ever more unbridled leer on the gondola that glided on before him" (55–56). The narrator's purple prose with its elaborate syntax and extravagant diction, its suggestions of illicit forbidden pleasures, and its emphasis on enervation and stagnation are features of the Decadent movement.

Venice and Aschenbach have become metaphors for one another, both disguising their inner reality and their motivations for their behavior by presenting themselves to the outside world as respectable. Yet both are living a lie. Alluding to the cholera epidemic and explicitly linking it to Aschenbach's denial of his pederasty, the narrator comments on "the unclean alleys of Venice": "The city's evil secret mingled with the one in the depths of [Aschenbach's] heart" (54).

Pathetically, Aschenbach makes himself up to look younger, mirroring the young-old man whom he despised on the boat to Venice. Like Venice in the midst of a cholera epidemic, Aschenbach's appearance disguises the rottenness within as the narrator reminds us in the scathing paragraph indicting Venice as morally bankrupt. In response to German (not Venetian) newspapers first reporting the cholera plague, the Venetian authorities published a statement that "the city's health had never been better; at the same time instituting the most necessary precautions" (64). The narrator's telling comment underlines the moral corruption that underlies the authorities' motives, namely to protect tourism and trade at all costs: "But by that time the food supplies – milk, meat, or vegetables – had probably been contaminated, for death unseen and unacknowledged was devouring and laying waste in the narrow streets, while a brooding unseasonable heat warmed the waters of the canals and encouraged the spread of pestilence" (64). In his *The Plague*, which I will be discussing in a subsequent chapter, Camus's depiction of Oran during the plague may owe something to Mann.

Aschenbach's Use of Classical Contexts

Mann uses what T. S. Eliot has called the mythic method as a way "of controlling, of ordering, of giving a shape and a significance" to his narrative (Eliot, "Ulysses, Order and Myth," 681).[9] But while Eliot used the method to describe what he called the "immense panorama of futility and anarchy which is contemporary history," Mann used the method ironically. The formerly ascetic Aschenbach reconfigures his lust in terms of an interest in classical concepts of beauty, an interest that Aschenbach expresses in terms which evoke the ancient Greeks' supposed permissive attitudes toward homosexuality and even pederasty: "[Tadzio's] face recalled the noblest moment in Greek sculpture. ... No scissor had been put to the lovely hair that (like the Spinnario's) curled about the brows, above his ears, longer still in the neck" (25–26).

The Spinnario, usually written Spinario, is the Greco-Roman sculpture called *Boy With Thorn* in which a beautiful, seemingly innocent, naked young boy is unselfconsciously removing a thorn from his foot. The sculpture has also been called *Il Fidele* or the faithful boy, because in legend a shepherd boy ran with a message to the Roman senate, stopping only to take out a thorn. For Aschenbach, evoking the sculpture is a way to think about Tadzio as an idealized boy rather than as a target of voyeurism or even pedophilia. But Mann expected us readers to understand that the temporarily disabling thorn – a rare anecdotal moment in classical Greek sculpture – has implications for *Death in Venice*. Tadzio, like the boy, is not perfect. Moreover, Tadzio will become a disruptive thorn in Aschenbach's world even while Aschenbach becomes a disruptive thorn in Tadzio's. Indeed, with Aschenbach's death, Tadzio has unknowingly extracted the pederast thorn that, whatever Tadzio's complicity, hovers over him.

According to Plato in the *Symposium* and the *Phaedrus*, Socrates was attracted to young boys and seems to endorse pederasty. The older man was called the *erastes*; his role was to educate and protect the boy called the *eromenos*, who was between 12 and 17 and the passive recipient in male–male sex with the *erastes*; the latter, like Tadzio, offered the appeal of youth and beauty. Indeed, relationships between an adult male and a younger male were very much part of the post-Homeric Greek culture. Yet, in the *Symposium*, Socrates himself is accused by Alcibiades of lusting after young men; by implication, Alcibiades is raising the issue of pederasty.

Aschenbach's putting his love in the context of the dialogue between Socrates and Phaedrus is his effort to justify his obsession with Tadzio in classical terms. The *Phaedrus*, we need to recall, discusses whether it is better for a boy to be loved by an older man who sexually desires him or someone who cares for him platonically; the Phaedrus also considers in which case it is better to return the older man's love. In the first case, which describes Aschenbach's love for Tadzio, the older lover abandons judgment, objectivity, and prudence. In fact, Aschenbach has given his passion to a younger man who disdains him.

Socrates knew the danger of submitting to passion: "Do you consider what happens to you after you have kissed a beautiful face? Do you not lose your liberty? Do you not become a slave? Do you not engage yourself in a vast expense to procure a sinful pleasure? Do you not find yourself in an incapacity of doing what is good, and that you subject yourself to the necessity of employing your whole time and person in the pursuit of what you would despise, if your reason were not corrupted?" (Xenophon, *The Memorable Thoughts of Socrates*).[10] Ironically and bathetically imagining himself as a modern-day Socrates but ignoring his wisdom on how passion distorts judgment, Aschenbach calls Tadzio "little Phaeax" (29), perhaps because Phaeax was the son of Poseidon, the Greek god of the sea, and he associates Tadzio with the sea.

Aschenbach calls Tadzio's friend, Jaschiu, whom he perceives as a rival for Tadzio's affections, "Critobulus," the son of Socrates' disciple Crito: "But you, Critobulus … you I advise to take a year's leave. That long, at least, you will need for complete recovery" (33). Basically, Aschenbach is suggesting that his imagined rival for Tadzio's affections has the same illness as he and should take a leave so as to be able to recover. Of course, the rereader understands that it is Aschenbach who should leave Venice and recover before he becomes enmeshed in the epidemic. Crito was chastised by Socrates for kissing the son of Alcibiades. Aschenbach imagines himself as Socrates dispensing wisdom to Jaschiu who, having just kissed Tadzio, has played the role of Crito, while Tadzio is a stand-in for Alcibiades' son.

Aschenbach at first rationalizes his interest in Tadzio as interest in a living beauty, "a masterpiece from nature's own hand" (31). The story he tells himself frames his interest in Apollonian terms, an aspect of his love of beauty for beauty's sake and a contemplation of the Greek ideal of beauty. For Aschenbach, Tadzio's face "recalled the noblest moment of Greek sculpture … with all this chaste perfection of form" (25). Unable to admit the real motive of his interest, Aschenbach "was astonished anew, yes, startled, at the godlike beauty of the human being" (29). As if Tadzio were a work of art, Aschenbach defines him in terms appropriate for a classical sculpture: "It was the head of Eros, with the yellowish bloom of Parian marble" (29).

Before finally redefining his interest in Tadzio to include passion, desire, and imagination, aspects of life that he has long denied, Aschenbach deludes himself in stages. At first Aschenbach thinks he is attracted by qualities in Tadzio that Aschenbach has heretofore admired and that he had honed within himself in Munich: "dignity, discipline, and sense of duty" (27). Next Aschenbach convinces himself that Tadzio is no more than a beautiful work of classical art and that his regard is Platonic rather than sexual. Thus he assumes "the patronizing air of the connoisseur to hide, as artists will their ravishment over a masterpiece" (29). Later he rationalizes that his being captivated by beauty has led him astray because it triggers desire and Dionysian frenzy that undermines his judgment.

Prior to being completely captivated by Tadzio, Aschenbach is aware that Tadzio is not the paradigm of beauty he would wish him to be: In fact, Tadzio, as Aschenbach realizes in an objective moment, has "imperfect" teeth, "rather jagged and bluish, without a healthy glaze" (34). Yet even as Aschenbach mythicizes Tadzio as a godlike figure, the narrator's deft rendering of Aschenbach's consciousness enables us to see that Tadzio is manipulative, temperamental, and perhaps less inexperienced and chaste than Aschenbach would like to believe. While Aschenbach tries to aestheticize his pursuit of beauty, the narrator emphasizes that he is sexually obsessed with a flirtatious adolescent boy who deliberately arouses Aschenbach's interest: "[Tadzio] would turn his head and assure himself with a glance of his strange twilit grey eyes that his lover was still following" (71). Indeed, Tadzio has much in common with the older doubles who insinuate themselves into Aschenbach's consciousness.

Aschenbach mistakes his Dionysian passion for a version of the Apollonian formal beauty he had been serving in Munich. In wooing Tadzio, Aschenbach renounces all that he had been and that had shaped his work, including devotion to a rigorous work ethic and a strong control over his style, form, and theme of passive heroism. What is being dramatized is Aschenbach opening his closed fist and letting go of the mask of control that he has created, but doing so with a shocking lack of self-awareness that he has become what he once despised. We remember Aschenbach's disparaging condescension to the old passenger who tried to look young on the boat to Venice: "Could they not see he was old, that he had no right to wear the clothes they wore or pretend to be one of them?" (17).

Aschenbach's Transformation and Demise

The narrator presents Aschenbach as someone who, in the final days of his life, has lost his intellectual moorings, perhaps in response to his contracting cholera, although the narrator does not describe any symptoms: "[T]he rouged and flabby mouth uttered single words of the sentences shaped in his disordered brain by the fantastic logic that governs our dreams" (72). Aschenbach lives on the borderland where physical deterioration, incipient senescence, depression, and madness meet.

Mann brilliantly renders the process by which the mind begins to fail as death approaches. Describing Aschenbach's very last day, the narrator uses a straightforward descriptive style rather than the Germanic master style with which he has been rendering Aschenbach's forced comparison of himself with Socrates. The narrator observes: "[Aschenbach] was not feeling well and had to struggle against spells of giddiness only half physical in their nature, accompanied by a swiftly mounting dread, a sense of futility and hopelessness – but whether this referred to himself or to the outer world he could not tell" (73).

In his final days of life Aschenbach redefines knowledge as something far more inclusive than the knowledge that had shaped his fiction and brought him fame. Taking refuge in his imagined role as Socrates, Aschenbach explains to himself in a poignant interior monologue: "For knowledge, Phaedrus, does not make him who possesses it dignified or austere. Knowledge is all-knowing, understanding, forgiving; it takes up no position, sets no store by form. It has compassion with the abyss – it *is* the abyss" (72; emphasis Mann's). Redefining language to justify his behavior, Aschenbach proposes an expanded concept of knowledge that encompasses all that he has repressed, including aspects of life that undermine judgment and link beauty to desire.

By redefining "knowledge," the confused and obsessive Aschenbach is abandoning the rigid aesthetic and moral values by which he has lived. Mann is very much aware of the irony of Aschenbach's adopting a humanistic cosmopolitanism that allows for relativism and pluralism. To "take up no position" is not so different from Ivan Karamazov's assertion in *The Brothers Karamazov* that without God "everything is permitted" (II.iv.5.263). Aschenbach tries to recoil from what for him is this very uncomfortable position to hold and embrace an Apollonian concept of beauty, but his distinctions are now blurred: "So we reject it, firmly, and henceforward our concern shall be with beauty alone. And by beauty we mean simplicity, largeness, and renewed severity of discipline; we mean a return to detachment and to form" (72–73).

In the frenzy of compulsive passion, distinctions as well as restraints dissolve. For Aschenbach, the dichotomy between the Apollonian and Dionysian breaks down. Concepts that had been associated with the Apollonian are redefined and reconfigured so that the Apollonian becomes a version of the Dionysian. Aschenbach had lived on the assumption that the alternative to Dionysian chaos, the protection against the abyss, was his dedication to the classical Apollonian beauty, and he rationalized that his interest in Tadzio was a version of his dedication to form that had driven his writing. But in fact, as he now knows, "detachment ... and preoccupation with form lead to intoxication and desire, they may lead the noblest among us to frightful emotional excesses. ... So they too, they too, lead to the bottomless pit" (71).

Aschenbach learns what he has denied, namely that life consists of more than work and that art is far more than its formal components; in both life and art there must be a place for passion, sexuality, and imagination. Yet paradoxically acting on that knowledge kills him because by remaining in Venice and pursuing his desires, he contracts cholera.

When Aschenbach says "I'll stop," Aschenbach means that he will stop and stay in a particular place in Venice. On rereading, we understand that he will stop living the life he has been leading and that he will stop living and die (30). Even after learning that Venice is in the midst of a cholera epidemic, he stays and presumably succumbs, although he does not seem to be suffering from the symptoms of cholera – diarrhea, vomiting, bloating, and other discomforts associated with that disease – or at least Mann does not specify them. However, untreated cholera and dehydration could cause very low blood pressure and a heart attack which seems to be how Aschenbach dies.

Ultimately, the narcissistic Aschenbach has modeled himself on the passive, persevering obsessive figure that he had proposed as a hero, although one could also say that he had created that version of a controlling hero from whom he was in Munich. To cite Stephen's theory in *Ulysses*, "He found in the world without as actual what was in his world within as possible" (IX.1041–1042). He had done so by turning his back on fancy, imagination, and passion and cultivated a very limited sense of what it is to be human. As the narrator steps back and reminds us a few days before Aschenbach's death: "[T]his was he who had put knowledge underfoot to climb so high; who had outgrown the ironic pose and adjusted himself to the burdens and obligations of fame; whose renown had been officially recognized and his name ennobled, whose style was set for a model in the schools" (71–72). Now Aschenbach, the author who, in a work called *The Abject*, had "in a style of classic purity renounced bohemianism and all its works, all sympathy with the abyss and the troubled depths of the outcast human soul," has become what he despised; Aschenbach is the abject (71).

As Aschenbach loses control, the pace of his deterioration and his race toward premature death increase. His violent, dissolute dream reflects his long stifled and repressed desire, sexuality, passion, and imagination. A pivotal turning point is his dream that evokes his country home overrun by men and animals in a confused orgiastic scene revolving around "[t]he stranger god" (67). His dream set in his rural retreat where all had been calm and ordered is, among other things, of sexual excess, perceived as a symptom of a breakdown of all moral barriers and of human devolution into animals:

· ·

From the wooded heights, from among the tree trunks, and crumbling moss-covered rocks, a troop came tumbling and raging down, a whirling rout of men and animals, and overflowed the hillside with flames and human forms, with clamour and the reeling dance. … He trembled, he shrank, his will was steadfast to preserve and uphold his own god against this stranger who was sworn enemy to dignity and self-control. But the mountain wall took up the noise and howling and gave it back manifold; it rose high, swelled to a madness that carried him away. His senses reeled in the steam of panting bodies, the acrid stench from the goats, the odour as of stagnant waters – and another, too familiar, smell – of wounds, uncleanness and disease. … They laughed, they howled, they thrust their pointed staves into each other's flesh and licked the blood as it ran down. But now the dreamer was in them and of them, the stranger god was his own. … [O]n the trampled moss there now began the rites in honour of the god, an orgy of promiscuous embraces – and in his very soul he tasted the bestial degradation of his fall. (67–68)

· ·

Note that Mann describes the dream in a much more graphic and precise style, but still one in which, as in German, the verbs are postponed to last. In his translation, Lowe-Porter wanted to capture the way a German sentence gathers its force as it accretes and coalesces to a crescendo.

Death in Venice ends in autumn, after most of the tourists have either died or departed. The narrator traces Aschenbach's deterioration and devolution into squalid degradation; soon he is stalking Tadzio: "He slunk under walls, he lurked behind buildings or people's backs" (71). The fatigue experienced a few short months ago from art now accompanies his obsession: "[T]he sustained tension of his senses and emotions exhausted him more and more" (71). In the final paragraph, Aschenbach whose name in German means "stream of ashes" – perhaps signifying dust to dust, perhaps a volcanic eruption depositing ashes – dies watching Tadzio playing in the ocean, seemingly summoned to death by Tadzio who awakened the libidinous self he had for so long denied. Yet, we ask, would it have been better for Aschenbach if he had stayed in Munich, living his stunted life, rather than expanded his knowledge and died prematurely?

Death in Venice reflects a cultural moment in early twentieth-century Europe when Mann believed materialism, selfishness, and narcissism were fore-grounded, while imagination and passion contracted and often found an outlet in perverse forms. But while *Death in Venice* is a critique of a dead world, the alternative, to evoke Matthew Arnold's "Stanzas from the Grand Chartreuse," seems "powerless to be born." Looking outward and within himself, Mann is

31

also asking poignantly and skeptically whether, within both an individual and a culture, balance is possible between the Dionysian and Apollonian aspects of life, between the needs of the intellect and those of the emotions.

Study Questions for *Death in Venice*

1. How do the various Aschenbach "doubles" function? Why and how does Mann present Aschenbach's various doubles and counterparts? Are they versions of himself?
2. How does the "master" style that Mann chose for his narrator relate to central issues within the narrative about Aschenbach?
3. What are the biographical, historical, cultural, and literary contexts for *Death in Venice*?
4. Why is Aschenbach attracted to Tadzio? Is Mann writing about pederasty?
5. Why is Socrates invoked? How does the rhetoric of allusions work in *Death in Venice*?
6. Why is Mann evoking Nietzsche's Apollonian–Dionysian dichotomy? Why does Aschenbach's Dionysian dream occur near the end? Can we use psychoanalytic terms – superego, id, repression, etc. – to discuss Aschenbach's trajectory?
7. Why the title? Why Venice? How is it contrasted with Munich? Does Mann use setting to represent different sides of Aschenbach's psyche?
8. How do both the beginning and ending function in terms of the way the structure affects the reader?
9. How does *Death in Venice* compare with other texts that use illness as metaphor?
10. How does Aschenbach's concept of heroism shape our response to him?
11. What is the function of Mann's narrator and what is his relationship to Aschenbach? Is Mann sympathetic or judgmental or both?

Notes

1. Thomas Mann, *A Sketch of My Life*, trans. H. T. Lowe-Porter (New York: Alfred A. Knopf, 1960), 43–44.
2. James W. Jones, "Mann, Thomas (1875–1955): *Death in Venice*." In *glbtq: an encyclopedia of gay, lesbian, bisexual, transgender, & queer study*; http://www.glbtq.com/literature/mann_t.html (accessed March 15, 2016; no longer available).
3. Leo Carey, "Love in Venice," *NYR* 61:1 (Jan. 9, 2014), 56–58; see 56.
4. See Gilbert Adair's *The Real Tadzio: Thomas Mann's Death in Venice and the Boy Who Inspired It* (Boston: De Capo Press, 2009).
5. Jones, "Mann, Thomas: *Death in Venice*."
6. Thomas Mann, *Death in Venice and Seven Other Stories*, trans. H. T. Lowe-Porter (New York: Vintage, 1930). Page numbers refer to this edition.

7. Peter Schjeldahl, "Then and Now: Bronzino at the Met," *The New Yorker* (Feb. 1, 2010); http://www.newyorker.com/magazine/2010/02/01/then-and-now-6

8. R. P. Blackmur, *Eleven Essays in the European Novel* (New York: Harcourt, Brace & World, 1964).

9. T. S. Eliot, "Ulysses, Order and Myth," *The Dial* 35 (1923), 480–483; reprinted in *The Modern Tradition: Backgrounds of Modern Literature*, eds. Richard Ellmann and Charles Feidelson, Jr. (New York: Oxford University Press, 1965), 679–681; see 681.

10. Xenophon, *The Memorable Thoughts of Socrates*, ed. Henry Morley, trans. Edward Bysshe (The Floating Press, 2013).

Chapter 3

Proust's *Swann's Way* (1913) and the Novel of Sensibility: Memory, Obsession, and Consciousness

> "It is thus the narrative, and that alone, that informs us here both of the events that it recounts and of the activity that supposedly gave birth to it."
>
> Gérard Genette, *Narrative Discourse: An Essay in Method*[1]

What Kind of Fiction Did Proust Write?

Proust's *Swann's Way* (1913) is one of seven novels that comprise *Remembrance of Things Past*, sometimes called *In Search of Lost Time* (*A la recherche du temps perdu*, 1913–1927). Proust took the English title *In Search of Lost Time* from Voltaire's translation of Shakespeare's thirtieth sonnet. The new translation by Lydia Davis beautifully renders Proust's sensibility, imaginative focus, encyclopedic knowledge of the arts, and the richness of his syntax.[2]

Gérard Genette aptly uses the term "disguised autobiography" to describe the genre of *Swann's Way* and indeed of *A la recherche du temps perdu* (Genette, 247). Genette reminds us: "[I]n free indirect speech, the narrator takes on the speech of the character, or, if one prefers, the character speaks through the voice of the narrator, and the two instances are *merged*; in immediate speech, the narrator is obliterated and the character *substitutes* for him" (Genette, 174; emphases Genette's).[3] Certainly, something like this happens in the middle section, "Swann in Love." But the narrator never completely cedes the floor to anyone. Genette calls *Recherche* "an autodiegetic narrative … where … the narrator-hero never yields the privilege of the narrative function to anyone" (Genette, 247).

Reading the Modern European Novel Since 1900: A Critical Study of Major Fiction from Proust's Swann's Way to Ferrante's Neapolitan Tetralogy, First Edition. Daniel R. Schwarz.
© 2018 John Wiley & Sons Ltd. Published 2018 by John Wiley & Sons Ltd.

Genette argues that we need to attend to the text rather than to parallels with Proust's life as our principal source of knowledge about *Swann's Way* and the whole of *A la Recherche du temps perdu*:

> It is thus the narrative, and that alone, that informs us here both of the events that it recounts and of the activity that supposedly gave birth to it. In other words, our knowledge of the two (the events and the action of writing) must be indirect, unavoidably mediated by the narrative discourse, inasmuch as the events are the very subject of that discourse and the activity of writing leaves in its traces, signs or indices that we can pick up and interpret – traces such as the presence of a first-person pronoun to mark the oneness of character and narrator, or a verb in the past tense to indicate that a recounted action occurred prior to the narrating action, not to mention more direct and explicit indications. (Genette, 28–29)

The question is how do we balance knowledge of Proust's life with our understanding that the narrator is a fictional character, an illuminating distortion created by Proust's imagination, but one whose experience is informed by Proust's life.

Thus when James Grieve tells us that "After 1899 … [Proust's] chronic asthma, the death of his parents, and his growing disillusionment with humanity caused him to lead an increasingly retired life," we need to resist simply attributing the cynicism and voyeurism of the section entitled "Swann in Love" to a few biographical facts which we can manipulate to provide various reductive explanations.[4]

Proust creates a fictional narrator and the narrator then uses his own memory to define himself, and that means speaking about personal memories of childhood to an imagined audience within the text. In the first part ("Combray") and third part ("Place-Names: The Name") of *Swann's Way* the unnamed narrator – a self-defined neurotic – examines his consciousness in excruciating detail in a process that we might call auto-therapy. Dramatizing the mind in action as it seeks to capture evanescent thought and feeling, sensations and reactions, desires and fears, the narrator is Proust's surrogate. Whether describing what really happened or summoning memories of elusive memories, the narrator is never given a name.

The narrator is an original: neurotic, depressed, obsessive, immersed in the life of the mind – art, literature, and music – and self-conscious in the extreme about all his feelings. He has an almost pathological interest in details which, combined with his rich array of sensory impressions, arrests the forward movement of plot. Thus he will suspend the narrative to share his pleasures in confronting nature, especially flowers. Often employing synesthesia, combining taste (food), visual impressions of art objects, and aural responses to music, the prose becomes a poetic experience transporting the reader to a timeless place where events take a back seat to the moment of immersed pleasure.

For Proust telling often takes precedence over showing. As Grieve observes: "Here is a novel written by a critic and literary theorist, both a novel in the form of an essay and an essay on the novel. … Proust's reflections, his enunciation of philosophical truths, his aesthetic theories, his opinions and system of thoughts are often more important to him than his verisimilitudes. … [A]ction must be performed perfunctorily, so that protracted analysis of it may ensue" (Grieve, xii). Yet, notwithstanding the narrator's propensity to reflect, Proust's idiosyncratic descriptions and ensuing reflections resist allegorical and even thematic readings. Our generalizations about what he has accomplished always seem to miss the mark and be reductive.

The time of memory is not clock time, and memory reaches backwards to give shape and form to transitory experience, but memory is a present tense event informed by imagination, and therefore memory is in part a memory of a memory. Another way of putting it: There is always a distinction between what happened and our memory of what happened, and a further distinction between our memory and how we organize it into language which necessarily transforms it. Readers of *Swann's Way* need to be quite aware on every page that the language – the agon of telling – is the final present tense event. Whether the narrator's memories of past sensory experiences and how they generate thoughts and feelings are memories or memories of memories, they are so strong that it is as if they were recurring at the moment he records them. Indeed, Proust's surrogate never speaks about the act of writing but about the act of remembering.

Space is defined by places and is a function of memory, and memory is always more of a personal impression than the encryption of an original event. Memory erases what time does to the past and replaces it with an image, fixed in the mind, even if as dynamic in its movement as events themselves. Memory itself is elusive and transitory, illusionary and deceptive. What fixes memory is writing, and *Swann's Way* is, in many ways, a Künstlerroman, that is, a novel about the development of an artist who, in this case, is writing the novel. Indeed, it creates a moving picture, and we realize that Proust is writing in the early days of film, although, as Allen Thiher remarks, we never know "the location of the narrator when he is narrating the story of his life" (Thiher, *Understanding Marcel Proust*, 113).[5]

It is not easy to pin down the chronology of *Swann's Way*, in part because Proust's point is that the inner life – memory, obsession, and consciousness – rather than external facts drives the narrative. My understanding of the temporal sequence is indebted to Mark Calkins's chronology,[6] which in turn owes a good deal to Genette's *Narrative Discourse*:

- Gilberte and the narrator are born in 1877 or 1878 (1878 (even experienced scholars differ on this date)
- Opening overture: takes place after 1925 (which is what Davis calls "Combray 1")
- Events described in "Combray 1": 1883–1892
- Episode of the madeleine: probably 1904
- "Combray 2": 1883–1892
- "Swann in Love": 1877–1878 (the narrator's mother is married while Swann is involved with Odette)
- "Place-Names: The Name": 1892–1895 (the narrator's fixation on Gilberte)
- Bois de Boulogne episode: probably 1903 (automobiles have replaced horse-drawn carriages)

Proust's Style

Even as the wonderful opening, with its memories of sleep, engages us readers, we may at first become impatient with what we perceive as the novel's glacial pace. That Proust deftly differentiates the essence of his characters' sensibilities, in part by precisely rendering idiosyncrasies of their personalties, personality, is a reason to put aside our impatience and immerse ourselves in the very slow reading of *Swann's Way*.

The slow, stately sentences often move outward from a radial center into concentric circles of sensory impressions, quirky visual observations, family and local history, and musical sounds until we get a full picture of the narrator's and later Swann's inner and outer world. The rendering of the narrator's perceptions, triggered early on if not throughout by his "nervous impulse," accretes to take us into the idiosyncratic but beautifully described worlds of the narrator and of Swann (33). Roger Shattuck observes:

· ·

The pendulum-like motion between solitude and sociability also strikes the reader in the rhythm of Proust's style. ... On the one hand, Proust is constantly tempted to fit his endlessly expanding, introspective universe into one proliferating, carefully built sentence whose syntax will articulate an order of subordination and temporality and causation holding all its parts in place. On the other hand, Proust knew the advantage of terseness. (Shattuck, *Proust's Way*, xviii)[7]

· ·

If terseness means the narrator's swift judgment on certain events, maybe, but if Shattuck means consistent, sharp, succinct distinctions in a few words, I am doubtful.

Given the narrator's boyhood "sadness," we consider depression part of his "involuntary ailment … a nervous condition for which I was not responsible" (38). We realize that he is a very special and not fully reliable or even – notwithstanding his exceptionally if not remarkably keen, polished sensibility – fully perceptive narrator around whom we need to draw our own circumference of judgment. Proust stresses the intricacies of his sensibility, but also, in a memorable way, the parallels between the frustrations of the narrator's childhood Oedipal love and Swann's disappointments as well as the preciousness of both narcissistic aesthetes. Like Swann, the narrator renders class distinctions in terms of bourgeois and aristocratic class division as well as smaller differences dependent on culture and style.

Proust's stylistic pyrotechnics are not streams of consciousness but controlled and disciplined sentences that reach outward into memory and prior experience – sometimes for what seems longer than is necessary and sufficient – but return to their original subject. "Proustian handling of inner speech," Genette observes, "is extremely traditional" because he avoids "an authentic interior monologue whose inchoateness supposedly guarantees transparency and faithfulness to the deepest eddies of the 'stream of consciousness' – or of unconsciousness" (Genette, 180). As Genette puts it, Proust's use of "gradations or subtle blends of indirect style and narrative speech ought not to blind us to the Proustian narrative's characteristic use of reported inner speech. Whether Marcel [whom I am calling the narrator] is involved or Swann, the Proustian hero, especially in his moments of ardent emotion, readily articulates his thoughts as a genuine monologue, enlivened by a fully theatrical rhetoric" (Genette, 176).

To enjoy Proust, the reader needs to empathetically surrender to the beauties of description and recreate in his mind – as if a sightseer – the experience of entering the church with the retrospective self-dramatizing narrator who is looking back on his youth and recalling in various ways the manner in which the sunlight coming through the windows affected the church: "[M]ore beloved than all these riches, a momentary smile of sunlight; it was as recognizable in the soft blue billow with which it bathed the precious stones as on the pavement of the square or the straw of the market place" (61–62).

Each sentence is an action of its own. Often sentences are at once meditative and reflective, but sometimes the narrator traces his own physical movement; his sentences mime his perambulatory bent and become travelogues reflecting his intense curiosity. Why, we need to ask, does Proust favor long sentences and paragraphs? We might say that the sentence and sometimes paragraph compose an interior monologue that renders in motion the complex consciousness of the narrator. Most sentences begin and end like normal sentences. But in between the beginning and the ending is what is different in Proust; references whirl out in a panoply of associations from the basic statement, covering swathes of time and space. We might call this tendency to postpone the ending of sentences "the long goodbye." Sentences transcend time by looking backward and sometimes forward, and transcend space by taking in many locations, even if often within the confined geography of Combray – sometimes filling up most or all of the page. To be sure, the focus is always on the limited world of the narrator.

"Combray 1": The Significance of the Opening Pages

The narrator and Swann have much in common, notably their fixation on mother and daughter, their aesthetic sensibility, and their hedonism punctuated by neurosis. It is ironic that both the narrator and Swann favor some paintings – the narrator: Giotto, Gozzoli, Gentile Bellini; Swann: Botticelli's *Primavera*, Ghirlandaio – reaching back to a world which contained religious truths and histories accepted by most educated people, although neither has much interest in religion.

Proust's unit is usually the sentence and sometimes the paragraph. The opening of each section introduces major themes that will be developed. The opening of "Combray 1" has been called the "Overture," as if it were setting up the epistemology and semiology for the rest of *Swann's Way* and the entire multi-volume *Remembrance of Things Past*, but while C. K. Scott Moncrieff used that term to describe the opening section in his 1928 Modern Library translation, Lydia Davis's more recent authoritative translation does not, preferring to divide the opening section into "Combray 1" and "Combray 2."[8]

We never know how old the narrator is in the opening and this indeterminacy has two paradoxical effects. It gives Proust leverage to include, whenever he wishes, whatever comparisons to art and music he chooses and whatever commentary on human behavior is on his mind. At the same time, the age indeterminacy also establishes the young narrator not only as brilliant and passionately drawn to the arts, but also as exceptionally perspicacious, polished, sensitive, nuanced, and in control of language well beyond his years.

From the outset, the reader is plunged into uncertainty and doesn't quite know when or where he is and the specifics of with whom he is dealing.

. . . .

For a long time, I went to bed early. Sometimes, my candle scarcely out, my eyes would close so quickly that I did not have time to say to myself: "I'm falling asleep." And, half an hour later, the thought that it was time to try to sleep would wake me; I wanted to put down the book I thought I still had in my hands and blow out my light; I had not ceased while sleeping to form reflections on what I had just read, but these reflections had taken a rather peculiar turn; it seemed to me I myself was what the book was talking about; a church, a quartet, the rivalry between François I and Charles V. This belief lived on a few seconds after my waking; it did not shock my reason but lay heavy like scales on my eyes and kept them from realizing that the candlestick was no longer lit. Then it began to grow unintelligible to me, as after metempsychosis do the thoughts of an earlier existence; the subject of the book detached itself from me, I was free to apply myself to it or not; immediately I recovered my sight and I was amazed to find a darkness around me soft and restful for my eyes, but perhaps even more so for my mind, to which it appeared a thing without cause, incomprehensible, a thing truly dark. I would ask myself what time it might be; I could hear the whistling of the trains which, remote or nearby, like the singing of a bird in the forest, plotting the distances, described to me the extent of the deserted countryside where the traveller hastens toward the nearest station; and the little road he is following will be engraved on his memory by the excitement he owes to new places, to unaccustomed activities, to the recent conversation and the farewells under the unfamiliar lamp that follow him still through the silence of the night, to the imminent sweetness of his return. (3–4)

. . . .

Adam A. Watt observes of the opening, "The slew of memories and reflections upon which we are cast adrift, however, in the first pages, serves a vital purpose; we share the Narrator's uncertainty; like him, we struggle to find our bearings" (Watt, *The Cambridge Introduction to Marcel Proust*, 47).[9] When we read the very first paragraph of *Swann's Way*, we know we have left behind the realistic tradition of Stendhal, Balzac, Flaubert, and Zola, all of whom I discussed in the first volume of this study, *Reading the European Novel to 1900*. Readers may recall that the aforementioned volume ended with Zola's *Germinal* and the study of the social and moral effects of the mining industry. Proust, along with Joyce and Woolf, takes the novel farther than past masterworks to render time, motion, touch, sensory experience as well as consciousness and even unconsciousness and dreams. What is striking is the extreme self-reflexivity and interiority of the narrator's consciousness and what it says not only about Proust but also about the direction of the modern novel in the twentieth century as it moves away from traditional realism. In a sense, Proust is playing with the conventions of the realistic novel by having the major plot event – the marriage of Swann and Odette – take place offstage, for this is a novel about the narrator's sensibility.

Swann's Way begins in darkness with a narrator trying to locate himself in the confusion of living by means of memory. He is a prodigy of perspicuity and memory. He reflects even while sleeping and sees himself as the subject of the book he is reading. Indeed, that self-immersion and narcissism, that sense that he is the measure of all things, dominates his life, and he has those qualities in common with Swann. Both he and Swann live in books, music, paintings, and history as much as in the world they inhabit.

The first paragraph opens out to the experiences of adulthood, to travels, exciting, perhaps erotic adventures ("unaccustomed activities"), including conversations and farewells at night, and these experiences look forward not only to the narrator's own love affairs and erotic fantasies but also to those of Swann in the second section entitled "Swann in Love." The traveler is not only himself and Swann, but also the reader who takes part in the opening out of the first paragraph to the world beyond the narrator's childhood bedroom when visiting Combray. For isn't the first paragraph a mental journey from childhood – almost the womb – to the larger world of trains, countryside, the pleasures of nature (a bird singing), human interactions, departures, and the implications of relationships ending with farewells? In a sense, the first paragraph encapsulates the entirety of *Swann's Way*.

For the story of Swann is also the story of how the mind responds to experience much less than to the experiences themselves. The narrative is about Swann's inner-life sensory, emotional, and aesthetic responses much more than about actual events. While "Swann in Love" has the scaffolding of traditional narrative – he meets Odette, has an affair, suffers from being cuckolded and rejected – the focus is on Swann's interiority: how he responds in terms of feelings, memories, and aesthetic experiences. Proust provides no more dating of events than in Part I.

Interestingly, as if to anticipate the presence of mistresses and the theme of rivalry – between the boy and his father for his mother's affections as well as among classes and persons, including seeking attention from lovers – the narrator on the very first page is reading about Charles V, Holy Roman Emperor from 1519 to 1556 (rather than Charles V of France who lived in the fourteenth century). Charles V opposed the Protestant Reformation and had several mistresses. His rival, the Protestant Francis I of France – patron of the arts, supporter of a standard French language, known as "Father and Restorer of Letters" – ruled from 1515 to 1547 and fought Charles V in the "Italian Wars." Francis I also had mistresses.

Proust's is an introspective world made of tiny victories and defeats. The Oedipal narrator, as a child, is obsessed with his mother's presence; she is for him a paradigm of "that goodness, that moral distinction which Mama had learned from my grandmother to consider superior to all else in life" (42). His victory is her staying with him all night: "My remorse was quieted, I gave into the sweetness of that night in which I had my mother close to me" (43). In the Davis translation, the narrator spends the 45 pages – the section begins on p. 3 and ends on p. 48 – recalling his fixation with his mother, while depicting the uniqueness of his family and their visitor, Swann.

The memory with which the narrator opens is a traumatic memory, namely that of being separated from his mother. Fearful of isolation, abandonment, and jealous when his mother's attention is on anyone but him, the unnamed narrator – whom we learn in a different volume is called Marcel – is manically obsessive about controlling bedtime routines. If there is an organizing principle, it is the narrator's memory rather than chronological order. In some ways the narrative of Part I is an anti-narrative following not the movement of events through time but the movement of memory. And memory is always uncanny, that is, familiar but strange in an unsettling way.

Young Marcel's awakening in the middle of the night – and memory of it – has an uncanny aspect; for we experience darkness when we awake without quite knowing where or even perhaps who we are. And isn't that dislocation of ourselves, that reaching back and sideways to define our decentered self, the essence of *Swann's Way*? Proust is implying that *Swann's Way* is an example of how reading itself, something to which his narrator is devoted, is necessarily strange and unsettling. Our response to reading and indeed all the arts has an uncanny aspect. We respond to the familiar and the strange. Our experience is always about the familiar because we see ourselves in characters' behavior that is, as Stevens (another aesthete and narcissist) put it in "The Idea of Order at Key West," "of ourselves and origins." But characters' behaviors are strange because we are observing others different from ourselves.

Swann's Way begins almost as if the narrator were a child discovering the world. Although about five years old, if we accept Calkins's chronology, the opening is cognate with an infant's registering first impressions and finding his place in the world. In the first pages we encounter the invalid narrator consigned to his bed in Combray, and meet the immediate family inhabiting the same house: grandmother, grandfather, great aunt, mother, and finally, Swann, the title character, who regularly visits the house. At first it seems that the narrator's feelings are in a dark, hypochondriacal tunnel, but gradually, as when he speaks of his uncle and the courtesan, we begin to move into a larger world and see social patterns beyond his own family.

What do we make of a narrator who obsesses about being sent to bed without a kiss from his mother and in the Davis edition weaves 45 pages around this obsession? Is this a prelude not only to Swann's obsession with Odette, which turns into disappointment and jealousy, but also his own obsession with Gilberte, Swann's and Odette's daughter?

For much of the novel's opening section, the narrator's focus is on his childhood, more specifically on rendering his sensibility on a night when Swann visits and the narrator is sent to bed early. Early on, before the first reader knows Swann's story, the narrator draws an implicit parallel between the pain of rejection Swann suffers due to his having an adulterous wife and the narrator's pain at being separated from his mother to whom he has a strong Oedipal attachment.

While the opening is retrospective, we are pulled up short with the brief sentence after his father has sent his mother to his room at Combray: "This was many years ago" (37). We are told that "life is now becoming quieter around me," but we don't know when "now" is and we realize that the relationship between memory and time will be a major theme and that the mind's time – what we might think of as significant time or *kairos* – can insert itself between the tick and tock of chronological time or *chronos* (37).

If there is an overarching theme in Proust, it is that art matters and, as much as our passionate and erotic life, defines us. One of Proust's major points is that artistic experiences are essential to who we are as much as or more so than other experiences. We are, as Marcel and Swann show, what we read in books, see in paintings, and hear in music. Because Marcel and Swann have heightened sensibilities, Proust's text is teaching us the importance of art.

For the narrator, as for Swann, artistic experiences are as intense and passionate as other life experiences. The narrator's knowledge of art (notably, Giotto and Botticelli), music, and literature informs his sensibility and often provides the context for responding to and understanding other kinds of experience. The way the narrator as a child and adolescent loses himself in books becomes a compelling and eloquent defense of reading and implicitly writing. Indeed, his reading becomes a model within the text of what books can do, what Proust is trying to do for his readers, and, specifically, how we readers should immerse ourselves in *Swann's Way*.

The act of memory always has an element of trauma because it contains an element of mortality. As a young boy, Proust's narrator awakes in darkness without knowing the time. Rereading, we understand time is what he seeks and can never find, that it is the darkness from which he tries to extract elusive meaning. Darkness represents time past which he is always chasing in his mind but never quite catching up to, and that inability to capture the originating event, to find one's way to permanent meaning as opposed to ephemeral moments of light and understanding, is, Proust believes, the human condition.

Proust is interested in how memory works. At the end of "Combray 1," the narrator is deeply affected when tasting a petite madeleine dipped in tea: "A delicious pleasure had invaded me, isolated me, without my having any notion as to its cause. It had immediately rendered the vicissitudes of life unimportant to me, its disasters innocuous, its brevity illusory, acting in the same way that love acts, by filling me with a precious existence" (45). What pleasurable memory does is interrupt time, provide a seeming space between the inevitable movement of time; what the narrator describes is like Eliot's "the still point of the turning world" or Joyce's epiphany, except that Joyce's epiphany is a moment of enlightenment within the present and Proust's narrator is finding his coherence in a memory of the past: "Smell and taste still remain for a long time, like souls, remembering, waiting, hoping, upon the ruins of all the rest, bearing without giving way, on their almost impalpable droplet, the immense edifice of memory" (47).

The madeleine is a paradigm for evoking the narrator's memories, but it is by no means the only stimulus for evoking the past. The Combray steeple also plays that role. Swann's very name acts as a madeleine because the narrator is infatuated with Swann's daughter, Gilberte.

Once Proust's narrator launches his comments, reflections, musings, he is not constrained by space or time. The reader lives in the narrator's mind more than in a world of external action. Proust's interest, unlike Balzac's, is not in the world beyond self, in the fabric of the city, the way material things reflect the social and political arrangements of life. Indeed, he often takes for granted how his major characters have the means to live and to live quite lavishly. Grieve puts it nicely:

....

Proust's real strengths lie in his analysis of the ordinary, his close acquaintanceship with feelings, the pessimism of his examination of consciousness, his diagnosis of the unreliability of relationships and the incoherence of personality, his attentiveness to the bleak truths he has to tell of time, of its unrelenting wear and tear, its indifferent outlast of all human endeavor, its gradual annulment of our dearest joys and even our cruelest sorrows, voiding them of all that once made them ours. Life, as Proust tells it, is disappointment and loss – loss of time … and loss of youth … loss of freshness of vision, of belief, and the semblance it once gave to the world; and loss of self, a loss against which we have only one safeguard, and that unsure: memory. (Grieve, xvi)

....

Nominally, the book's title, *Swann's Way*, refers to a walk from the narrator's Aunt Leonie's house past Swann's elaborate house. But it also refers to Swann's obsessive way of loving, his aestheticism, his narcissism, his self-delusion, that is, all the things that make Swann who he is.

If there is a recurring neurosis shared throughout by both the narrator and Swann, it is obsessive and compulsive behavior. The first part of Part I revolves around the young boy's Oedipal relationship with his mother and the triumphant night his father assigns her to the narrator's bedroom. But he knew even then that such an epiphanic night – existing now only as a precious memory – was unique.

These opening oscillations in the narrating boy's mind between moments of fulfillment and anxiety as well as disappointment are repeated in Swann's relationship to Odette in Part II, "Swann in Love." "Swann in Love" revolves around Swann's obsessive, even emotionally sado-masochistic relationship with Odette, a relationship that descends into self-degradation. Leopold von Sacher-Masoch's *Venus in Furs* (1870), which stressed female dominance and sado-masochism, was published a handful of years before Swann met Odette. Since it was well known in Paris, the very literary up-to-date Proust was certainly familiar with it. The oscillations between poignant moments of fulfillment and disappointment are again repeated in the narrator's own adolescent yearnings for – indeed, fixation with – Odette's daughter Gilberte, in Part III, "Place-Names: The Name."

Economically comfortable, Proust stresses that our identity depends as much on idiosyncratic quirks as upon social caste. Proust emphasizes that we create our real self – the inner self which shapes much of our personality and who we are – from our thoughts, feelings, and experiences. Notably, in Proust who we are depends on how memory distills what transpires. What matters as much as what happened is how our mind organizes what happened from the retrospective narrative that our memory creates. But as the narrator puts it, "our social personality is a creation of the minds of others," although that seems reductive in view of how the interior self modifies the social personality in the cases of Swann and the narrator (19).

Yet if what matters most is our inner life, the reader knows that much of the life Proust describes depends on the luxury of having considerable means. Proust focuses on the distinction between the social self and the inner self, often hidden in a myriad of secrets, including anxieties, obsessions, quirks, compulsions, and unacknowledged needs. We are in fact myriad selves, Proust urges. This concept of self is very different from the older concept of coherent self with a sturdy character, but very much a concept that Virginia Woolf, perhaps more of an English counterpart to Proust than any other English author, would have understood.

Published in 1913 on the threshold of the outbreak of World War I but looking back into the nineteenth century, *Swann's Way* takes us into the narrator's personal and private world where his sensibility seems enmeshed completely in his own feelings and memories and indifferent to external events. Unlike Joyce's *Ulysses*, *Swann's Way* does not have unity of time and in fact has several beginnings, implicitly raising questions about the very nature of beginnings of life, love, creativity, personality, how we each perceive, and what we live for.

Is Proust's theme, we might ask, the danger of solipsism (and concomitant neurosis) and aestheticism or is he himself immersed in those very values he criticizes? Or does he walk a fine line between awareness and criticism – especially when presenting Swann, perhaps less so the narrator to whose faults he is more tolerant than he is to Swann's? By contrast, James Joyce renders interior consciousness – notably, in *Ulysses*, of the narrator and Bloom, but also Stephen-Dedalus – without losing touch with politics, history, and the transformation of urban culture.

What Proust paradoxically does is foreground every nuanced sensory response and emotion, even while showing that perspicacity and self-knowledge are what we strive for and yet pathetically lack. The narrator dismisses "the eyes of an observer who sees things only from the outside, that is to say who sees nothing," but we realize that what we see from the inside depends on our emotional life and that each of us perceives as a function of who we are at a given moment and that these moments are ephemeral and ever changing (406). Thus while seeing from the outside may be limited, savoring every feeling, dipping into the context of every other feeling, sensory response, and artistic experience may have its limitations, too.

Multiple Selves

Proust is very much aware that how one experiences the world depends on who is having the experience, where one is situated at a given moment, and, if one is an artist, how that experience can be transmuted into a formal arrangement which enables it to be shared by an audience. In the visual arts, Cubism – and in particular Picasso and Braque – stressed the need for multiple perspectives as a way of understanding reality. Modern literature from Conrad to Joyce and Woolf stresses that knowing depends on individual perspectives and we all know differently.

The narrator discovers multiple versions of himself. As Roger Shattuck observes: "Marcel, the boy who grows to manhood in these pages, spends the early part of his life absorbed in his own sensations, which give him a powerful sense of life concentrated upon himself. Nothing is more precious than this physical, organic, inward sense of his own existence as himself in the world's zoo. Yet, after every move to an unfamiliar place and a new bedroom, Marcel must build this sense of himself all over again. At the same time ... [h]e wants to know and to touch what is not part of him. He yearns to live beyond himself" (Shattuck, xvi–xvii).

Perhaps an example of Proust balancing multiple selves is his attitude towards Jews. Proust, like Swann, had a Jewish parent; his mother was Jewish although his father was Catholic. As a strong supporter of Dreyfus, Proust expressed in later volumes of *Remembrance of Things Past*, notably in Vol. 3, *The Guermantes Way*, strong outrage when Swann's friends turn against him during the Dreyfus affair because of his Jewish heritage. But Proust himself reveals his ambiguous attitude towards Jews in his condemnation in *The Guermantes Way* of Bloch for being gauche.

Surely, what the narrator and Swann see depends on their own fixations and idiosyncrasies as well as their own experiential history. Neither is consistent because both have complex psyches that answer to multiple needs. As the narrator puts it towards the end of "Combray 2": "Facts do not find their way into the world in which our beliefs reside; they did not produce our beliefs, they do not destroy them; they may inflict on them the most constant refutations without weakening them" (151). Not facts, but our response to them matters; that is, our feelings about them and our memory of them filtered through our present consciousness that is shaped by experience subsequent to the original facts.

One of Proust's points is that we are all more complex than we imagine and we all have multiple selves. In part, this is because we are all necessarily hypocrites; no one is who he/she seems, and no one has full self-knowledge. Depending on the circumstances, including with whom we are speaking, we wear different masques. Thus the Swann dining with the narrator's family, who disapprove of Odette, is not the Swann obsessed with Odette.

The narrator and Swann continually illustrate how we have multiple selves. Isn't the narrator dividing himself between his younger and present self as well as implicitly between himself and Swann? But every character from Odette and Swann to the minor characters is a complex self with multiple aspects. Legrandin's talking self is a Jacobin, but his darker, private self is a snob. On those rare occasions when she extricates herself from her compulsive hypochondria, Aunt Leonie believes that social status is equivalent to merit. Except for the family she serves and for whom she cares a great deal, the maid Françoise believes she is better than others and thus lacks a capacity for empathy for anyone outside the family.

Combray 2

Evoking the place where the narrator awoke as a boy in "Combray 1," "Combray 2" has a more solid beginning, but again depends on the narrator's memory:

· ·

[T]hese streets of Combray exist in part of my memory so withdrawn, painted in colors so different from those that now coat the world for me, that in truth all of them, and also the church that rose above them on the square, appear to me more unreal than the projections of the magic lantern [of his childhood memory that were part of the special night with his mother in Combray 1]; and that at certain moments, it seems to me to be able to cross the rue Saint-Hilaire again, to be able to take a room in the rue de l'Oiseau … would be to enter into contact with the Beyond in a manner more marvelously supernatural than making the acquaintance of Golo or chatting with Geneviève de Brabant. (49–50)

· ·

What is real, Proust asks, through his narrator? Is it memory or what we encountered as we experienced a place or event? Or is it neither, but what our imagination creates and what words we use to express that creation in the very novel we are now reading? But, paradoxically, what Proust's narrator is also implying here is that he cannot go back to that memory because life has affected the original impression and something is forever lost. So, memory itself is part of the process of change and metamorphosis, and while it can provide temporary respite, it too is affected and shaped by time. Therefore memory is as much a part of mortality as life itself. What can forestall time is writing because that survives our life.

For Proust, to paraphrase Wallace Stevens, the words of the world are the life of the world, malleable things, which he plays with just as a painter works by blending colors, shading lines, and defining space. Words are a material substance to be worked like clay, shaped, reshaped, and presented as art. Memories of, say, the church at Combray are opportunities to explore how language can use synesthesia to render sights and textures; while on other occasions, as with the madeleine, the focus is on taste and smells – as with his recalling the talk downstairs while he lay in bed – auditory sensations. In the case of the Combray church, the stress is on the poetic possibilities of the aperçu rather than on theme and idea.

The pink and white hawthorn hedge on the Swann property from which he hopes for Gilberte's emergence captivates him and plays a role not unlike the madeleine. What triggers the synesthesia is a sense of smell and the pink color. He appropriates religious language – informed by his boyhood Catholicism – to describe the hawthorn hedge:

The hedge formed a series of chapels that disappeared under the litter of their flowers, heaped into wayside altars; below them, the sun was laying down a grid of brightness on the ground as if it has just passed through a stained glass window; their perfume spread as unctuous, as delimited in its form as if I were standing before the altar of the Virgin, and the flowers themselves adorned also, each held out with its distracted air its sparkling bunch of stamens, delicate radiant ribs in the flamboyant style like those which, in the church, perforated the balustrade of the rood screen or the mullions of the window and blossomed out into the white flesh of a strawberry flower. (141–142)

To be sure the image is overdetermined, but we realize that he associates the flowers – notably the pink ones – with his first sighting of Gilberte, "a little girl with reddish-blond hair, who appeared to be coming back from a walk" (143). Because he had met Uncle Adolphe's lady in pink (who we now know is Odette), pink is associated with sexuality.

With his almost pathological interest in details, the narrator is an acute (and at times comic) observer of human foibles; in fact, *Swann's Way* is more comic than I remembered, particularly the valetudinarian Aunt Leonie who is certain

48

she faces imminent death and is loathe to leave her sickbed, and the maid Françoise feeding and protecting Leonie's illusions. Eulalie stops by Sunday to humor Leonie and not so incidentally to get her weekly tip for doing so.

Proust is an observer of human foibles and expects us to smile at the behavior of his narrator and Swann as well as that of the characters he presents. For example, he speaks euphemistically of sex as "music" in the household of M. Vinteuil, the composer of the phrase in the sonata that so moves Swann; Vinteuil shares the same female lover with his daughter. Dr. Percepied observes, "There's certainly a good deal of music-making going on in that establishment [M. Vinteuil's home]. … They play too much music, those people" (151). Among other things, the narrator and Proust are smiling that the composer had feet of clay.

The narrator's introduction to sexuality is the sordid scene in which he looks through a window and sees Mlle. Vinteuil and her friend having sex in part to desecrate the memory of her father, who had been, among other things, his aunt's piano teacher. M. Vinteuil had lived for his daughter and was so deeply saddened by her lesbianism that, according to the narrator's mother, it adversely affected his health.

To be sure, the narrator had seen Uncle Adolphe with a courtesan whom we suspect – and learn in a later volume – is Odette. But Adolphe's affair, as far as we know, was sex as play and pleasure, albeit also commerce. While Adolphe's relationship with Odette had its sordid aspect inflected by his parents' disapproval, this relationship is something different, not because of its lesbian nature but because of its devious and nasty overtones.

The narrator is appalled by the women's behavior. The women deliberately leave the window open when having sex and revel in M. Vinteuil's death. The narrator describes how they figuratively dance on Mlle. Vinteuil's father's grave – they deliberately have sex in front of his picture – and the narrator uses the word "sadism" (162, 167) and "sadist" (167–168) to describe their behavior. Mlle. Vinteuil encourages her friend, who also had sex with Mlle. Vinteuil's father, to spit on his picture (162, 167). Note the narrator's retrospective view when he begins this anecdote: "As will be seen later, for quite other reasons the memory of this impression was to play an important part in my life" (162).

The complexity of Mlle. Vinteuil's sexual responses anticpates Swann's and the narrator's own. She, like them, does not understand herself. In the narrator's analyses, Mlle. Vinteuil's sadism and cruelty give her no pleasure: "Sadists of Mlle. Vinteuil's kind are creatures so purely sentimental, so naturally virtuous that even sensual pleasure seems to them something bad, the privilege of the wicked" (168).

That Proust emphasizes the bathetic distinction between M. Vinteuil the musician and M. Vinteuil the sometimes fool – between the man who creates and the man who lives as an idiosyncratic outsider – may reflect his own awareness that in his social world he was regarded with some ridicule notwithstanding his brilliance as an artist.

By embedding in the closing pages of "Combray 2" examples of how the narrator's youthful writing summons his memories of the two steeples of Martinville and the one at Vieuxvicq, Proust anticipates the mature writing of the novel.

Swann

Swann (and perhaps Proust but certainly his narrator) needs to be understood in the context of the Decadent Movement. Swann has inherited great wealth from his father, a successful banker. The narrator (and we suspect Proust agrees) speaks of "the current philosophy of the day … where one's intelligence was understood to be in direct ratio to one's skepticism and nothing was real and incontestable except the individual tastes of each person" (289). Swann is a solipsist who lives for his own pleasure like Des Esseintes in Huysmans's *A Rebours* (1884) or Wilde's title character in *The Picture of Dorian Gray* (1890). Swann has no interest in politics or what the future will be like when he dies. Nor is he interested in religion.

Swann is the man Proust feared becoming but someone whose lifestyle had resemblances to his own, especially prior to his beginning to write *Remembrance of Things Past*. Swann is an obsessive, lazy narcissist, wrapped in his own pleasures. While the narrator and Swann have much in common, one major difference is that while Swann wastes his life and creates nothing, the narrator by writing about Swann and his own parallels does create something substantive. His telling is a sustained, committed, and powerful response to Swann's lazy aestheticism. The prose we are reading demonstrates not only his creative passion but also, in its way, his immersion in life.

Partly in the novel of manners tradition, Part II, "Swann in Love," reads much faster because it is more focused on actual events. The narrator becomes cynical as he describes Odette's group, revolving around the Verdurins; this group is presented as composed of self-deluding and pretentious arrivistes. But in his pursuit of Odette, Swann puts aside his reservations about the Verdurin circle. Odette gives Swann's life definition, but like Aschenbach in Mann's *Death in Venice*, he lets go of his social standards and judgment. We might say that Odette is his Tadzio and the corrupt, morally dense, and socially outré Verdurin circle, his Venice. Swann aestheticizes Odette as Aschenbach does Tadzio and we not only realize that the narrator also aestheticizes people but that he and Swann turn people into works of art. Aestheticizing people is a feature of the Decadent Movement – including Huysman and Wilde – as well as an indication of the role of painting in defining literary characterization in this period. As Anka Muhlstein has shown, the presence of painters and painting loomed large in nineteenth-century French fiction (Muhlstein, "Painters and Writers").[10] It is hardly a stretch, as I have argued in my *Reconfiguring Modernism: Explorations in the Relationship between Modern Art and Modern Literature*, to show the influence of French painting on the literature of other nationalities, particularly British (Joseph Conrad, D. H. Lawrence, Virginia Woolf), Irish (James Joyce), and American (Henry James, Wallace Stevens, T. S. Eliot).

The narrator ironically observes Swann's lack of self-knowledge. As Allen Thiher remarks, "Swann's association with this clan because of Odette threatens to undermine his own sense of values. He is drawn down by Odette, who in her lust for social ascension has adopted the shallow values, vulgar mannerisms, and absurd style of what she takes to be the 'smart' set. ... Swann's love cuts him free from the moorings of his own upper-class values" (Thiher, 113). Odette, who is at first impressed with Swann's social prestige, is soon, if not at first, playing Swann for money.

After meeting Odette, the lazy and often depressed Swann returns to working spasmodically on his unfinished – really, the narrator tells us, "abandoned" – study of Vermeer. In the nineteenth century, Vermeer was not the towering figure he is today. But his thematic appeal to Swann and Proust would have come from his focus on domestic matters with strong hints in many of his paintings of sexual intrigue. Examples are *The Procuress* or the subtler *The Music Lesson* or *Lady at the Virginals with a Gentleman* or *Girl Reading a Letter at an Open Window*.

We need to think about the form that heterosexual love takes in the section entitled "Swann in Love." Swann and Odette use a euphemism for intercourse: To "make cattleya" means to have sex because their first physical intimacy occurs when she was wearing cattleyas (cattleya is a genus comprising 113 species of orchids), but that they need such a phrase may suggest a way of bridging Swann's awkwardness in speaking of sex with a far more experienced woman whose full experience and profession he wants to deny. Interestingly, the narrator recalls Swann's courtship of Odette and the orchids on her breast when he remembers in the closing pages "the bouquets of violets crushed at [Gilberte's] breast" (442).

Is Swann's pursuit of Odette about heterosexual passion or does that take a backseat to obsessive behavior that becomes masochism? Isn't Proust writing about love that is unbalanced, where one loves far more than the other, where one is dominant and the other submissive? Does Swann play the submissive role akin to the receptor in homosexual male sex? We might ask, too, why Swann is revolted by Odette's having sex with another woman. One could argue that this news is another soiling of his idea of Odette, but the virulence of his response seems to reflect that of both the narrator and his creator;

we recall how Proust turned sex between Vinteuil's daughter and her lover into something sordid and sadistic.

As Shattuck acutely observes:

. . . .

The stations of Swann's love for Odette begin and end in indifference, and between those terms his sentiments, still covered by the generic term "love," pass through multiple, overlapping stages: aesthetic appreciation of Odette's beauty, passive acceptance of her company, suffering because of being deprived of her company, urgent physical need for her, brief happiness in the satisfaction of that need, the torments of jealousy, social disgrace in her eyes because of importunate behavior, a sense of physical and nervous sickness, despair at the recollection of his happier moments, incapacity to act in order to rescue himself, and the slow cooling of affection. (Shattuck, 128)

. . . .

Although obsessed with Odette, Swann seems of limited sexual passion and what sensuality he has is that of a collector rather than a lover. And what is a collector if not a voyeur who needs to possess what he regards as valuable, either in monetary or sentimental terms? He invokes Botticelli – notably a painting called *Primavera*, also known as "Allegory of Spring" and featuring Venus – in his perception of Odette (Fig. 1). Lonely and feeling empty, despite

Fig. 1   Sandro Botticelli, *La Primavera* (*Spring*) (1481–1482). Uffizi Gallery, Florence.

his being sought by the bourgeois and aristocracy, he seeks in her what he lacks within himself, but of course she has even less substance than he does.

Odette is a courtesan who takes advantage of Swann's obsession. What, we might ask, does Odette have in her favor? Swann does not find her particularly attractive. She is greedy, often nasty, and a solipsist whose only concern is herself. She knows he is in the throes of jealousy because of Forcheville. Swann is tortured by her seeing another man and having an erotic life outside the one he shares with her. It bothers him even early on that "Odette had a life which did not entirely belong to him" (249), but he is at first something of an ostrich in hiding her promiscuity from himself. Indeed, there is an aspect to their relationship that is emotionally sado-masochistic as if she enjoys hurting him and he enjoys being hurt.

Odette is hardly intellectually gifted: "[Swann] fully realized that she was not intelligent" (249); nor does she have anything more than superficial refinement or know anything about the arts. She is part of the Verdurin clique that lacks taste and substance. We learn in a later volume that the narrator's Uncle Adolphe's kept woman is none other than Odette. The more Swann learns of her, the more obvious it is that she has been extremely promiscuous, and that bothers him a great deal (325). The narrator draws a contrast between Odette's voracious sexual appetite – her "riotous" prior life and her "passion" (do we not recall Emma Bovary or Gina in *The Charterhouse of Parma*?) – and Swann who, in contrast to her, is an "aesthete examining the extant documents of fifteenth-century Florence in order to penetrate further into the soul of Botticelli's Primavera, bella Vanna, or Venus" (325). Swann's aestheticizing Odette is a kind of sublimation, which enables him to shift his thoughts and feelings into a less painful, safer, and more comprehensible plane. And isn't the narrator a doubleganger who also sees the world through the eyes of a connoisseur of Italian painting also an aesthete?

Swann's relationship with Odette is increasingly defined as a "disease" as if he suffered from consumption or had a morphine addiction:

. . . .

And, in fact, Swann's love had reached the stage where the doctor and, in certain affections, even the boldest surgeons, ask themselves if ridding a patient of his vice or ridding him of his disease is still reasonable or even possible. … And this disease which was Swann's love had so proliferated … that it could not have been torn from him without destroying him almost entirely: as they say in surgery, his love was no longer operable. (319–320)

. . . .

Because Odette is defined as a disease, Swann is "suffering" from an "illness" and that illness becomes the combination of love and jealousy (382). The disease is exacerbated when he discovers that Odette's sexual experience includes women: "He wanted to devote more care to her, as to a disease which one suddenly discovers is more serious" (377).

For Swann the musical phrase from the Vinteuil sonata serves the same evocative role as the madeleine does for the narrator; it evokes Swann's passion for Odette and, later, the sorrow and jealousy he feels for being cuckolded. Vinteuil was an imaginary figure. Proust was unequivocal about the origin of the *petite phrase*: As he wrote to Jacques de Lacretelle, "the 'little phrase' of the Sonata – and I have never said this to anyone – is … the charming but mediocre phrase of a violin sonata by Saint-Saëns [Violin Sonata No. 1 in D Minor, Op. 75 (1885)], a musician I do not care for."[11]

Swann's Way is structured like a musical composition with recurring motifs and leitmotifs. Swann, like his creator and the narrator, experiences life in terms of art. Perhaps the most poignant moment in "Swann in Love" is when Swann hears the Vinteuil sonata after he knows he has been relegated to the position of cuckold (which he probably was before he knew about it) by Odette. Swann recalls the moments when he seemed to be pre-eminent in Odette's heart: "Of those sorrows of which [the phrase of the sonata] used to speak to him and which, without being affected by them, he had seen it carry along with it, smiling, in its rapid and sinuous course, of those sorrows which had now become his own, without his having any hope of ever being free of them, it seemed to say to him as it had once said of his happiness: 'What does it matter? It means nothing'" (361). As Thiher observes, "Swann's wistful meditation on how likely is any permanent form of existence marks the beginning of the end of his love. After his meditation on music, the quickly ensuing succession of degrading revelations about Odette's sexual adventures concludes the tale of his love" (Thiher, 151).

Proust's psychological subtlety includes an understanding of how dreams reflect both our conscious waking minds and our deep-seated anxieties. The importance of dreams as a reflection of reality is part of Proust's modernist exploration of the inner self. In a crucial dream passage the narrator draws a parallel between Swann and himself, even while stressing the coexistence of Swann the younger lover and the retrospective disillusioned dreamer who sees his younger self saddened by decisions that he the dreamer has made: "Thus did Swann talk to himself; for the young man he had not been able to identify at first was also himself; like certain novelists, he had divided his personality between two characters, the one having the dream, another he saw before him wearing a fez" (393). In the same dream Forcheville (with the name's echo of the sexually explicit *foutre* or "fuck") becomes Napoleon III who took power in 1851 in a coup d'état after he was blocked from running for a second term as President by the Constitution and Parliament. Thus Forcheville for Swann is an illegitimate rival and a disreputable putative successor. We realize, too, that Proust's narrator has divided himself into "two characters": himself and Swann.

But this dream, where he divides himself into a younger and an older self, is anticipated by a former dream where he sees both selves on a train: "One day [Swann] dreamed he was leaving [Paris] for a year; leaning out the door of the railroad car toward a young man on the platform who was saying good-bye to him, weeping, Swann tried to convince him to leave with him. The train began to move, his anxiety woke him, he remembered he was not leaving, that he would see Odette that evening, the next day, and almost every day after" (367). The younger man is the Swann who fell in love with Odette and has now become miserable because of what ensued.

Why Does the Narrator Need to Tell Swann's Story?

Swann's story is part of the narrator's own life experience, in this case an introduction to the emotional complexity of the adult sexual world. A fellow aesthete who becomes more and more neurotic and depressed, Swann, the reader comes to understand, is the narrator's doubleganger as obsessed with Odette as the narrator is with his mother and with Combray and will be with Swann's daughter Gilberte. Sobbing, thinking of death, imagining he discovered a "fatal tumor," Swann reverts to infantile behavior that recalls the way the narrator behaved in the opening episode when he is desperate for his mother's attention (329). That the narrator speaks of Swann's obsession in terms of illness not only reveals something of the narrator's obsession with health and neurosis, but also stresses the parallels between the novel's two central characters. Like the narrator in his childhood anxiety and later in his attraction for Gilberte, Swann has a repetition compulsion and thus does the same things over and over.

As his narration evolves, the narrator begins to stress specific parallels between himself and Swann. In a process that the adolescent narrator repeats when Gilberte loses interest in him, the more Odette ignores Swann, the more attached Swann becomes. The narrator's Oedipal fixation on his mother had anticipated Swann's fixation with Odette, except Swann "did not have, as I had at Combray in my childhood, happy days during which to forget the sufferings that will return at night" (306–307). Suspecting Odette of having sex with others, Swann, the narrator observes, "went to bed as anxious as I myself was to be some years later on the evenings when he would come to dine at the house, at Combray" (308). But unlike Swann, who does not complete his study of Vermeer and who is an aesthete and dilettante, the narrator, Proust's surrogate, does tell his story.

Using as he often does the second person pronoun as if to reach out to the reader and imply a community of those who would respond as he has, the narrator alludes to the sonata phrase and other "certain notions without equivalents" in his own memory. The reader thinks of the narrator's fear and loneliness in the Combray bedroom when he desperately awaits his mother: "But as long as we are alive, we can no more eliminate our experience of them than we can our experience of some real object, than we can for example doubt the light of the lamp illuminating the metamorphosed objects in our room whence even the memory of darkness has vanished" (363).

There is something of a paradox in the narrator's emphasizing the idiosyncratic behavior of the aesthete and claiming that the behavior is shared by a much larger category of readers? He wants to stress human commonality: "[F]acts do not find their way into the world in which our beliefs reside," even while preserving the originality of his sensibility and that of Swann (150–151).

Part III: The Narrator's Obsession with Gilberte

In Part III, "Place-Names: The Name," the narrator's plethora of sexual references makes us aware that he is pubescent. Gilberte has become the fantasy of a forward woman coming on to him in places he treasures, and he refers to his recurring masturbation as "a natural trail left by a snail added itself to the leaves" (161).

The youthful narrator's pursuit of Gilberte parallels Swann's of Odette. Lest we miss this, and it is hard to do so, he reminds the reader, when he sees Swann picking up his daughter, of his own earlier Oedipal fixation and does so in one of his prolonged sentences. By its very length and complexity, the sentence asks the reader to live in the former time to which the sentence takes us back: "[S]ince nothing had any value for me anymore except to the extent that my love could profit from it, it was with a burst of shame and regret at not being able to erase them that I returned to the years when, in the eyes of this same Swann who was at this moment before me in the Champs-Elysées and to whom, happily, Gilberte had perhaps not mentioned my name, I had so often in the evenings made myself ridiculous by sending word asking Mama to come up to my room and say goodnight to me, while she was having coffee with him, my father, and my grandparents at the table in the garden" (424). Proust's brilliantly inclusive sentence alludes to the main themes of *Swann's Way*, including a synopsis of the opening episode, the narrator's fixation on Swann, Swann's on Odette, and the narrator's on Gilberte.

Parallels to what has preceded in the earlier parts abound. The narrator divides Gilberte into two selves; his playmate and his beloved; she responds only as playmate. We realize the parallel: Odette had never given Swann her heart and has used Swann as a playmate. The agate marble Gilberte brought the narrator as well as the book by Bergotte (a fictitious author based on Anatole France) she gave him become his madeleines for remembering her.

That the narrator is Swann's doubleganger is quite explicit. So taken is the adolescent narrator with Swann's daughter and so shaped by his reminiscence of the high regard he as a child had for Swann and by his fascination with what he knows about Swann – although he is years from writing about him – that he comically and poignantly tries to look like Swann: "As for Swann, in order to try to resemble him, I would spend all my time at the table, pulling on my nose and rubbing my eyes. … He seemed to me a person so extraordinary that I found it amazing that people I knew actually knew him too" (430).

The novel concludes with a nostalgic awareness that place, like time, belongs to memory and the imagination. Going back to the Bois and discovering automobiles there pollutes for him not only the original event but also the memory of it. He learns, to his regret, "what a contradiction it is to search in reality for memory's pictures, which would never have the charm that comes to them from memory itself and from not being perceived by the senses. The reality I had known no longer existed. … The places we have known do not belong solely to the world of space in which we situate them for our greater convenience. They were only a thin slice among contiguous impressions which formed our life at that time; the memory of a certain image is but regret for a certain moment; and houses, roads, avenues are as fleeting, alas, as the years" (444). What has happened to the magic of the past? Is it always tinged with nostalgic and elegiac regret for something that cannot be recaptured?

Study Questions for *Swann's Way*

1. What is distinct about Proust's style?
2. What can you say about the narrator's psyche and character?
3. Why is Swann attracted to Odette?
4. What are the parallels between Swann and the narrator? Why does the narrator tell Swann's story?
5. What does the madeleine do? Are there other memory triggers?
6. How is *Swann's Way* a social satire?
7. How is *Swann's Way* part of Modernism and Decadence? How is *Swann's Way* both a deviation from and continuation of nineteenth-century realism?
8. What is Gilberte's role?
9. How does the opening define the imagined world of *Swann's Way*?
10. How is the narrator introduced to sexuality?

Notes

1. Trans. Jane Lewin (Ithaca: Cornell University Press, 1986), 28.
2. Marcel Proust, *Swann's Way: In Search of Lost Time*, Vol. 1, trans. with intro. and notes by Lydia Davis (New York: Penguin, 2003). Page numbers in the text are to this edition.
3. Gerard Genette, *Narrative Discourse: An Essay in Method*. trans. Jane Lewin (Ithaca: Cornell University Press, 1986).
4. James Grieve, introduction to Marcel Proust, *In the Shadow of Young Girls in Flower: In Search of Lost Time*, Vol. 2, trans. with intro. and notes by James Grieve (New York: Penguin, 2002), ix.
5. Allen Thiher, *Understanding Marcel Proust* (Columbia: University of South Carolina Press, 2013), 113.
6. Mark Caulkins, "Chronology of the Novel," *ProustMatters*; https://proustmatters. files.wordpress.com/2015/09/chronologyofthenovel.pdf.
7. Roger Shattuck, *Proust's Way: A Field Guide to In Search of Lost Time* (New York: W. W. Norton, 2000), xviii.
8. Marcel Proust, *Swann's Way*, trans. C. K. Scott Moncrieff, intro. by Lewis Galantiere (New York: Modern Library, 1928).
9. Adam A. Watt, *The Cambridge Introduction to Marcel Proust* (Cambridge: Cambridge University Press, 2011), 47.
10. Anka Muhlstein, "Painters and Writers: When Something New Happens," *NYR* 64:1 (Jan. 19, 2017); http://www.nybooks.com/articles/2017/01/19/painters-and-writers-when-something-new-happens/
11. Quoted in Susan Scheid, "Will the Real Vinteuil Sonata Please Stand Up?" *Prufrock's Dilemma* (blog), August 26, 2012; http://prufrocksdilemma.blogspot.com/2012/08/will-real-vinteuil-sonata-please-stand.html

Chapter 4

The Metamorphosis (1915):
Kafka's Noir Challenge
to Realism

"A text is not a text unless it hides from the first comer."
Jacques Derrida, "Plato's Pharmacy"[1]

Some fiction, notably modernist fiction, introduces non-realistic events to make a point. Rather than describing the world as it is, such fiction introduces an element of magic that transports the reader from the world he inhabits to another world with different physical rules. For example, in Kipling's "The Gardener" (1926), Helen Turrell is welcomed by Christ when she looks for a son who died in World War I. In Lawrence's "The Rocking Horse Winner" (1926), the adolescent child, when riding his rocking horse in frenzy, can predict the winners of horse races.

The Kafka Universe

The Metamorphosis (1915) is the longest of the Franz Kafka (1883–1924) fiction that was published during his lifetime. Most of Kafka's work was published posthumously under the auspices of his friend Max Brod, who fortunately did not follow Kafka's request that Brod destroy his unpublished work after he died. Kafka would agree with Macbeth that life is a tale told by an idiot, full of sound and fury, signifying nothing, the very line with which Woody Allen, his heir in metaphysical pessimism, begins *You Will Meet a Tall Dark Stranger* (2010).

Reading the Modern European Novel Since 1900: A Critical Study of Major Fiction from Proust's Swann's Way to Ferrante's Neapolitan Tetralogy, First Edition. Daniel R. Schwarz.
© 2018 John Wiley & Sons Ltd. Published 2018 by John Wiley & Sons Ltd.

When we read Kafka, we are often taken beyond our recognizable world, whether to a nightmare world of secret and incomprehensible legal procedures in *The Trial* (1925) or the bizarre, sadistic noir world of "In the Penal Colony" (1919). In *The Metamorphosis* (1915) a man who has lost his ability to think and act independently and who has become no more than a cog in the wheel of his family's and employer's needs turns into a giant beetle before eventually dying. The focal points in *The Metamorphosis* are on Gregor's employer bullying him, on the lack of jobs with dignity for either Gregor or his father, and on the devolution of the traditional family and community as a centerpiece of cultural identity.

Published three years after *Death in Venice* (1912), *The Metamorphosis* can be read as a metaphor for Central Europe in social and historical disarray during the period when World War I was taking place. Industrialism and capitalism are failing or dependent on parasitic relationships; personal and family relations no longer provide compensating satisfaction. Do we not notice the complete absence of community institutions and cultural activities in Gregor's world?

What Kafka does is undermine our expectations of the possible and explicable and introduce into his imagined worlds the fantastic and bizarre. What we think can't happen does happen. Thus focusing in "The Hunter Gracchus" (written 1917, published posthumously in 1933) upon the seemingly aimless journey of the hunter Gracchus who has been dead hundreds of years, Kafka imagines that the dead inhabit the same space as the living rather than going to heaven or hell.

Much of what we now call magic realism in Kafka's world was once called surrealism. Kafka's nightmare fantasies have much in common with the noir apparitions and uncanny images of the painters Giorgio de Chirico, René Magritte, Salvador Dalí, and Joan Miró. Rendering the unconscious mind, the reality that realism had traditionally not reached, was the project of Surrealism – literally surrealism means "above realism" – the movement originally defined by André Breton's *Surrealist Manifesto*. Dreamscape and the actual world are both present in the same work but intentionally not resolved by the artist's imagination or presentation (Fig. 2).

While Miró wanted to "assassinate" painting – that is, breach aesthetic and visual expectations, even those of his recent Cubist predecessors – Kafka wanted to assassinate the assumptions of realistic fiction. Characters like Gregor or Joseph K. in *The Trial* find themselves in a world freed of expected cause and effect where inexplicable events occur. In this surreal universe the characters adjust to alternative realities without much questioning.

Kafka's originality derives from his wildly inventive imagination. He takes a situation to its exponential extreme. He is mischievous in his ingenuity as well

Fig. 2   Joan Miró, *Dog Barking at the Moon* (1926). Philadelphia Museum of Modern Art.

as frightening and alarming in the dreadfulness of his dreamscapes. Reading Kafka, one feels uncomfortable and that discomfort remains – indeed is intensified – on each rereading.

Yet, paradoxically, Kafka often depends on his audience to identify with his protagonist. We are drawn into the plights of Gregor Samsa and Joseph K. despite the seeming remoteness of the narrator. By means of his rendering the internal confusion and decency of his characters, Kafka demonstrates that their essential humanity can't be forgotten or patronized; in fact he creates a structure of affects that evokes our sympathy. The characters may have limited imaginations, but we feel their troubles – their anxiety, dread, guilt, and puzzlement – because the text teaches us to empathize with the major characters' pain even while other less central characters in the text try to ignore what terrible things are happening to the protagonists.

Often using allegorical and parabolic narratives, Kafka examines the fixations, obsessions, and desires of the subconscious. Without moralizing and with little overt historicism, his narrators present a fable that takes place in an alternative universe which accepts assumptions that are antithetical to those we accept as normal, but yet on closer examination bear a striking resemblance to the universe we know. Take, for example, "In the Penal Colony" in which the officer's blind obedience to his former Commandant is a premonition of blind obedience to the demagogues of twentieth-century history: Hitler, Stalin, Mao. Kafka has a unique ability to get inside the minds of the marginalized and even the very weird: the slightly deranged trapeze artist and his manager in "First Sorrow" (1922) or the fasting artist in "A Hunger Artist" (1922), and, in the case of "In the Penal Colony," the psychotic officer.

The word Kafkaesque describes an absurd and irrational world where consequences are not directly related to actions, where hopes are dashed, and where
unseen forces intervene in private lives. His works have an aspect of fable in which
he demonstrates how in his cosmos things turn out badly – or worse. Kafka often
opens up an "as if" world; that is, we are invited to see an alternative to the real
world, an alternative that is organized according to different rules and conventions.
In a sense that world is a subjunctive contrary to fact, an "if it were," but with, notwithstanding exaggerations, frightening similarities to the real world.

Humankind, in the Kafka universe, tries unsuccessfully to make sense of
the world, but as Gregor and Joseph K. learn, the world is irrational and
beyond comprehension. Moreover, humans are the victims of mysterious
legal and penal systems informed by perverse logic. Often Kafka's worlds
have the incongruity of nightmares – sadistic punishment and metamorpho-
ses – and seem to elude understanding. It is as if a mischievous god had
invented a world contrary to the "good" one described at the outset of
Genesis, a world in which human consciousness is at odds with the capricious conditions in which the individual finds himself. Kafka turns on their
heads the optimistic and organizing Christian beliefs of the Fortunate Fall,
Christ's infinite compassion for mankind, and death as the birth of the soul.
Kafka's is a world of guilt, shame, threat, a compulsive sense of duty, fixation
on authority, and terrifying punishment.

Kafka's Jewishness

Something of a socialist, Kafka lived in Prague and was fluent in Czech, but
wrote in German. Although not religious, he was Jewish and interested in
Jewish cultural life. That Joseph K, the protagonist of *The Trial* (and not specifically Jewish), is haunted by guilt without knowing the crime can be read as an
allegory of the discomfort Jews – and Kafka himself – felt in Prague and, implicitly, in cosmopolitan Middle European cities where they were always regarded
as outsiders.

Kafka's world is rife with paranoia, and a source of that paranoia was the
anti-Semitism that was very much part of Kafka's Prague. (One of Kafka's sisters
was gassed at Auschwitz, although by that time he was dead.) As Walter H.
Sokel has observed, "Living under the double threat of German racism and
Czech pogromic populism, the Jews of Prague lived with an undertow of anxiety, a siege mentality of which, even though few admitted it, Kafka's nightmare
fiction has become the eloquent testimonial" (Sokel, "Kafka as a Jew").[2] Kafka
was alienated from Judaism in his early years, in part because of his disdain for
and physical fear of his father.

Rejecting Judaism as a religion was also a way for Kafka to reject his father and to turn towards Germanic culture, especially since German was the language in which he spoke and wrote. As Sokel observes,

. . . .

[Y]oung Kafka became an atheist, toyed with Socialism, and for a time turned to German culture as his refuge and gate to freedom. ... The German culture to which Kafka tried to flee did not accept him and his kind. It had become thoroughly impregnated with a nationalist and racist ideology, a substitute religion, in which anti-Semitism played a dominant part. Kafka found that his flight from his Jewish family to German culture was a flight from one alienation to another even worse. (Ibid.)

. . . .

Kafka found solace in Jewish culture, especially Yiddish theater, but his stories and in particular *The Metamorphosis* are about shame and punishment, isolation and the curse of feeling always as other, an outsider. In part these themes may derive from Kafka's realization that as a Jew he could never be part of the dominant Germanic culture.

Sokel attributes to Kafka the view that: "Modern Western Jews are split between their emancipated rational façade, their official self that they show to the world, and their hidden ghetto past, their truth, which they do not acknowledge, but which still rules them." He continues:

. . . .

This division of the self constitutes a dominant structural principle of Kafka's three tales of punishment, the most widely read of his works – *The Judgment, The Metamorphosis*, and *The Trial*. ...

    Gregor's consciousness is that of a dutiful son and family member, an ordinary hardworking salesman. But his reality, into which he wakes after a night of restless dreams, is that of a giant species of vermin, an unspecified combination of bed bug and cockroach perhaps. The cool, objective narration provides no explanation. (Ibid.)

. . . .

To be sure, a pluralistic reading will attribute this split consciousness to several factors besides Kafka's Judaism, including his own relation with his father, his disappointment with three engagements that did not eventuate in marriage, his frustration with having to write part-time while working for an insurance company, his failure to receive recognition as a writer, his poor health (that resulted in his dying of tuberculosis at forty), and finally the idiosyncrasies of his gloomy, despairing psyche.

Kafka's World: *The Trial* and "In the Penal Colony"

Before turning to a close reading of *The Metamorphosis*, let us turn briefly to other Kafka works that provide a context for understanding *The Metamorphosis*. With its secret judicial system that displaces constitutional government and preys upon guiltless citizens, *The Trial* helps us understand the paranoia of Gregor's perspective and the claustrophobia of Gregor's world. Even before his transformation, Gregor is psychologically imprisoned not only by his parents and employer but also by his submissive nature, especially his lack of self-esteem.

At the conclusion of *The Trial*, Joseph K., a thirty-year-old junior bank official, is brutally murdered by thugs operating under the auspices of a capricious and arbitrary legal system that arrests him and assumes his guilt without revealing the crime. "I've been accused of something but can't think of the slightest offense of which I might be accused."[3] We see Joseph K.'s already narrow world contract to the ritual of his hopeless defense and interaction with the arbitrary legal system, just as Gregor's small world contracts to his surviving as a bug. Poignantly, despite moments of resistance, Joseph K. is always trying to please his accusers. On the threshold of being murdered, he blames himself: "I've always wanted to seize the world with twenty hands, and what's more with a motive that was hardly laudable. That was wrong; do I want to show now that even a yearlong trial could teach me nothing?" (*The Trial*, 228).

In Kafka, the world contracts to a few compulsive gestures as if the characters were imprisoned in their own minds as well as in the social and legal conditions in which they find themselves. Neither the characters nor the narrators have any historical sense. The characters are isolatoes, even if they seem connected. Like Gregor, Joseph K. resents being treated with "carelessness and indifference" (*The Trial*, 39) by an alternative legal system he didn't know existed. But doesn't that also define Gracchus in "The Hunter Gracchus" and the psychotic officer in "In the Penal Colony"?

When "In the Penal Colony" the officer suicidally puts himself in the dreaded execution machine – to have written on his body over twelve hours "Be Just" – the explorer, a European dignitary, knows that the torture is inhuman but is touched by the officer's zeal and by how the officer is mesmerized by the former Commandant; we are horrified when the narrator presents the explorer's conclusion: "[I]n his place the explorer would not have acted otherwise."[4] Perhaps the aforementioned acquiescence by the explorer to masochistic self-torture is the most shocking moment in all of Kafka not only because the sadistic machine and the justification for its use foreshadow the Holocaust, but also because the entire ritual, embodied in the legal system of an isolated island, shows how easy it is for humankind to lose its moral bearings.

Kafka shows us the folly of relying on reason in an irrational world; perhaps he is critiquing the Enlightenment's assumption that we can build a rational system of life. The complicated and abusive legal system in *The Trial* lacks both humanity and reason. We are reminded of a definition of paranoia attributed to William Burroughs: "Sometimes paranoia is just having all the facts."

Kafka's characters live in a world where mysterious forces connive to make the unthinkable possible. Part of Kafka's dark comedy is the characters' efforts to understand the incomprehensible and to rely on reason in situations where reason doesn't work. His characters assume the world is organized logically, and they cannot deal with a world which makes no sense. Thus Gracchus insists because his labors were blessed he doesn't deserve his fate; Gregor pathetically and poignantly tries to rely on his routines when he awakes as a giant bug; Joseph K. never abandons logical and rational thought even when he is beset by every reason to do so. Early on he thinks, "Committing suicide would be so irrational that even had he wished to, the irrationality of the act would have prevented him" (*The Trial*, 11). Later Joseph K. argues to the examining magistrate: "I'm completely detached from this whole affair, so I can judge it calmly" (*The Trial*, 49).

Like Gregor and Joseph K. the explorer in "In the Penal Colony" seeks to understand by reference to his reason. The officer who serves as judge in "In the Penal Colony" declaims to the explorer, "Guilt is never to be doubted" (198) and smugly explains, "If I had first called the man before me and interrogated him, things would have got into a confused tangle. He would have told lies, and had I exposed these lies he would have backed them up with more lies, and so on and so forth" (199). The officer has a reactionary love of the past procedures without any moral sense of the inhumanity involved. He writes the crime of the perpetrator on the latter's body with needles and takes sadistic pleasure watching the victim die as the script "embellishes" the body for twelve hours (203).

The explorer's limited moral sense and rationalizations are hardly encouraging to readers who believe in the evidentiary test: "The explanation of the judicial procedure had not satisfied him. He had to remind himself that this was in any case a penal colony where extraordinary measures were needed and that military discipline must be enforced to the last" (199). Just as no one intervenes to help either Gregor or Joseph K. although Gregor's family could have done so before the metamorphosis and various characters promise to intercede on Joseph K.'s behalf, no one intervenes to stop the torture of the condemned prisoner. The explorer thinks: "It's always a ticklish matter to intervene decisively in other people's affairs. He was neither a member of the penal colony nor a citizen of the state to which it belonged. … [H]e traveled only as an observer, with no intention at all of altering other people's methods of administering justice" (206). The reader recalls that the only crime of the perpetrator was failing to salute his captain's door "every time the hour strikes" one night because he was asleep (198). The officer in charge of torturing the victim sadistically asserts that "more than a hundred men have already slobbered and gnawed [on the same felt gag] in their dying moments" (207).

In Kafka's nightmare world, things inevitably turn out badly. Even the narrator's clinical detachment – his lack of affect – is itself troubling unless the reader believes he is anesthetized to what he is saying, and that seems unlikely. At times we wish his narrators, especially in *The Trial*, "The Hunter Gracchus," and *The Metamorphosis*, were less accepting, felt more, and were more sympathetic and empathetic. It may be that Kafka's focus on allegory and parable is at odds with the human drama, and it is the latter which engages most readers. That Kafka's universe knows neither charity nor justice and that its rules are not discernable counts for the effectiveness of his stories even while we may be shocked at the distance between the suffering characters and the cynical teller.

Kafka's characters are often caught in the maelstrom of an arbitrary legal and/or bureaucratic experience. Kafka was an insurance lawyer, and in *The Trial* we feel his disdain for an enigmatic, capricious legal system that is indifferent to the needs of the accused and petitioners for justice and fairness. If there is humor in *The Trial*, as some claim, it is noir humor at the expense of the characters, and that kind of humor makes most readers uncomfortable, but I think that is Kafka's intent.

We as readers are entangled in the text as we experience with Joseph K. the incomprehensible world of legal gibberish and impenetrable legal procedures that Kafka's narrator describes. Kafka brilliantly shapes his text to make us as baffled and frustrated as Joseph K. – and as deflected from our sense-making – as we experience the odyssey of reading. Law in "In the Penal Colony" is associated with sadistic torture, but even in *The Trial* it is a labyrinth that becomes mental torture. As Joseph K. discovers when he visits the offices of the court, "the farther he went, the worse things would get" (74). As he puts it after hearing the parable of the man who waited until his death to get past the Law's first doorman, "Lies are made into a universal system" (223). Kafka stresses the absurdity of the legal world Joseph K. encounters and the impossibility of understanding its logic and rules. At the conclusion of the penultimate chapter entitled "In the Cathedral," the prison chaplain tells Joseph, "The court wants nothing from you. It receives you when you come and dismisses you when you go" (224).

The Metamorphosis

Major writers, as T. S. Eliot reminds us in "Tradition and the Individual Talent," are not only aware of the tradition in which they write, but often make a conscious effort to redefine it. In *The Trial*, Kafka relies on the conventions of the realistic novel – strongly rooted in the rationalism of the European Enlightenment and concomitant scientific revolution – to present his protagonist's consciousness, even while proposing an alternative reality. In *The Metamorphosis*, Kafka uses the interior monologue of the realistic novel side by side with a grim noir fairy tale to invent a parable that draws upon both fable and bestiary, a genre where animals take on human patterns of thought and feeling.

It is worth thinking about *The Metamorphosis* in the context of other modernist texts, especially *Notes from Underground* (1864) and *Death in Venice*. In each the protagonist is suffering from an illness that is a metaphor for insufficiency of character. Aschenbach's obsessive fascination with Tadzio leaves him vulnerable to the cholera epidemic. In Dostoevsky's *Notes from Underground* the narrator's various symptoms are a result of his emotional chaos and lack of faith in God. Gregor's bizarre transformation is a direct result of his failure to respond to his emotional and physical needs.

How, all three texts ask, does one find meaning without religious belief? In Kafka, as in Dostoevsky and Mann – and in Joyce, too, where Dublin is a center of paralysis in *Dubliners* (1914), although in 1915 Kafka probably wouldn't have read it in English and it does not seem to have been translated – the city is claustrophobic, imprisoning, and limiting. Often there seems to be a lack of useful work in the modern city and of chances to realize one's potential. The routines demanded of urban life are anathema to a fully realized life, one that includes space for intimacy, passion, creativity, and imagination. Tedious and meaningless work dehumanizes and saps one's ability to experience the day-to-day pleasures of life. Urban life can become routinized, defining its denizens by work that is unfulfilling and demanding and reduces life to mechanical repetition. Gregor is a traveling salesman whose life is so regulated by his company that when he awakens as a giant beetle or cockroach all he can reference is his work: "It's much more irritating work than doing the actual business in the office, and on top of that there's the trouble of constant travelling."[5] Desperate to pay off debts incurred by his father, he is beholden to the chief clerk's will and whims.

To be sure, all imaginative literature has an "as if" component, but the "as if" component is inflected in Kafka. People simply do not turn into giant bugs. Yet what is so frightening in Kafka is that we recognize so much of our world. Kafka asks us what if someone is being patronized and ignored as if one were not human by one's employment associates and even one's own family? The ignored person is Gregor, who is the sole economic support of his father who is not only in debt, but like Gregor's mother and sister doesn't have a job.

What if, Kafka also asks, becoming a host in a parasitic relationship at home and at work could actually deprive one of one's humanity? Hasn't Gregor's humanity been devoured by the responsibilities imposed on him by his family and employer? What if, Kafka finally asks, one becomes an automaton, a mechanical cog in the service of the lives of others, while depriving oneself of love or self-regard or joy? Thus, so inculcated with a sense of serving others, the first thing Gregor thinks about, even while knowing that he has metamorphosized, is going to work!

Although Kafka did not suffer from tuberculosis until 1917, he wrestled with depression and insomnia throughout his life; emotional and physical illness were never far from his mind. When the narrator describes the metamorphosis of Gregor as if he were taken ill, the reader is aware that Gregor's gradual transformative experience does have resonance with how a major illness – tuberculosis, cancer, Parkinson's disease, or multiple sclerosis – reduces us to a shadow of ourselves. Not only does Gregor's response to his metamorphosis speak to our fear of becoming repulsive in appearance, but it also speaks to our fears of loneliness, abandonment, and deprivation. Because, Gregor can't find insect food in his room, lacks the teeth necessary to eat human food, and is therefore starving. Ironically, Kafka himself died of starvation, in his case when eating became too painful in his last months.

Another important autobiographical aspect of *The Metamorphosis* is that the story mirrors tensions with Kafka's oppressive, authoritarian father who intimidated both him and his mother. With its five letters, the second and final ones of which are "a," Samsa deliberately resonates with Kafka's name. The abusiveness of Gregor's father and the later betrayal by his sister Grete underline the fragility of family ties when someone becomes other or different. Although Grete had been close to Gregor and was at first sympathetic to his plight, it is she who definitively announces, "We must try to get rid of it. ... He must go" (447–448). Responding to his sister's music more intensely than before ("Was he an animal, that music had such an effect on him? He felt as if the way was opening to the unknown nourishment he craved") Gregor becomes in some ways more human as an insect (445).

Gregor's sexuality has been reduced to looking at a picture of a woman with "fur cap on and a fur stole" on his bedroom wall (409). The pictured woman may be a reference to Leopold von Sacher-Masoch's *Venus in Furs* (1870). Certainly Gregor Samsa is a masochist; his name Samsa may derive from the letters in Sacher-Masoch's name.[6]

Gregor's metamorphosis into an insect is a dynamic process that began before the actual moment of transformation and continues until he dies of starvation, starvation that results not only from lack of food but also from lack of love. As in *The Trial* or "The Hunter Gracchus," we never know why Gregor is punished. He seems to have done everything right in terms of serving his family. Yet, isn't that submissive service a major part of his problem?

At the outset of *The Metamorphosis*, Gregor is on the borderland between human and insect but gradually he becomes more and more insect. His words are garbled but have some resemblance to human speech, at least in his mind.

He takes solace in the false premise that people "were ready to help him" (418). He desperately wants to believe he is simply ill and that something can be done. Ironically he relies on reason, optimism, and a desire not to be other: "He felt himself drawn once more into the human circle and hoped for great and remarkable results from the doctor and the locksmith, without really distinguishing precisely between them" (418).

In the sense that Gregor after his transformation asserts his own needs, he becomes more human as a gentle, giant cockroach or beetle than he is as a man. Meanwhile, as if the entire family had a parasitical relationship with the giant insect – as if they were grotesquely feeding off his body and gathering strength – his father, mother, and sister become healthier and more functional. In a weird way, the family members become more and less human. They become more human as physically fit, functioning adults taking on new responsibilities. But they become less human by separating themselves from a son who has become radically different. Do we not think about how some families react to a child with Down's syndrome or a parent with dementia? I have heard people say of an elderly parent suffering from Alzheimer's, "He is not my father any more." When I was growing up, people didn't speak about mentally, physically, or emotionally impaired family members. Just as Gregor's family does when Gregor becomes an embarrassment, they pretended that those family members didn't exist.

Given the emphasis on walls and doors separating Gregor from others, it is not surprising that the narrator speaks of his situation as "imprisonment" (428). When Gregor realizes that the very sight of him repels Grete, "In order to spare her that [discomfort] … one day he carried a sheet on his back to the sofa – it cost him four hours' labor – and arranged it there in such a way as to hide him completely" (430). But the self-imprisonment is something that began long before the metamorphosis when Gregor's own compulsive conscientiousness put up walls between himself and others and when he began to live only for others. When he repressed and suppressed interests and needs to the point where he was reduced to mechanically doing the bidding of others, he built the walls of his own prison. A traveling salesman used to awaking in strange rooms where he needed to lock all doors during the night, Gregor had taken to doing the same at home.

In some ways, he has become so insignificant to his employer and his family that he is hardly more than a speaking biped whom no one thinks of in human terms. Yet he is hardly a supernumerary to his family, who depend on him for financial support until his metamorphosis requires them to release themselves from the parasitic relationship and metamorphosize into human beings who can themselves function within the economic system that helped destroy Gregor.

Kafka's parabolic fable has a folkloric aspect and may owe something to the German fairy tale, collected and popularized by the Grimm brothers in the early nineteenth century. As with many fairy tales, three plays a significant role. After Gregor's metamorphosis, the three family members live in an apartment and take in three lodgers. The story has three parts; the first ends with his father chasing Gregor back into his room; the second part ends with his father throwing apples at him, perhaps an ironic reference to the Fall when Adam takes a bite out of Eve's apple; and the third part ends with Gregor's dying.

We would today regard *The Metamorphosis* as science fiction. What Kafka does is take the metaphor, "He is like an insignificant bug," one step further and creates a fantasy of a man turned into a bug. Until he becomes a bug Gregor cannot assert his own needs. By eavesdropping he learns that he had been misled about his father's financial condition; Gregor learns the latter is better off than he was led to believe and that his father had put away some money. Gregor is not outraged that he had been taken advantage of – as we would expect – but, rather, "rejoiced at this evidence of unexpected thrift and foresight" (429). As readers, we become impatient with Gregor for his always seeing the point of view of his family rather than asserting his own needs, and we realize that this is not only a long-held pattern before his metamorphosis, but is a cause of the metamorphosis (if we can speak of cause and effect in Kafka's uncanny universe).

What makes Gregor sympathetic is the narrator's rendering of Gregor's consciousness as a bug that not only has human feelings and strong memories of his life as a human but is also introspective. Indeed, while Kafka departs from the realistic novel in so many ways – giving us little in the way of time or place – he relies strongly on the convention from the realistic novel of an omniscient narrator rendering the consciousness of his protagonist by means of free indirect discourse, even while maintaining an ironic perspective. Within this convention, the distinction between the two points of view is central to our reading experience.

The disjunction between Gregor's thoughts, especially his sense of purpose, and his actual plight as a huge bug, emphasized by the narrator, is the essence of the story's noir comedy and grim tragedy. We are sympathetic with Gregor's perspective even while we become impatient with his generosity to his increasingly hostile family. We know how he has been virtually reduced to nothingness, even as he gradually learns that. He not only experiences guilt, shame, and an obsessive sense of responsibility, but also runs through an entire gamut of often-nuanced emotions, including loneliness and anomie. Yet Gregor loves his mother and sister, and is a respectful son to his bullying father. He is the host in two parasitic relationships that define his life. Were he not in the primary parasitic relationship with his parents whose debts will take another five or six years to pay off, he thinks that he might have broken the other destructive one with his "chief": "If I didn't have to hold my hand because of my parents I'd have given notice long ago" (410). Committed to working for a firm whose chief is owed money by his parents, Gtrego is almost an indentured servant.

There is, as I have been stressing, a parabolic and allegorical dimension to all of Kafka's works. He renders Gregor's neuroses, anxiety, and self-doubt as representations of modernist angst, an angst that informed Kafka's own life. Gregor is depressed and feels he is not good enough to have a better life than the one he is living at the outset. He lives in fear of his father and boss, fear of being fired, and fear of not fulfilling his responsibilities. His overarching emotion is the free-floating anxiety of someone who feels that he is undeserving. Nothing will deflect him from his work and family responsibilities, no matter how arduous or unfair they are. Only when he is turned into a bug does he begin to discover a self that will take account of the needs and desires of his "I."

How *The Metamorphosis* Begins

In one of the great opening lines, *The Metamorphosis* begins at the denouement; the first sentence catches the moment when Gregor Samsa, a traveling salesman, awakens in his room in the family apartment only to learn he has been transformed into a bug: "As Gregor Samsa awoke one morning from uneasy dreams he found himself transformed in his bed into a gigantic insect" (409).

The most common translation of the German description *ungeheures Ungeziefer* is "monstrous vermin." Translators have usually rendered *Ungeziefer* as "insect," although Kafka would have known in Middle German that it means "unclean animal not suitable for sacrifice."

The incongruity between the narrator's detachment and what he is actually describing is part of the novel's formal genius. With clinical detachment, the matter-of-fact narrator describes Gregor Samsa's condition as if Gregor had awakened with a cold. At first he and his family treat the incredible transformation as if it were within the ken of indispositions with which they can deal. How humans domesticate and naturalize the unimaginable is a recurring Kafka theme, and really a major focus of *The Trial* and the other Kafka texts I have cited.

At first Gregor treats his transformation as if it were an indisposition and encumbrance that he needs to overcome. But neither his family nor the chief clerk of his employer – who comes to see why Gregor has not turned up to work – can understand what he is saying. Even as Gregor thinks like a human, his bugness asserts itself. He is "unusually hungry" (411), and he hears his own voice soon after the transformation: "Gregor had a shock as he heard his own voice answering [his mother's], unmistakably his own voice, it was true, but with a persistent horrible twittering squeak behind it like an undertone that left the words in their clear shape only for the first moment and then rose up reverberating round them to destroy their sense, so that one could not be sure one had heard them rightly" (411). Notwithstanding the noir humor, we feel Gregor's isolation and loneliness as well as his victimization by circumstances out of his control.

Soon his voice will entirely disappear, for the metamorphosis is a continuing rather than static process. On one hand, Gregor's sight continues to deteriorate. But on the other, as an insect, he discovers within himself a greater range of human emotions than he has been experiencing.

Brilliantly, Kafka gives his narrator the ability to render in detail Gregor's thoughts and pathetic feelings as a bug – his anger, frustration, dedication to task, and sense of family responsibility – as if Gregor were a human. With great understated irony he juxtaposes the reality of Gregor's transformation with Gregor's rationalizations, rationalizations that are all-too-human as he tries to deny the absurd reality of what has occurred: "What has happened to me? he thought. It was no dream" (409). Kafka's interior monologue renders Gregor's desperate effort to pull together his world which is falling apart. As if denying an illness that might keep him from going to work, Gregor puts his head in the psychic sand and pretends that he is having a bad dream: "What about sleeping a little longer and forgetting all this nonsense. … This getting up early, he thought, makes one quite stupid. … [T]o catch [the next train] he would need hurry like mad … and he himself wasn't feeling particularly fresh and active" (410–411). But ostriching does not work, and he has lost control of his body along with his ability to order his life.

Not realizing, as the reader does, that his metamorphosis is the result of suppressing his human needs, "[H]e felt great pride in the fact that he had been able to provide such a life for his parents and sister in such a fine flat" (424). Pathetically, Gregor "would rather starve" than make his needs felt for something other than milk (425). He feels that he has let his family down; whenever he hears his family talking about "the need for earning money," "he felt so hot with shame and grief" (429).

One continuing trope Kafka uses to define Gregor's plight is that of illness. When Gregor is attacked by his now more energetic and employed father at the end of Part II, "He was already beginning to feel breathless, just as in his former life, his lungs had not been very dependable." After he has been wounded by the apples his father throws at him, the narrator describes his mobility problems and his "disabled condition" (448).

Metamorphosis as Transformation and Transvaluation

Gregor begins to have an authentic emotional life when he is a bug. Rather than maintain the fiction of a coherent self, as he had while serving his parents and company, he begins to adopt a number of different stances: "At other times he would not be in the mood to bother about his family, he was only filled with rage at the way they were neglecting him, and although he had no clear idea of what he might care to eat he would make plans for getting in the larder to take the food that was after all his due, even if he were not hungry" (440). He is more authentic as a bug than he was as a human; feeling rage is a realization of the human emotional range that he had denied himself in service to his company and family. As we readers take his side and feel sympathy if not empathy, we almost cheer him on: "Gregor hissed loudly with rage because not one of [his family] thought of shutting the door to spare him such a spectacle [of a family quarrel about the condition of Gregor's room] and so much noise" (441). In selfishly asserting his desires in a contradictory and often irrational way – and expressing anger at the world in which he finds himself – he not only becomes more human but also resembles the speaker from *Notes from Underground*.

Arthur Pita's innovative, eerie, and powerful ballet *The Metamorphosis* (2012), based on the Kafka novella, calls attention to the role of movement in the claustrophobic apartment. Gregor desperately tries to move as a huge insect but has nowhere to go. When Gregor seeks to leave his room at the end of Part I, "Pitilessly Gregor's father drove him back, hissing and crying 'Shoo!' like a savage. … If only he would have stopped making the unbearable hissing noise! … He had merely the fixed idea of driving Gregor back into the room as quickly as possible" (422). Interestingly, in another metamorphosis, "the hissing" sound reduces Gregor's father to a creature who has damaged another creature in a fight for the survival of the fittest: "[H]is father gave him a strong push which was literally a deliverance and he flew far into the room, bleeding freely" (423).

Accompanied by "bleeding," the "deliverance" mimics a grotesque birth to what Gregor thinks of as a "new life" (437). Do we not as readers see an ironic reference to "new life" in the form of religious transfiguration when the narrator tells us: "Gregor had plenty of time to meditate at his leisure on how he was to arrange his life afresh" (424)?

Kafka's narrator stresses the metamorphosis of Gregor's father's attitude to his son now that the latter is different and no longer useful in extricating him from debt. Long before Gregor's metamorphosis his father thought of Gregor as the family breadwinner but, the narrator strongly implies, not with the love, tenderness, and empathy that one would expect from a father. Now employed as a bank messenger, Gregor's father has become an abusive and domineering bully and is "angry and exultant" when he confronts his son (436). (We recall Kafka's fear of his own father depicted in his *Letter to my Father* (1919).) Part II ends with another nightmare scene of Gregor's abusive father attacking his son by throwing apples at him. Gregor is "aware as he had been from the first day of his new life that his father believed only the severest measures suitable for dealing with him" (437). As a result of his father's attack, he feels "startling, incredible pain" and "a complete derangement of all his senses" (437).

Grete has her own metamorphosis. At first she is sympathetic to Gregor, but later she pushes his food into his room with her foot and finally she is the one who urges his banishment. Grete's metamorphosis from a loving sister to the person who calls for Gregor's removal is the immediate cause of his death. Gregor's hearing and understanding of human speech are unaffected by his transformation. He overhears Grete scolding her father for thinking that "this is Gregor. The fact that we've believed it for so long is the root of all our trouble" (448). Hearing his beloved sister's verdict that it is his responsibility to die, Gregor sets in motion the process by which he dies: "The decision that he must disappear was one that he held to even more strongly than his sister" (449).

As a beetle Gregor's range of feelings increases. He has begun to throw off the guilt and shame that transformed him into a neurotic self-denying cog in his family's and company's machine. Gregor develops a sense of being wronged and of suffering unjustly. In his claustrophobic world, the only object of his affection is Grete. While Gregor thinks lovingly if perversely of how he can protect Grete by having her live in his room with him, he also is becoming less worried about the views of others and begins to put his own needs and desires first. Gregor abandons moral constraints and fantasizes about an incestuous relationship: "He would never let her out of his room, at least, not so long as he lived; … but his sister should need no constraint, she would stay with him out of her own free will" (445).

In the weird scene when he leaves his room – instead of hiding so as not to embarrass his family – and kisses Grete in front of the lodgers, he is asserting his presence. Seeking "the unknown nourishment he craved" (445) in the form of music, he ventures out of his room to hear his sister's violin playing for the lodgers: "He felt hardly any surprise at his growing lack of consideration for the others; there had been a time when he prided himself on being considerate" (444). His awakened human imagination responds to music, specifically his sister's violin, but also to the eroticism of his sister's presence.

As if she intuitively understands his incestuous fantasy as his bizarre, pathetic, and pathological version of intimacy, Grete declares, "He must go" (449). By using the pronoun "he" not "it," she is acknowledging Gregor's gender and by implication that he is her brother. Even as Gregor feels "love and tenderness" towards his family, he instinctively knows he must disappear if they are to flourish, and for that reason he stops eating. Kafka stresses the irony that as an insect, Gregor "thought of his family with tenderness and love" (449), while they as humans think of him as an encumbrance that is better dead. By getting rid of the corpse, the unnamed charwoman acts on – or perhaps we should say acts out – the family's wishes. Acting purposefully, yet instinctively, the charwoman is the opposite of the self-conscious Gregor and his duplicitous and hypocritical family with their various secrets. When she sees that Gregor – or rather the large bug which she calls by the pronoun "it" – is dead, she opens the door to the Samsa bedroom and yells: "just look at this, it's dead;

it's lying here dead and done for!" (450). Because she knows the family secrets and knows that the family has violated the convention that families protect their own at all costs, they need to fire her. We modern readers think of a family expelling a member who is other whether the person be disabled, gay, or mentally or emotionally troubled or of a community expelling the aforementioned or those of different races. At some level, how Gregor is treated both before and after the metamorphosis represents how we judge humans in terms of their utility.

In Kafka there is a weird principle of Conservation of Energy where some flourish at the expense of others. He does not focus on traditional cause and effect, but rather relies on uncanny coincidences. When Gregor dies, the family's metamorphosis into humans is complete. The family was using Gregor as a host in a parasitical relationship and they flourished at his expense. Gregor had been his parents' principal support and had wanted the family to live in a comfortable apartment. Without the need for a room for Gregor, they will move to a smaller, less expensive apartment that they can afford. By spring, Grete has become a nice-looking, sexually attractive, and marriageable young woman who in the last sentence "sprang to her feet first and stretched her young body" (453). The remaining members of the family have good jobs. Grete is ready for a husband (another child the parents are rid of), and they can put their dead son behind them. Expecting the readers to see the horror of the transaction in which the death of a son leads the remaining family to better futures, Kafka's narrator ironically presents the "new dreams" of the parents (453).

Study Questions for *The Metamorphosis*

1. Why does Gregor turn into a bug?
2. What do we learn about his father and mother?
3. Are Gregor's father and employer partly responsible for his transformation or is it entirely his own doing? How does Kafka offer a critique of the contemporary urban world, a world which seems to offer meaningless jobs in a money-driven economy?
4. What is Gregor's sister Grete's role and why does her behavior change as *The Metamorphosis* evolves?
5. Does the novella begin at the end?
6. What is the charwoman's role?
7. What is the function of each of the three parts?
8. What is the evolving role of the narrator in shaping our response to Gregor?
9. Does a reader respond differently to non-realistic stories, including parables and folk tales, than to realistic ones? How does *The Metamorphosis* draw on both fairy tale and realism?
10. What are the qualities of the Kafka universe? What does *The Metamorphosis* have in common with other Kafka fiction, including *The Trial*, "In the Penal Colony," and "The Hunter Gracchus"?

Notes

1. In *Disseminations*, trans. Barbara Johnson (Chicago: University of Chicago Press, 1981), 63.
2. Walter H. Sokel, "Kafka as a Jew," *New Literary History* 30:4 (Autumn 1999), 837–853; http://muse.jhu.edu/article/24490
3. Franz Kafka, *The Trial*, trans. with preface by Breon Mitchell (New York: Schocken, 1998), 14. Page references in the text are to this edition.
4. Franz Kafka, *In the Penal Colony: Stories and Short Pieces*, trans. Willa and Edwin Muir (New York: Schocken, 1961), 221. Page references in the text are to this edition.
5. Franz Kafka, *Metamorphosis*, in *Classics of Modern Fiction: Eight Short Novels*, ed. Irving Howe (New York: Harcourt, Brace & World, 1968), 410. Page references in the text are to this edition.
6. See Mark Anderson, *Kafka's Clothes: Ornament and Aestheticism in the Hapsburg Fin de Siècle* (Oxford: Oxford University Press, 1992).

Chapter 5

Camus's Indifferent, Amoral, and Godless Cosmos: *The Stranger* (1942) and *The Plague* (1947) as Existential Novels

"Everything ends badly, otherwise it wouldn't end."

Cocktail, 1988 film[1]

"I summarized *The Stranger* a long time ago, with a remark that I admit was highly paradoxical. 'In our society any man who does not weep at his mother's funeral runs the risk of being sentenced to death.' I only meant that the hero of my book is condemned because he does not play the game."

Albert Camus[2]

Introduction

Albert Camus (1913–1960) won the Nobel Prize in 1957 at age forty-four. He was a hero of the Resistance because he was (anonymously of course until after the war) a major editor and writer for the clandestine resistance newspaper *Combat*. But he became a pariah to the left because he opposed the creation of an independent Algeria. He condemned the terrorism of the National Liberation Front (Front de Libération Nationale, FLN), the group that led Algeria to independence in March 1962.

For Camus, as Adam Gopnik puts it, "meaning is where you make it and life is absurd" (Gopnik, "Facing History," 72).[3] In an indifferent universe without God, the only meaning is what an individual can make on his own, and, Meursault, when we meet him, has few ordering principles other than the belief that there is no God. Or to reference my epigraph from the film

Reading the Modern European Novel Since 1900: A Critical Study of Major Fiction from Proust's Swann's Way to Ferrante's Neapolitan Tetralogy, First Edition. Daniel R. Schwarz.
© 2018 John Wiley & Sons Ltd. Published 2018 by John Wiley & Sons Ltd.

Cocktail, all things being equal, things turn out badly, sometimes sooner, sometimes later, but always because we die and death is the end, not, as religion tells us, the beginning of something new. In his long philosophical essay *The Myth of Sisyphus,* Camus argues that, as Gopnik summarizes, "we are all Sisyphus … condemned to roll our boulder uphill and then watch it roll back down … until we die. … Telling Sisyphus that he'll get the stone up there someday is an empty hope. He won't. Camus imagines Sisyphus committed to his daily act; he doesn't encourage him to hope for a better stone and a shorter hill" (Gopnik, 72).

Camus's characters live in an amoral, indifferent cosmos where God does not exist, albeit some live with the fiction that there is a God watching over them. One who subscribes to that naïve view is the priest in *The Plague* named Paneloux, whose name recalls Pangloss, the optimistic teacher-mentor in Voltaire's *Candide.* Pangloss teaches the title character that "all is for the best in the best of all possible worlds." But in fact, Camus believes, we live in an absurd world where, like Sisyphus, we are condemned to repeatedly roll a boulder up a hill only to have it roll down again.[4]

Our lives, Camus stresses, are defined by the inevitability of death without the reprieve of an afterlife and this view is central to his fiction. How do we humans, Camus asks, live within these conditions? With his contemporary Jean-Paul Sartre, Camus believed that existence precedes essence; we do not fit into predetermined patterns and we must create our own meaning. Put another way, if we are fully alive, we humans must make our own choices and form our own identities rather than allow ourselves to be defined by vague abstractions about human nature or extrinsic concepts provided by religions or political systems.

We might recall Joseph Conrad's famous letter, written in the very late 1890s, where he uses the ironic trope of the world as an indifferent knitting machine to rebut Christianity: "It knits us in and it knits us out. It has knitted time, space, pain, death, corruption, despair and all the illusions – and nothing matters. I'll admit however that to look at the remorseless process is sometimes amusing."[5] According to Conrad, humanity would like to believe in a providentially ordered world vertically descending from a benevolent God; that is, a world embroidered to humankind's tastes rather than a world knitted without reference to our needs and desires.

If death is the inevitable ending for all of us and if God does not exist, Camus asks, what gives life meaning and purpose? Can we transform life from a condition into a value? Camus believes that the best we can do if we are emotionally and morally healthy is to be engaged in the lives of others and to sympathize and empathize with their joys and sufferings. But this engagement will always be partial and limited.

Humans do the best they can in a world not organized for their happiness or salvation. They are imprisoned by their existential condition in which existence precedes essence and essence is elusive. Belief in abstractions and systems – whether in the form of religion or historical inevitability – in the face of an unintelligible world deflects humans from the possibility of living authentically and passionately by making conscious choices in response to actual experience.

Camus's *The Stranger* (1942)

Introduction

Meursault's transgressive act of violence defines his entire life. For no apparent reason other than momentary hatred and panic, he kills an unnamed Arab on the beach. While the Arab is a friend of the brother of the girlfriend whom Meursault's friend Raymond Sintès has beaten, Camus's point is that Meursault has no relationship of consequence with the Arab and the shooting is, to use Coleridge's term for Shakespeare's Iago, virtually "motiveless malignity." After shooting the Arab on the beach, he then inexplicably fires four more shots.

Let us consider the title. The French word *étranger* is defined as: 'foreign', 'unknown', 'extraneous', 'outsider', 'stranger', 'alien', 'unconnected', and 'irrelevant'. But the meaning depends on how the word is used. As a noun, it means foreigner, stranger, alien, outsider. As an adjective, the word also means foreign, strange, unknown, unconnected, and alien and has implications of extraneous, irrelevant, and even outlandish. Thus *corps étranger* means 'extraneous body', reminding us that Camus is depicting an Algeria where the Arabs not only have no place in the French world, but Meursault also has no place in the moral universe.

Arguably, the title might be translated as *The Foreigner*, because Meursault, the anti-heroic protagonist, is culturally foreign to Algeria; or as *The Outsider*, because Meursault *feels* alien to the Arab Muslim society in which he lives as a colonist. As he is oblivious to the reasons for which he lives, he is unencumbered by any meaning exterior to his sensory experience, a character trait rendering him *foreign* to his contemporaries; thus, most English translations of the French title *L'Étranger* are rendered as *The Stranger*, and less frequently as *The Outsider*.

As we read a text (in English or French) in which relatively few words are printed on each page, in which Meursault's contribution to dialogue is almost nil, and in which for the most part the sentences are straightforward, the very whiteness of the spare, sparse pages becomes a metonymy for Meursault's loneliness. Just as there isn't much in Meursault's life to which he responds with emotion, there is not much on the pages that present him. That sometimes a sentence is in an oblique relationship to the prior or ensuing one not only reflects Meursault's idiosyncratic thoughts and responses, but also emphasizes his quirkiness and social isolation.

Historical Context

Algeria was considered a part of France, with departments like those of the mainland. In 1913, the year of Camus's birth, 750,000 French people (but many, including naturalized French citizens – Jews, Spaniards, Italians, etc. – were not descendants of French settlers) lived there and dominated a much larger Arab and Berber population. After Algeria was conquered by the French in the 1830s and French immigration was encouraged, most Arabs had few political rights, although some had been given the right to vote in 1919 in return for abandoning their Islamic traditions. Meursault, like his creator, was a Frenchman born in Algeria; such Frenchmen were called "pied-noir" or black foot to indicate that they were besmirched by having one foot in black Africa and/or perhaps were doing humbling and dirty tasks which would temporarily darken their feet such as trampling grapes or having to work in swampy areas. Another possible explanation of the term: The French soldiers wore black boots while many of the poorest Arabs went barefoot. All these explanations emphasize the strong sense of separation and difference between the colonists and the Arabs, and that racist perspective enables Meursault's murder of the unnamed Arab.

Although the novel takes place before World War II, we need to recall that Hitler had conquered France in 1940 and, under the Vichy government, France was collaborating with Hitler. Algeria, with more than a million French citizens and considered not a colony but part of France, was under Vichy control. Indeed, the Vichy government took citizenship away from the considerable number of Jews there.

But Eisenhower liberated Algeria in November 1942. In the last years of World War II, David Carroll observes, "the Algeria of *The Stranger* was for Sartre and other readers not the site of colonial oppression but of the possibility of freedom and revolt" (Carroll, 11). Sartre praised and discussed the novel in his 1943 essay "An Explication of *The Stranger*".

Later the book became for some readers a colonial text, one that endorses racist and imperialist attitudes, but this is a reading that ignores the fact that Meursault is an imperceptive narrator from whom Camus strongly distances himself. Conor Cruise O'Brien's indictment of Camus as a colonialist is an example of how a text evolves through time. In contrast to Sartre, O'Brien argues that "underneath the mask of the progressive, antiracist, European humanist and defender of the oppressed can be found Camus's true face: that of a partisan colonialist."[6]

The Stranger: *Part One*

Beginnings of novels are like Genesis; we enter into an imagined world that has nothing preceding and the words we read are the imagined ontology to which we are transported. At the same time, we bring our experience that exists anterior to our reading; that experience defines how we initially respond emotionally and how we make judgments. But, as we read, the fictive world interacts with prior experience and may change our responses.

Camus writes, "*Aujourd'hui, maman est morte*," which Stuart Gilbert translates as "Mother died today."[7] In 1988, Matthew Ward corrects Gilbert's translation to "Maman died today."[8] By retaining the intimate French word "maman" instead of "mother," Ward's translation emphasizes the centrality of the loss. More recently, Sandra Smith's 2012 translation begins "My mother died today," which connects the speaker even more reflexively to his loss.[9]

Meursault, the protagonist in *The Stranger*, is also the retrospective narrator. He lives on the borderland between past and present. Much of the novel's effect on the reader depends on the frisson between now and then. Thus looking back to the day of his mother's funeral in Marengo, Algeria, Meursault recalls: "And I can remember the look of the church. The villagers in the street, the red geraniums on the graves … the wait outside a café for the bus, the rumble of the engine, and my little thrill of pleasure when we entered the first brightly lit streets of Algiers, and I pictured myself going straight to bed and sleeping twelve hours at a stretch" (22). Somewhat anesthetized to feelings, he responds to discrete visual images as if he were a camera rather than a person experiencing the loss of his mother. Later, in prison, he is more adept at evoking things of the past than understanding the social and economic world in which he lives.

Adele King observes that in *The Myth of Sisyphus* (1942), Camus "defines the 'absurd man' as one who is always conscious of tragedy and death, free from any illusions either of eternal life or of the saving power of some goal within life, and passionately interested in accumulating sensual experiences."[10] But Meursault is the antithesis of the absurd man in Part One. He is not conscious of the world in which he lives and, indeed, he is hardly proactive in seeking passionate or even sensual experience. When he has the opportunity for intimacy, he responds almost mechanically to the physical act of sex; even though he seems to be familiar with his partner Marie, he is not at all emotionally engaged.

Meursault is also strange as in "odd" and "quirky." Camus has created a character who keeps his audience at a distance. Rather than take us into his world and gain our trust and sympathy, Meursault's behavior is off-putting. Moreover, Meursault's telling is at an oblique angle to the events he describes rather than a precise version of those events. Because Meursault refuses to observe the social amenities when his mother dies or does so perfunctorily, because he seems to be without a moral compass in responding to the nastiness he sees around him, because he seems emotionally stunted, and, for some readers, because he refuses to acknowledge God, we see him as Other.

At times, much of what Meursault says expresses the darker self we all fear to acknowledge. He and his mother have little to say to one another; even if he loves her within his severely limited capacity for feeling, we suspect that at some level he may be wishing for her death and the release from a burden of moral responsibility.

To understand what Meursault does, one needs to know who he is, and that is not so easy. While seemingly taking us inside Meursault's consciousness, Camus actually does not give us much information. And Camus does this for a reason. He wants to dramatize a figure who does not have a refined moral sensibility and who is incapable of subtle distinctions. Accident and propinquity, rather than proactivity, shape his behavior. While we sense that he has serious psychopathological issues and that he cannot communicate his emotions, we are not sure what or if he is suppressing and displacing.

At the outset, Meursault's emotional responses to his mother's death at about age sixty – he is not sure about her age – are short-circuited. The very next day, after her funeral and his return to Algiers, he has casual sex with Marie, whom he happens to run into at the beach. While she becomes attached to him as soon as they have intercourse, he is relatively indifferent to her except for seemingly enjoying the physical act. He realizes "nothing in his life had changed" (30). He had put his mother in an old age home, but for the past year had rarely gone to see her because getting there was too much trouble for him. With typical inconsistency, he explains, it would have "meant losing my Sunday," even though he has told us "I've never cared for Sundays" (25, 30). When he and his mother lived together, they had rarely spoken.

Meursault is at once socially inept, paralytically self-conscious – "embarrassed," "uncomfortable," worried that he is not saying the right thing – and indifferent as if suffering from anomie. In contemporary terms, he has Asperger's syndrome and is also paranoid; he imagines that he is being blamed for inappropriate and awkward behavior, even though there is scant evidence that such is the case (1, 3). His sensory responses to the sun generate odd physical discomforts, and his descriptions of these moments give us a window into a mind that oscillates between indifference and hyperbolic if not eccentric responses. Thus when he describes his walking to his mother's funeral: "It gave one a queer, dreamlike impression, that blue-white glare overhead and all this blackness round one: the sleek black of the hearse, the dull black of the men's clothes, and the silvery-black gashes in the road" (20).

One of Camus's major points – indeed, the focus of his fictional inquiries – is that without a moral sense humans are no different than animals as creatures of nature responding instinctively to physical phenomena like a hot sun as he does when he murders the Arab. But how does one develop a moral sense in a godless universe? Why does Rieux in *The Plague* have it and Meursault lack it? His shooting the Arab encapsulates his reactive personality; the metaphor of a steel spring is appropriate: "Every nerve in my body was a steel spring, and my grip closed on the revolver" (76).

Because Meursault is defined purely by sensory experience as if he were an animal rather than by values, his behavior is shaped by physical phenomena. Before shooting the Arab on the beach, he recalls: "[I]t crossed my mind that one might fire, or not fire – and it would come to the same thing" (72). The heat of the sun, which bothered him at his mother's funeral, seems again to be disorienting to Meursault. During these crucial, defining moments of the confrontation, the sun's heat creates extra pressure on him and exacerbates his losing control. Before the murder he aggressively moves forward to escape discomfort caused by the hot sun even though he knows he could turn and walk away (75).

Meursault's capacity for empathy and sympathy are drastically underdeveloped. Indeed, at times he has the moral compass of an infant. More and more, he seems defined by whomever he is with at the moment. Thus he has few compunctions about writing a letter for the hoodlum Raymond Sintès. Meursault's willingness to write a letter on behalf of the disreputable and disgusting Raymond – who seeks sadistic revenge on his girlfriend whom he thinks betrayed him – shows that Meursault's ability to make moral distinctions is flawed; he "quite understood [Raymond]'s wanting her to suffer for it" (40).

In Part One, Meursault lives in his senses but not in values. He does not care about love, marriage, business success, or promotion. What he doesn't feel in the moment barely exists for him. Beginning, even if we allow for Ward's and Smith's slightly more nuanced translations, with his inability to express conventional feelings of loss when his mother dies, Meursault deviates from adhering to the expected patterns of European behavior. He has little feeling for Marie, the woman with whom he has sex, and he is indifferent to killing a man.

Meursault is a stranger to himself and an outsider not only to the Arab community but also within his own social network and even his family. When he uses memory, especially in Part One, it is to summon disconnected objects, rather than substantive experiences from which he has learned to make choices.

Indeed, despite his seeming indifference, from our perspective, Meursault is depressed and a borderline psychotic. As a depressive, he sleepwalks through life. At times, it is as if he were an outsider observing himself, and his retrospective telling is a kind of client-centered therapy. Why does he fire four more shots? Is he deliberately following through on an action to which he has accidentally committed himself? Is he responding to a self-destructive urge that underlies most of his behavior or is his motive racial hatred? Or to a combination of all three? Retrospectively, as the final sentence of Part One indicates, Meursault knows that "each successive shot was another loud, fateful rap on the door of my undoing" (76).

While one could argue that conventional feelings are inadequate and inappropriate in an absurd, amoral universe, Camus makes clear, especially in *The Plague*, that such human feelings are the glues of decency and commonality which hold civilization together.

When Meursault refuses to respond to Marie's queries about whether he would marry her or whether he loves her, Camus wishes us to see her poignant proposal as a cultural oddity reflecting frustration and puzzlement with Meursault's indifference, depression, and his alienation from traditional amenities and social rituals. The reader takes a further step back from this unfeeling and inconsiderate man: "Then she asked me again if I loved her. I replied, much as before, that her question meant nothing or next to nothing – but I suppose I didn't" (52). "Nothing" becomes a metonymy for who he is. When she affirms her love again and speculates that one day the love might turn to hate – no doubt because he is rejecting her – he reports: "To which I had nothing to say, so I said nothing" (53). Indeed, that Meursault is defined by the recurring negatives he uses is stressed by the last word of Part One after he has killed the Arab: "undoing" (76).

It is not long before we realize Meursault is not only depressed and misanthropic but also deeply disturbed and morally obtuse. That he enjoys Salamano's sadistic relationship with his dog or Raymond Sintès's abusive relationship with a former lover, further puts Meursault at arm's length from the reader who begins to regard him as a *strange* other rather than as a fellow human. In conversation with Salamano, who mourns the loss of a dog that he had regularly abused (as Sintès physically abuses his Arab former girlfriend), Meursault once more defines himself in terms of what he is not, as vacancy and emptiness: "I found him rather boring, but I had nothing to do and didn't feel sleepy" (57).

Meursault's Literary Ancestors

We might think of Meursault's literary ancestors and how they influenced Camus. While much less intellectual than the speaker in Dostoevsky's *Notes from Underground*, Meursault is equally deracinated and estranged from the social and political world that he inhabits. Even though Meursault has friends and a mistress, he is what Melville calls an "isolato." We are aware of Meursault's strong resemblance to Gregor Samsa, the protagonist in Kafka's *The Metamorphosis*. Like Gregor, he feels like a functionary at work and lacks ego or purpose. Meursault is "embarrassed," apologetic, and guilty; he feels the need to "excuse" himself because his mother died (3).

But in fact Meursault could have the promotion Gregor wants as well as the love and sexual satisfaction that Gregor ostentatiously lacks. Meursault has been offered a position in a new office that was opening in Paris. He summarizes what he said to his boss: "I told him I was quite prepared to go; but really I didn't care much one way or the other" (52). Meursault's indifference, ennui, and lack of ambition further distance the somewhat puzzled reader from Meursault.

Social Contexts for Meursault's Behavior

Rather than rely on a reductive "absurdist" explanation for the mindless and senseless killing of an Arab, we need to examine the social conditions that create Meursault as well as why his grammar of motives is obscure to us. Gopnik's explanation is representative of the "absurd" approach: "Meursault thinks (and Camus seconds), because, without divine order, or even much pointed human purpose, it's just one damn thing after another, and you might as well be damned for one thing as the next; in a world bleached dry of significance, the most immoral act might seem as meaningful as the best one" (Gopnik, 70). But I am reluctant to fully accept Gopnik's account and want a more pluralistic explanation that includes psychological, social, economic, and physical factors.

Camus's political focus originally was the French presence in Algeria, but by the time of the publication of *The Stranger* he had witnessed the occupation of much of France by Germany and the establishment of the puppet Vichy regime in the South. Although Camus has created a stiff impersonal language appropriate for Meursault, it is also a prose that emphasizes the distance between the personal feelings of an emotionally mature responsive adult and the self-deluding bombastic language of officialdom not only in Algeria but also during the 1940–1944 period of Vichy government which nominally controlled Algeria. Thus Meursault learns of his mother's death by a coldly efficient official telegram.

The Stranger had to be cleared by the German propaganda authorities. To get the book passed, Camus may have deliberately disguised his intentions. In Part Two, he parodies the language of officialdom that the Germans would have found acceptable, but in such a way that the censors would not have noticed. When Meursault is imprisoned and condemned to death in a show trial marked by arbitrary and capricious procedures, Camus's readers would have been aware that the deprivation of freedom paralleled what happened to Jews in Vichy France. In Part One, it is possible that Camus wished us to take Meursault as a metonymy for the moral vacancy and heartlessness of the German occupation and the Vichy government (the supposedly independent French government responsible for Southern France) and his killing of an Arab as a metonymy for the senseless killing of Jews.

Meursault's anomie has both personal and historical implications. Given the year of publication, 1942, and Camus's identification with the have-nots, the Communists in Algiers and, later, the anarchists, as well as his sympathy for the French Resistance, we need to be alert to historical contexts and historical nuances. Like France during Vichy and the German occupation, Meursault is self-immersed and unwilling to look at the moral implications of his behavior. Meursault's indifference and lack of remorse parallel that of France to its Jews as well as Algeria's towards its Arabs.

That Meursault kills an Arab, who has no given name, emphasizes the racial implications of the murder. The victim is the brother of the Moor woman (also nameless) whom his friend Raymond Sintès beats up, although she has been his mistress. To Meursault, as for many of the French Algerians, the Arabs are no more human than the Jews were for the Vichy government.

But Camus has a complex vision and also sees Meursault as a member of the French underclass to which he himself belonged. Camus was a Communist who did not have much tolerance for the social and political elite, especially for the way that they condescended to and disregarded the interests of the anonymous lower middle class and poor people like Meursault. Meursault associates with the disreputable Sintès, and he has no ties to the governing class or the administrative and legal authorities that preside over his trial. Camus does not like bullying, whether it results from imperialism (French colonial administration versus Arabs), ethnic divisions (European Caucasians versus Berbers and Arabs) or class differences (the social elite and administrative and political elite versus the underclasses), or the power of the Catholic religious hierarchy in Algeria and the rest of France versus other religions, agnostics, and atheists.

We need to remember Camus's own experience as a poor son of a working-class family, a marginalized outsider, and barely part of the dominant colonial culture by means of his French ethnicity. We need to remember that his father died of a World War I wound when Camus was an infant, and his mother cleaned houses. Camus was deeply conscious of the racial and economic divisions in Algeria – he belonged to a family of poor uneducated people (his mother could neither read nor write), a group that thought of themselves as more Algerian than French (Carroll, 4) – and "believed in … [an] idealized vision of a multiethnic, multicultural Algerian people" (Carroll, 4–5).

If *The Stranger* is an example of the failure of the modern state and its political economy to develop conventional moral feelings in its citizens, it is even more so an indictment of how authoritarian colonialism, imperialistic aspirations, and military conquest – here Camus has in mind the German occupation of France – inflects this failure by creating arbitrary class distinctions based on ethnicity and color. Meursault is an example of those who have been left behind by the work ethic of the industrial revolution; he does not have any interest in participating in the meritocracy. Lacking ambition or desire to excel, he simply does not care about advancement and lives within his own sensory experience. Self-immersed, Meursault is unwilling and unable to look at the moral implications of his behavior.

The Stranger: *Part Two*

While there is an immense ironic distance between Camus and Meursault in the first part of *The Stranger*, there is still considerable distance in the early pages of the second part even though Meursault begins gradually and partially to come to life and to realize he is a victim of a judicial system worthy of Kafka or of Lewis Carroll's *Alice in Wonderland*. Indeed, in Part Two, Meursault undergoes his own metamorphosis.

At first in Part Two, as in Part One, Meursault misunderstands and misinterprets what is going on. But in Part Two, as we shall see, Meursault paradoxically recovers his humanity after his crime and behaves as if he were regaining his emotional life. He becomes engaged in the legal process and is no longer anesthetized to its serious implications.

Even as his humanity and imagination expand, Meursault still embraces the everlasting no, but in ways that are more focused and proactive. To an extent the iteration of negatives paradoxically defines a positive curve because he is making decisions and choices rather than being acted upon. His very first word in Part Two, when he is asked if he has a lawyer, is "No" (77).

In Part Two, the man defined in Part One by silence begins to talk to himself. Meursault gradually begins to care a little more about life when he suffers deprivation in prison. His previous life at liberty from the Law – going to the beach, swimming, and his relationship to Marie – takes on a different meaning. He finds Marie attractive the one time she visits; she is not permitted to return because they are not married.

The magistrate and chaplain have values to survive in the amoral, indifferent cosmos in the form of their Christian faith, but Camus views their reductive and narrow faith from an ironic and condescending perspective. When asked by the magistrate if he believes in God, Meursault again answers a simple "No" (85). Reiterating later his lack of belief to the chaplain, he never abandons his rejection of God (145).

If we were to return to psychological terms, we might say Meursault's indifference and anomie indicate serious depression from which he is somewhat roused by his imprisonment, trial, and approaching execution. But one could also argue that Meursault is bipolar and cite as evidence his spasms of manic activity, especially when he kills the Arab and then shoots four more times for good measure. Another manic outburst occurs in his very last days when he loses control and begins to shout as he takes the chaplain "by the neckband of his cassock, and, in a sort of ecstasy of joy and rage, I poured out on him all the thoughts that had been simmering in my brain. ... [T]he jailers rushed in and started trying to release the chaplain from my grip" (151, 153).

Meursault's prison cell recalls his apartment which had contracted to his bedroom after he moved his mother to the old-age home, itself a kind of prison: "[T]he rest of the flat was never used, so I didn't trouble to look after it" (25). He realizes that "[T]here is no way out, and no one can imagine what the evenings are like in prison" (101). The rigid procedures of what becomes a show trial for murder are at odds with his own growing self-awareness. "I wasn't to have any say and my fate was to be decided out of hand. ... I found I had nothing to say" (124). Note how he is still defining himself in negatives, but now it is because he is *choosing* to erase himself from the social system even before his execution.

Within the walls of Meursault's cell, his imagination becomes far more active just as Gregor Samsa becomes far more human after he becomes a giant cockroach. Meursault imagines that were he to get out of jail, he would attend every execution: "[T]he mere thought of being an onlooker who comes to see the show and can go home and vomit afterward alone, flooded my mind with a wild, absurd exultation" (138). His fantasy comes alive with framing "new laws, altering the penalties" (139).

Compared to Part One, his prose becomes more complex as a result of his awakening consciousness. Realizing the limits of the claustrophobic prison world and denying the presence of God, he informs the chaplain: "I'd been staring at those [prison] walls for months; there was nothing, nobody in the world, that I knew better than I knew them" (149). To the chaplain's request to kiss Meursault, he once again says "No" (149).

The prison walls define the space of his world. Once the Law speaks, the sequence of events leading to the reality of his approaching death is inevitable: "[F]rom the moment the verdict was given, its effects became as cogent, as tangible, as, for example, this wall against which I was lying" (138).

In prison, Meursault discovers a range of emotions. After hearing the prosecutor's certainty and triumphant tone, he realizes he is loathed as Other and responds with feelings that had been previously absent: "I felt as I hadn't felt for ages. I had a foolish desire to burst into tears" (112). Then, when his friend Céleste testifies somewhat ineffectually on his behalf and looks at him, he felt that "for the first time in my life I wanted to kiss a man" (116). Deprived of – indeed, estranged from – the routines of his life, he begins to imagine the life he once lived and with some nostalgia to appreciate the small pleasures of life:

. . . .

As I was being taken from the courthouse to the prison van, I was conscious for a few brief moments of the once familiar feel of a summer evening out-of-doors. And, sitting in the darkness of my moving cell, I recognized ... the characteristic sounds of a town I'd loved, and of a certain hour of the day which I had always particularly enjoyed. … Yes, this was the evening hour when – how long ago it seemed! – I always felt so well content with life. (122–123)

....

Ironically, what humanizes Meursault the most is how the Law – as a cultural expression of the absurdity of the world in which humans live – defines his inevitable path to the guillotine. While it is the very nature of Camus's narrative strategy to keep his reader off balance, we know how wrong the prosecutor is when he at this point calls Meursault "a criminal devoid of the least spark of human feeling" (129). Once convicted, Meursault thinks of possible loopholes to forestall the inevitable.

In Part Two, Meursault convincingly presents himself as the victim of the Law's failure to understand him as anything but the Criminal and Murderer. Neither the magistrate, the prosecutor, his lawyer, nor the chaplain really knows Meursault; they merely go through their own ritualized routines. Increasingly, he is caught in a labyrinth of legal and religious babble to which he responds with a mixture of anomie, frustration, anger, and passive aggression.

Meursault is unaware of the possibility that he has been suffering from a mental illness such as depression and perhaps what we think of as a bipolar disorder. He is barely aware of how heat is affecting him, although in the courtroom, he is "conscious only of the steadily increasing heat" (128). Meanwhile, the Law – which Camus anthropomorphizes into an aggressive entity – relentlessly grinds forward to the capital punishment that Camus abhors (128). Indeed, the Law's indifference to Meursault's humanity mirrors Meursault's indifference to anything outside his sensory responses in the first part.

Even as Meursault's consciousness becomes more complex, the legal system suppresses his voice. He hears his defense attorney speak in the first person, as if Meursault's identity had been subsumed in the legal procedure: "'It is true I killed a man.' He went on in the same strain, saying 'I' when he referred to me. … It seemed to me that the idea behind it was still further to exclude me from the case, to put me off the map, so to speak, by substituting the lawyer for myself" (130).

Meursault the perpetrator of a senseless act has now become the victim of a senseless system. He is the stranger. Meursault has no answer as to why he hesitated after his first shot before he fired four more shots into the victim's inert body. The man who didn't sleep now sleeps sixteen to eighteen hours a day in his last months of prison (99). Sleeping that much we know is a sign of depression.

Yet, as Meursault discovers his "I," his claim is credible that "[O]nce I'd learned the trick of remembering things, I never had a moment's boredom" (98).

In some ways, he escapes from his personal imprisonment in prison; among other things, he learns to recall some aspects of the past and to imagine the future.

That the murderer Meursault, as he begins to express a range of emotions, make choices, and discover temporal connections, thinks of himself as "normal" in Part Two is not only frightening to the reader, but also not so off the mark (80). The result of our partially acceding to Meursault's self-definition as normal gradually draws us into his perspective as Victim of an indifferent State Law. Moreover, like many of us, he discovers value in things he can no longer have, as he realizes conviction is becoming likely if not inevitable: "[A] rush of memories went through my mind – memories of a life which was mine no longer and had once provided me with the surest, humblest pleasures: warm smells of summer, my favorite streets, the sky at evening, Marie's dresses and her laugh. The futility of what was happening here seemed to take me by the throat" (132).

What Meursault gains – and what makes him less the stranger and outsider – in Part Two is awareness and articulateness, even eloquence. Thinking of his mother's fiancé he asserts:

. . . .

With death so near, Mother must have felt like someone on the brink of freedom, ready to start life all over again. No one, no one in the world had any right to weep for her. And I, too, felt ready to start life all over again. ... [F]or the first time, the first, I laid my heart open to the benign indifference of the universe. To feel it so like myself, indeed, so brotherly, made me realize that I'd been happy, and that I was happy still. (154)

. . . .

By asserting the value of his mother's life and then his own, he is claiming somewhat proactively that his life is his own, that he is human and capable of moral judgments rather than the bundle of instinctive, senseless reactions that in Part One brought him to a terrible murder. He is now more than the "nothing" which defined him in Part One. Haltingly and inadequately, he is reclaiming his life by thinking outside the boundaries defined by the Law, but he cannot change the result of his being executed for murder. Nor do we readers fully participate in Meursault's naïve "yes" to the "benign indifference of the universe" because the Law, constructed by humans to cope with that universe, is often socially and politically malevolent and authoritarian. This is the Law which Meursault confronts and the Law experienced by Jews in Europe and Arabs in Algeria.

In Part Two Meursault transforms living in an amoral, indifferent cosmos from a condition to a value. This results from a fundamental shift in how he regards his life. Meursault asserts that his life is his and this is the existential moment when essence precedes existence. Paradoxically, he wants to face the Law boldly and what he – asserting morality, passion, and commitment in the face of the Law's indifference – regards as its false view of who he is. Notwithstanding that he has killed a man, he regards the verdict as well as the punishment as unjust. Yet he will existentially reverse the "undoing" of Part One by looking the Law in the eye: "For all to be accomplished, for me to feel less lonely, all that remained to hope was that on the day of my execution there should be a large crowd of spectators and that they should greet me with howls of execration" (154).

Camus, opposed to capital punishment, expects us to see the parallels between two kinds of murder. As Meursault once imagined witnessing executions, he now imagines witnessing his own. Even as he regains his humanity, he will be persecuted as Other, as stranger to his fellow humans. Aware of what he has done in Part One, his being murdered by the Law completes in his mind an inevitable cycle. He wants a crowd aligned with the Law, even if it is one that sees him as murderer and curses him, because he needs to see himself as a victim. But we should not miss the nuance of "lonely" in the above passage; unlike in Part One, he wants to be part of an almost tribal social ritual which involves others, to be acknowledged as part of the human community even if as an ostracized stranger eliciting hate.

Presumably the telling of Part Two takes place very shortly before Meursault's execution. While we cannot be sure that the execution takes place, we have no evidence that it does not.

In his essay "Reflections on the Guillotine" (1957), Camus takes an uncompromising position on behalf of the abolition of the death penalty, believing that "In every guilty person, there is some innocence. It is that which makes all absolute condemnation repulsive."[11] For Camus, "Capital punishment ... is the most premeditated of murders, to which no criminal's deed, however calculated it may be, can be compared."[12]

In many respects the structure of Part Two echoes that of Part One and in a formal sense "undoes" it. Part One begins with the death of Meursault's mother and ends with the violent death of the Arab. The closing scenes of Part Two anticipate Meursault's own violent death, and emphasize that the Law's guillotining him is as senseless as his killing the Arab. Both are equally inhumane, anonymous assassinations. Meursault's refusal to talk to the chaplain about his own death mirrors his response to expected social amenities surrounding his mother's funeral. His grabbing the chaplain in a moment of excitement mirrors his killing of the Arab, except that in this instance he shows genuine passion when he grabs the chaplain and discovers the ability to express feeling. While his physical movement narrows, his emotional world expands; when, after his sentencing, he hears a steamer's siren, he thinks, "People were starting on a voyage to a world which has ceased to concern me forever" (153).

Conclusion

The Stranger is often discussed as an "existential novel," because existence precedes essence in an absurd world. If the first part reveals Meursault as a moral idiot who defines himself by a senseless act, the second shows how circumstances push him not only to take part in the conventional world he detests but also to define himself in relationship to the circumstances in which he finds himself.

Meursault does not believe in God or organized religion; nor does he adhere to accepted social customs for mourning his mother's death. At his trial that failure to behave as expected within the contours of his culture becomes evidence of his heartlessness. That he hadn't wanted a last view of his mother is a major (and for Camus a ludicrous) reason that the Law judges him guilty of murder and executes him.

Thus he is convicted of premeditated murder and sentenced to death when he probably, by our contemporary judicial standards, should have been convicted of manslaughter. To be sure, we should be aware that French legal definitions and practices in the 1940s were not the same as ours today. But we realize that when the Arab's "hand went to his pocket" and remained there, Meursault is justified in feeling threatened (74). Another reason we might expect a manslaughter conviction rather than one for murder is that Meursault shot only after the Arab drew a knife; at that point Meursault quite reasonably imagined the threat of the knife to his safety: "A shaft of light shot upward from the steel, and I felt as if a long, thin blade transfixed my forehead" (75).

The crimes for which Meursault receives the death sentence include not adhering to social conventions at his mother's funeral and not accepting repentance within the Catholic tradition when the judge offers it. While the prosecutor argues that Meursault is worse than a parricide in being "morally guilty of his mother's death," we realize that the prosecutor – and the legal system he represents – have become morally and emotionally anesthetized (128). Within the terms of the Law, Meursault has become as much an outsider as the Arab he shoots; he is a Frenchman who needs to be purged as an embarrassment and disgrace. To the magistrate, who is appalled by Meursault's atheism and considers that his failure to believe in God makes Meursault the most "case-hardened" soul he had ever met, Meursault becomes "Mr. Antichrist" (87–88). As David Carroll has accurately observed,

"The trial is staged rather to prove that Meursault is not French and in fact is not even human, not in legal terms but more importantly, in moral, religious, and metaphysical terms" (Carroll, 33). We might slightly resist Carroll's vague use of "metaphysical," but the prosecutor accuses Meursault of having "no soul, there was nothing human about me, not one of those moral qualities which normal men possess" (127).

Carroll is correct that Meursault is condemned by what the court, representing society, has decided he is, namely an outsider to French culture and, more locally, to the pied-noir culture of French Algeria. His verdict expels him from society as what Carroll calls a "monstrous other" (Carroll, 35).

The verdict tests Meursault's newfound humanity. At first, he uses sensuous memory to scorn the chaplain's orthodox Catholic ideology as well as the way he imagines that the chaplain lives: "[N]one of [the chaplain's] certainties were worth one strand of a woman's hair. Living as he did, like a corpse, he couldn't even be sure of being alive" (151). Even if Meursault may still not be capable of love, he is proactive about what it means to be a living human being connected to another in sensual embrace.

Just as the sun seems to exert extra pressure that releases violence within him when Meursault shoots the Arab on the beach, the chaplain's persistence in presenting repentance and God's forgiveness – as the magistrate had earlier – triggers a violent response from Meursault. Losing control and seizing the chaplain's cassock – and somewhat echoing his shooting of the Arab except now he expresses himself passionately – Meursault yells: "Nothing, nothing had the least importance, and I knew quite well why. ... Every man alive was privileged. ... All alike would be condemned to die one day" (152). But, and the difference between what happened when he shoots the Arab in Part One and what happens here is crucial, he does not physically harm the chaplain. We note, too, how "nothing" has become a much richer term, one associated with rejection of nihilism and embrace of life.

Afterword

Let us recall Claire Messud's observation, cited in my Chapter 1: "Translation is inevitably to a degree subjective. The quality of a translator will depend, then, not merely on her understanding of the mechanics of a language, or on her facility as a writer of prose, but also on her capacities as a reader of texts, her sense of subtext, of connotation, of allusion – of the invisible textures that give a narrative its density and, ultimately, shape its significance" (Messud, "A New 'L'Etranger,'" 6).[13] The 1946 translation by Stuart Gilbert was supplanted by two in the 1980s, that of Joseph Laredo and that of

Matthew Ward. Messud observes: "Ward's highly respected version rendered the idiom of the novel more contemporary and more American, and an examination of his choices reveals considerable thoughtfulness and intuition" (Messud, 6).

But Messud prefers the more recent translation by Sandra Smith, retitled *The Outsider* (2012), because it is a more nuanced translation of French: "Meursault emerges, in the crisp clarity of [Smith's] prose, emphatically not as a monster, but as a man who will not embellish or elaborate. ... [W]e are not to understand ... that Meursault is unfeeling or heartless. He is, rather, painfully without pretense" (Messud, 6). As Smith explains: "In French, *étranger* can be translated as 'outsider,' 'stranger,' or 'foreigner.' Our protagonist, Meursault, is all three, and the concept of an outsider encapsulates all these possible meanings: Meursault is a stranger to himself, an outsider to society, and a foreigner because he is a Frenchman in Algeria" (quoted in Messud, 6).

Study Questions for *The Stranger*

1. How would you define Meursault's psychological condition in Part One?
2. How does Camus regard the world in which humans live? Does he give humans a chance to make meaningful choices in what he presents as an indifferent and absurd cosmos where God does not exist?
3. Why does Meursault kill the Arab? Why does he fire four more shots than needed?
4. Is Meursault an emotional and moral dwarf? Can he love? Can he see the difference between right and wrong?
5. What is the relation between Part One and Part Two? Is Part Two an affirmation of existentialism?
6. How does Meursault grow and evolve in Part Two? In what ways does he become more imaginative, passionate, and conscious of the past, and how does that transformation reshape our response to him?
7. How does the Law speak? Is it responsive to who Meursault is and who he has become? Why is Law personified as a caricature, seemingly human, yet oblivious to individual human feelings?
8. How would you define the legal proceedings against Meursault? Do you see crucial resemblances between *The Stranger* and *The Trial*?
9. How would you respond to the verdict that Meursault is guilty of premeditated murder? Does the reader regard Meursault as moral monster or does the reader find himself sympathizing with Meursault against his or her better judgment?
10. What does Camus think of capital punishment?
11. How would you compare Meursault to Kafka's Gregor Samsa and Dostoevsky's Underground Man in *Notes from Underground*?

The Plague (1947)

"[L]ove is never strong enough to find the words befitting it."

The Plague, 253[14]

"For the mothers, husbands, wives and lovers who had lost all joy, now that the loved one lay under a layer of quicklime in a death-pit or was a mere handful of indistinctive ashes in a gray mound, the plague had not yet ended."

The Plague, 257

Introduction

The Plague is a moving humanistic response to *The Stranger*. The values it emphasizes are love, compassion, and understanding. It is a philosophic and political novel; indeed, sometimes the narrator's meditations and dialogues recall discussions in Thomas Mann's *The Magic Mountain* (1924) between Naphta, representing decay and radicalism, and Settembrini, representing humanistic Enlightenment thought and values. Camus no doubt knew of Mann's use in *The Magic Mountain* and *Death in Venice* of physical illness as a metaphor for moral rot and moral decrepitude.

When we think of nature, we think of spring daisies and summer roses and maybe even in Ithaca, where I live, the fall apple harvest and the winter landscape. Nature is the gorgeous seascape in "The Idea of Order in Key West" and landscape beauty of Constable and Monet. But nature includes hurricanes, tsunamis, earthquakes, and volcanoes. As Camus emphasizes in *The Plague*, nature includes carriers of pestilence like rats and fleas. Nature also includes us humans and our behavior in response to the world in which we find ourselves.

The ostensible subject of *The Plague* is an outbreak of bubonic plague in Oran, a port city in the French colony of Algeria. Oran suffered a terrible cholera epidemic in 1849 following France's conquest, and that may be one historical reference point for the novel. (Camus may also have had in mind the typhoid plague in Morocco in the early 1940s.) Oran had a large European population, including a considerable number of Jews.

While the physically terrifying illness is rendered with searing realism, *The Plague* is also an allegory of how vulnerable humans are to conditions that we cannot control as well as how we exist as lonely creatures, each in our own separate world.

Oran is actually quite a pretty city, according to all sources, although it is not a place that I have visited. But in *The Plague* Camus depicts it as an ugly place; the narrator asks at the outset: "How to conjure up a picture, for instance, of a town without pigeons, without any trees or gardens, where you never hear the beat of wings or rustle of leaves – a thoroughly negative place, in short? ... During the summer the sun bakes the houses bone-dry ... In autumn ... we have deluges of mud" (1). Yet the narrator somewhat qualifies his description a few pages later when he mentions that Oran is "ringed with luminous hills and above a perfectly shaped bay"(3).

The dull weather is a metaphor for "bored" citizens who care only about getting rich, that is, "making money, as much as possible" (2). They live a routinized life where love-making is saved for weekends, vices are unexciting – "addiction to bowling" and gambling – and "the passions of the young are violent and short-lived. … [Oran's] life is not particularly exciting" (2–3). Oran's residents live by organizing their time to pursue ordinary pursuits and banal habits, but not to explore ideas, poetry, causes, values or sustained passionate love; they often die without sympathy or empathy. We recall e. e. cummings's "anyone lived in a pretty how town" because if we think of plague as a metaphor for bigotry, social injustice, and narcissistic complacency, Oran could be anywhere. Or, as Rieux, Camus's surrogate, remarks in his closing sentence, "[Plague] can lie dormant for years and years" before "it would rouse up its rats again and send them forth to die in a happy city" (269).

Camus assigns Oran a population of 200,000 and describes the efforts of authorities to underplay what is happening in order to protect commercial interests. The fictional events recall Mann's *Death in Venice* where Venetian authorities pretend cholera doesn't exist and anticipate Aharon Appelfeld's *Badenheim 1939* where a plague decimates the population of a Jewish resort town in Austria.

Camus's Oran is the opposite of a utopia. Indeed, because of the introduction of an incomprehensible and virulent fatal epidemic, *The Plague*'s imagined world is a dystopia, that is, a place where the quality of life deteriorates into the chaotic antithesis of that of an ideal community. *The Plague* examines how various individuals respond to a community in severe crisis and how they balance their own needs with those of the community.

In Camus's narration, the anonymous and indifferent plague, affecting the innocent and bypassing the corrupt, is also a metaphor for our pathetic human vulnerability to conditions we cannot control rather than individual failings. Some resistant readers may object to Camus's using the literary convention of illness as the responsibility of the ill – in this case, the responsibility of a corrupt community – because this convention often carries the implication that the person suffering from cancer or schizophrenia or the community suffering from plague or Zika could have done something to prevent illness.

What Kind of Fiction is The Plague?

The Plague is a powerful read. Yet it does have a confusing and problematic aspect because Camus has some trouble juggling its hybrid form, with its components of realism, allegory, and philosophy. The realistic narrative often conflicts with the political allegory; the philosophic novel – in which the speaker meditates on the metaphysical question, "How and for what do we humans live?" – conflicts with both.

With a strong interest in character, personality, psyche, and a grammar of motives, *The Plague* as a realistic narrative explores how people behave when a disease ravages a community. Some grow in stature; others like Cottard, who has a sketchy past, become parasites. Interestingly Cottard, who exploits the plague for profit, is immune from the disease, in part because, in terms of the allegorical construct, he can't be a Nazi perpetrator and a French and/or Jewish victim.

As an allegory, *The Plague* moves too slowly and does not always have a consistently clear correspondence between story and signification in which the moral meaning is clear. At times discussions between characters as well as the narrator's observations are prolix as opposed, say, to the taut allegory of the uncivilized, brutish Yahoos and the rational, intelligent Houyhnhnms in Swift's *Gulliver's Travels* or the onset of the Holocaust in Appelfeld's *Badenheim 1939* where the sanitation workers represent the Nazis. Moreover, as an allegory *The Plague* includes too much philosophic discussion about God and death as well as perhaps too much information about the physical symptoms of the plague.

As a philosophic novel *The Plague* foregrounds and tests various metaphysical positions, including absolute faith in Christianity. It also examines ethical positions, including the common responsibility for one another we humans all share as well as the guilt some feel for not doing enough to fulfill that responsibility. When Tarrou, whose core beliefs center on our social responsibility to other humans, says, "I have realized that we all have the plague," he means that no one can be exempt from inadvertently taking part in injustice to others (219).

The Onset of the Plague

Let us consider how Camus renders the physical presence of the plague. Spring days are ironically juxtaposed with the encroaching bubonic plague: "Beyond [the window] lay the tranquil radiance of a cool spring sky; inside the room a word was echoing still, the word 'plague'" (33). Dead and dying rats begin to appear on April 18. Even before people become ill, the rats are described in graphic terms that introduce revoltingly disruptive images of illness: "People out at night would often feel underfoot the squelchy roundness of a still warm body. It was as if the earth on which our houses stood were being purged of its secreted humors; thrusting up to the surface the abscesses and pus-clots that had been forming in its entrails" (13). It is as if a deviant birthing of a monstrous disease were occurring with the resulting events somehow deriving from the outburst of "secreted humors" – be it hate, racism, or genocide – into the open.

When the weather turns uncomfortably hot, the plague bursts out in all its venom. Camus shows in every way possible how the virulent plague distorts the individual and the community. On the very spring day when the narrator-physician Rieux (along with others) feels optimism and hope, the concierge of Rieux's building dies: "His limbs spread out by the ganglia, embedded in the berth as if he were trying to bury himself in it or a voice from the depths of the earth were summoning him below, the unhappy man seemed to be stifling under some unseen pressure" (18).

Rieux reminds us that disease – and human suffering and death – are part of the "observed facts" that Rieux confronts in his patients suffering from the plague: "stupor and extreme prostration, buboes, intense thirst, delirium, dark blotches on the body, internal dilatation" (33). Even though humans rather than rats are dying, denial in Oran still has the upper hand: "No, all these horrors were not near enough as yet even to ruffle the equanimity of that spring afternoon" (34). A few days later, as the plague reaches out its tentacles, the narrator describes "a serene blue sky flooded with golden light each morning" (53). But Rieux (the still anonymous narrator) also reminds us of another template of nature, namely the sea, which "told of the unrest, the precariousness, of all things in this world. … A picture rose before him of the red glow of the pyres mirrored on a wine-dark, slumberous sea" (34). With the epithet "wine-dark" to describe the sea, Rieux evokes Homer's funeral pyres in Book 23 of *The Iliad* and links the "unrest" and "precariousness" of the 1940s world to prior eras. Using the past to measure the present and vice versa is a pattern in several texts in this study, namely *Swann's Way*, *Death in Venice*, *My Name is Red*, and *The Leopard*, as well as in such modernist texts as Joyce's *Ulysses* (1922) and Eliot's *The Love Song of J. Alfred Prufrock* (1915) and *The Waste Land* (1922).

Excessive summer heat brings with it an increasing number of victims of the illness: "And then the sun took charge, incessant waves of heat and light swept the town daylong. … The sun stalked our townsfolk, along every byway, into every nook; and when they paused, it struck. … Everyone realized with dismay that hot weather would favor the epidemic" (96–97). The August wind is blamed for spreading the plague. When cold returns, the plague abates, with January 25 as the turning point. Perhaps Camus, the non-believer, is playing with the received significance of December 25 as the day of the miracle of Christ's birth.

The Plague as Allegory

What, we must ask, is the significance of the plague in this novel, and does it develop because something is morally amiss in Oran? Is Oran a metonymy for France? Camus has asserted that *The Plague* is an allegory of "The

European resistance against Nazism. The proof is that even though this enemy is never named, everyone recognized it."[15]

Carroll reminds us that Nazism is "unnamed and unrepresented" (Carroll, 54). Certainly it is true that, in terms of the allegory, the signifier (the story) is clearer than what the story signifies in historical and political terms. We must acknowledge that Camus rarely mentions in his writing what happened to Jews in France or Europe. Yet in his November 11, 1942 journal entry, Camus compared the Germans to "rats."[16] Camus was probably responding to the November 10 German invasion of the Vichy-controlled Southern Zone which took place after the successful launch of the Allies' crucial North African campaign called "Operation Torch," which began on November 8, 1942.

Within the allegory, those who die are victims of hatred, and the plague is the disease of intolerance that becomes genocidal. The virulent pestilence is a social disease, incomprehensibly and irrationally searching for victims, and those affected and dying are Holocaust victims, the disadvantaged, the Communists, or any group that is Other. Resisting the bacteria or virus causing the plague requires far more than "common decency," but rather the kind of proactive human caring and intervention demonstrated by Rieux and Tarrou.

Camus is evoking the Nazi invasion of France and France's inept resistance as well as the virulent social disease in Europe of the Holocaust. By setting the novel in the 1940s Camus probably had in mind the treatment of Jews by the Nazis, and in particular the active collaboration of the French with Nazis in persecuting Jews. Somewhat reductively, one could argue that those who catch the plague are the Jews, those who organize to resist the plague are the Resistance, and the rest of the population are the Vichy collaborators.

While the novel's allegory does not have a one-to-one correlation between the nuanced narrative and historical reference points, Camus expected us to see the parallels between victims of the plague and Jews who are arbitrarily separated from their fellow citizens as if they were criminals. He also had in mind the way the Vichy government isolated and harassed its enemies – notably those in the Resistance – and imprisoned or executed them. Once the city gates are shut and the entire city is quarantined, the citizens of Oran "came to know the incorrigible sorrow of all prisoners and exiles, which is to live in company with a memory that serves no purpose" (62). Not unlike Kafka's Joseph K. in *The Trial*, Oran's citizens feel "that they had been sentenced for an unknown crime to an indeterminate period of punishment" (86).

Camus's story can also be read as an account of how the disease of anti-Semitism led to concentration camps. To stress the parallel between victims of the plague and Jews sent to camps, Camus's narrator uses the language of prisons. Once Oran is closed to entrances and exits, Oran becomes a ghetto.

Those catching the plague are sent to hospitals where they are quarantined; the hospitals themselves resemble concentration camps. Doctors are accompanied by police to be sure that sick people are removed from their homes. To get out of Oran, one needs to bribe sentries, and some parasites make a living smuggling material into the city. Indeed, we recall that one reason given by the Nazis for quarantining Jews in ghettoes was that the Jews were supposedly typhoid carriers. Two other ways that Camus evokes the Holocaust are: (1) the burying of bodies in pits; and (2) the use of streetcars to provide a transport system for dead bodies to outlying crematoriums.

Camus emphasizes the imprisonment motif. What, he asks, does being a prisoner and being an exile mean? Is imprisonment not only external – as when the gates of Oran are shut – but also internal for each individual? Once the deadly plague and the imminence of death become the fundamental facts of day-to-day life, and once Oran is cut off from the world due to the quarantine, personal and community assumptions radically change. Only a moral idiot, Camus shows, can immerse oneself in private comforts without regard to the ubiquitous presence of terrible suffering and imminent death.

While we need to note that sometimes the allegory is partially at cross-purposes with the narrative of individual human responses to the disease, we also need to stress that a major point of reconciliation between the realistic narrative and the allegory is when Rieux and his colleagues, notably Tarrou and Dr. Castel, assume responsibility for finding the etiology of the disease and caring for the ostracized victims.

Existentialism, as defined by Sartre and in his own even more gloomy way by Camus, is not only a response to decisions people were forced to make during the German occupation, the Vichy regime, and the deportation of Jews, but also has a strong humanistic component. Whatever else Camus intended, *The Plague* is a humanistic novel, stressing how caring physically and emotionally for other people is the only way to build community and to fulfill oneself. Rieux is the ultimate existentialist defining his moral and emotional essence – his commitment to his fellow citizens – in response to the dire circumstances in which he finds himself.

Camus has been criticized, notably by Conor Cruise O'Brien (*Camus*), for ignoring the Arab majority when rendering Oran and the effects of the plague. Yet it is worth noting that within the novel the journalist Raymond Rambert has come from a leading Paris newspaper to report on "living-conditions prevailing among the Arab population, and especially on the sanitary conditions" (9). Nor does the plague seem to attack females. Given that Arabs and European women would certainly not be immune to the plague, we may assume that they are among the victims. But it is curious that Camus's narrative focuses on males of European ancestry because during the Holocaust women were certainly as much victims of racism and genocide as men. In Algeria the Arabs – men and women – were victims of indifference, harassment, and consignment to lower social classes. But if Camus intended the Arabs to be victims, he should have been explicit by including them among those catching the plague.

The Human Drama: Rieux as Protagonist and Narrator

Both the protagonist and the source of the understated third person narrative, Rieux is insistent that nothing be held back in the way of truth. He is an Oran denizen, a thirty-five-year-old physician, and a war veteran. Because he speaks of "our town" and "our townsfolk" and is committed to Oran's suffering community, and because he is the only one who could have reported many scenes and dialogues, we suspect early on that Rieux is the narrator. Only at the end of *The Plague* does Rieux reveal himself as the source of the narration: "Dr. Rieux resolved to compile this chronicle, so that he should not be one of those who hold their peace, but should bear witness in favor of those plague-stricken people; so that some memorial of the injustice and outrage done to them might endure; and to state quite simply what we learn in a time of pestilence: that there are more things to admire in men than to despise" (268).

We have probably guessed that Rieux is the only possible source since Tarrou is dead, and Rieux clearly has access to Tarrou's diaries. Speaking in the third person, Rieux claims to be an "impartial observer" (262), but there are clearly implicit and explicit judgments deriving from his values on every page. Certainly he has been not only a "conscientious witness," but also a conscientious participant in organizing medical and empathetic resistance to the plague (262). As he admits, "this self-imposed reticence cost him little effort" (263).

Rieux is Meursault's opposite; if, as Germaine Bree puts it, Meursault "acts in a human situation as though human relationships, and therefore responsibilities do not exist," Rieux is defined by responsibility (Bree, *Camus*, rev. ed., 112).[17] Yet while far more engaged than Meursault, Rieux – somewhat defined by his categorizing sensibility and scientific temperament – needs to learn the value of love as something other than an abstraction. His understanding and humanity develop in breadth and range as he commits himself to those ravaged by the plague and develops human relationships with those who resist the disease and those who finally succumb to it. Within both the story of how individuals respond to the plague and the allegory, Camus suggests the need to, as E. M. Forster puts it in the epigraph to *Howards End* (1910), "Only connect."

The narrator – whom rereaders are always aware is Rieux – traces the devolution of civic order, the casting off of the trappings of civility, and the ineffectuality of public institutions, including the Catholic Church. He mocks Father Paneloux, the Jesuit priest who sees the plague as a judgment of God and who resents the failure of Oran's citizens to pay enough attention to him. Public order breaks down. People set fire to their own houses to purge them of germs or they attack sentries that keep people from leaving or entering the quarantined city that has become a prison and a charnel house.

As the plague takes hold, the surviving citizens become apathetic, indifferent, and lose their capacity for sustained emotions. Those separated from the ones they love reduce the absent persons to abstractions and do not feel the same passion for them that they once felt. With few exceptions, the entire city of Oran has lost the capacity for intimacy: "For there is no denying that the plague had gradually killed off in all of us the faculty not only of love but even of friendship" (158). But we do recall that throughout the narrative, and notwithstanding when Rieux as narrator makes the above observation, Tarrou and Rieux have become closer and closer friends.

Would it have been better for the novel had Camus identified the narrator at the outset? I could imagine Rieux as a self-dramatizing first person narrator seeking adequate terms to understand the invasion of large numbers of human bodies by a terrifying visitation of illness. As it is, when rereading we notice the possibility of a first person telling peeking through almost as if Camus had seriously considered such an approach. Reflecting his own sense of mortality, as well as his sense of encroachment and enclosure brought on by the disease, Rieux as narrator is reaching for terms to comprehend the inexplicable and unimaginable. Were the story told in the first person, more emphasis might have been on Rieux's epistemological quest to understand and his semiological quest for the language to explain. But perhaps with a first person narrator throughout, Camus might have had even more difficulty balancing allegory and realist narrative and at times taking an ironic, detached view of events and behavior.

In the third person, Rieux oscillates between, on the one hand, providing a log of the evolution of the plague as if he were writing a public health document and, on the other, describing his deeply felt personal engagement. The clinical detachment with which Rieux as narrator traces the etiology of the disease's progress is modulated by the humanistic commitment on the part of Rieux and his colleagues to trying to find a way to control symptoms and stop the progress of the disease, even while caring for the ill.

Rieux's narration is shaped by his personal pain. To some extent, Camus solves the aforementioned formal issue of mixed genres – or perhaps I should say circumvents it – with stunning images which the reader understands reflect Rieux's sensibility, engagement, and commitment to his medical profession, even though the narration is in the third person: "At that moment he had a preternaturally vivid awareness of the town stretched out below, a victim world secluded and apart, and of the groans of agony stifled in its darkness" (90).

Rieux idealizes Tarrou, who is accepting of human frailty at the same time that he feels the guilt and pain of his own compromises. Finally, Rieux argues we are all plague-ridden in that every day we disregard inequities and injustices. But, we might ask, does Rieux feel more specific guilt than he acknowledges? Does his choice to immerse himself in the plague compensate for something in his life? He does not focus as much as the reader would expect on his wife, who passed away in a sanatorium outside Oran while trying to recover from a prior illness. Does Rieux's lack of attention suggest that perhaps he feels responsibility for her death because their marriage lacks sustained passionate love? He seems to have been more drawn to his mother, whom he depicts as a saint, than to his wife.

The Human Drama: Choice

Camus asks the questions Conrad asks in *Lord Jim*, *The Secret Sharer*, and elsewhere: Why do some people respond well to emergencies and excruciatingly difficult circumstances while others do not? Why do some people have the moral imperative necessary to do humane acts, even when faced with danger and the possibility of death, while others fail to respond?

The Plague is populated by male characters of European ancestry whose behavior in response to the disease often becomes increasingly obsessive and peculiar. One of Camus's points is that extreme conditions bring out the core of who people are, notably their potential for courageous or cowardly behavior as well as their suppressed desires and quirks. That is, the conditions of crisis define a person. In the face of the external threat to descend into chaos, the choices individuals make reveal who they are, but choice comes from a complex mixture of motives. Tarrou, a well-to-do cynical loner who is vacationing in Oran, and Rieux make conscious choices when they decide to immerse themselves in the day-to-day, often hopeless activities of fighting the plague in Oran. Tarrou's diary becomes an important source for Rieux's narration.

A resistant reading would note that Rieux's greatest intimacy, and one with strong homosocial overtones, is with Tarrou, with whom he swims naked one night in the sea while the plague is still at high tide: "Turning to Tarrou, he caught a glimpse on his friend's face of the same happiness, a happiness that forgot nothing, even murder" (223). When the plague recedes enough to allow normal life to resume and the exile to end, Rieux observes heterosexual lovers, but he seems physically drawn to idiosyncratic males like the functionary Grand, who keeps statistics on the plague for those desperately trying to control what is going on. Rieux is even fascinated, perhaps erotically, by Cottard, the parasitic figure flourishing during the plague's siege.

Grand is the counterpoint to Tarrou and Rieux, men of words whose observations become the warp and woof of the novel. For most of his adult life, Grand, an elderly civil servant who has little verbal facility, chooses to privilege his writing over his clerical service: "[T]his difficulty in finding his words had come to be the bane of his life" (40). Grand is pathetically trying to write a novel but is stuck on the opening sentence. Yet Grand reaches beyond his obsessive effort to compose the perfect sentence and chooses to play a role in battling the epidemic. Rereading, we see that Grand's regret for his lost marriage has some echo in Rieux's experience, for Rieux knows that something needs to be fixed with his marriage if he survives the plague. Grand survives, and he finally writes a letter to the wife who has left him.

Camus emphasizes the heightened role of miscommunication and misinterpretation in historical crises such as the onset of the plague. Camus implies that our struggle with language is part of our Sisyphean effort to find meaning in an absurd world. Grand's struggles with language crystallize Camus's continued focus on the inadequacy of language within the imagined world of the novel.

Rambert, a visiting journalist from Paris, schemes to escape Oran so as to return to his beloved. Finally, he changes his mind and commits to the choice of fighting the plague. After abandoning his efforts to leave Oran, he asserts to Rieux: "This business is everybody's business. … But you know that as well as I do, damn it! Or else what are you up to in that hospital of yours? Have *you* made a definite choice and turned down happiness?" (181; emphasis Camus).

At first, Rieux's response to Rambert is one of the puzzling moments in the novel, for he seems to be saying that human engagement is more important than love: "For nothing in the world is it worth turning one's back on what one loves. Yet that is what I'm doing, though why I do not know. … [A] man can't cure and know at the same time. So let's cure as quickly as we can" (181). Rieux is implying that his own absent wife has become an abstraction as opposed to his living fully and existentially moment to moment in real time and engaging with the always present and terrible illness besieging the city and his patients. We realize that the above passage is also true of Rambert's choosing commitment to the plague victims rather than fleeing to his absent lover. Nor is there anything Rieux could be doing to participate in his wife's cure in the sanatorium from which he is cut off by the quarantine. Camus's lesson is clear: We cannot ignore the present demands on our humanity if those demands mean turning our back on people fighting for their very lives.

In his refusal to do anything to help fight the plague, Cottard, whom we first meet in an unsuccessful suicide attempt, makes – and never deviates from – a different kind of choice. He turns the plague into a temporary oasis – an opportunity – where he can pursue disreputable activities while his anticipated legal difficulties are suspended. Cottard is a kind of darker doubleganger for Rieux and

Tarrou, a selfish, unprincipled figure who highlights the values of those who do existentially commit to community.

Within the allegory, humanity finally triumphs. Sometimes the narrative voice anthropomorphizes the plague so that it is an enemy stalking the unsuspecting and innocent: "[I]ts energy was flagging, out of exhaustion and exasperation, and it was losing, with its self-command, the ruthless, almost mathematical efficiency that had been its trump card hitherto" (234). If there are weapons to deal with the voracious plague, they are human sympathy for victims, individual acts of kindness, and a refusal to give up when "Pestilence" appears. It is almost as if there is a cause and effect between the efforts of those who care – Rieux, Tarrou, Castel, Rampart, Grand – and the retreat of the plague. Self-abnegation and empathy matter. Rieux says, "I feel more fellowship with the defeated than with saints" (222). In a great image – and Camus is not continuously a writer of striking images – the lifting of the plague is compared to a rent in an airless shroud: "The truth was that for many months the town had been stifling under an airless shroud, in which a rent had now been made, and every Monday when he turned on the radio, each of us learned that the rift was widening; soon he would be able to breathe freely" (235).

Like *The Stranger* where the Law grinds inexorably forward toward Meursault's execution, *The Plague* explores whether there can be any justification for a culture choosing capital punishment. Within *The Plague*, capital punishment becomes a metonymy for cruelty and exploitation on the part of those in power as they mete out punishment to less powerful victims. Tarrou had despised his father for advocating capital punishment for those guilty of murder, and had joined those who wanted to change the current system only to realize that by "approving of acts and principles which could only end … in the deaths of thousands of people," he was as guilty as those who supported capital punishment, and that in a sense so are we who participate in the rituals of civilization: "For many years, I've been ashamed, mortally ashamed, of having been, even with the best intentions, even at many removes, a murderer in my turn. … I have realized that we all have plague" (218–219). Camus asks, what can any of us do to avoid implication and complicity in society's evils (the nameless "acts and principles" evoked by Tarrou), including cooperation with the German occupation and the Vichy government as well as active approval of anti-Semitism? Can we do anymore than Tarrou and Rieux to absolve ourselves of guilt and responsibility for human failings or must we all share the guilt for history's outrages?

Underlined by Tarrou's awareness that no one has a claim to purity, one of the paradoxes of *The Plague* is that many of those who embrace humane abstractions, and who thus seem to wear the mantle of justice, may have the plague, while those without sustaining ideas may do more of what needs to be done during crises in terms of sympathy, empathy, and courage. In other words, thinking too much can be debilitating and narcissistic. It is not necessarily the intellectuals or most imaginative who best take care of our fellow humans who have the plague. An odd assortment of people create the best possible conditions for stifling the plague. In fact, after witnessing the death of a child named Jacques Orton, the formerly deluded priest Paneloux comes to the same conclusion when he exclaims in his final sermon: "'My brothers, each one of us must be the one who stays!'" (196). Recovering his humanity, Paneloux takes ill and dies, but whether he dies from the plague is uncertain. Identifying with the victims, he becomes one with them in a world that is not, as claimed by his near namesake, the Voltaire character Pangloss, the best of all possible worlds.

Conclusion

Camus is aware of how we want to believe we live in a benign universe – no matter the evidence to the contrary – and how we personally and collectively live in the illusion that we can control our lives and overcome adversity. He stresses how many of us continually adjust our beliefs to fulfill our needs for satisfactory endings:

. . . .

> Stupidity has a knack of getting its way; as we should see if we were not always so much wrapped up in ourselves. ... Our townsfolk ... thought that everything was possible for them; which predisposed that pestilences were impossible. ... How should [our townsfolk] have given a thought to anything like plague, which rules out any future, cancels journeys, silences the exchange of views. They fancied themselves free, and no one will ever be free as long as there are pestilences. (31–32)

. . . .

Such passages make sense when we realize that the plague is both an illness and an allegorical signifier for something with larger historical and moral implications.

With full awareness of the historical contexts of his novels, Camus wrote *The Stranger* during World War II and *The Plague* just after the War. What ties these seemingly different novels together is their insistence that we must define ourselves in relation to personal and historical circumstances within a godless, absurd world. In many ways the highly developed and conscientious Rieux is the emotionally and morally stilted Meursault's polar opposite, but each is responding to what they see as a meaningless cosmos, and each defines himself by his behavior. After murdering the Arab for no real reason and without feeling guilty, the loner Meursault takes the first steps towards asserting himself while caught in the legal labyrinth that has imprisoned him; after he is convicted of murder and awaits the death sentence, he continues to discover flickers of what it is to be human, in part by responding to memories of the past. From the outset of *The Plague*, Rieux, a conscientious physician, is defined by his highly evolved conscience and moral compass that permit him to risk his own health to help others.

Camus expects the reader to understand how difficult it is to make sense of a complex, absurd world that lacks easy answers and requires choices. He reminds us that reading his novels leaves us with puzzles about what passages mean and why characters behave as they do. Absolute certainty is itself a plague and, Camus implies, novels that don't leave us with interpretive issues and puzzling moments oversimplify in their efforts to demystify life. Or as Derrida has put it, "A text is not a text unless it hides from the first comer" ("Plato's Pharmacy," 63).[18]

Study Questions for *The Plague*

1. How does Camus's graphic imagery underline the horror of the plague?
2. How is *The Plague* an existential novel? How would you define existentialism?
3. How does *The Plague* work as a political and historical allegory? How do the novel's allegory and realistic depiction of the plague at times work at cross-purposes?
4. What does Camus gain by withholding the identity of the narrator and narrating most of the novel in the third person? Would the novel be better with Rieux as a first person self-dramatizing narrator?
5. How would you compare and contrast Rieux with Meursault?
6. How do we respond to Rieux's tendencies towards abstraction as well as his propensity to emphasize numbers when confronting the plague? Are these limitations that he overcomes?
7. What is the role of Grand, the compulsive and ineffectual writer who commits to the project of resisting the disease? How does he represent the difficulty if not the inability to transform experience into language? In what ways might he be someone Camus and/or Rieux, the narrator, fear becoming?
8. What is the function of Tarrou, the young visitor, whose diaries give us another perspective, and who organizes the sanitary volunteers? In what ways are the volunteers, whom Rieux is careful not to praise excessively, representations of those who participated in the French Resistance? Or is the allegory less specific than that?
9. What is the function of Rambert, the journalist, who wants to escape Oran before realizing that he needs to stay and join the fight against the plague?
10. How are Rieux and Tarrou surrogates for the various moral positions to which Camus subscribes? Or is the novel dialogic in the sense that various views are tested, modified, and reconfigured?

Notes

1. Directed by Roger Donaldson and written by Heywood Gould; Coughlin's words to young Flanagan.
2. Quoted in David Carroll, *Albert Camus the Algerian: Colonialism, Terrorism, Justice* (New York: Columbia University Press, 2007), 27.
3. Adam Gopnik, "Facing History: Why We Love Camus," *The New Yorker* (April 9, 2012), 70–76; see 72.
4. See Camus's 1942 essay, *The Myth of Sisyphus*, trans. Justin O'Brien (New York: Penguin, 2013).
5. Dec. 20, 1897; in Joseph Conrad, *Collected Letters of Joseph Conrad, Vol. 1: 1861–1897*. Eds. Frederick Karl and Laurence Davies (New York: Cambridge University Press, 1983), 425.
6. Conor Cruise O'Brien, *Camus* (London: Fontana, 1970), 12.
7. Albert Camus, *The Stranger*, trans. Stuart Gilbert (New York: Vintage, 1946). Because this is the standard edition, I will use this translation.
8. Albert Camus, *The Stranger*, trans. Matthew Ward (New York: Alfred A. Knopf, 1988).
9. Albert Camus, *The Outsider*, trans. Sandra Smith (London: Penguin, 2012).
10. Adele King, *Camus* (New York: Capricorn, 1971), 25–26.
11. Quoted in John Foley, *Albert Camus: From the Absurd to Revolt* (New York: Routledge, 2014), 100.
12. Quoted in Carroll, 195, from Albert Camus, "Reflections on the Guillotine," in *Resistance, Rebellion and Death*, trans. Justin O'Brien (New York: Alfred A. Knopf, 1961), 199.
13. Claire Messud, "A New 'L'Etranger,'" *NYR* 61:10 (June 5, 2014), 6.
14. Albert Camus, *The Plague*, trans. Stuart Gilbert (New York: Time Inc. Book Division, 1962). Page references are to this edition.
15. Camus, *Théâtre, récits, nouvelles*, 73; quoted in Carroll, 54.
16. See Herbert Lottman, *Albert Camus* (Garden City, NY: Doubleday, 1979), 265.
17. Germaine Bree, *Camus*, rev. ed. (New York: Harbinger Books, 1964), 112.
18. Jacques Derrida, "Plato's Pharmacy," in *Disseminations*, trans. Barbara Johnson (Chicago: University of Chicago Press, 1981), 63.

Chapter 6

Why Giorgio Bassani Matters: The Elegiac Imagined World of Bassani and the Jews of Ferrara

One of the most odious forms of anti-Semitism was precisely this: to complain that the Jews were not *enough* like the others and then, vice versa, having ascertained their almost total assimilation into their surroundings, to complain of the opposite: that they were just like the others, not even a bit different from the average, the ordinary.

Giorgio Bassani, The Garden of the Finzi-Continis, 114[1]

Introduction: Making the Case for Bassani's Stature

In the United States, Giorgio Bassani (1916–2000) is undoubtedly the most neglected major European Jewish and Holocaust writer. Yet in Italy Bassani is considered along with Primo Levi as one of the two pre-eminent writers of Italian Jewry as well as one of the most important Italian writers of the twentieth century. Like many European writers who lived through World War II and especially like other Jewish writers, Bassani writes out of an ethical and psychological compulsion to revisit historical forces that were beyond his control.

This chapter is in the genre of making a strong argument for a writer who deserves to be read more than he is, in this case a figure I regard as an essential author whom few people I know have read, even though many know the 1970 film *The Garden of the Finzi-Continis* that is based on the work of his that is best known in the Anglophone world. Thus my main purpose is to introduce

Reading the Modern European Novel Since 1900: A Critical Study of Major Fiction from Proust's Swann's Way *to Ferrante's Neapolitan Tetralogy*, First Edition. Daniel R. Schwarz.
© 2018 John Wiley & Sons Ltd. Published 2018 by John Wiley & Sons Ltd.

Bassani's entire corpus and to show how his Ferrara novels and stories hold together as one coherent fictional history.

Bassani's novel, *The Garden of the Finzi-Continis* (1962), for which he won the Viareggio prize, was made into a major film by Vittorio De Sica (1971); the film won the 1971 Oscar as the Best Foreign Film. But barely known today in the English-speaking world – even though translated – are such wonderful fictions as *Five Stories of Ferrara* (1956; reissued in 1973 as *Inside the Wall*), for which he won the prestigious Strega prize, *The Gold-rimmed Eyeglasses* (1958), *Behind the Door* (1964), *The Heron* (1968), and *The Smell of Hay* (1972) (which includes *The Gold-rimmed Eyeglasses*). Bassani's first book, *Una città di pianura* ("A City of the Plains"), a collection of short stories set in Ferrara, was published in 1940 under the pseudonym Giacomo Marchi – the name of Bassani's Catholic paternal grandfather – to evade the Italian anti-Semitic racial laws, which were introduced in 1938. He also wrote poetry that was collected in *Stories of Miserable Lovers and Other Verses* (1945), *To You Before the Close of Day* (1947), *Another Freedom* (1951), and *Rolls Royce and Other Poems* (1982).

As befits someone who wrote film scripts for Italian directors, Bassani has a strong visual imagination and often focuses on particular objects and settings as the centerpieces of his narratives: a plaque on the Ferrara Temple commemorating the Jews who didn't return, a parade in honor of a leftist heroine after the Liberation, a place where anti-Fascists or Fascists who were willing to compromise were assassinated, and the omnipresent Jewish cemetery in Ferrara. Apparently influenced by cinema, his narratives move backward and forward and sideways in time, shift from close to distant views of characters, and, despite a relatively enclosed geography, move rapidly from place to place in unexpected ways. Vignettes obliquely peel layers away from historical and cultural illusions as Bassani invites his readers to share with his narrators their muted outrage at the dehumanizing behavior committed against Jewish, political, or sexual victims.

Bassani as Italian-Jewish Writer: Why History Matters

Bassani was part of the Jewish community in Ferrara that dates back hundreds of years. Focusing on twentieth-century Ferrara, Italy, he has written a series of magnificent historically inflected dramas of the human psyche living on the edge. Unlike his father, Bassani himself wasn't deported to the concentration camps, but he was jailed in the spring of 1943 for anti-Fascist activities. After Bassani was released, he moved with his new wife to Florence where he lived under a false name and took part in the Partisan resistance to German occupation.

Reading the Bassani oeuvre in translation, we learn what it was to be a Jew in Italy between World War I and the years immediately following the Holocaust and World War II. We learn how the Jewish minority in Italy strove to balance assimilation with preserving its own cultural identity, even while the Catholic majority at every turn could – and often did – pull the rug out from under its very existence.

For Bassani, crucial to Italy's deterioration in the first half of the twentieth century was Mussolini's becoming Prime Minister in 1922 and later taking on the title Il Duce in 1925. Whether identified by name or anonymous, Bassani's Jewish narrators and characters are often surrogates and metaphors for himself, as much in replicating feelings and attitudes – especially detachment, estrangement, shame, guilt, and embarrassment – as in actual facts. Thus the anonymous narrative voice of *The Garden of the Finzi-Continis* has an autobiographical aspect. Such self-inscription is also notable in the recurring Bruno Lattes, a young Jewish Ferraran who is ostracized by the 1938 racial laws and isolated from his former acquaintances, including the beautiful gentile Adrienna Trentini. Later, the fictional Lattes makes his way to Rome (as did Bassani, although Bassani first spent some months in Florence) after July 25, 1943, the month of Mussolini's overthrow, in time to avoid deportation and death – the fate of his parents – and then (unlike Bassani) emigrates to America in 1945. Lattes is the retrospective narrator of "The Last Years of Clelia Trotti" – first published in the journal *Paragone* in 1954 – and three stories collected in *The Smell of Hay* as well as a character in *The Garden of the Finzi-Continis*.

Bassani's stature grows when one reads his major works one after the other because they are episodes in a fully rendered fictional history of Ferrara that is strongly related to actual history. Not only recurring characters but also recurring references to real historical events give authenticity to Bassani's Ferrara. Interlocking characters and events make his oeuvre one coherent text. One could use Bassani's fiction to construct a timeline of Italy's political history from 1918 to 1948.

Examples of Bassani's rich historical fabric include the deportation of Jews in autumn of 1943 – including actual Ferrara residents like Dr. Elia Corcos – and the assassination on December 15, 1943 of eleven Ferrara citizens who opposed the Fascists for collaborating with the Nazis. Specified, too, are historic political figures such as the socialist Matteotti, who was murdered in 1924 for opposing the Fascists. In "A Plaque on Via Mazzini," Bassani reminds his readers of the 183 deported Ferrara citizens who became "shadows devoured by Buchenwald, Auschwitz, Mauthausen, Dachau, etc."[2]

Bassani created a unique imagined world out of the provincial city of Ferrara, one that crystallized important ingredients of nineteenth- and twentieth-century Italian history, with a strong inflexion of Italian Jewish history. Bassani's Ferrara is what Wessex is to Hardy or Yoknapatawpha County is to Faulkner. Bassani's history, based on facts, fleshes out history that takes the reader back to

Garibaldi, who Doctor Elia Corcos's father heard speaking from the balcony of Palazzo Costabelli close to the time he remembered that the gates of the ghetto were torn down in the 1860s.[3]

In Bassani's fiction, history matters – and matters most to Jews – and it is the lesson learned not only by the young Jewish narrators in both *The Garden of the Finzi-Continis* and *The Gold-rimmed Eyeglasses* but also by the characters in the *Five Stories of Ferrara*. Bassani speaks to those readers who know the broad history of Europe between the two World Wars as well as during and immediately after World War II, but may not know about Italy. In that period, Jews discovered that they could not control their lives or seek refuge in aestheticism or personal relationships. They may have dreamt of reconfiguring or reinventing themselves, of realizing their potential, of transfiguration through love and politics, but history usually mocked those dreams. Their imagination offered the possible; history responded all too often with disappointingly harsh reality.

The Jewish Community in Ferrara

The small city of Ferrara and the surrounding area – notably Bologna – is a major protagonist in all of Bassani's fiction. For Bassani, the Jews of Ferrara are both a special case with a unique history and a representative group of Italian Jews. On every page is the living, quivering presence of the past, and that past is often shaped by crucial events in twentieth-century Italian history. Bassani writes of the rise of Mussolini and Fascism and its effects on Italy's political and social tolerance, the 1938 anti-Jewish laws in Italy, and Italy's collaboration with Hitler, which opened the door to the persecution and, in 1943 after Mussolini was deposed and the Germans invaded, the extermination of Jews in Italy, including Ferrara. He never forgets Italy's political history and how Fascism undermined and corroded the quality of Italian life in turning people against one another, encouraging class and social divisions, and opening the door to barbaric behavior, most notably virulent anti-Semitism, including betrayals by Christians who had lived together with Jews for generations. He writes, too, of wartime devastation, and the aftermath of rebuilding Italy politically and morally.

Let us turn to the Ferrara Jewish community, many of whose families had lived in Italy for centuries and thought of themselves as Italians who happened to be Jewish rather than as Jews living in Italy; they were more central to civic life than in most Italian cities. Yet as much as the Jews would have liked to forget that they were confined in a ghetto from the 1620s to the first years of the 1860s, the ghetto area remained and many Jews occupied that area.

Historically, the Ferrara Jewish community prospered from the thirteenth to early seventeenth century under the Este family rule, but in 1624, under papal administration, Jews in the ghetto had to wear yellow badges. During French invasions, Jews experienced freedom, but it was soon squelched; for example, during the 1802–1814 Napoleonic period in Italy, Jews were briefly emancipated. Even after Jews were forced to return to the ghetto in 1826, they retained land acquired during the French years. In the early 1860s confinement ended with a unified Italy under a constitutional monarch granting rights to all citizens.

For many Italian Jews – including those of Ferrara – the way to escape social isolation had been through assimilation. Yet, paradoxically, within their community the Ferrara Jews sought to maintain their own identity as Jews of separate origins, with three distinct Jewish communities: German, Italianate, and Levantine. Culminating in the racial laws of 1938, the gradual anti-Semitism of the 1930s became a cause of their renewed isolation. According to Bassani, for the Jews of Ferrara, the ghetto became an image for a state of mind. Lingering always in the imagination and memory of the Ferrara Jews were stories passed down about ghetto times when the Jews were forced to listen to sermons inviting them to convert and when their funerals had to be held at nighttime.

Jews in Ferrara had emerged in the 1860s and established themselves as important citizens in the professional and merchant community. Some upper-middle-class and prosperous Jews, including a few large landowners, cast their lot with Fascism in the 1920s and the early 1930s, thinking it would provide social order in the face of international Communism. But they came to realize that in the minds of the Fascists they would always be residents of an invisible ghetto.

Except for its requirement that Jewish students attend public school on Saturday, the Law on Jewish Communities of 1930–1933 was actually viewed favorably by many Italian Jews because it helped organize their communities. But the plight of Italian Jews worsened. In 1933 anti-Semitic campaigns began in Italy, culminating in Italy's collaboration with Germany on the side of Franco in the Spanish Civil War. In 1936 anti-Semitic slogans appeared in Ferrara where 800 Jews were a powerful presence.

Paolo Orano's 1937 diatribe *Gli Ebrei in Italia* blamed the Jews for supporting degenerate cultural expressions, for Zionist sympathies, and for a lack of loyalty to the Fascist state that claimed to be the successor to Imperial Rome. Mussolini was trying to please Hitler with whom he cast his destiny. Mussolini's anti-Semitic measures began with a manifesto on race prepared by Italian "scientists" on July 14, 1938, claiming that Italians, like Germans, were Aryans. The 1938 race manifesto was accompanied by harsh racial laws eliminating Jews in Italy from civic life, depriving them of their civil rights, preventing them from using public libraries, and expelling them from the armed forces. Jews were banned from public schools and universities although they could finish degrees on which they were working, as Bassani did in 1939. Certain Jews were exempted from various exclusions on account of their membership in the Fascist party or because of prior patriotic service, but those exemptions disappeared when Germans took over after Mussolini was deposed in 1943.

After Mussolini's fall and after Italy signed an armistice with the Allies, the Nazis occupied Northern and Central Italy. Their subsequent puppet regime was called the Italian Social Republic, informally known as the Salò republic because its headquarters were in Salò, a small town on Lake Garda. Mussolini was installed as the nominal head by the Germans with the support of the German army and Fascist supporters who were organized into the paramilitary Black Brigades. Before the German occupation, foreign Jews were interred, but conditions were not like those in Nazi camps. After the German occupation, the puppet regime pursued Nazi policies of arresting, deporting, and ultimately liquidating Jews in Northern and Central Italy until it was overthrown by Partisans on April 25, 1945. Mussolini and his coterie were shot three days later.

Bassani is an angry writer, emphasizing the noir history of Ferrara. He rages against Ferrara not only for allowing its Jewish community to be decimated but also for allowing itself to lapse into cultural mediocrity while its neighbor Bologna flourished. Indeed, death is omnipresent in Bassani as if the entire oeuvre were an elegy for a lost culture. Images of the city's cemeteries – in particular but not exclusively the Jewish cemetery – as well as a prison become interchangeable with the area of the Jewish ghetto. In a Ferrara cemetery before the ensuing deportations, Bruno Lattes notices "The shadows of the funerary columns and the gravestones stretched across the graves."[4] The cemetery is frequented by young lovers from whom Bruno as a racial outcast feels estranged and to whom he feels resentful: "Their blood was better than his, their soul was better than his! … Oh, to be one with them, one of them in spite of everything!" (160). *The Garden of the Finzi-Continis* begins with the unnamed Jewish retrospective narrator visiting Etruscan tombs and thinking of the Finzi-Continis whom he "had known and loved" and who had built a huge tomb in the Jewish cemetery of Ferrara: "[A]ll deported to Germany in the autumn of '43, who could say if they found any sort of burial at all" (10).

Given Bassani's focus on the demise of Jewry in Ferrara, we might recall his citing Henry James in his epigraph to "The Walk Before Supper": "Why does my pen not drop from my hand on approaching the infinite pity and tragedy of all the past?" (41).

Bassani wants his readers to remember how the Jewish culture in Ferrara was destroyed and he hardly spares anyone – including many of the Jews – from his indictment. Like Joyce's Dublin, Ferrara became dominated if not infested by mediocrity, self-delusion, and paralysis, but in Ferrara the consequences were much greater. In Ferrara, cemeteries, prisons, ghetto walls, and plaques honoring the martyred are the physical correlatives to loneliness, isolation, and, of course, death. So, too, are bullet holes and other damage caused by bombing during World War II.

The Jewish cemetery is a central landmark in *The Garden of the Finzi-Continis* and *Five Stories of Ferrara*. It is a metaphor for a once vital Jewish presence in Ferrara's cultural, social, and political landscape that will never be revived by the remnants of the Jews who are left. Ostentatiously missing from the cemetery are the bodies of the 183 deported Jews, including four members of the Finzi-Contini family who had rather poignantly built an enormous family tomb there.

What Kind of Fiction Did Bassani Write?

While Primo Levi foregrounds what happens in the concentration camps, particularly Auschwitz, Bassani's contribution to Holocaust narratives is to write mostly about the before and after – before the liquidation campaign and after the World War ended – while leaving out most of the torture and killing. Bassani focuses on the gradual deprivation of civil rights and the social marginalization of Jews in a city where they had played an important economic and political role. Bassani's more oblique approach to this subject emphasizes the gradual marginalization and isolation of Ferrara Jews, the developing complicity of much of the rest of the Ferrara citizens with racism, and their even worse involvement during the Salò regime when the unspeakable deportations occurred. In Bassani's fiction, what happened to Jews who disappeared from Ferrara shadows the telling, almost like pentimento in painting, where a painted-over subject insistently peeks through.

Bassani is an ironist, so much so that in the guise of writing historical novels, he also writes about strong and complex emotions such as fear, guilt, and shame. He understands that there is no escape from history and that manners become a luxury when people are caught up in terror and genocide. He knows how brutality and barbarism can scar private lives to the point where ordinary living becomes impossible and what results may be suicide, necessary exile, or going into hiding. Whether in the guise of first person or third person narrators, Bassani creates a world-weary voice that is often distant and clinically detached as if he would be surprised at nothing; he is skeptical if not cynical about human motives and the possibility of self-knowledge. He is under few illusions about the mediocre nature of most of humankind, although his disdain for the lies we tell ourselves and his contempt for bullies are mitigated by his pity for victims.

In *The Gold-rimmed Eyeglasses*, Bassani's first person Jewish narrator looks back at the dissolution of Italy's social fabric that began to accelerate in the early 1930s but had its seeds in the post-World War I years beginning in 1919. The narrator experiences racial discrimination, while tracing similar intolerance heaped on the homosexual physician Dr. Fadigati, for whom he feels sympathy as a fellow victim of rapid social ostracism. Tormenting the doctor, the decadent bully Deliliers is a grotesque parody of Il Duce and a by-product – if not the quintessence – of Fascism.

Dr. Fadigati reminds us that Bassani's focus is not only on Italians of Jewish descent whose lives are disrupted by the racial laws but also on non-Jews who are among the lonely, the marginalized, the ostracized, the socially outré. Abandoned with child by her well-to-do Jewish lover, the peasant title character in "Lida Mantovani" later finds some respectability and stability in marriage to a religious Catholic who had been orphaned and became a middle-class bookbinder, Oreste Benetti. In "The Last Years of Clelia Trotti," the socialist activist title character is virtually quarantined in the Fascist era and ironically rehabilitated after her death. In "The Walk Before Supper" – first published in 1951 in the periodical *Botteghe oscure* – Luisa Brondi, the "little woman with the black shawl and bony, spinster fingers," takes the place of her late sister, Gemma Brondi, the nurse from a peasant family whom Dr. Elia Corcos married after impregnating her (65).

Behind the Door (1964), which takes place in 1929 and 1930, dramatizes the bullying, intimidation, and exploitation of a Jewish adolescent in an Italian liceo. Emphasizing how the Catholics regard the Jews – and especially himself – as *others* rather than as fellow Italian citizens, Bassani's retrospective first person Jewish narrator has experiences that foreshadow the more virulent anti-Semitism that follows in the later 1930s. The star student Cattolica (the word ironically means Catholic) asks the narrator whether "Israelites didn't believe in the Madonna … [and if] it was true that we were still waiting for the Messiah. … And I answered him, point by point, with feverish, exaggerated enthusiasm, not even noticing how elementary his questions were, how generic and vulgar, not to say insolent his curiosity was" (31).

Bassani writes about how personal memory distorts what really happens. He is aware of the ironic disjunction between originating events and how we remember them. Bassani's target is those who retrospectively reconfigure history – and who pretend history to be something different from what actually happened – to support their self-serving current social and moral needs.

"A Plaque on Via Mazzini": A Story about Jewish Deportation and a Lone Single Return

Perhaps the most important story for understanding Bassani is "A Plaque on Via Mazzini" – a story that first appeared in the periodical *Botteghe oscure* in 1952 – in which Geo Josz returns from the concentration camps in August 1945 to find his name on the Temple plaque that is just being completed and that honors the 183 members of the Jewish community who did not return. I am using Bassani's figures, which he believed to be accurate (and which included his own father), although as Guia Risari points out in *The Document Within the Walls: The Romance of Bassani* (1999), others have different counts.[5] The lone survivor of the 183 – a number including the ninety-year-old Elia Corcos, the parents of Bruno Lattes, and members of the Finzi-Contini family – Geo becomes a touchstone for how Ferrara, and by implication Italy, dealt with deporting some of its own citizenry.

Geo Josz's father was once exempted from racial laws because he had been a Fascist but he, too, "had vanished with his wife and children into the ovens of Buchenwald" ("A Plaque on Via Mazzini," 87). (In fact, we now know what Bassani didn't know, namely that Buchenwald, for all its horrors, was not an extermination camp and people were not incinerated.) Some Jews managed to escape, such as Geo's uncle, lawyer Geremia Tabet, a "Fascist from the first days" whose political and business wiles enabled him to survive the war, while cowering in his home. Tabet is still wearing the characteristic beard of the Fascist when Geo returns from the concentration camps. But for most Jews, neither assimilation nor withdrawal – the path chosen by the Finzi-Continis – or prestigious social position was a guarantee against deportation.

The concentration camp experience has turned Geo into what Melville calls an "isolato." Bassani presents a schism between the former Fascists, represented by Uncle Geremia who wants to forget the deportations and sanitize the past, and the Partisans, represented by his Uncle Daniele who loathes Geremia and who wants to remember the persecution of Jews and the Fascist regime. But to Geo this schism between Fascists and Partisans is irrelevant. Bassani renders the changing response of citizens of Ferrara who do not know what to make of Geo's erratic behavior, including his embracing his sycophantic Uncle Geremia. At first, the city's denizens assume that Geo's refusal to re-enter Ferrara life is a consequence of his terrible concentration camp experiences, but gradually they lose patience with what they see as eccentricity if not petulance.

Bassani never penetrates Geo's consciousness or explains the motives behind his behavior. We as readers assume – but don't know – that his single-minded concern with regaining his Palazzo is a natural outcome of the necessary narcissism that enabled him to survive. We never learn how he survived and what compromises he made, if any were necessary, and what role luck played. Barely disguising his suppressed anger at the limited sympathy and empathy of the unimaginative and narrow-minded citizens of Ferrara, Bassani's point is not only that we cannot know or judge someone who has had Geo's experience, but also that vestiges of intolerance of difference remain even after the war. When Geo returns, the Ferrara citizens want him to reassimilate but he refuses and becomes a thorn in their conscience.

The point of view of "A Plaque on Via Mazzini" is that of a Ferrara citizen who is not Jewish and who seems to be a choral figure speaking for the compromised moral position of the citizenry. They need to rationalize their prior and present behavior in the face of Geo Josz's insinuating reappearance and refusal to adhere to social expectations. When the narrator remarks, "He came from afar, from much farther than the place he actually had come from!" he is not only recognizing that Geo has emerged from the depths of hell but is also already anticipating Geo's estrangement from Ferrara's post-war rebirth (82).

Speaking as the voice of the community, the narrator criticizes Geo for "carry[ing] around that obsessive, ill-omened face of his: surely to add new fuel to the wrath of those who would make it their business to avenge him and all his people" (85). Geo begins to wear the ragtag outfit he wore when he returned to Ferrara. Geo will not let Ferrara live in the past any more than Bassani will let his readers forget. No one wants to be reminded of either collaboration with the Fascists or the compromises of the Liberation era.

As the narrator renders Ferrara's changing attitude to Geo over the next three years, he adopts the community's increasingly critical view of Geo, who continually reminds the citizens of Ferrara of their complicity in Holocaust atrocities. Finally, shortly after the Partisans Association finally moves out of Geo's palatial home that it was occupying and allows him to have it back, Geo disappears for a second time, presumably never to return.

Expressing the view of post-war Ferrara that wants to put aside the past, Bassani has his first person narrator – a detached, puzzled but myopic outsider rather than a surrogate for Bassani – present an alternative optics to that of Geo's whose behavior he describes. That alternative optics – which Bassani expects the reader to join him in condemning – implies with growing intensity as the story progresses that it is Geo who is in error and that Geo is not only exaggerating what happens, but is guilty of disrupting the reconfigured historical tapestry that Ferrara and Italy are weaving: "[T]he anguished, atrocious yesterday, with the today so much more serene and rich in promises. … We had the impression that we were all involved. Geo Josz on one side and the rest of us on the other" (98–99). Speaking of Count Scocca, who had been a paid informer of the Secret Police of the Italo-German Cultural Institute, the overly tolerant and historically dim narrator observes: "[Scocca] had allowed that little Hitler mustache to grow … and he kept it still; now didn't it lead you to consideration tinged with fondness, and even – why not? – even with gratitude?" (100). Carefully laying the ground for a condemnation of his narrator by including the bare facts of the Fascist collaboration and betrayal, Bassani invites his reader to answer a resounding "No" to the insidious aforementioned question. If there is a crystallizing image in Bassani's reserved and often passive-aggressive oeuvre, it is the moment when Geo Josz slaps this former Nazi sympathizer.

Differentiating true seeing from self-serving versions of seeing is crucial to Bassani's technique. For his epigraph to this story Bassani takes a line from Rimbaud's "Le Bateau Ivre": "And I have sometimes seen what men thought they saw" (77). The epigraph ironically applies to Geo's insistence on foregrounding what truly happened and making sure that Ferrara's self-serving citizens do not forget that they stood by while their Jewish brethren were deported. The epigraph differentiates Geo – and Bassani himself – from the narrator who is the choral voice of Ferrara's citizens. Bassani shows how citizens of Ferrara and, indeed, of Italy transformed *what they saw* into *what they thought they saw.*

Bassani's Psychological Realism

Bassani's Jewish characters are often in trouble because of their moral and social limitations and flawed psyches. Caught up in the maelstrom of twentieth-century history, they respond with fear and anxiety to events that they cannot control. Evading history, ignoring history, pushing history into the background is impossible. In the case of the Jews, they are not only at the mercy of events, but for a time they are pushed outside the official historical chronicle of what happened. In the case of those deported, they are virtually erased only to be pathetically reified by something like a not fully accurate memorial list of names such as that described in "A Plaque on Via Mazzini."

Bassani's fiction is driven by the memory and imagination of both his narrators and characters, although his narrators – whether self-dramatizing first persons or a third person – may have a very different perspective than the other characters. Often his novels and stories juxtapose first and third person tellers' suppressed rage with the insouciance, naïveté, and often self-delusion of his characters. Very much a modernist in the James and Conrad tradition, Bassani may ask the reader to see that a first person narrator – even if at first seemingly something of an autobiographical speaker – is myopic, self-immersed, and not fully in touch with his own motives. Even at a distance of years, his first person narrators often lack self-knowledge. Indeed, one notable aspect of Bassani's fiction is that, while eschewing Freudian terminology in terms of his characters' behavior or his narrators' self-analyses, he is well aware of how characters act out obsessions, fixations, and dimly acknowledged needs.

Bassani revels in the inexplicable mysteries of human behavior and finds refuge in the uncanny, and that is why Bassani on occasion frustrates his reader who may want less of what we now call magic realism and more of a grammar of motives to understand characters' behavior. An example of the uncanny is the virtually silent Luisa Brondi who, in "The Walk Before Supper," has been obsessed with Dr. Corcos from the outset when he first arrived at the very modest family home, and, after her sister Gemma's death, mysteriously becomes his housekeeper and perhaps his lover.

We might note that the stress on walls – *Five Stories of Ferrara* was reissued in 1973 as *Inside the Wall* – emphasizes the division not only between Jews and Gentiles (especially the dominant Catholics), but also between Fascists and Partisans, the well-to-do and poor, and homosexuals and heterosexuals. Walls divide those whose passion and romance run into religious and social codes. Indeed, walls separate people from different social classes both within the general population of Ferrara and within the Jewish community. Walls separate the Finzi-Continis from the rest of Ferrara, including other Jews, but internal psychic walls also separate characters from understanding external events and personal motives.

Dreaming as a way for entrapped characters to escape from repressive reality – notably the imprisoning walls of ghettoes and the horrors of the concentration and death camps – is a recurring motif in Holocaust fictions. Thus in "The Last Years of Clelia Trotti," Bassani's autobiographical Bruno Lattes finds refuge "in the lonely dreams, the desperate pastimes, the sad miserable prisoners' dreams of his own traveling companions" – that is, fellow Jews, moving "toward an inevitable future" (147). Bruno Lattes retrospectively recalls a dark snowy night when he was aware of the parallel between Clelia and his father: "Although finished, although near death, neither one stopped dreaming, each in his way, of liberty still" (146). Bruno Lattes emphasizes the parallel between Clelia, the aging socialist put under surveillance by the Fascists and imprisoned within the walls of her sister's house, and the plight of Jews who have been metaphorically imprisoned and returned in their minds if not yet physically to the ghetto by racial laws: "[The] snow would have spread over the whole city, this common prison and ghetto" (147).

Bassani's irony is directed at all the distinctions that divide humankind. Walls represent how each character is enclosed in his or her own perception of reality and cut off from others, even those we imagine close to us. Social and moral walls are central to "Lida Mantovani" – which appeared in 1949 in *Botteghe oscure* but was published in an earlier version in "A City of the Plains" under the pseudonym Giacomo Marchi – where Lida is judged by rigid Catholic practices about what love is. She is pushed by her mother and social convention into marrying a man twenty years older than she and whom she doesn't love after being abandoned by a Jew whose child she bore out of wedlock after he reconciled with his family. Such social walls divide not only the economically comfortable Corcos family from the peasant Brondi family in "The Walk Before Supper," but also the aloof Corcos – who is unique in his ability "for keeping people at a distance" – from his fellow citizens; this particular division is metaphorically represented by "the wall that separated the [Corcos] garden from the [city] bastions themselves" (64, 68). Cared for by his wife, Gemma Brondi, but barely connected emotionally to anyone but her and his father, he has erected invisible walls and recused himself in his professional life.

The walls of the fifteenth-century fortifications of Ferrara represent the dark threat of violence hovering over the city, a threat that for Jews dates back to the ghetto walls and climaxes in the aforementioned plaque on the red brick façade on the Temple on Via Mazzini. Similarly for Ferrara citizens, haunting memories of violence are associated with the wall where those – several of whom were Jewish – who refused to submit to Fascist zealots were shot by them in "A Night in '43" (originally published in *Botteghe oscure* in 1955).

Isn't the door in *Behind the Door* another wall? At the most obvious level, it is the door behind which the depressed first person Jewish narrator hides when his rival Cattolica sadistically arranges for Luciano to cast aspersions on his and his mother's generosity. It also refers to the wall he has built between himself and his classmates, in part as a defense against their patronizing if not hostile attitude deriving from anti-Semitism. It refers to how the adolescent narrator – and to an extent the retrospective adult narrator – is bottled up and not in touch with his sexual feelings. He finds Luciano despicable and yet he is fascinated with his open discussion of sexuality as well as his enormous penis. He is taken, too, with Cattolica, whose physicality – a "forehead … broad, pale, calm, very handsome" – fascinates him even though Cattolica disdains traditional sports.[6]

The Garden of the Finzi-Continis as Holocaust Text

The Garden of the Finzi-Continis takes place in the 1930s as Fascist Italy turns against its forty thousand Jews. The Finzi-Continis are wealthy Jews who have the illusion that they can recuse themselves from the vicissitudes of life and history. For complex reasons – snobbery, comfort, and the desire to control life after the loss of a son to meningitis in 1914 – the Finzi-Continis have even before the 1938 racial laws already subtracted themselves from Ferrara and its Jewish community.

The Palazzo Torlonia in Rome and its gardens are Bassani's source for the palace and elaborate grounds of the Finzi-Continis. The gardens are a refuge, an example of nature tamed and controlled and an ironic and ultimately ineffectual example of the Finzi-Continis' effort to turn their backs on history and control their self-created insularity. The naïveté of trying to recreate a pre-lapsarian world is grimly and methodically exposed. As if the Finzi-Continis were a tiny municipality, family property and conventions are presided over by Professor Ermanno, a learned "professor" whose title – the source of which we never learn – seems odd considering he lacks a university appointment.

A metaphor for the Jews of Ferrara and Italy who fail to recognize the threat to their existence, the self-deluding Finzi-Continis, living in an anesthetized state of arrested political and historical development, segregate themselves behind walls that ironically recall the ghetto. When the Fascists pass the Race laws, the Finzi-Continis invite other Jews, including the first person narrator, deprived of membership in the tennis club to be part of the garden retreat. Bassani expects the reader to notice the pathos and bathos of this invitation in the context of the gathering Holocaust storm that will soon result in roundups and deportations.

What Bassani makes clear is that the Finzi-Continis – their names suggest "fake little counts" in Italian – cannot isolate themselves from history either by surrounding themselves with luxury, technology (telephone extensions in every room, elevators), and protective walls, or by retreating into a world where small daily pleasures, beautiful objects, and the pursuit of knowledge for its own sake – the recondite research of the professor in his private library – take precedence over political engagement.

For a while the Finzi-Continis seem immune from the deprivation of rights but finally they, too, are caught in the labyrinth of racial laws. The juggernaut of twentieth-century European history relentlessly crushes the personal and career aspirations of the young people as they try to define their identity and sexuality. Living within the Finzi-Continis' estate walls like orchids in a hothouse are Alberto and Micòl, Professor Ermanno's two self-immersed, narcissistic adolescent – and later young adult – children. But walls cannot protect them from either illness or history. Alberto dies of a blood cancer, "a lymphogranuloma"; lymphogranuloma venereum is a rarely fatal sexually transmitted disease but Bassani seems to have in mind something like Hodgkin's disease. Micòl is deported with the rest of the family and never returns.

Looking back from a post-war perspective, the unnamed first person narrator gives voice to a mixture of melancholy, sadness, reminiscence, and regret. Often the narrator seems anesthetized as if he were recapturing an elusive dream, but that is part of Bassani's artistry; for isn't the escapism, simplicity, and unreality of a dream appropriate for the way that the Finzi-Continis attempted to suspend time and retreat into their aesthetic world? There is a narcoleptic quality to the behavior of the narrator, Micòl, and Alberto. The narrator and Micòl dream about romantic love, yet, with each other, they seem unable to define their emotions or move beyond flirtation. During this period, the immature narrator sees women in terms of a virgin–whore dichotomy, where whores are sexual and found in brothels, while Micòl, the woman to whom he is attracted, is so idealized as to make her untouchable. Recalling his clumsy wooing of Micòl, the narrator continually returns to a handful of sightings and brief meetings. When he finally does make sexual overtures, she is no longer responsive and self-indulgently – if not a tad sadistically – does everything possible to make him uncomfortable with his awkward sexuality.

Bassani's Last Novel: *The Heron*

In his final short parabolic novel *The Heron* (1968), which takes place in 1947, Bassani's anger and bitterness are even more foregrounded, his style is more direct, and his narrator less elusive and subtly ironic. He focuses on the last day in the life of Edgardo Limentani, his depressed and suicidal Jewish protagonist. Ironically, the story takes place at the onset of the Christmas season. Limentani is alienated from post-war Italy after being forced to flee to Switzerland during the years of Jewish persecution. A substantial landowner, Limentani feels his ways of farming are obsolete and that his land is in jeopardy due to the rising tide of Communism sweeping Italy after Liberation; he cannot even visit his own farms without facing social protest. He wonders whether today's Communists are any better than the Fascists.

Like his creator, Limentani's memory is haunted by his personal history. He identifies with a dying red heron who was shot by his hunting guide: "[T]he heron must have felt much as he felt now: hemmed in on all sides, without the slightest possibility of escape."[7] He is estranged from his wife, who is a former mistress whom he had to marry so he could transfer his property to her to get around racial laws. Like his creator, Limentani still feels deep resentment towards Italy for turning on its Jewish citizens. While Bellagamba, the host of a small hotel he visits to go to the bathroom, welcomes him with a glad hand, Limentani remembers that in 1938 and 1939 as Corporal of Militia, Bellagamba strutted around in a uniform and had given him "menacing and contemptuous glances" (30). Limentani has contempt for his cousin Ulderica, who converted to Catholicism and before that had accepted the offer of a Fascist party card in 1932.

Far less brilliant than *Five Stories of Ferrara* and *The Garden of the Finzi-Continis*, Bassani's last two novels, *Behind the Door* (1964) and *The Heron* (1968), have a more straightforward chronological structure and present a less dense and allusive historical and political vision; nor do these later novels have either the probing presentation of a grammar of historical and political cause and effect, or the deeply felt if loquacious descriptions and reminiscences that demand rereading.

Bassani the Modernist

Let us conclude by thinking about Bassani the modernist. Bassani's novel has much in common with Mann's *Death in Venice* (1912) where, like the Finzi-Continis, the major character seeks refuge from personal and social turmoil in the aesthetic. Often Bassani's characters, like Mann's Aschenbach, seem unaware of their ambiguous sexuality. Other influences are Henri-Pierre Roche's semi-autobiographical *Jules and Jim* (1953), written when Roche was seventy, and the source for François Truffaut's *Jules and Jim* (1962), which, with his strong interest in film, Bassani surely knew. The introverted writer-narrator of *The Garden of the Finzi-Continis* recalls Jules while Malnate, a non-Jewish socialist visitor to the Finzi-Contini estate, recalls Jim. In Bassani's novel, as in Roche's novel, these males bond and develop a strong homosocial relationship. Malnate and the narrator are not only rivals for Micòl's love but are attracted to one another as well as to her brother Alberto.

As editorial director of Feltrinelli publishing house, Bassani was responsible for the posthumous publication of the anti-Fascist Giuseppe Tomasi di Lampedusa's *The Leopard* (1958) with which his work has much in common. Just as *The Leopard* – focusing on the effects of Unification on Sicily – covers fifty years of history from 1860 to 1910, so does Bassani's history of Ferrara stretch back to 1880 and even before. Anticipating Professor Ermanno, the patriarch of the Finzi-Continis, the protagonist of *The Leopard*, Don Fabrizio Corbera, says: "I am sorry; but I cannot lift a finger in politics. It would only get bitten."[8] It is worth recalling what Don Fabrizio's nephew Tancredi says: "If we want things to stay as they are, things will have to change" (*The Leopard*, 40) – something that the ostrich-like Finzi-Continis don't understand, even before the racial laws.

Rereading *Five Stories of Ferrara* and *The Garden of the Finzi-Continis*, one sees in the hands of a skilled empathetic translator like William Weaver the balance, richness, and subtlety of Bassani's elliptical and elusive style. Mann, Henry James, Marcel Proust, Joseph Conrad, and William Faulkner come quickly to mind. Like Proust and James, Bassani often writes in elegant complex sentences that suggest the nuanced if not ambivalent attitudes of self-dramatizing, ironic and sometimes imperceptive narrators. With his nuanced perspective in which he takes a multi-dimensional and ironic view of his major characters, his ambiguous and complex endings that draw upon the uncanny and unexpected, and his understanding of moral paralyses in the face of history's remorseless process, Bassani takes his place among modernists.

To be sure, Bassani's prose, especially in the *Five Stories of Ferrara* and *The Garden of the Finzi-Continis*, can be a tad prolix, and at times sentences seem to be leisurely Sunday journeys through the country where the scenery matters more than the destination. Thus descriptions of Ferrara's geography, the weather, or the contents of a character's room may, particularly at first, provide more information than is necessary. But isn't this true of Proust, Mann, and James? With its circumlocutious sentences, frequent qualifying parentheses, interrogatives, abundant if not seemingly excessive inclusion of proper names, use of snow and winter fog for moral opacity, and intimations of attitudes and feelings that are not quite confirmed, Bassani's elusive style creates at times a puzzling penumbra of doubt in the reader who is not always sure what is being said and what is being suggested. But with each subsequent reading, we see that Bassani's indirect style is part of his richly woven tapestry that is essential to each text's significant form.

Study Questions for the Fiction of Giorgio Bassani

1. How does Bassani's microcosmic examination of the Jews of Ferrara stand as a metonymy for the Jews of Italy?
2. How does Bassani interweave personal, political, and historical perspectives?
3. How do the recurring characters and themes create a unity for Bassani's entire body of fiction?
4. Why does Bassani choose a first person narrator for *The Garden of the Finzi-Continis*?
5. In what ways is Bassani critiquing the Finzi-Continis?
6. How would you compare the film and the book of *The Garden of the Finzi-Continis*?
7. What are the unifying themes of *Five Stories of Ferrara*? How is "A Plaque on Via Mazzini," particularly Geo, central to the collection?
8. What are the significant parallels to other texts in *Reading the Modern European Novel Since 1900*?
9. How are walls an important metaphor in Bassani's fiction?
10. What are some of the features of Bassani's form and, as rendered in translation, Bassani's style?

Notes

1. Page numbers are from Giorgio Bassani, *The Garden of the Finzi-Continis*, trans. William Weaver (New York: Alfred A. Knopf, 2001).
2. "A Plaque on Via Mazzini," in Giorgio Bassani, *Five Stories of Ferrara*, trans. William Weaver (New York: Harcourt Brace Jovanovich, 1972), 78.
3. See "The Walk Before Supper," in *Five Stories of Ferrara*.
4. "The Last Years of Clelia Trotti," in *Five Stories of Ferrara*, 159. All references to the stories are from the 1972 edition of *Five Stories of Ferrara*, trans. Weaver (reissued in 1973 as *Inside the Wall*; the stories are arranged in the following order: "Lida Mantovani," "The Walk Before Supper," "A Plaque on Via Mazzini," "The Last Years of Clelia Trotti," and "A Night in '43").
5. Guia Risari, *The Document Within the Walls: The Romance of Bassani* (Leicester: Troubador, 1999).
6. *Behind the Door*, trans. William Weaver (New York: Harcourt Brace Jovanovich, 1971), 16.
7. *The Heron* (New York: Harcourt Brace Jovanovich, 1972), 145. Page numbers are from this edition.
8. Giuseppe di Lampedusa, *The Leopard*, trans. Archibald Colquhoun (New York: Pantheon, 1960), 213.

Chapter 7

The Novel as Elegy: Giuseppe Tomasi di Lampedusa's *The Leopard* (1958)

"If we want things to stay as they are, things will have to change."

Tancredi, in Lampedusa, *The Leopard*, 40[1]

Introduction

Written by Giuseppe Tomasi (1896–1957), the 11th prince of Lampedusa, and published posthumously, *The Leopard* (1958; in Italian *Il Gattopardo*) is one of the great historical novels of twentieth-century European literature and, with its manageable length, has become a classic of Italian literature and a staple of European novel courses. The novel is an elegy for Sicily as well as for a patrician class represented by Don Fabrizio Corbera, the Leopard.

The Leopard owes much to the life of Tomasi's great-grandfather, Don Giulio Fabrizio Tomasi, but of course ultimately to the mindset of its author (whom I will refer to as Lampedusa) who was depressed after Allied bombs damaged the family palace. The resulting destruction seemed to inspire Lampedusa's need to fictionally historicize what he felt was the progressive transformation – indeed, devolution – of the Sicilian way of life. Focusing on the effects of the Unification of Italy (what is called "the Risorgimento," which translates as the Resurgence) on Sicily and covering fifty years of history from 1860 to 1910, the novel alludes to what happened in the more immediate aftermath of Garibaldi's invasion of Sicily. In the novel, we find parallels between two historical periods: the Savoys, in the name of Unification, displacing the Bourbons as the rulers of Italy and in

Reading the Modern European Novel Since 1900: A Critical Study of Major Fiction from Proust's Swann's Way to Ferrante's Neapolitan Tetralogy, First Edition. Daniel R. Schwarz.
© 2018 John Wiley & Sons Ltd. Published 2018 by John Wiley & Sons Ltd.

particular Sicily, and the Allied invasion, Mussolini's fall, and the resulting rebirth of a federal Italy different from the Italy of the Unification.

The original title *Il Gattopardo* refers to an African wild cat, the serval – in fact, something less than a leopard in size and charisma – which was the coat of arms for Lampedusa's family and which was hunted to near extinction in the mid-1880s just as, in the novel, the aristocratic class, represented by Dom Fabrizio, is being pushed from the stage. Don Fabrizio is often called "The Prince" to empha-size his social difference and his own self-regard and perhaps to reference Machiavelli's *The Prince*, where glory and survival are the necessary goals of princes and actual facts are more important than abstractions. He is also referred to as a lion to signify his difference from those rational post-Enlightenment fig-ures who will succeed him. For Don Fabrizio is a man who responds to his natu-ral instincts, even as he seeks to maintain a tradition of customs and manners.

After rejection by two major publishing houses and after Lampedusa's death, *The Leopard* became a major literary and financial success. This occurred despite the political Right's original dislike of the novel's cynical view of Catholicism as another self-interested and self-perpetuating power player in Italian politics with little more concern for poverty and violence than the nobility. *The Leopard* also addresses the passing of Europe's traditional class structure. The crucial words of the protagonist, Don Fabrizio, Prince of Salina, might have been spoken by Levin in *Anna Karenina* (1877): "I am sorry; but I cannot lift a finger in politics. It would only get bitten" (213). Moreover, the Italian Left objected to the novel's criticism of Unification and its focus on the pleasures and perquisites of the nobility.

Historical Context

The novel begins in May 1860 when the fiercely anti-Catholic Garibaldi (1807–1882) landed in Sicily. On May 11, 1860, with some help from Sicilians favoring Unification, he came ashore with a force of about eight hundred men. After conquering the island across the Straits of Messina and conquering Naples – and thus ending the Kingdom of the Two Sicilies – Garibaldi handed his forces to the Piedmontese House of Savoy. Put another way, Garibaldi con-quered the island in the name of a unified Italy ruled by the northern King Victor Emmanuel II.

King Ferdinand ("Bomba"), the Bourbon king of the Two Sicilies, who in 1837 had violently suppressed discontent in Sicily and sent troops to quell a rebellion in 1848, died in May 1859 and was succeeded by his son Francis II, who was deposed in 1861 following Garibaldi's riding victoriously into Naples on November 7 with King Victor Emmanuel II at his side.

Because Lampedusa's skepticism as a conservative about Garibaldi and how the latter's erratic, revolutionary, and anti-papal bent informs the novel, we might recall a little more history. Garibaldi split from King Victor Emmanuel II. In June 1862, without government approval, Garibaldi led a campaign to take the Papal States but was prevented from crossing from Messina to the mainland by a force loyal to the king. He then set sail from Catania but was defeated by Colonel Pallavicino, in part because, although he had been badly wounded in the ankle, he did not want to fire on fellow subjects of the United Kingdom of Italy. He was taken prisoner but treated as an honorable figure and later released.

Lampedusa, like Tolstoy, does not, as Gershon Gurenberg writes in another context, "fall for the fallacy that all historical events are intended" or presume that "there is a clear policy choice behind great historical shifts. ... History is messy, complicated, often morally ambiguous. It is not as simple as the stories nations tell about their past" (Gurenberg, "The War to Begin All Wars," 38).[2]

If ever a novel demonstrates my mantra, "Always the text; always historicize," it is *The Leopard*. Some novels, like those of Tolstoy, derive from the author's looking outward to present a vision of the world, while others derive from the author's inner necessity to speak of things that weigh on his mind. Most novels do some of both. While the historical scope of *The Leopard* seems to put it mainly in the first category, it is Lampedusa's necessity – even compulsion – to speak about what happened to Sicily over its history, and in particular to the way of life of a social class as expressed by both Don Fabrizio and Lampedusa's narrator, that gives the novel its uniquely elaborate, dense, almost operatic verbal texture. Using as his point of departure Garibaldi's May 1860 landing on the coast of Sicily, Lampedusa balances his elegiac and nostalgic vision of the world with a desperate need to tell his story in his own way.

Don Fabrizio's title is Prince of Salina, one of the Aeolian islands off the coast of Sicily that Lampedusa's Italian readers would have known is a small enclave with a tiny population, even now numbering only four thousand. The Prince, who lives in a palace close to Palermo and has a country house on the mainland, never within the novel thinks of visiting Salina.

Sicily as Character

The history and geography of Sicily are foregrounded throughout the novel. Indeed, Sicily is the major subject of the novel and in a sense its central character. When the Prince speaks bitterly, chauvinistically, and with a hint of racism, about Sicily's colonial past, we hear Lampedusa's recurring elegiac voice aligned with his character, mourning an island that has seen its best days and is not interested in or ready for unification:

For more than twenty-five centuries we've been bearing the weight of a superb and heterogeneous civilization, all from the outside, none made by ourselves, none that we could call our own. ... We're as white as you are, Chevalley, and as the Queen of England; and yet for two thousand and five hundred years we've been a colony. ... [I]t's our fault. But even so, we're worn out and exhausted. ... [O]ur sensuality is a hankering for oblivion, our shooting and knifing a hankering for death; our laziness, our spiced and drugged sherbets, a hankering for voluptuous immobility, that is for death again. (205–206)

The reader hears the poignancy and enervation in Don Fabrizio's analysis. His resignation and passivity derive from Lampedusa's regretful and reluctant acceptance of the course of history. As resistant readers, we also hear a note of white superiority as Don Fabrizio reminds his listener that even if some Sicilians are dark-skinned – no doubt in part from intermixing with various conquerors, including those with Moorish blood, which neither Fabrizio nor Lampedusa's narrator mention – they still are considered Caucasian. In the nineteenth century some Sicilians were sensitive about their whiteness, and that sensitivity may linger today.

Individual human lives and aspirations are mere spots of time in history; the Prince's size and ability to conjure a life that suits him, even the artist's conjuring the larger perspective of Sicily's history, all are dwarfed by natural processes over which humans have little control: "All around quivered the funereal countryside, yellow with stubble, black with burned patches; the lament of cicadas filled the sky. It was like a death rattle of parched Sicily at the end of August vainly awaiting rain" (68).

The omniscient narrator oscillates between microcosmic focalization on the Prince and, in the last chapter, on the Prince's heirs and a macrocosmic perspective on Sicily's history and culture. For Lampedusa and his surrogate, the omniscient narrator, Sicily's miseries derive in large part from its "violence of landscape" and "cruelty of climate" (208). In a passage in which the author aligns his narrator's views with those of Don Fabrizio, the latter harangues a delegate of Piedmont's Savoy King about why Sicily is what it is in 1860:

[T]he atmosphere, the climate, the landscape of Sicily. Those are the forces which have formed our minds together with and perhaps more than foreign dominations and ill-assorted rapes; this landscape which knows no mean between sensuous slackness and hellish drought; which is never pretty, never ordinary, never relaxed, as a country made for rational beings to live in should be; this country of ours in which the inferno around Randazzo is a few miles from the loveliness of Taormina Bay; this climate that inflicts us with six feverish months of a temperature of a hundred and four. ... [From May through October] six times thirty days of sun sheer on our heads; this summer of ours which is as long and glum as a Russian winter and against which we struggle with less success ... and then the rains, which are always tempestuous and set dry river beds to frenzy, drown beasts and men on the very spot where two weeks before both had been dying of thirst. (207–208)

. . . .

In *The Leopard* climate is a factor in destiny. The climate is a major cause of Sicily's poverty and history of violence. That humankind suffers from nature in Sicily is a recurring motif in the novel. Sweltering heat without rain becomes another image of a desiccated culture. In August 1862, the Prince – along with his family and entourage – make their way from his city palace to his country home, Donnafugata, in stifling heat: "Never a tree, never a drop of water; just sun and dust. Inside the carriages, tightly shut against that sun and dust, the temperature must have been well over 120 degrees Fahrenheit" (66). Drawing upon his macrocosmic and microcosmic historical perspective that spans centuries and includes a myriad of relevant details, some of which he chooses not to reveal fully as if it were wise not to, the narrator remarks on a deep village well that "mutely offered various services: as swimming pool, drinking trough, prison or cemetery. It slaked thirst, spread typhus, guarded the kidnapped, and hid the corpses of both animals and men till they were reduced to the smoothest of anonymous skeletons" (66).

In many ways, Sicily with its history, hypocrisy, intractability, dark secrets, intolerable summers, is itself both protagonist and antagonist. As Don Fabrizio's daughter Concetta in 1910 tries to sort out the truth of what happened in Sicily fifty years ago, the narrator tellingly remarks: "Nowhere has truth so short a life as in Sicily; a fact has scarcely happened five minutes before its genuine kernel has vanished, been camouflaged, embellished, disfigured, squashed, annihilated by imagination and self-interest; shame, fear, generosity, malice, opportunism, charity, all the passions, good as well as evil, fling themselves onto the fact and tear it to pieces; very soon it has vanished altogether" (314). But isn't this true of most descriptions of human behavior, even if it is, as the novel implies, exacerbated in Sicily? The reader should be a tad resistant to the narrator's categorizing sensibility that insists (echoing Don Fabrizio) on Sicily's uniqueness and specialness. For the narrator's self-pitying and self-indulgent analysis says as much about himself – his iconoclastic values, sense of privilege, and rigid, inflexible, controlling psyche – as it does about Sicily.

Don Fabrizio, the Prince of Salina

An aristocratic vestige of Sicily as it once was, Prince Don Fabrizio is an enormous mountain of a man, a "huge bulk" who bestrides the novel like a Colossus (82, 84). Although Lampedusa's grandfather was named Don Giulio Fabrizio, we may wonder whether the echo of *Charterhouse of Parma*'s self-indulgent and manipulative hero's name, Fabrizio, is deliberate.

Don Fabrizio is middle-aged; at one point the age of forty-five is implied by the narrator. He has lived through Garibaldi's May 1860 invasion of Sicily, which, as I have mentioned, overthrew the monarchy of the Bourbon state of Naples and Sicily (known as the Kingdom of the Two Sicilies). He has seven children, a wife, and a mistress. He has a priest in residence, but it is Don Fabrizio who presides over daily family prayers, although he does not take God too seriously.

Knowing well before his last days that his world is finished, Don Fabrizio oscillates between upholding traditions and organizing his life to fulfill his own pleasures and desires. Although Tancredi, Don Fabrizio's nephew, had taken part in the overthrow of the Bourbon king – who represented to Fabrizio the older ways which he regrets losing – Don Fabrizio loves Tancredi more than his own children because he sees himself in Tancredi.

Tancredi's words run through the Prince's mind all day. "If we want things to stay as they are, things will have to change" (40). Don Fabrizio knows the days of his authority and privilege – derived from belonging to Sicily's feudal aristocracy – are coming to an end. Yet he tries to maintain some position in the new order by merging his family – notably his nephew Tancredi – with the rising bourgeois family of the nouveau riche Don Calogero in the form of a marriage to the latter's daughter, Angelica. That marriage and its implications, including the Prince's response, are the central foci of the novel.

Don Fabrizio is a sexist, a womanizer, a sybarite, an elitist, and a cynic. He has a serious intellectual interest in astronomy for which he has received some recognition. He is a condescending iconoclast who looks down on everyone from an enormous distance. He enjoys his own company and savors his sense of privilege.

He is a practicing Catholic whose embrace of religion has to do with tradition rather than belief. For Don Fabrizio, Christianity exists not on the vertical dimension in relation to God, but as part of the fabric of a routine that he sustains: "That half hour between Rosary and dinner was one of the least irritating moments of his day and for hours beforehand he would savor its rather uncertain calm" (19). It is part of the day-to-day life which he both actively revels in – including the joy he takes in astronomy – and cynically accepts.

Thus while wearing the mantle of Catholicism, it is not clear that the Prince believes in an omniscient God, Christ's intervention as God's son on behalf of humankind, or that death is the birth of the eternal soul. But, within the world that Lampedusa's narrator presents, the function of Catholic rituals, customs, and institutions is not to provide gateways to either salvation or damnation of the eternal soul, but to give order to the confusion and complexities of living, and living includes personal and historical challenges. In the Prince's and the narrator's minds, death, sex, and the practice of Catholicism are aspects of day-to-day life as much as eating and sleeping. All are parts of the business of living; they are linked metaphorically and metonymically as if to imply that they are all equally part of the cycle of human life and the tick tock of passing time.

Don Fabrizio desperately wants to hold on to a world of privilege and wealth that he knows is slipping away. Parvenus like Don Calogero Sedara have been accumulating wealth and have become as rich as, if not richer than, Fabrizio. He understands that Tancredi must marry Angelica and that power depends on money. As a defensive response to historical change that he cannot control, he retreats into the hunting world – similar to Faulkner's wilderness – where, temporarily, political time seems to stand still.

Don Fabrizio is also a lazy, if not incompetent, manager of his financial resources. Because he cannot manage his financial affairs, he is hopelessly outflanked by Don Calogero who casts his lot with the Piedmontese Savoys. Although without class and style, Don Calogero is triumphing, in part because he has his beautiful daughter Angelica as a material resource to trade for the prestige of the Salina name.

Tancredi

Tancredi is a younger double of his uncle, Don Fabrizio. As representative of the next generation and responding to different socio-economic and political conditions, Tancredi relies a bit more than his uncle on reason rather than on passion, privilege, and instinct. Like his uncle, Tancredi is wily and elitist. Tancredi's father – Fabrizio's brother – has dissipated his share of the family fortune. Notwithstanding his involvement with a woman named Schwarzwald and his attraction to his cousin Concetta, he knows he needs to marry Angelica, although he somewhat despises himself for his materialistic decision. Knowing that an economic merger will sustain his career, he cynically turns from Concetta to Angelica. To be sure, he is attracted by Angelica's beauty, but his ultimate motivation is his knowledge that he needs to marry wealth.

Don Calogero is fully aware that he is dealing "with a young noble as cynical as himself, capable of striking a sharp bargain between his own smiles and titles and the attractions and fortunes of others" (161). When Tancredi learns how a seventeenth-century Saint-Duke scourged himself as "penance" and/or was blackmailed by religion to give up worldliness, he realizes that he has succumbed to "blackmail through beauty" in selling the Salina name and exchanging his love for Concetta for material advantage. Very harshly Tancredi says to Angelica, "[Y]ou're like the whip there, you're used for the same ends" (187). Such a perception on the part of Tancredi, derived from his knowing that marriage to Angelica is his scourge to root out his passion for Concetta and to give the Salina heritage an opportunity to survive if in an eviscerated form, gives bitter irony to Tancredi's words to his uncle Fabrizio: "If we want things to stay as they are, things will have to change" (40).

The Penultimate Chapter

With its iteration of phrases and its physical images associated with individual characters and places, and with eight baroque scenes taking place in elaborate settings with colorful clothing, *The Leopard* has an operatic structure as well as, as I have implied, an operatic verbal texture.

Each chapter is a kind of set piece in the transformation of Sicily. Dated July 1888, when Don Fabrizio is seventy-three, and opening with Don Fabrizio's name, the seventh and penultimate of eight chapters, "The Death of a Prince," is a powerful exploration of the process of dying: "Don Fabrizio had always known that sensation. For a dozen years or so he had been feeling as if the vital fluid, the faculty of existing, life itself in fact and perhaps even the will to go on living, were ebbing out of him slowly but steadily. … [T]his imperceptible loss of vitality was itself the proof, the condition so to say, of a sense of living" (277–278).

Although indifferent to an accounting of his financial resources as if it were beneath him, Fabrizio renders an accounting of his life. He thinks of his vital past; in evoking the opening chapter for the reader, Lampedusa brilliantly dramatizes how aging is a narrowing of possibility, a constricting of opportunity, but also how the Prince himself had become intellectually, politically, and socially obsolete: "[H]e thought of his own observatory, of the telescopes now destined to years of dust; of poor Father Pirrone, who was dust, too; of the paintings of his estates, of the monkeys on the hangings, of the big brass bed in which his dear Stella had died. … He was alone, a ship-wrecked man adrift on a raft, prey of untamable currents" (284–285). Hadn't the interest in astronomy indicated that the Prince was a forward-looking man, an heir to the Italian scientific tradition of Galileo rather than a hostage of the Catholic Church's retrograde view of anything that got in the way of its teachings? That he regards the dead as "dust" underlines his basic agnosticism as he approaches death.

That Fabrizio's eldest son, Francesco Paolo, is not a worthy heir and that Giovanni, his second son, had turned his back on Sicily and his Salina heritage – and even

Italy – underlines how the Salina line is coming to an end. Giovanni has become a diamond merchant in London, the quintessence of materialism and a trade associated with Jews (although this aspect is not mentioned, Lampedusa's readers would have known it). As Fabrizio is dying, he knows that "in Concetta's beauty and character was prolonged the true Salina strain" (290).

Empathetic, the narrator summarizes how the Prince's mind works in his final hours, particularly his stress on moral accounting that emphatically reminds the reader of his failures in keeping accounts of his estates: "He was making up a general balance sheet of his whole life, trying to sort out of the immense ash-heap of liabilities the golden flecks of happy moments" (288).

The distinctiveness and uniqueness of Fabrizio's perceptions combined with the taut verbal texture are crucial aspects of why we reread *The Leopard*. We recall the poetic last sentence of the prior chapter, "A Ball," when the Prince is already in November 1862 thinking about his death – and reminding us that he, like Natasha in *War and Peace*, has a poetic sensibility as well as a scientific one. He conjures his reality as an alternative to the world swirling around him: "When would [the star Venus] decide to give him an appointment less ephemeral, far from carcasses and blood, in her own region of perpetual certitude?" (273).

The chapter "Death of the Prince" closes with an iteration of that charged Venus image – again linking sex and death and ironically undermining Christian eschatology – now imagined as a sexually appealing young woman coming for a rendezvous: "When she was face to face with him she raised her veil and there, modest, but ready to be possessed, she looked lovelier than she ever had when glimpsed in stellar space" (292). Always a sensualist and intellectual, he imagines death not in terms of the Catholic religion he nominally practices but as a beautiful "yield[ing]" young woman emerging from "stellar space" (291–292).

The Ending

Structurally, the novel depends on repetition that not only anticipates what is to come but also resonates and modifies what has occurred. Nowhere is this more striking and essential to form and meaning than in the last section, which takes its richness from what has preceded. The last chapter might well have been called "Ghosts," for the sisters live with the presence of the past and Concetta in particular is frozen in time with her regrets about the stillborn romance with Tancredi.

The eighth and last chapter is entitled "Relics," referring not only to aging characters whose lives are no longer relevant, but also to the remnants of what had existed before Italy's Unification of the House of Salina and feudal Sicily. "Relics" also refers to the memories in May 1910 – not long before World War

I will sweep Europe in a historical maelstrom – that haunt the minds of the surviving daughters, in particular Concetta whose room is described in a splendid metaphor as "an inferno of mummified memories," including the corpse of Don Fabrizio's dog, Bendicò, embalmed forty-five years ago (305). When Angelica visits, she recalls losing Tancredi and his death after a "tempestuous and interrupted" forty-year marriage, including a brief affair with Tancredi's friend Tassoni. She thinks of how "the road she'd taken then had led her here, to this desert not even inhabited by extinct love or spent rancor" (308, 310).

After Don Fabrizio's death, the three sisters living in the palace install an oratory and create a kind of decadent parody of Catholicism in which death and sexuality play a part. With the decline of wealth and power, their remaining prestige depends on the respect that the Church gives them. They have collected bogus relics "in their religious exaltation as custodians of supernatural treasures" (302). In contrast to the Prince, Concetta is presiding over a much-reduced "family fortune" which is "very much smaller than that of some rich industrialists" (306).

That the proud and elitist Concetta – in whom her father has inculcated the importance of taking pride in the Salina heritage – has heart problems in her early sixties reminds us that after Tancredi chooses Angelica, Concetta's heart metaphorically turned to stone because her life has stopped. Concetta's great enemy is herself and her own rigidity. The only Prince in the house in 1910 is that of the Church official, and he is there to inspect the relics of the surviving spinster sisters' oratory (316).

For Lampedusa, the Catholic Church's assault on the independence of individual home chapels – even if these chapels are quirky and peculiar – mirrors the assault fifty years earlier on feudal families in the name of political unification. This effort to standardize chapels has only meaning and purpose in terms of the Vatican's extending its political reach by asserting its control. While Lampedusa is hardly a believer, the dramatization of the Vatican's aggressive behavior becomes another piece of the narrator's elegiac mosaic for the passing of the aristocratic life he values. But we readers understand the culture and system that he elegizes benefit the leisure and pleasure of the fortunate few at the expense of the many and allow for the narcissism of the privileged.

The Salinas are an anachronism; the family home is as obsolete as the sisters' pretensions. Don Fabrizio had taken satisfaction that "in Concetta's beauty and character was prolonged the true Salina strain," (290) but we see that she is living in the past: "The prestige of her name had slowly disappeared" (306). Concetta had established herself as mistress of the house; she doesn't care about the removal of the relics except that this will further reduce the family prestige: "the Salina chapel was the best known in the city" (296). Prestige is the major currency that matters to her: "To her the removal of those objects was a matter of indifference; what did touch her, the day's real thorn, was the appalling figure the Salina family would now cut with the ecclesiastical authorities, and soon with the entire city" (306).

The concluding chapter of *The Leopard* begins with what the current Church authority regards as a sacrilegious painting and one that echoes Don Fabrizio's fantasy with which the penultimate chapter closes. The sisters regard it as the "Madonna of the Letter," depicting a scene in which Mary answers the letter supposedly sent to her by those converted by St. Paul in Messina: "I bless you and your city." But the Vicar-General of the Church construes this particular painting as depicting a young woman receiving a letter from her lover, specifically, a "girl with a rendezvous waiting for her lover" (303). To the reader, the letter ironically suggests Concetta's optative relationship with Tancredi – the one for which she fervently wished – a relationship mocked by economic necessity and subsequent events.

The last chapter of *The Leopard* is as much a death rattle as an elegy for lives wasted, a culture that has become a façade for eviscerated values, hidden passions, secrets, and lies. Like Sicily itself, Concetta's room is one of those rooms with "two faces, one with a mask that they show to ignorant visitors, the other which is revealed to those only in the know, the owner in particular, to whom they are made manifest in all their squalid essence" (304).

As in Mann's *Death in Venice*, a central figure's death stands for the death of a stultifying overripe culture. "Enclosed between three walls and a side of the house," the "seclusion" of the house's garden "gave it the air of a cemetery": "Every sod seemed to exude a yearning for beauty soon muted by languor. But the garden, hemmed and almost squashed between these barriers, was exhaling scents that were cloying, fleshy, and slightly putrid, like the aromatic liquids distilled from the relics of certain saints" (19–20). We think not only of the repression of Mann's turn-of-the-century Munich as well as the sensual riot of Venice but also of Aschenbach's effort to wear the appearance of a conventional bourgeois while complex desires increasingly shape his behavior.

Do we not recall Chapter One when Bendicò's unruly vitality was an anarchic principle and one that represented the turmoil of desire and emotional life – the Dionysian aspect of Fabrizio and of Sicily – contrasted with the Apollonian rules and conventions of life, including Catholicism? Of course the continuing tensions and dialectic between Dionysian and Apollonian aspects of life recall *Death in Venice*, which takes place about 1910, the very year that *The Leopard* concludes. Indeed the narrator evokes the Ear of Dionysus at Syracuse "which makes the lightest sigh resound for fifty yards around" as a metaphor for the impossibility of keeping secrets in Sicily (306).

With a comic noir touch, Lampedusa stresses how the stuffed remnants of Don Fabrizio's dog Bendicò remain with his children to whom they represent Don

Fabrizio and his world. In 1910, decades after their father's death, Don Fabrizio's children are aged spinsters, stuck in the past and living together in the Prince's house. Two of the sisters are quite ill (Concetta has heart problems [304]; Caterina has paralyzed legs [297]) and all three are moving towards their death in a house that has become a mausoleum.

Approaching and representing the end of a cultural era, the surviving sisters recall the aging sisters (Kate and Julia) in Joyce's "The Dead." As in "The Dead," the richness of the verbal texture reinforces the events. Death, decay, nullification, emptiness are writ large on virtually every page and especially in the final two chapters. The very last paragraph sounds the death knell: "As the carcass [of Bendicò] was dragged off, the glass eyes stared at [Concetta] with the humble reproach of things that are thrown away, that are being annulled. ... Then all found peace in a heap of livid dust" (320).

Dissolution is what is happening to the oratory, the relics, and indeed to the Prince's home, family, and heritage. The aforementioned word "livid" not only means ashen and pale (another suggestion of aging and decay) as well as discolored by bruising (a physical metaphor of mortality as well as the psychological pain of the survivors), but also suggests the furious rage on the part of the narrator.

That in the English translation the last word is "dust" – referring to the discarded stuffed body of Bendicò, Fabrizio's ghoulishly preserved dog – echoes the effects of the parched climate and the devolution of Fabrizio's feudal world. The carcass is a metaphor for a world gone and lives deceased or about to end. *The Leopard* ends with the "moth-eaten and dusty" carcass of Bendicò being tossed out the window; we hear an echo of Ecclesiastes 3:20 and 12:7: "Then all found peace in a heap of livid dust" (320) and remember that in Genesis 2:7 and 3:19 man was made from dust. In the King James Bible, Ecclesiastes 3:20 reads: "All go unto one place; all are of the dust, and all turn to dust again."

Decadence

Notwithstanding his interest in astronomy, Fabrizio represents nobility that is used up, at the end of its line, and prone to ennui, enervation, and sloth: "His family for centuries had been incapable even of adding up their own expenditures and subtracting their own debts. ... Between the pride and intellectuality of his mother and the sensuality and irresponsibility of his father, poor Prince Fabrizio lived in perpetual discontent under his Jovelike frown, watching the ruin of his own class and his own inheritance without ever making, still less wanting to make, any move towards saving it" (18–19).

That world for which Don Fabrizio nostalgically longs was not without strong limitations, limitations underlined by the languor of the prose. The self-indulgent syntax and images of overripeness if not corruption, putrefaction, and rot are symptomatic of Decadence. Don Fabrizio has "contempt for his own relatives and friends, all of whom seemed to him mere driftwood in the languid meandering steam of Sicilian pragmatism" (18). Brilliantly, Lampedusa creates for his narrator an involved, circumlocutious syntax that parallels the slow pacing of the plot and the indirect, illusive, and languorous way the Prince's Byzantine mind often works.

One feature of the Decadent movement in European literature was its depiction of the self-indulgent and hedonistic sloth of an idle aristocracy that is estranged from bourgeois society and values. Because in *The Leopard* the narrator has an iconoclastic voice that is often oblivious to the effects that the conspicuous consumption of the wealthy have on the have-nots, and virtually ignores the feelings of those whose lives are defined by eking out an existence within poverty-stricken Sicily, the novel has a strong kinship with the Decadent movement in Europe.

Another feature of the Decadent movement is the lack of idealism and the blatant cynicism that informs relationships. Marriage – such as the one between Angelica and Tancredi – is not about love but rather about settling family financial issues.

With its Baroque, even Rococo, fin-de-siècle style, *The Leopard* needs to be read in the context of the Decadent movement, most notably Mann's *Death in Venice*, but also, to a lesser extent, Huysmans's *A Rebours* and the works of Wilde, Beardsley, and Baudelaire. Don Fabrizio is a direct descendant of a line that includes Des Esseintes in *A Rebours* – a character based on his creator, Joris-Karl Huysmans – Wilde's Lord Henry Wotton and Dorian Gray in his *The Picture of Dorian Gray*, and, first and foremost, Mann's Aschenbach in *Death in Venice*.

Aren't both *Death in Venice* and *The Leopard* about the last days of a figure that represents a culture that has declined into Decadence? Isn't the self-reflexive prose a stylistic metaphor of the self-indulgence and narcissism of the major figures and perhaps of the cultures that shaped them? Both Don Fabrizio and Aschenbach begin as heroic figures within their culture, but are caught in a web of history that reduces their stature. In both texts, the slow languorous pacing suggests the slow demise of both these figures' lives just as the circumlocutions and qualification suggest the indirectness of their approach to their real goals. Yet in both texts, the Rococo style also calls attention to – and at times parodies – the gap between the protagonists' self-deceiving rationalizations of their motivations and what actually drives them.

With its focus on the Prince's pleasures and presumptive privilege and the elitist snobbery including his hatred of parvenus that offend his sometimes fastidious sensibility, *The Leopard* takes its place along with *The Garden of the Finzi-Continis* as Italian versions of the European Decadent movement. Like Mann's *Death in Venice* and *The Garden of the Finzi-Continis*, the novel explores a culture that is in crisis and decline. These novels dramatize how aging men – Aschenbach, Don Fabrizio, and Professor Ermanno – who are representative of an enervated culture, turn their back on their public responsibility and retreat into themselves. While the historical circumstances vary, all three are passive men for whom pleasure is more important than public accomplishment or moral leadership.

There are strong autobiographical components to both *Death in Venice* and *The Leopard*. Mann feared becoming Aschenbach, and Lampedusa is writing not only about his paternal great-grandfather but also about a world he at least partly knew. Just as Aschenbach represents and is the artistic spokesman for a Decadent culture in historical crisis (*Death in Venice* takes place just as World War I is about to break out), Fabrizio represents a cynical, aristocratic culture that is interested in perpetuating itself at all costs, even while knowing that perpetuation is unlikely if not impossible.

One crucial difference is that while Mann emphasizes the ironic distance between his omniscient narrator and Aschenbach and uses his master style to parody Aschenbach's pretensions and limited artistry, Lampedusa often doesn't separate himself from Don Fabrizio's perspective. Lampedusa shares through his surrogate, the narrator, Don Fabrizio's disdain for the newly emerging materialism and opportunism and his nostalgia for the way the aristocracy once lived.

Both Aschenbach and Don Fabrizio want to retreat from history into their own sensual and voyeuristic pleasures. For Aschenbach, those pleasures reside for the most part in his repressed homosexual – and pederastic – desires that Tadzio evokes; for Don Fabrizio, those pleasures derive from the mistress he visits in Palermo and the indulgences that his wealth and position permit. Both Lampedusa and Mann's protagonists seek refuge in their intellectual pursuits – Aschenbach in his writing, Don Fabrizio in his astronomy – as well as in subtle, even erudite, analyses and rationalizations, although Don Fabrizio, for all his cynicism, is much more aware of his historical situation than Aschenbach.

The Narrative Voice

Let us look in greater detail at Lampedusa's artistry and, in particular, his narrator. It is not too much to say that *The Leopard*'s genius depends on Lampedusa's subtle creation of the narrative voice. The voice balances scathing cynicism and snobbish iconoclasm as well as a macrocosmic historical sweep inflected with nostalgia for a more leisurely feudal era. The voice also balances a delight in worldly, even sensual pleasures, with the ordering and mystical value of Catholicism. The narrator's ironic awareness of Fabrizio's limitations combines effectively with an affection for his imperious and self-serving ways, including his sensuality and his rationalizing justifications for his behavior. *The Leopard*'s efficacy depends too on the narrator's stress on the inextricable relationship between the personal and political and the narrator's historical awareness of actual events and personae – especially Garibaldi – in combination with his Conradian awareness that politics is composed of small stories driven by individual motives. Writing nostalgically from a temporal distance, but very much aware of the present, the narrator's elaborate sentences and paragraphs – notably his wide-ranging references and allusions, including allusions to such present realities as jet travel – give the novel a multi-focal perspective that yields more textual richness on each rereading.

The Leopard depends on the narrator's worldly, quietly ironic voice that juxtaposes the rising nouveau riche with the falling aristocracy; the Unification of Italy with the passing of the hope for an independent Sicily; the powerful Church with the rise of secular authority; time-consuming customs, rituals, and routines in an insulated world in which the Prince provides protection, security, lodging, and food with a more hectic world dominated by materialism and politics; and the appearance of a controlled, routinized, and staid existence with hidden sexuality and latent youthful passion. From the outset, Catholicism is a principal target of satire. The Prince and his family's daily recital of the Rosary – in veneration of the Virgin Mary whose focus was Christ – takes place in the Rococo drawing room decorated with naked and sensuous mythological figures. After the Prince's death, the sisters pray in front of a sexually provocative painting above the altar that they pretend is a spiritual painting.

With his macrocosmic perspective, the narrator looks beyond May 1910 towards the Sicily to come, as when he speaks of "all the furniture in a breezy local craftsmanship" which Concetta thought of as "antiquated and in very bad taste, which, sold at auction after her death, is today the pride of a rich shipping agent when his wife gives cocktails to envious friends" (304). Of course in an elegiac novel focusing on mutability, it is not surprising that the narrator includes the deaths of the remaining central characters, namely Concetta and her rival Angelica: "[T]he illness which was to transform [Angelica] into a wretched specter three years later was already active" (307).

Fully aware of the terrible carnage of World War I, the narrator, with his memory of Italy's civil wars, speaks ironically about the intimacy in 1910 between Concetta and Angelica – who hate each other and despite outward amenities live in fierce opposition – in terms of "an intimacy similar in closeness and feeling to that which was to bind Italians and Austrians in opposing trenches a few years later" (307). His forward reach extends to the American bombing of Sicily during World War II.

The usually retrospective narrator writes at a distance of a hundred years and is very much aware of social and political comedy, for *The Leopard* contains rich, if poignant, comic moments. Rereading, I was much more aware of the novel's playfulness than in my earlier readings. For example, when Don Fabrizio negotiates with the nouveau riche Mayor about the marriage of his daughter Angelica to Tancredi, the narrator compares the dialogue with Fabrizio's devouring a toad: "The last shreds of toad had been nastier than he had expected" (152). In a wonderful comic scene the narrator juxtaposes Fabrizio's snobbery and elegance with Don Calogero's "ignorant vulgarity" (154): "Don Fabrizio felt as if he were assailed by numbers of stinging hornets" (147). In the foregoing two sentences, the narrator penetrates Fabrizio's mind and renders metaphorically how repellent and disgusting Don Calogero is to him, even while Fabrizio outwardly observes the amenities.

Notwithstanding the comic moments, many of which are noir, the entirety of *The Leopard* is informed by a bitterly ironic cynicism deriving from the mood of the author when he wrote the novel. Recognizing the passing of his privileged way of life and the relationship of the nobility to the rest of the Sicilians, Fabrizio says: "'We were the Leopards, the Lions; those who will take our place will be little jackals, hyenas; and the whole lot of us, Leopards, jackals, and sheep, we'll all go on thinking ourselves the salt of the earth'" (214). As if discovering a new creature occupying his own habitat, Don Fabrizio sees Don Calogero as another species rather than a fellow human: "Free as [Don Calogero] was from the shackles imposed on many other men by honesty, decency, and plain good manners, he moved through the jungle of life with the confidence of an elephant which advances in a straight line, rooting up trees and trampling down lairs, without even noticing scratches of thorns and moans from the crushed" (159).

To a large extent, we need to regard the narrator not only as the centerpoint of focalization, but also as a character with his own voice. Thus the worldly narrator seems almost enervated when he ruefully and judgmentally informs us that Tancredi and Angelica never regain the eroticism in marriage that they have in their engagement and that their marriage is something of an anticlimactic disappointment, perhaps echoing Fabrizio's own marriage: "These [sensual] days were the best days in the lives of Tancredi and Angelica, lives later to be so variegated, so erring, against the inevitable backgrounds of sorrow. ... Those days were the preparation for a marriage which, even erotically, was no success" (188).

The Leopard raises an aesthetic issue that has moral implications for the reader's response to what he is reading. Can a narrator be so worldly, can he take such a long view and be so knowing that his presence undermines the very drama that he describes and leaves us with an empty sense that nothing human really matters? As Ecclesiastes puts it, "vanity of vanities; all is vanity."

Yet, do we not as readers at times resist the narrator and begin to see him as having tunnel vision and as not fully perceptive? But in spite of that, as resistant readers drawing at times a circumference of judgment around the narrator's perspective, we do care about Don Fabrizio because the narrative voice renders Don Fabrizio's perspective sympathetically and respectfully, showing us that, for all his failings, he is a figure of considerable stature who is concerned about his family and Sicily.

Afterword

Before closing, I might mention the excellent film of *The Leopard*. Starring Burt Lancaster, Luchino Visconti's 1963 epic film *The Leopard* focuses on two events: the battle in the streets of Palermo when Garibaldi's army – with Tancredi among them – routs the local forces, and the social gala two years later in the novel (but undated in the film) when Angelica debuts and is accepted by the Sicilian aristocracy.[3]

Study Questions for *The Leopard*

1. How is *The Leopard* an elegy and what is being elegized? How is it a historical novel?
2. How does Lampedusa regard Fabrizio? Why does he call him "The Prince?" How does Lampedusa use characterization, focalization, and narrative structuring to render Dom Fabrizio's life?
3. What is the function of the last two chapters?
4. Why does the novel end with Bendicò's long-dead carcass being tossed out the window and an echo of both Ecclesiastes and Genesis?
5. What does the marriage of Angelica, daughter of the parvenu Don Calogero, to Tancredi represent?
6. How would you describe the voice of the narrator? Is he too worldly, knowing, and cynical? Sympathetic to Don Fabrizio?
7. When does the narrator tell the story? Is his almost hundred-year perspective effective? How does he know the kind of marriage Tancredi and Angelica will have? And how does he know about the American bombing of Sicily?
8. How would you compare the aging disillusioned Don Fabrizio with Mann's Aschenbach? Are both novels about the last days of a figure that represents – is a metaphor for – a culture that has declined into decadence? What does *The Leopard* owe to the Decadent movement in literature?
9. In both *The Leopard* and *Death in Venice*, how is the self-reflexive, circumlocutious prose a stylistic metaphor of the self-indulgence and narcissism of the two protagonists?
10. Is there a strong autobiographical component to both *The Leopard* and *Death in Venice*? Are there parallels between Lampedusa's relationship to his protagonist and Giorgio Bassani's relationship to his fiction, especially *The Garden of the Finzi-Continis*?

Notes

1. Page numbers are from Giuseppe di Lampedusa, *The Leopard*, trans. Archibald Colquhoun (New York: Pantheon, 1960).
2. Gershon Gurenberg, "The War to Begin All Wars," *NYR* 56:9 (May 28, 2009), 38–41; see 38.
3. See Dave Kehr, "After the Leopard, the Deluge," *New York Times* (June 27, 2010); *Arts and Leisure* 8, 10.

Chapter 8

Günter Grass's *The Tin Drum* (1959): Reconfiguring European History as Fable

So as not to have to rattle a cash register, I stuck to my drum and didn't grow a finger's breadth from my third birthday on, remained the three-year-old who, three times as smart, was towered over by grownups, yet stood head and shoulders above them all, who felt no need to measure his shadow against theirs, who was inwardly and outwardly fully mature, while others driveled on about developments well into their dotage, who merely confirmed for himself what others learned with difficulty and often painfully, who felt no need to increase his shoe and trouser size from year to year, to prove he was growing.

Günter Grass, *The Tin Drum*, 49[1]

There was so much confusion after the war, especially in literary circles, because the generation that grew up during the war – my generation – was either uneducated or badly educated. The language was tainted.

Günter Grass, "The Art of Fiction No. 124"[2]

Introduction

If there is a successor to the historical and imaginative sweep of *War and Peace*, Tolstoy's epic of the Napoleonic era, it is Günter Grass's powerful and original *The Tin Drum*, a remarkable novel which substantively addresses the major events in Germany and Central Europe from Hitler's rise to the early days of the divided post-war Germany. In awarding Grass (1927–2015) the Nobel Prize in 1999, the Swedish Academy praised him for embracing "the enormous task of reviewing contemporary history by recalling the disavowed and the forgotten: the victims,

Reading the Modern European Novel Since 1900: A Critical Study of Major Fiction from Proust's Swann's Way *to Ferrante's Neapolitan Tetralogy*, First Edition. Daniel R. Schwarz.
© 2018 John Wiley & Sons Ltd. Published 2018 by John Wiley & Sons Ltd.

losers and lies that people wanted to forget because they had once believed in them."[3] It called *The Tin Drum* "one of the enduring literary works of the 20th century." (ibid.) But Grass's approach deviates from the naturalism of the nineteenth-century novel, presenting history at an oblique angle through the eyes of a physically and emotionally challenged figure whose judgment is suspect and whose grasp of reality is often unreliable. *The Tin Drum* is a wildly inventive and high-spirited novel with important political implications.

Grass's own behavior during the period about which he writes has come under question. In 2006 Grass revealed he had been a member of the Waffen-SS, a military branch of the Nazi party; this tarnished his reputation as a "good" German who had recognized the Nazis at an early age. Despite the controversy surrounding Grass and his involvement with the Nazis, I believe *The Tin Drum* – the first volume of his *Danzig Trilogy* along with *Cat and Mouse* (1961) and *Dog Years* (1963) and the book regarded as its centerpiece – is one of the most important novels of post-war Europe and deserves inclusion in this study.

Grass tells his story from the retrospective point of view of his self-dramatizing narrator Oskar Matzerath whose physical growth is stunted by his own decision to remain a small child on his third birthday and who communicates by means of a tin drum that he gets as a gift on that birthday. But his mental growth continues; he pretends to be retarded as a way of avoiding adult responsibility. Dreadful and disturbing things happen to those around him, but he survives; his complicity usually falls in a gray area.

In a gesture to show his lineage to major twentieth-century predecessors, especially German authors, Grass draws on the theme of physical illness paralleling moral illness which is present in Mann's *Death in Venice* and *The Magic Mountain* as well as in Kafka's *Metamorphosis*. Of course, this is a theme with a long heritage dating back to Shakespeare's *Richard III* and Greek and Roman litertature.

Oskar's preposterous claim that at birth he hears and understands everything adults say confirms that he is not to be taken as a realistic character but one that has ties to magic realism, folk tales, and fairy tales: "I was one of those clairaudient infants whose mental development is complete at birth and thereafter simply confirmed. … [W]hat my ear took in, my tiniest of brains immediately evaluated, and I decided, after devoting sufficient thought to all I had heard, to do certain things and most certainly not to do others" (35).

On his third birthday, Oskar willfully arrests his development because he disdains the behavior of the bourgeois adults around him, notably his mother's adultery with his uncle. Oskar's refusal to grow up begins as a personal response to his awareness of his mother's hypocrisy, but it also includes a strong element of narcissism. He chooses not to grow physically, although he develops mentally. Rather than speak, he expresses himself by drumming. With its evocation of the military, the drumming may anticipate the rousing noise of Nazism.

He maintains his distance from the world around him but not his innocence. Indeed, one important irony is that while Oskar thinks he has an adult sensibility, from the outset the growth of his moral judgment is arrested more than he realizes; this is true even at the novel's end when he is about to be released from the asylum in which he has been placed.

This is not to deny that at times, particularly in rendering the rise of Nazism in Danzig, the drum has a moral function since bearing witness to immoral events can be a moral act. But one of the novel's many paradoxes is that for the most part the drum is simply an outlet for Oskar's narcissism.

Given his early reluctance to speak at all, it is ironic that when telling the story at thirty, Oskar has logorrhea; he simply loves narrating the events of his life, sometimes digressively, and he enjoys experimenting with ways of writing in terms of different styles, genres, and metaphors. We as readers are captive to words rushing like a torrent as if his pent-up feelings can know no limits. Towards the end of the final chapter, when he twice says "I have run out of words now" (562–563), we don't believe him for a minute. The torrent continues to recapitulate (once again) the high points of the narrative we have been reading. Indeed we wonder if his increasing backward looks indicate that, even while anticipating release from the asylum, he is stuck in the past without any idea how he will resume his life and move forward.

Using my rule that the maximum self-revelation of the narrator is an important clue to how the author expects us to respond to that narrator, we must be suspect about a character whom we meet in a psychiatric institution at the age of thirty and who on occasion confuses himself with Jesus when he is not fearful of the dreaded Black Cook, a metonymy for the specter of mortality that haunts Oskar's imagination.

We realize that Oskar is not always a reliable or perceptive narrator and that he often lives in his fantasies. When Oskar describes his mother to Herr Bebra, claiming he himself is responsible for his mother's death, he admits, "I was exaggerating wildly" (157). We should take that as a warning to be skeptical about his tale. That Bebra sees through Oskar becomes another indication that we need to be on our guard.

To some extent Oskar personifies Danzig, both in its Polish and German ethnicities, as well as Poland and Germany themselves. Having said this, we need to also be aware that one of the issues in reading *The Tin Drum* is when and how to assign allegorical and parabolic readings without being reductive.

Oskar's arrested physical and moral development parallels Nazism's rise and fall in Europe and its effects on civilians. Death is a major presence in *The Tin Drum*. Grass's novel is punctuated with corpses, often of those who suffer bizarre and violent deaths. Oskar not only loses his three parents, his dwarf lover and dwarf counselor, as well as the Jewish man who provides him with tin drums, but anonymous death caused by military aggression permeates the entire novel.

At the time of its publication in 1959 Grass, by showing that many Germans were complicit in one way or another, disabused his compatriots of the view that there was nothing that could have been done when the Nazis took over. Grass shows how the hypocrisy, selfishness, and tunnel vision that defined the personal lives of individuals at least partially enabled the Nazis' rise to power. But he also dramatizes how the day-to-day personal lives of citizens are shaped by political and historical circumstances.

With their desire to feel important by belonging to a social movement as compensation for emptiness and loneliness, many of the Danzig bourgeois created an environment for the Nazis to grow and flourish. Others were so caught up in petty concerns and dysfunction in their personal lives that they ignored what was happening. And Danzig's German citizens become a metonymy for the larger body of people of German nationality not only in Germany but also in Europe whose failure to protest gave tacit support to the rise of Hitler.

Self-interested, self-immersed, blind to the implications of their behavior and indifferent to its consequences for others, the Danzig middle class provided, Grass strongly suggests, a fertile ground for Nazism. The members of the Jan/Agnes/Alfred troika make little effort to disguise their behavior, which is carried out under Oskar's nose and indeed in the presence of their entire social circle. Oskar's father, Alfred Matzerath, slides into Nazism "little by little … piec[ing] together his [Nazi] uniform" for Sunday rallies (103). Grass implies that Alfred finds his identity in politics as compensation for his being cuckolded. In other words, private frustration and public humiliation are driving him and, by implication, others who desperately need to be part of a group in which they can feel superior to their peers.

What makes *The Tin Drum* a challenging read is that Grass never lets the reader be comfortable with any one perspective, whether it be tragic, comic, satiric or parodic. Instead, he introduces uncertainty and ambiguity to challenge the reader's complacency. One of the distinguishing characteristics of *The Tin Drum* is the rapid change in tone from judgmental to ironic to facetious to cynically noir. Very much a modernist who rejects the idea of a fixed self, Grass shows us that each character has different selves depending on circumstances.

What we read is at times dissonant with our expectations and would have been even more troubling to Grass's original post-war readers. For example, in 1959 Grass knew many of his readers would think his sexual explicitness went beyond conventional standards. In fact, he was accused of pornography. By dramatizing the rise of Nazism and the behavior of his characters, Grass also debunks cherished values of Western civilization: humanism, romantic love, logic, and the idea that life is gradually improving.

The Autobiographical Element

All fiction (and literary criticism) has an element of autobiography, and in *The Tin Drum* it is barely disguised. Like Oskar, Grass had a mother who was Catholic Polish-Kashubian – Kashubians are a Western Slavic ethnic group – and a German Protestant father. Grass was born in Danzig in 1927, three years after his fictional Oskar Matzerath, who tells – or rather writes – his story in 1954 when he is thirty years old and hospitalized in a psychiatric hospital, the location where the novel begins and ends. Oskar stops growing at three feet when he is three, that is, in 1927 the year Grass was born, although Oskar does grow to four feet and acquires a hump on his back later as a result of a bizarre accident after he is hit by a rock thrown by a boy who may be his son. The accident and its effects remind us that Grass takes us into a world where cause and effect are often suspended and where the illogical, the inexplicable, and the magical rule.

After World War II, Grass went to Dusseldorf where he studied sculpture and graphics; in 1953 he moved to Berlin. Once the Wall dividing Berlin was constructed in 1961 by the East German regime, he lived in West Berlin. Both Oskar's stone-working apprenticeship and his career as a model for artists owe something to Grass's experience. Grass's proficiency in the field of graphics enabled him to design his own cover for *The Tin Drum*.

After World War I, Danzig was set up by the Treaty of Versailles as a semi-autonomous city-state under the auspices of the League of Nations. The majority of Germans in Danzig resented their separation from Germany and treated the Polish minority badly, and in 1933 the local Nazis took over Danzig's government. In 1939 after the German invasion of Poland, Danzig was annexed by Germany. Jews and Poles were sent to concentration and death camps. In early 1945, Danzig fell to the Soviets and the Potsdam agreement among the major victorious allies (USA, UK, and the Soviet Union) made Danzig part of Poland. Danzig is now the Polish port of Gdańsk. The Germans were expelled and the Poles became the dominant group.

Grass stresses that while the Germans were the perpetrators of European chaos and many participated in Nazi atrocities – and a great many more were complicit – they were also victims. Germany was left devastated and 5.3 million German soldiers died, while close to a million German civilians were killed. Germany's military losses exceeded those of all Western Europe.[4]

What Kind of Fiction is *The Tin Drum*?

It is the purpose of Grass's novel to show that many genres are required to present the complex reality of the period which Oskar is describing. For whatever magical sounds Oskar may think he is making, Grass expects us to remember, too, that we are listening to a tin drum. Grass insists that Germany look at its past and present and shows how the country has anesthetized and simplified its history.

To understand how Grass accomplishes his goals, it may be wise to consider the novel's form. Often the way into a work of art is to ask, "What kind of fiction does its author write?" And that question can often best be rephrased as, "What genre or genres does a work belong to?" One does not read *Gulliver's Travels* or *Candide* as a realistic novel. Nor should one read *The Tin Drum* as a realistic novel, although it at times has aspects of that genre.

As with most major works of art, Grass's wide-ranging innovative novel challenges traditional expectations. Indeed one of the focal points of my study of the modern European novel since 1900 is to show how the novel is transformed in the twentieth century as a result of experiments in other arts and of new political realities. In part, *The Tin Drum* is a response to insular novels of manners that neglect political and historical events. Grass's novel is a unique mélange of many genres and that is part of its originality. *The Tin Drum* is not realism, fable, allegory, surrealism, picaresque, fantasy, Bildungsroman, romance, or political and social satire but takes from all these genres and often moves rapidly from one to another without warning. By giving the year of actual historical events, the novel also has aspects of docu-fiction, tracing the rise and fall of the Third Reich (with a focus on Danzig). An example of the novel's historical range is when Grass has Oskar mention the American Olympic athlete Jesse Owens, who was snubbed by Hitler at the 1936 Olympics (126). Finally, *The Tin Drum* is often a picaresque novel, a form in which the question of the parenthood of a roguish protagonist of little social standing – in this case Oskar – is often an issue.

Grass has written a big, sprawling novel where organic unity and a traditional grammar of motives take a back seat to his making thematic points, as he takes us through German history from 1899 to 1953 with a focus on Danzig and, after World War II, Dusseldorf. Even in translation, however, we are aware of Grass's dazzling stylistic variety and love of words. The reader's odyssey becomes a journey through wildly diverse modes of presentation. The reader, like Oskar, becomes something of a picaro working his way through an elusive and fragmented text – and one with rough formal edges – that does not quite hold together as a traditional narrative.

As a picaro trying to survive by his wits in a corrupt world and taking part in adventures that reveal the values of the society in which he lives, Oskar bears a resemblance to Cervantes's Don Quixote. Grass uses Oskar in many different ways to show what happened not only to Danzig but also to Germany and Europe and to inquire into the nature of the human motives that made history take such a bizarre turn. He is witness to the gradual rise of Hitler in Danzig,

Germany, and Europe. Oskar is present at such major historical events as Kristallnacht; the fall of Danzig to the Nazis and, later, to the Russian army; and the Normandy invasion.

With its innovative use of magic realism to inflect political themes, Grass's novel is an important work in the history of the European novel. To be sure it is a continuation of a tradition, foregrounded in the early twentieth century by authors writing in German such as Kafka and Mann, where the author uses fantasy elements to supplement realism. Grass, like Kafka and Mann, also draws upon the tradition of German folk tales, including fairy tales, in which the lesson is as important as the story and in which there is a suggestion that characters are punished for transgressive behavior by forces beyond human control.

One way that Grass challenges our expectations of the realistic novel is that his concept of Oskar's function changes. Rather than give Oskar a comprehensible grammar of motives, Grass makes him an example of the uncanny, that is, a mysterious and strange presence whose behavior is supposed to be weird, incomprehensible, and at times bordering on the psychotic.

It is difficult to see Oskar as a consistent character since he is at times a sociopath and, at other times, a satirist. Often Oskar is also a fictional device – Grass's surrogate – for satirizing Nazism as well as various forms of social hypocrisy. A notable example of the latter is Oskar's presentation of his mother Agnes, who, while continuing her affair with Bronski, confesses weekly to a Catholic priest; her confessions become for her a psychological refuge from guilt.

While Grass often uses Oskar's ability to hypnotize his listeners as a parody of Hitler's demagoguery, sometimes *The Tin Drum* evokes – but in ironic and parodic ways – the traditional German genres of Bildungsroman (in the tradition of Goethe of *Wilhelm Meister's Apprenticeship*) and Künstlerroman (the story of the development of an artist in the tradition of Mann's *Tonio Kröger* or Joyce's *A Portrait of the Artist as a Young Man*). Oscar's supposedly autobiographical telling is a kind of parody of the Bildungsroman since he never grows into a fully functioning adult. Even while the novel's world expands, Oskar contracts to a patient in a mental hospital where he is dictating his memoirs. In this sense, it might be best to think of *The Tin Drum* as a Bildungsroman and Künstlerroman manqué.

Grass knew James Joyce's work.[5] Like Joyce's *Ulysses*, *The Tin Drum* mixes genre and includes most ways of writing that were current when Grass composed the novel. Grass may owe something of his scathing satire of Catholicism to Joyce. Perhaps because of the Catholic Church's failure to respond adequately to the rise of Nazism in Europe, it is a major target of Grass's wrath. That Oskar sees himself as Jesus is a parody of the way Hitler considered himself as Germany's savior and convinced his followers that he was a combination of Santa Claus and Jesus if not God, and would save Germany from chaos and lead her to greatness. On one of the few occasions Oskar speaks, he takes on the quality of a demagogue when he convinces the Dusters and perhaps himself that he is Jesus, and the Dusters mindlessly follow him as the Germans followed Hitler (347–348).

Thus Oskar identifies with the three-foot statue of Jesus in his mother's church, the Church of the Sacred Heart: "Oskar's exact build, my healthy flesh, my strong, slightly plump knees, my short but muscular drummer's arms" (337). Fascinated with his physical resemblance to Jesus, he puts his drum around the neck of the statue and rests the drumsticks in its hands. He awaits the miracle of the statue of Jesus playing the drums but nothing happens. Later, as the Germans are nearing their defeat after the Normandy invasion, he returns to the same church with Maria and positions the drum and drumsticks the same way and imagines that Jesus is playing the drum (337).

In addition to the mélange of genres, the novel presents the reader with a number of other challenges. One is simply Oskar's strangeness as a character. Grass presents him as a chameleonic if not an inconsistent figure. Grass challenges our expectations of an admirable protagonist as the moral center of historical chaos. Often Oskar is complicit in the moral morass which he observes; when we think he is a satirist observing immorality from a steep and icy peak, he reveals aspects of his own behavior that are almost as disreputable as those he is satirizing.

Another aspect of *The Tin Drum* that makes reading the novel and making sense of it challenging is the oscillating distance between Grass's narrator and Oskar. The unusual and rapid shifts between first and third person prevent the reader from feeling comfortable within the fictional world. These rapid and seemingly arbitrary shifts undermine traditional expectations and announce that Grass is calling into question the conventions of traditional novels whereby the narrator is either a character speaking about his life (homodiegetic) or an outsider speaking about events he observes (heterodiegetic).

There is also a question about whether Oskar develops or regresses. Does he learn anything from his experiences? Oskar often observes without criticizing or analyzing the cause of the rise of Nazism. Are we to take him as an unreliable narrator or is his perspective at times closer to Grass's than we as resistant readers find comfortable? Is Oskar a surrogate for Grass when Oskar is almost as critical of post-war Germany as he is of the Nazi regime as if the two periods were moral twins rather than radically different not merely in details but in kind?

One can see parallels between Grass and his first person teller, who seems to avoid moral responsibility for the events taking place around him. Is Grass himself a tin drummer who is avoiding his responsibility? But while there is some truth in such a reading, this reductive perspective does not do justice to this complex work of art. To simply equate Grass with Oskar is to ignore the often scathing irony that is present throughout, whether it be towards government, religion, sexuality, middle- and upper-class assumptions, and even love itself.

In the pages that follow I shall explore some of the novel's formal complexities, including issues that pertain to Grass's characters and characterizations as well as his narrator's reliability and perspicacity. Since form and content are inextricably related, I will be showing how, in presenting Oskar, Grass's choices inform and shape content and vice versa.

Magic Realism and the Uncanny

Dreams contain the uncanny, and the uncanny is at the heart of *The Tin Drum*. *The Tin Drum* often has the texture of dreams, something underlined by Oskar's living in his bed in a mental hospital. Illogic, incongruity, exaggeration, distortion, inevitability, strangeness, and fantasy – the components of dreams – often find their way into imaginative literature. Janet Malcolm has shown how Tolstoy uses the illogic and inevitability of dreams, including the "archetypal … dream of lateness," to structure *Anna Karenina* (Malcolm, 10).[6] Malcolm contends that "the dream is father to imaginative literature" and we certainly see this in *The Tin Drum*, where daytime realism gives way to a nightmare world inhabited by distortions and inexplicable weirdness (5). Beginning with his willing himself to stop growing, Oskar's continuous feeling that he could have done more to prevent disaster is a version of the intrusion of an uncanny nightmare world.

Often comic in introducing the uncanny and incongruous into a seemingly realistic world, *The Tin Drum* belongs to the genre of Magic Realism, where fantasy inflects pedestrian events and gives them allegorical meaning. Dating back to Kafka and the German folk and fairy tale tradition, fantasy has a long heritage in Germany. Grass uses Magic Realism to show that the rise of Nazism depended in part on the introduction of folklore, magic, and myth into its discourse. Grass wants to stress that when this occurs, history and facts can be distorted by demagoguery and propaganda. Grass attributes the rise of Nazism in part to Germany's implicit and explicit rejection of the Enlightenment's emphasis on logic and reason and its concomitant system of laws derived from historical experience. Nazi ideology relied on substituting the mythology of an alternative Norse tradition, which supposedly supported the superiority of Aryans in place of the Greek and Roman mythology that was assimilated into Western European Enlightenment tradition.

The uncanny and dreamscape both lack a logical cause and effect, a why, and that often defines the world of *The Tin Drum*. Grass foregrounds war as an instance of how the historical uncanny dominates history. The crystallizing scene that takes its cue from dreamscape and that undermines the realistic code is when Oskar as a three-year-old arranges his own fall and stunts his growth by will, even while he continues to develop intellectually if not morally. As the figure whose picaresque adventures defy logic, history, and rational explanation, Oskar embodies the uncanny.

Rather than romanticizing or idealizing sex as love, Grass presents sex, like hunger and warmth, as a necessary human function. Yet Grass's treatment of sex often draws upon magic realism and the uncanny. Sex is part of the uncanny because of the irrationality of human desire. Grass's presentation of sexuality may owe something to the German playwright Frank Wedekind's indictment of bourgeois attitudes towards sex in such works as *Spring Awakening* (1890–1891; first produced 1906).

To be sure, some of the sexual scenes would seem deliberately offensive to the middle-class German audience in 1959. Grass may be stressing, like Milan Kundera in the *Unbearable Lightness of Being*, that sex becomes foregrounded in times of political turmoil as an outlet for stress and fear. In *The Tin Drum*, sexual desires have unforeseen complications; Alfred's turn to Nazism is related to his passively accepting an untenable domestic situation because his wife Agnes is having an affair with her cousin Jan. Her obsessive-compulsive behavior has an uncanny aspect when she eats herself to death. Grass chooses magic realism to show how Agnes is gorging herself on eels as a way of avoiding having another child and committing suicide.

Similarly, Oskar's own passion for Maria, who responded to Oskar when she was an adolescent, leads him into irrational behavior. When he clumsily proposes to Maria on the heels of her husband Alfred's dying after swallowing his Nazi pin, he is rejected although he is probably father to her son Kurt. Linda Greff takes Oskar to bed because she is not fulfilled by her homosexual husband. Because Oskar is a misshapen dwarf, sex with anyone except other dwarfs would have been unacceptable to conventional middle-class society. Grass is quite explicitly indicating that such differentiation, whether it be dwarfs or Jews, was central to Nazi ideology.

Allegory and the Uncanny

The uncanny plays a role in *The Tin Drum*'s complex political allegory. Think of the scene in which a fisherman fishes with a horse's head or the scenes in which Oskar's mother gorges herself with fish. The first scene, with its plenitude of eels, may be a perverse parody – in a world where generosity and unselfish love are in short supply – of the miracle of the loaves and fishes when Christ feeds five thousand people with five loaves and two fish. Interestingly, Alfred, increasingly sympathetic to the predatory Nazis, is fascinated by this mode of fishing, while Agnes, Oskar's sensitive and guilt-ridden mother, is disgusted by it. While Agnes's obsessive fish eating – especially gorging on the phallic eels that she detests – may be a misplaced effort to induce a miscarriage lest she have another child about whose father she is unsure, Grass could do better here at giving us a grammar of motives to help us understand his events.

Among the major reasons that *The Tin Drum* is a difficult read is that the political allegory is not consistent or sustained. One of the novel's problems, seen in the horse head scene under discussion, is that the novel both invites and frustrates allegorical readings. The fisherman using a dead horse to attract eels – the odd mixture of life and death – might be a metaphor for how the Nazis try to reinvigorate a seemingly dead past (the horse) by preying upon the weak (the fish), notably the Jews. But, to take another track, when rereading one can see the horse's head as an anticipation of defeated Germany, the fisherman as Hitler, and the eels (caught and eaten) are not only the Jews but also the Germans caught up in the Nazi hysteria without being fully conscious of what is going on. But we need to concede that the meaning of the allegory here is unclear.

At times, might the allegory be more effective if Grass's wildly inventive imagination had been more controlled? On first reading, the second to last chapter of Book One, the chapter in which Herbert tries to have sex with a large wooden figurehead, is overwrought as realism even though we understand that Herbert with his scars is a metonymy for Danzig and the indifferent figurehead represents Europe. But if we think of it as a nightmare of sexual desire resulting in death or in other horrific consequences to the person having the nightmare, the scene does have a kind of absurd logic. The scene has resonances with other weird sexual scenes that may tell us as much about Grass as they do about Oskar. In Grass's world, sexuality tends to be part of the same tough-edged ontology as politics and to undermine humanistic assumptions that might link sex to romantic love or indeed to anything other than to desire and physical needs.

The Tin Drum and German Expressionism

To appreciate *The Tin Drum*, we need to imagine Grass's creative process as well as think about his finished novel. Grass first drew public attention as co-founder of Group 47, a group of post-war writers concerned with developing a democratic tradition in Germany; the group met a few times a year to hear a writer read from his work. Grass won their Literary Prize in 1958. In his 1991 *Paris Review* interview, Grass, echoing Oscar Wilde, identified creativity with lying, and that of course opens the door to deviations from realism, including fantasy (Grass, "The Art of Fiction No. 124").

In some ways Grass is the heir to Modernism's expressive, romantic impulse rather than its classical one. His visual counterparts are the German expressionists in film (Wiene, Lang, Pabst, Murnau) and painting (Schiele, Nolde, Kirchner, Kandinsky, Klee) with their focus on madness, betrayal, and deviations from realism. Grass was trained as a sculptor and graphic designer; his cover illustration – part of the reading experience of *The Tin Drum* – owes something to expressionism in painting, much of which had been banned as "degenerate" during the Nazi period. It is worth noting that Bruno, Oskar's "keeper" in the mental hospital, is an abstract visual artist who transforms Oskar's written stories into knotworks made from pieces of string he gathers from his patients' rooms before dipping the strings in plaster and mounting them.

Grass created *The Tin Drum*'s expressionist cover design which, as Keith Miles notes, emphasizes that "The drum is at once an organic part of Oskar, and something quite separate that has to be strapped on to him: a gaping red wound, and a proudly-held weapon. ... The drumsticks, too, are both organic and separate; monstrous growths or bone-like sticks held by embryo hands" (Miles, *Günter Grass*, 56).[7] We might think of Schiele's paintings, with their tortured distortions of himself and the women in his life. The white top of the drum suggests emptiness, and the triangles below suggest teeth. The hat suggests that of the jester, and the left arm seems detached from the body.

An important influence on Grass was, I believe, Kandinsky. When Kandinsky showed *Komposition V* in Munich in December 1911, "abstraction not only began to seem plausible but took on the character of an imperative"[8] (Fig. 3). Later that year Kandinsky published *On the Spiritual in Art*. He was influenced by Arnold Schoenberg's musical innovations that in turn depended on borrowing ideas from painting. Kandinsky's book was influential in arguing that we need an art for emotions that cannot be expressed in words. Obviously literature could not discard words, but it became much more self-conscious about the ability of form and style to influence how behavior and cultural context were presented and how they shaped reader response. We might think of Joyce's experimental novel *Finnegans Wake* (1939).

As Karen Rosenberg observes, Kandinsky brought "the Wagnerian concept of *Gesamtkunstwerk*, or total artwork into the 20th century. Kandinsky advocated clashes of sound and color, 'multiple dissonant stimuli,' the better to disrupt complacency" (Rosenberg, C28).[9] Following in this tradition, Grass's novel is an example of the *Gesamtkunstwerk*, combining movement from place to place within Danzig and, later, in Europe by train and, in the last episode, airplane (the dance, motion, and energy of *Gesamtkunstwerk*). If letters and words are represented in Grass's cover design (the text of *Gesamtkunstwerk*), colors and shapes (the visual aspect of *Gesamtkunstwerk*) take the form of the statue of Jesus and Kroneff's gravestones, both the paintings made of Oskar and Ulla, and the brown of the Nazi uniforms as well as of the asylum guard Bruno's eyes

Fig. 3 Wassily Kandinsky, *Komposition V* (1911). Museum of Modern Art, New York.

watching Oskar through a keyhole. The weaponry, including the military aircraft, and the escalator in the final episode represent technology (its utility and necessity) that is an aspect of the *Gesamtkunstwerk*. The response of the body to physical objects (drum, fizzy powder, onions) represents the tactile aspect of the *Gesamtkunstwerk*. The sounds of the *Gesamtkunstwerk* are highlighted by Oskar's drum and glass-breaking screams as well as by the moths drumming on the light bulb when Oskar is born, and later, the sounds of industrialism, which often take military form such as the cacophonous, violent siege of the Polish Post Office. Of course, one could make a case for putting other twentieth-century novels, most notably Joyce's *Ulysses*, in this tradition.

Grass's Historiography: Oskar, Hitler, and the German Nation

Because discussion of the novel has often equated Oskar's fictional biography with the rise of Nazism, we need to address that mode of reading the novel. Perhaps some twenty-first-century readers, ignoring the revolutionary nature of Grass's critically examining German history in 1949, might find such readings oversimplified.

But it would be naïve to think that Grass's novel was intended as anything less than a scathing critique of German history and German behavior in the period from the early 1930s up to the late 1940s. On the other hand, sometimes Grass's political allegory is contradictory if not muddled, and there can be disagreement about the allegorical meaning of events and characters. The question arises whether this really is a major novel if at certain times we are puzzled by rapid shifts in genre and how we are to understand certain passages. The answer is that so much of the novel is a compelling and unique macrocosmic panorama of the rise of Nazism presented with microcosmic examples brilliantly created by Grass's fantasy – highlighted by Oskar and his drum – that for the most part we can overlook the novel's failings.

Sometimes Grass does use Oskar to satirize Germany itself; his infantilism represents a nation in a state of arrested development. His willful falling down the stairs can be read to represent Germany's self-destructive behavior after its defeat in World War I. Oskar's aggressive drumming then becomes Germany's taking on a militaristic posture in response to perceived wounds of the humiliating Versailles Treaty.

Grass uses Oskar's family to make fun of the Nazi claims of racial purity. To be sure, since his grandmother is Kashubian, of Slavic descent, Oskar's lineage is hardly pure Aryan, but Grass's point is also the ambiguity of lineage. Oskar does not know whether Alfred Matzerath, his mother's husband, or Jan Bronski, her lover, is his father. Oskar is certain he is Kurt's father, but since both he and his father ejaculated inside an unprotected Maria, how can he be sure? Kurt is the second generation in a row where the identity of the father is in doubt.

Like Oskar, Hitler has ambiguous lineage. His father was the illegitimate son of Maria Anna Schicklgruber. His younger brother's death when Hitler was eleven seemed to have turned him into a morose, lonely child. Like Oskar, one source of Hitler's displacement and anger seems to have been his estrangement from his father.

At times Grass uses Oskar as an eye witness to atrocities, such as the painter Lankes, the man who on the orders of his superior, Herzog, gunned down nuns before the Normandy invasion. Upon Lankes's return to Normandy, he rapes a young nun. In between these two Normandy episodes, Lankes physically beats Ulla, his adoring model. Does Lankes, the artist as scoundrel, reflect Grass's own view – perhaps driven by his then hidden Nazi past – that artists, despite their supposed sympathy and perceptiveness, do not behave better than others?

Oskar's extraordinary arrogance and consummate belief in his own specialness, both of which seem to date from his birth, differentiate him from most other young boys. Grass expects us to see the irony of this physically challenged figure whose symptoms mirror autism and who exhibits obsessive-compulsive behavior (for example, in his stalking of the nurse Dorothea) thinking of himself as a physical and moral paradigm. As "the gnome, Tom Thumb" weirdly express-ing himself on a tin drum, Oskar *knows* he is better than others (48). Grass wants us to understand that Oskar's certainty about his superiority recalls Hitler's belief in his own superiority, notwithstanding many early disappointments. Grass is also reminding us how the myth of Aryan superiority – that is, *knowing* that they are racially superior – became a centerpiece of Nazi political ideology that con-demned the Jews and Slavs as members of inferior races. Yet it is ironic that despite his Aryan blue eyes, Oskar is a dwarf and, from a physical standpoint, would hardly be considered as belonging to the supposedly fit and beautiful master race.

Very much like Arthur Miller in *Incident at Vichy* (1964), Grass is exposing Western and in particular European pretensions of human progress. He does this by showing some of Oskar's protests as those of an enraged infant. The non-verbal drumming and Oskar's shrill scream that breaks glass suggest the way that the Nazis substitute noise and ritual and folk tales for reason. Breaking glass as a means of communication and an outlet for anger implies that German culture is an illusion, as fragile as the glass that breaks.

Grass has invented a post-Enlightenment figure who often disdains rationa-lity and substitutes drumming for language. Oskar takes the reader into a topsy-turvy world which defies the logic, order, and clarity valued by the Enlightenment and rather seems to proceed by randomness and illogic. The rapid oscillation, sometimes in the same sentence, between first and third person narration emphasizes this. The very meaning of words like "love," "reform," "morality," and "history" is up for grabs.

Rather than a persistent outsider, Oskar represents the trajectory of the emo-tions and trends of ordinary Germans. While Oskar does subvert one Nazi rally by playing waltz music and despises his presumptive father's Nazi uniform – in part because he despises his presumptive father – his strongest commitment is to himself. We need to recall that his disruption of the Nazi rally takes place before the Germans occupy Danzig in 1939 after which Oskar gradually loses his independence. At first resistant to the Nazis, he then becomes implicated as an entertainer who does their bidding and lives lavishly.

That Oskar is playing a child's drum and later, after the war, being acclaimed as a pop star by banging on his drum as he had as a three-year-old alludes to the Nazis' subversion of German musical and cultural heritage. A child drummer playing a tin drum is in fact making basic sounds on an instrument that has a very limited range, even if the performer thinks his drum is making subtle sounds. Grass is reminding us, too, that despite Germany's elite cultural tradi-tion, notably in music and opera but also in art and literature, Germans became entranced by the simplistic rhetoric of Hitler. Oskar's drumming along with his screaming suggest the displacement of Germany's cultural tradition and

European Enlightenment. Whatever audiences think they hear when listening to Oskar's drumming, we readers understand the tin drum's limitations in terms of evoking complex sounds and emotions.

Oskar's screaming that breaks glass and his drum beating are means of controlling others, and his controlling others – we might think of Hitler's hypnotic effect on his audiences – often derives from pure selfish narcissism. The screaming and drumming – Keith Miles quotes Hitler as wanting "to become a drummer" (Miles, 48) – surely suggests the irrationality, bullying, and loudness of Hitler. Screaming takes the place of thinking as it does for a very young child who uses screaming to manipulate and get his own way.

Grass shows that bullying begets bullying. The bullying to which Oskar as a child is subjected – he is forced to swallow soup with urine – plants the seeds of his own bullying leadership of the Dusters, a combination of street gang and anti-Nazi protest movement that has some basis in reality. But as with the Nazi claim that others – Communists, Jews, the victors in World War I – are undermining Germany, Oskar's claims of being bullied can lead to justifying proactive violent behavior that is, among other things, egregious bullying.

Like Hitler, the demagogic Führer – a term which means "guide" or "leader" – Oskar believes that he knows better than anyone else. In that sense his knowing suggests Hitler's in *Mein Kampf* (1925–1926) – *Mein Kampf* translates as "my struggle" – which was published at about the time when Oskar, born in 1924, willed himself to remain a three-year-old. As we read about Oskar trying to turn his dwarfism into an asset, we realize the memoir Oskar is writing while in the mental hospital could have been called *Mein Kampf*.

Germany suffers from a collective illness in the form of psychosis throughout the novel, and that psychosis is imaged by the dwarfism and amorality of Oskar. Grass uses Oskar's psychotic behavior in 1941 to make an urgent political point. When Oskar bites Maria because she has slept with his forty-five-year-old father – she is seventeen and Oskar sixteen – and then attacks her pregnant belly with scissors, he shows symptoms of a psychopath. If Grass is suggesting that Oskar's insanity in 1941 mirrors Hitler's in that year when the latter invaded Russia, the political allegory could be clearer. We also know that in 1941 Hitler was making decisions, culminating in the January 1942 Wannsee Conference, that committed him fully to the eradication of European Jewry, but, given how Grass understates the Holocaust, we can't be sure if he has this central aspect of Hitler's psychosis in mind.

Idolized by Oskar to whom he is a mentor and ideal, Bebra, an older dwarf, is perhaps even more than Oskar a parody of Hitler. A figure of magic realism who reappears when least expected, Bebra is kind of a double who leads Oskar astray. Oskar responds to Bebra – whom he meets at the circus where Bebra performs as a musical clown – the way the Germans respond to Hitler. Oskar is mesmerized by Bebra's confidence and becomes a follower. Grass is also alluding to Hitler's theatricality and role-playing, while implying, as he does on many occasions, that the Germans are a hypnotized audience. We think of Hitler's ideas about racial superiority when Bebra advocates the specialness of dwarfs and the way that they must direct the action: "We have to perform and direct the action, otherwise our kind will be manipulated by those who do" (102). Bebra expresses his fear that a group will emerge to displace the dwarfs: "They're coming! They will take over the festival grounds. They will stage torchlight parades. They will build grandstands, they will fill grandstands, they will preach our destruction from grandstands" (102). Grass is parodying the logic of demagogues who justify themselves with the claim that if their group doesn't proactively protect themselves, they will be victims. As a supposed descendant of Prince Eugene of Savoy (1663–1736), who although physically deformed was an important general and statesman, Bebra claims his own version of Aryan heritage.

Evoking Hitler's rabble-rousing argument that Others – the Jews, the Communists – are about to take over Germany, Bebra's paranoia makes us think specifically of the Nazi leadership speaking of Jews as "They" and warning that They will take over Germany. Lest we doubt this reading, Bebra has "close connections with the Reich's Ministry of Propaganda" (289) and access to Goebbels and Göring; he becomes a major in the German army and takes a position as "director of the Theatre at the Front," a troupe of dwarfs on an entertainment tour for the German troops (302). Bebra's justification for joining the Nazis resonates with various testimonies provided by Germans after their defeat: "He spoke of difficult times, of the weak, who must temporarily give way, of resistance that blooms in secret, in short, the phrase 'inner immigration' was uttered" (289–290).

Before revealing the dwarfs as complicit with the perpetrators, Grass teases us into thinking of the dwarfs as helpless victims, perhaps themselves metaphors for Jews. As an excuse for his actions, we recall, Hitler claimed that the Germans were victims of the Versailles Treaty that officially ended World War I, the Weimar Republic, hyperinflation, and the Jews. The dwarfs are in danger from those who will take over the "grandstands" and create an alternative spectacle, one that will displace their circus. After all the dwarfs, like the Nazis' stereotype of Jews, do not fulfill the paradigm of Aryan physical stature and beauty. Because of the circus setting, we might even think of the Weimar world as presented in *Cabaret* (1966) and its source, Christopher Isherwood's *Goodbye to Berlin* (1939). But Grass pulls the rug from under his own subversive reading when Bebra becomes a Nazi, and we realize that it is the Nazis who are the dwarfs, with Bebra representing Hitler.

As a moral dwarf who does what is best for himself, Bebra later suggests Germany itself when he reappears in Book Three as the head of the West Concert Agency. He manipulates Oskar into signing a contract to drum as a soloist by reminding Oskar of his complicity (and perhaps implying that Oskar could be exposed) in the murders of Jan Bronski, Roswitha, and Matzerath. By making Bebra a successful music promoter in post-war Germany, Grass uses him as an example – as part of Grass's searing critique of post-war Germany – of how former Nazis seamlessly became part of the new Germany and how one kind of charlatanism replaced another. Bebra represents the decadence of German capitalism and its amnesia about its past.

The Rise of Nazism: The Chapter Entitled "Faith Hope Love"

In *The Tin Drum*, there are powerful moments when Grass focuses on the Nazis' emergence and their atrocities, and these are among the novels' most effective episodes. The best example of this and perhaps the most brilliant chapter is the last chapter of Book One, "Faith Hope Love," an ironically titled chapter about the opposite of those qualities that could be entitled "Violence Pathology Hatred." Mentioned at the outset, the ominous disaster "that was donning larger and larger boots, taking longer and longer strides in those larger and larger boots, and had every intention of spreading" is Nazism (181). The chapter is about the onset of Kristallnacht.

The "Faith Hope Love" chapter begins with the burial in a cemetery of Herbert Truczinski, whose scarred back represents the abuse he suffered first as a citizen of Danzig and later, with the encroachment of the Nazis, as a Polish citizen of Danzig. Herbert's funeral takes place at the onset of Kristallnacht when the Nazis are in full control of Danzig. Herbert himself stands as a metonymy for Danzig; the scars he accumulates while serving others as a waiter are those that Danzig suffered from various interlopers – "Finnish, Swedish, Polish, Free Port, and German" – over the centuries (167). Oskar seems to have a particular penchant for cemeteries, summoning in his and the reader's mind needless and senseless deaths.

"Niobe," the prior chapter, focuses on Herbert Truczinski who, in a bizarre episode, died trying to have sex with the figurehead of a ship named *Niobe*. We might recall that Niobe is the proud and fertile daughter of Tantalus who lost all her children, the sons killed by Apollo, the daughters by Artemis. We might take Niobe as another trope for the impossible and hopeless situation of Danzig, as well as for the Poles seeking an amicable relationship with the Germans who are indifferent to their desires in Danzig and beyond. By implication, the children of Niobe are all those who are not German.

Containing various narratives told from a folk perspective – underlined by Oskar's iterative "Once upon a time" – this compellingly effective "Faith Hope Love" chapter gradually zeroes in on Kristallnacht and the specific and disgusting anti-Semitic outrages committed against the toymaker Sigismund Markus. Supplier of tin drums to Oskar and putative lover of his mother Agnes, Markus responds to the destruction of his shop and the vile Nazi behavior by committing suicide in his own office. Grass has Oskar repeat, "Once upon a time" over and over again to remind us how Germans were telling themselves a fairy tale even while committing atrocities. Yet by evoking fairy tales, Grass also reminds us that while the Nazis created a world of make-believe, that world had dire consequences for the Jews and finally the entire nation.

In formal terms, Grass stresses the way a narrative can be manipulated and how many ways a tale can be told. At first, the telling does not focus on the crucial historical events and how they impact individuals as if there were a way of telling the story of Kristallnacht without zeroing in on what really happened. Yet each successive paragraph that begins with "once upon a time" becomes a little less evasive and a bit more pointed and revelatory.

Present at Herbert's funeral is Meyn, an SA member, whose full name we never learn. A paramilitary organization, the SA – standing for *Sturmabteilung* ["assault division"] – were also known as Brown Shirts or Storm Troopers, often World War I veterans too old to be soldiers; the SA played a major role in Hitler's rise to power. A trumpeter, Meyn rides a brown horse, brown being the Nazi color. Meyn was once a friend of Herbert's when they both were Communists in the 1920s and members of the Socialist young people's group known as the Red Falcons. Meyn wears his civilian coat over his uniform to hide his Nazi sympathies. But Crazy Leo, the seemingly omnipresent cemetery guardian who is associated with death and becomes something of an allegorical figure, withholds his sympathy and white glove from Meyn, for whom the lure of Nazism – the fulfillment of his need to belong to something – has become a substitute for alcohol. Grass's point here and elsewhere is to relate joining the Nazis to individual frustration and disappointment and to see Nazism as a compensation for loneliness. Meyn is a recovering alcoholic who has turned "from the drunken excesses of a wasted and unstable youth" to Nazism (183).

Meyn is depicted, as are so many of the novel's characters, as unstable if not a borderline psychotic. When he returns from Herbert's funeral, he gets drunk and kills his four cats that had been his only companions. But another Nazi, Laubschad the clock-maker, notices the cats in the garbage when he saw movement because they were not all dead. He reports Meyn, who, despite his "conspicuous bravery" while participating in the atrocities of Kristallnacht, was expelled from the SA for "dishonorable conduct" in killing his cats (185).

Grass's heavy irony emphasizes that for the Nazis killing cats is a crime while burning synagogues and taking part in behavior that drives Jews to suicide is not.

The ironically titled chapter "Faith Hope Love" continues with graphic events on Kristallnacht. Oskar's German father Alfred Matzerath, a grocer who has cast his lot with the Nazis, takes him to a burning synagogue as if he were taking him to the circus: "Outside the ruins, civilians and men in uniforms were piling up books, sacred objects, and strange pieces of cloth. The mound was set ablaze and the grocer took the opportunity to warm his hands and his passions at the public fire" (185). The phrasing is Grass at his best. The strange pieces of cloth are Jewish prayer shawls (tallit, pl. tallitot) worn by men at prayer. Oskar sees that his father is "so involved and inflamed" (185). Note the zeugma: Oskar's father warming his hands is radically different from warming his passions in the form of hatred for Jews and enthusiasm for Nazi atrocities. Here more than in any other passage, Grass comes closest to effectively and graphically rendering the atrocities suffered by the Jews during the Nazi era.

Knowing that Markus, whose toy shop is the source of his beloved tin drums, is a Jew, Oskar slips off to protect the drums, but he is too late; Markus's shop has been ravaged. Oskar sees that "Jewish Swine" has been written on the shop window; the perpetrators are "at play" – a scathingly ironic phrase – destroying toys and defecating on them (186). By the time Oskar arrives, Markus has already committed suicide by taking pills.

After taking three of his treasured drums from the shop with him, Oskar encounters some poor people handing out religious tracts under a sign from 1 Corinthians 13: "Faith – Hope – Love." Oskar thinks, "An entire gullible nation believed faithfully in Santa Claus. But Santa Claus was really the Gasman" (187). Equating Santa Claus with Hitler, Oskar gives an ironic voice to the German reaction in 1938 to a demagogue who promised everything. But equating Santa Claus with the Gasman is also a retrospective comment from Oskar's present memoir. Continuing in the ironic mode, Oskar proclaims the Advent season which in fact comes the fourth Sunday before Christmas: "He's Coming! He's Coming! And who came? The Christ Child, The Savior! Or was it the heavenly Gasman … ?" (187). Hitler, the Gasman, commits genocide by gassing Jews, but for the Germans Hitler is a surrogate for Jesus: "[F]aith in the Gasman was proclaimed the state religion" (188).

The Function of Oskar

Oskar, the first person narrator-protagonist, is a complex figure with multiple selves. As a picaro in Book One, he observes corruption and outrageous behavior without getting overly involved: He is an outsider and a detached observer.

At times Oskar's drumming is a means of protest against social and historical situations of which he disapproves. When in his picaro role he uses his drum to disrupt the Nazi rally, he is able to dupe the society he observes. In fact until Kristallnacht, Oskar is an anti-Nazi.

One aspect of his drumming is his resistance to dogma, whether Catholic or Nazi. It enables him to maintain his individuality and reductive views whether of family or community hypocrisy or national policy. In 1934, as his supposed father Alfred Matzerath turns to Nazism, Oskar plays a waltz on his drum to disrupt a Nazi rally, and he continues to do this until 1938: "For a long time, till November of thirty-eight to be exact, crouching under grandstands with my drum, with greater or lesser success I broke up rallies, reduced speakers to stutters, and turned marches and hymns into waltzes and foxtrots" (111).

But Grass often stresses Oskar's arrested development, self-immersion, and selfishness. Frequently, Oskar's adolescent drumming expresses his narcissism and possibly autism. There is also an aspect of decadence and aestheticism to Oskar's behavior. Oskar relies on the drum not only to communicate but also to give order and shape to what he sees and hears. In that sense, the drum has an aesthetic function, and that aesthetic function often has a personal component as if Grass were attributing the rise of Nazism to earlier forms of moral blindness in Europe as represented by the hypocritical behavior of Oskar's mother, father, and uncle and their social circle.

Through the influence of Bebra, Oskar gets sucked into a role in the Nazi juggernaut and becomes complicit in the very world from which he at first stood apart. Grass does not give us a sufficient grammar of motives to understand the change. The drumming on a child's toy is associated with Oskar's willfulness and refusal to take part in the bourgeois adult world. But we are sympathetic to his willful detachment because that adult world itself is regressive, without admirable social values, and indifferent to the rise of Nazism, a rise fueled in part by misfits and malcontents.

Oskar's arrested development suggests what happened to Germany in terms of ceasing to grow as a country offering civility, tolerance, respect for diversity, and openness to multiple perspectives. Oskar's impulse to protest burgeoning Nazism fades. By the time Oskar reaches the "summer of [nineteen] thirty-three" we realize his life parallels the rise of Nazism (97). Oskar's ability to shatter glass also aligns Oscar with the perpetrators of Kristallnacht, when the Nazis on November 9, 1938 coordinated attacks against Jewish synagogues and businesses and arrested more than thirty thousand Jews. Although once resistant to the rise of the Nazis, Oskar comes to represent Germans who gradually got caught up in the fervor of Nazism. He betrays his Polish uncle/father soon after Kristallnacht.

Oskar's Divided Self: The Paradigms of Goethe and Rasputin

Oskar's mind at times oscillates between two paradigms: the German Romantic writer Goethe, statesman and cultural icon, and Rasputin, the Russian faith-healer who influenced Nicholas II, the last Tsar of Russia, and his wife. Goethe is known for *The Sorrows of Young Werther*, although Oskar prefers Goethe's *Elective Affinities* in which human relationships are imagined in scientific terms. Grass is aware, too, of Goethe's *Faust*, in which Faust makes a pact with the devil. Isn't there some suggestion of a parallel when Oskar entertains Nazis and lives flamboyantly during the occupation of France as well as when, in the wake of the German defeat in World War II, he takes part in manipulating post-war German emotions in the Onion Cellar? Perhaps the ultimate parallel to Faust's pact with the devil may be Oskar's arranging his fall at the age of three, an event that draws on the fantasy of folk tales.

Oskar's development is also shaped by a book about Rasputin entitled *Rasputin and Women*. While books about Rasputin existed in twentieth-century Germany, I could find no such title. For Oskar, Goethe represents both the Romantic idealist but also the respectable and reasonable, something akin to Nietzsche's Apollonian way of life. By contrast, Rasputin represents Oskar's illogical, illicit, darker side, the disreputable, chaotic, and Dionysian self. Grass would have expected us see the irony of the Romantic bisexual Goethe with his multiple love affairs being considered Apollonian. Given that Oskar has Rasputin's larger than expected penis and Goethe's reputedly blue eyes, his physical appearance has aspects of both the Dionysian and Apollonian poles.

Oskar's duality is mirrored in Alfred Matzerath's living room containing pictures of Beethoven and Hitler; as Oskar recalls, "Hitler and the genius hung opposite each other, stared at each other, saw through each other, yet found no joy in what they saw" (103). Beethoven, like Goethe, stands for the tradition of German culture that is undermined by the Nazis. Rasputin represents the dark side of the German psyche to which Hitler gave voice. Hitler also becomes the Black Cook, a recurring bogeyman from the German folk tradition that hovers over *The Tin Drum*.

The Relationship Between the Personal and Political: Oskar's Drumming and Glass-shattering Screams

One of Grass's major points is the interrelationship between the personal and political. Without the personal there can be no political; individual needs, including the need to belong to a larger community and the need to feel superior to others, drive the political.

An outsider by choice, Oskar nevertheless suffers from loneliness. Even as he writes, he wants to marry Maria who has rejected him. Underlying Oskar's narrative is the human need for companionship and the poignancy of loneliness, loneliness that shapes the sexual longing mirrored in the various triangles: Agnes–Jan–Alfred; Maria–Alfred–Oskar; Bebra–Roswitha–Oskar, not to mention the secondary triangles: Lankes–Ulla–Oskar and Oskar–Greff–Mrs. Greff.

Oskar uses his tin drum, his glass-shattering scream – and later, when writing, his pen – as a buffer to compensate for hurt, loneliness, suffering, disappointment, unfulfilled desires, and rejection. As a young boy he pretends that he cannot speak and does not let on that he can read; he wears what John Reddick calls "the guise of infantility" (Reddick, 65).[10] For Oskar, the drum and the scream are desperate means of self-expression. On his first and only day of school, when a teacher tries to take away his drum, his screaming breaks her spectacles.

Oskar seeks refuge under his grandmother's skirts and in the wardrobe of his mother's bedroom. Oskar has an Oedipal relationship with his mother which is inflected by his continuing awareness of her adulterous sexual relationship with her cousin Jan Bronski. What he wants most emphatically is his mother's understanding. For the most part he seeks the protection of isolation and darkness, venturing out to placate sexual desires and practical needs but preferring his own world to social interaction. When he chooses social interaction, he usually has a sexual or materialistic motive or a need to preserve or replace his drum. Indeed, in Freudian terms, the drum for him is a way to express his ego and superego, while his scream is pure id. Oscar's "singshattering" – breaking glass with his screams – derives from his own narcissistic willfulness. But in Freudian terms his willfulness is a response to his knowledge that his beloved mother's adultery sullies the ideal he wants to keep.

What Grass emphasizes in Oskar's retrospective telling is solipsism and avoidance of confrontation when the historical stakes require it. Oskar's breaking glass with his voice derives from private pique as well as an obsessive need to show his power as when he breaks store windows to see if people will steal. In Oskar's mind his drumming is a justifiable protest, but his personal pique is usually an important cause of his behavior. Yes, his drumming breaks up a Nazi rally, but what about all the times he breaks glass with his screams to satisfy himself? When Oskar entertains for the Nazis as a collaborator and later participates in the business conventions of post-war Germany, we realize again that his narcissism and selfishness are important motivations.

Expressing himself for years by drumming rather than speaking, Oskar is both victim and perpetrator. Those close to him die prematurely and he feels some responsibility. Yet his behavior is often manipulative and reprehensible. He is difficult to like and that affects how we respond to the novel. We are in the anomalous and uncomfortable position of not liking a disabled person for whom we feel we should have sympathy. Yet Oskar is responsible for arranging his fall at the age of three. One of the worst instances of Oskar's bad behavior is his betrayal of his "presumptive father" and actual uncle, Jan Bronski, resulting in "the assumption of my second great burden of guilt" (230). The first burden of guilt results in his blaming himself for his mother's death. He believes that the misery he caused her by his dwarfism meant that the thought of having a second child after becoming pregnant not only drove her to compulsive eating but also exacerbated her guilt as a Catholic for her long-term adultery.

In the early chapters of Book Two, Grass uses Oskar's focalization to evoke crucial episodes in the rise of Nazism. Grass is ironic in his presentation of the Danzig Poles. They live in a fantasy world, expecting the intervention of the French and British who in fact do nothing. During Grass's rendering of the attack on the Polish Post Office in Danzig on September 1, 1939 (considered in fact the first battle of World War II), Oskar and his father-uncle, a Danzig Pole, are in the Polish Post Office that is under siege. This episode brings home the horrors of war; using rifles against the tanks and howitzers of the Home Guard – an auxiliary Danzig wing of the German forces – many of the defenders are killed.

Consider the bizarre scene of Jan and Oskar's playing the card game skat with a wounded and dying man during the climax of the siege. In a scene combining scathing realism and the uncanny, Jan finds refuge in playing cards with a dying man. Jan becomes catatonic, revealing himself as a coward. After the Germans rout the Poles and they surrender, Jan is unconscionably (uncannily?) betrayed by Oskar's "accusatory gestures" (229). Jan's construction of a house of cards while the Home Guard's attack reaches its climax is a metaphor for the Polish obliviousness to reality: "Jan had already entered the eternal realm of card houses, dwelt happily in one of those houses that trust in good fortune, whereas the Home Guard and I … stood amid brick walls, on tiled corridor floors, under roofs with stucco cornices" (230).

In the Post Office episode, Oskar's only concern is taking possession of a toy drum that he finds in the nursery of the postmaster's family residence. After the people in the Post Office surrender, his uncle is executed, and Oskar feels responsible because he had convinced the Home Guard that Jan was "a villain who had dragged an innocent child to the Polish Post Office in typically barbaric Polish fashion to use as a human shield" (229) when in fact the only reason Oskar was accompanying Jan was that Jan was trying to help Oskar get his tin drum repaired. Once the Poles defending the Post Office surrender, "Oskar counted himself among the Home Guard" (230). At this point he had chameleon-like cast his lot with the seemingly triumphant Nazis. Recalling the sequence of events, Oskar remarks: "Today … I'm occasionally ashamed of my disgraceful behavior" (230). In this case, Oskar's deception and betrayal suggest the complicity of the German civilians in cooperating with the Nazis.

How *The Tin Drum* Begins: Oskar as a Self-Dramatizing Narrator-Protagonist

With the help of his tin drum to summon memories, the thirty-year-old Oskar is writing his memoirs in an insane asylum, while being watched by Bruno, an asylum employee. We are presumably reading those memoirs. The asylum, like Oskar's recurring refuge in his grandmother's skirts and his mother's wardrobe, is a kind of escapist regression to the womb: "[M]y bed is a goal I've finally reached, it is my consolation" (3). When we meet Oskar, he seems a borderline psychotic, resenting visitors and embracing the notion that he is being constantly watched by his "keeper" as if he were a circus animal. In a phrase that recalls Poe's sociopath in "The Tell-Tale Heart," he asserts: "[M]y keeper's eye is the shade of brown that can't see through blue-eyed types like me" (3). How can we trust such a narrator? At Oskar's request, the keeper has brought him five hundred blank pages on which he will write his "recollections, which I hope will be accurate" (4).

Oskar is conscious of his audience. He addresses the audience as "you" to narrow the distance between himself and his audience, that is, readers "forced to live confusing lives beyond the confines of my mental institution" (5). In claiming with – as rereaders understand – bitter irony that he and Bruno are heroes, Oskar is separating the two of them from a "nameless mass devoid of heroes" (5). Presumably the direct address is a way of differentiating from the mass his audience who, like himself, can "claim ... individual loneliness" (5). In a sense, Oskar, in all his physical and personal idiosyncrasies, is rescuing individuality in its purest form from mass behavior. One point of Grass's novel is that we all have our own stories and make our own choices, even if our unique stories are in part a function of historical events we cannot fully control.

While *The Tin Drum* begins in an asylum, it quickly moves outward diachronically and synchronically. Oskar begins with, and soon returns to, the first generation of his family chronicle. Lacking a serious grammar of motives, the simple story of his grandparents has aspects of a folk tale. Oskar relates the tale of the police catching up with his grandfather in 1913 and some tall tales surrounding his grandfather's disappearance.

The first chapter is entitled "The Wide Skirt," an image that suggests the openness of his grandmother's thighs to the escapee Koljaiczek who hides under her skirt. Perhaps she could have closed her thighs, although she may not have had any choice, and what has taken place may be rape. Yet in a high-spirited comic mode that belies what follows in the novel, Grass presents this event as a consensual one. In fact we don't know if Oskar's grandmother is a virgin or even whether Koljaiczek is Agnes's father, a confusion echoed in the ensuing ambiguity about the identity of Oskar's father and, later, of his son's father.

In the early chapters, Oskar calls attention not only to his own situation but also to that of post-war Germany and its division (91). He conflates past and present, even while sustaining an historical sweep. He rapidly oscillates between contemporary Germany and the recent and even distant past; thus he elegizes Poland, which during World War II was occupied by Germany and then, after Germany's defeat, by Russia; "I search on my drum for the land of the Poles and drum: lost, not yet lost, lost once more, lost to whom, lost too soon, lost by now, Poland's lost, all is lost, Poland is not yet lost" (95).

Juxtaposing present and past is essential to Grass's technique in the early chapters with the result that we readers are simultaneously on two tracks. We are with Oskar in the asylum, experiencing the sequence of personal events that got him there as well as the historical events in Danzig and Germany that helped define him.

To begin the second chapter, entitled "Under the Raft," Oskar returns to his hospital bed and mentions the role of the tin drum which, thanks to the institute's permission, "speaks[s] three or four hours each day" as a crucial aid in summoning his recollections (13). Indeed, he has anthropomorphized his drum to speak of the past as if the drum had a life of its own: "My drum says" (13).

In this second chapter, Oskar takes us back to his birth: "I'm burning to announce the beginning of my own existence" (17). His self-consciously reminding us that he is writing about himself and digressing whenever he wishes recalls Laurence Sterne's *The Life and Opinions of Tristram Shandy, Gentleman* (1759–1767). As Keith Miles suggests in *Günter Grass*, Sterne's novel has long fascinated German novelists. Oskar speaks of his "love of the labyrinthine" (38), which recalls Tristram Shandy's love of digression. But while both novels are conscious of time and mortality, Grass's harsh cynicism in *The Tin Drum* is far different from Sterne's sentimentalism and gentleness.

It is not long before we are aware of the complexity of Oskar's telling. He begins the fourth chapter, "The Photo Album," by referring to a 120-page album – "this open family grave" (38) – which helps jog his memory while writing. After Germany's defeat in World War II, when Oskar and his family were forced to leave Danzig with other Germans, he recalls taking the album out "during the trip in the boxcar" (38). He spends a great deal of time pondering over one "indecent snapshot" of his mother on a balcony sitting on the lap of Jan, her cousin and lover, with Alfred, her husband, smiling; knowing the entire story, the reader appreciates the bitter irony of Oskar's speaking of "their tripartite happiness" (45). That another photo of the threesome shows the "same tense peace" makes us aware of the bitterness of Oskar's memories (45).

He returns to his baby pictures before his fall and stresses his "clenched fists": "The little clutched hands hover gravely gathered at my temples ready to strike, to sound the beat. What beat? The drum beat" (47). He concludes this chapter with a picture of himself on his third birthday when, equipped with his drum, "I decreed … that I would never be a politician and most certainly not a grocer, that I would make a point instead of remaining as I was – and so I did, remained that size, kept that attire, for years to come" (48). Yet something was growing, "[u]ltimately taking on messianic proportions" (49); what that is, we realize upon rereading, is Oskar's penis, his id, his screaming ability, his intelligence, his perspicacity about what is happening in Germany.

Book Three: Grass's Satiric Visions of Post-War Germany

Breaking down into discrete episodes with less unity than the earlier two books, Book Three, the final book, dramatizes post-World War II Europe, including the indignities and humiliations suffered by both soldiers and civilians on the losing side. Book Three satirizes the economic renewal of defeated Germany after the war. That Bebra forgets his Nazi enthusiasm and becomes a cynical master of capitalism, once again involving Oskar in his machinations, is Grass's way of reminding us how the Nazis survived by reinventing themselves within a society in denial. The second chapter in Book Three entitled "Fortuna North" is named after a power plant near a cemetery linking the energy of the new Germany with death in the old Germany. Oskar as apprentice to Korneff becomes quite economically comfortable making tombstones, sometimes bartering the tombstones rather than selling them. But death, rejection, and loneliness hover over the chapter and the success of the tombstone business is a metonymy for the new Germany.

The various ways Oskar makes his living in Book Three emphasize the irony of the economic miracle following currency reform. Rather than produce necessary goods or create jobs for workers, the economic miracle in *The Tin Drum* revolves around tawdry or narcissistic activities dependent on a parasitic relationship to the past. Making gravestones, Oskar lives off the dead, recalling the fisherman who uses a dead horse to catch eels. To emphasize Oskar's dependent and obsequious relationship to Korneff, the man who makes gravestones after the Germans are defeated, Grass has Oskar squeeze Korneff's festering boils. He models – often with Ulla, a beautiful woman – as a physical curiosity for painters and sculptors.

After the war, the adult Oskar becomes a famous soloist performing on a tin drum to fifteen hundred to two thousand people, mostly over the age of forty-five, "as I did when I was three and as I did again in Schmuh's Onion Cellar" (530). Oskar's appeal is that he reminds his listeners of Germany's past. That Oskar can seamlessly move from entertaining Nazis to becoming a pop star in post-war Germany is Grass's way of satirizing how former Nazis prospered during the recovery. The great popularity Oskar achieves after the war not only recalls the response to Hitler's *Mein Kampf* before the war, but also reminds us that many former Nazis had prominent positions in post-war Germany.

Like the Germans captivated by Hitler, Oskar's audience – especially the age group that two decades before had been captivated by Hitler – responds to his drumming as if Oskar were "a magician, a faith healer, messiah" (531). Oskar's drumming with "its childish babbling and prattling" echoes his drumming as a three-year-old (531). He even "rediscovers [his] glass-slaying voice" (531). His audience hears the sound of "black fright" (531), and, Oskar tells us, "the term 'Oskarism' made its first appearance, and soon became a catch-phrase" for curing memory loss (532). But the cure is partial and distorted, allowing audience members to return to their bourgeois lives with little awareness of the victims of the Nazi era.

At first the Onion Cellar, the nightclub manqué where Germans pay an entrance fee to come and show emotions about their dark past, seems to be a satire on how Germans' excessive sentimentalism alternates with their repression of the past. In order to express their feelings, the patrons of the Onion Cellar need the extrinsic stimulus of onions: "People wept. At long last, people wept again. Wept openly, wept without restraint, wept honestly" (503). After weeping, the nightclub patrons talked to one another about their experiences, including "revelations, self-accusations, confessions, exposures, and admissions" (503). The Onion Cellar is a darkly comic example of how post-war Germany's exploitive capitalists profited from the tears of others. It may also refer to how bourgeois Germans reveled in their own sentiments rather than addressing the needs and claims of the victims.

The occasional lack of clarity in the political allegory comes from Grass's complex feelings, some of which he is loath to acknowledge. What is off-putting and has a strong anti-Semitic nuance is that the Onion Cellar owner Schmuh is probably a Jew; in Yiddish, *Schmuh* means deception or sham. Schmuh is depicted as an eccentric who abuses his female employees and after shooting sparrows feeds them to other birds. Even if Grass is satirizing the handwringing and remorse that avoid coming to terms with the actual facts of the past in which so many Germans like Oskar's father were complicit, Grass seems to be blaming Jewish victims for exploiting German feelings of guilt.

Rereading, I feel at times that Grass's novel is a metonymy for the Onion Cellar. In other words, for all his critiques, Grass is sympathetic to the defeated Germans and those who, like Oskar, were expelled from Danzig and other venues. Grass implies that it was incumbent upon the Danzig Germans to disguise their complex feelings about the rise of the Nazis and their repression was not entirely their fault. Grass never eschews the theme of how history and politics shape the lives of people who simply want to have their own private existences but who are inevitably drawn into the historical maelstrom. To an extent this claim of being caught in overarching teleology transformed into "What could I have done?" became an excuse for ordinary people – not only in Danzig but also throughout Germany and German-occupied Europe – who participated in the Nazi regime, as if that excuse relieved them of some responsibility.

Oskar, too, is often oblivious to moral considerations but feels on occasion some, but hardly overwhelming, guilt in retrospect. In the retelling at age thirty Oskar acknowledges his guilt for the deaths of the three adult figures in his life – namely Agnes, Jan, and Alfred – as well as his dwarf lover, Roswitha. But is that guilt another version of sentimental excess like the cabaret in the Onion Cellar? In this way Grass is equating Oskar's behavior with that of the German public's retrospective response to its Nazi past.

What dominate the closing chapters are fear, anxiety, and psychopathology. Oskar sought to be arrested as a way of subtracting himself from a world he detests. When captured by the police for killing Sister Dorothea, which he didn't do, he claims, "I am Jesus," but we are not sure if he is being ironic or believes what he says, although the latter is more probable (562). At this point, he is increasingly delusional and thinks he is being observed by the nightmarish figure of the Black Cook with her "terrifyingly calm countenance" (562). Carrying vestiges of Catholicism's reductive duality, the Black Cook is Satanic: "[W]hat would Catholicism be without the Cook who blackens every confessional?" (563). In Oskar's disturbed mind, he is taking on the sins of the world because he allows himself to be arrested for a crime he didn't commit. But the reader sees that he has lost his connection with reality.

The Black Cook represents both the unknowable and the shadow of mortality. Isn't the Black Cook that was once behind him and now comes towards him the unknown future that Oskar – and, by implication, Germany – is afraid to confront now that his release from the mental hospital is imminent? Yet if Grass means Oskar's breakdown to personify Germany, once again the political allegory is not clear.

Even as the novel closes, Oskar's thinking of himself as savior has resonances of the rise of Hitler and the possibility of future self-deluded but

172

convincing demagogues leading people astray. Now thirty, Oskar thinks of the parallel to Jesus. "Today I am thirty." (Apparently he has been in the asylum for two full years since he was arrested at twenty-eight.) Jesus began his ministry at thirty (Luke 3:2) and that is the age when David became king (2 Samuel 5:4). Knowing he will soon be released, Oskar thinks of "gather[ing] disciples" (554). Yes, he is still out of touch with reality, but his still pathologically thinking of himself as a savior reminds us that the political demagoguery that ravaged Europe in the form of totalitarianism, Nazism, and Fascism is always a threat.

Resistant Reading: *The Tin Drum*'s Failure to Render the Holocaust

Notwithstanding my praise for the chapter entitled "Faith Hope Love," I do think that Grass could and should have done more with the Nazis' elimination of most of the Jewish population of Europe.

By including the return of the Poles and Jews as well as the resettlement of Germans, Grass emphasizes the chaos at the end of the war. But his stress seems to be on the Germans as victims. In Danzig, we are informed that the men of the Volkssturm – a national militia set up at the end of the war by the Nazi party as a last defensive gasp – are hanged as traitors, but what about about specifics of how Jews were treated? In 1933 Danzig's population of over four hundred thousand included about ten thousand Jews. That Grass focuses on those of German ancestry who were shipped off in boxcars from Danzig after the war but omits mention of the earlier deportation of Jews is an example of how his novel understates the Holocaust and/or leaves it offstage.

In his presentation of the Nazi regime's behavior and policies, Grass does not have much time for the Jewish victims. Downplaying the Jews as victims needs to be put on Grass's doorstep since this spacious, prolix, repetitious, and over-determined novel seems to have space for everything else. Surely, an epic novel about Germany should show much greater awareness of the plight of Europe's Jews. In the entire novel, there are two characters identified as Jews. The first is the aforementioned toy store owner Sigismund Markus, whose shop is destroyed on Kristallnacht right before he commits suicide. He would be a more sympathetic character had he not been so infatuated with Agnes that he invited her to leave her husband and, with Oskar, go to London with him.

The second Jewish character is Mariusz Fajngold, who survives Treblinka but whose wife died there. He is depicted as willing to displace Oskar's family from their shop and apartment. Not only is this retributive justice of which the novel disapproves elsewhere, but Fajngold is viewed as something of a parasite. In fact the idea that soon after the war a healthy Fajngold, who survived the Treblinka extermination camp, would turn up in Danzig to take over someone's shop and apartment is far-fetched and hardly representative of the effects of the Holocaust. Grass seems to suggest that misplaced sentimentalism towards surviving Jewish victims is in part responsible for Germans having to leave Danzig after the war when, in fact, the major reason was the return of the Polish population seeking the fruits of allied victory.

Neither Jewish character is fully realized or sympathetic. Both Jews are depicted as insensitive. As I have mentioned, a probable third Jew is the imposter Schmuh who presides over the Onion Cellar. Grass could certainly have shown a greater awareness of and sensitivity to the suffering of Jews and provided more dramatized examples of how they were victims.

Afterword: The Film of *The Tin Drum*

The excellent 1979 film of Grass's *The Tin Drum* directed by Volker Schlöndorff somewhat simplifies Oskar's motivations. More efficiently than the book, the film makes clear that his desire not to grow up is based on his confusion about the domestic arrangements in his home and his distaste for them. The film stresses that the drumming is a response to his mother's sexual behavior with her cousin, much of which goes on under her husband's nose. By streamlining the unruly plot, the film's political allegory is more consistent and clearer than Grass's novel.

By foregrounding the relationship with Bebra and Roswitha as another triad in which Bebra is a willing or at least submissive cuckold very much like Oskar's legal father and by stressing how Bebra's troupe, including Oskar, become collaborators as entertainers for the Nazis, the film also makes clear that the dwarf world mirrors the world of larger people.

The film is somewhat more sympathetic to Jews than is the novel. Fajngold, the Jew who in the book takes over Oskar's family flat and store, is absent. Markus is a more complex character. Although he has been baptized as a way of surviving virulent anti-Semitism, he returns to Agnes's grave to say Kaddish after being chased away from her funeral. When Markus commits suicide, he is wearing a yarmulke to stress the Jew as victim.

Thus it is not too much to say the film is something of a correction and clarification, but also a reductive distortion of a novel that is often unruly, contradictory, inconsistent, muddled in terms of its allegory, and, when it comes to Jews, unsympathetic, oblivious, and even judgmental.

Study Questions for *The Tin Drum*

1. What is the significance of Oskar's arrested development? Why does he throw himself down the cellar stairs?
2. What do his drumming and glass-shattering screaming signify?
3. How does Grass relate the personal to the political, including the rise of Nazism, and vice versa?
4. How do we reconcile Oskar's self-identification with Jesus with the satire of Hitler and Nazism?
5. How does Oskar evolve as a character?
6. What is gained by Grass's mix of genres, including allegory, satire, Bildungsroman, picaresque novel, and family chronicle?
7. How do inconsistencies and confusion in some parts of the political allegory affect our reading?
8. Why is Oskar in a mental hospital for criminals throughout the novel?
9. What is the role of Bebra?
10. What could Grass have done differently in terms of presenting the Holocaust as perhaps the most crucial event in the period about which he writes?
11. Why does the novel lose some of its power and focus in Book Three?
12. How do the rapid shifts between first person and third person narrator work? How do they shape our reading? Why does Grass use this technique?

Notes

1. Page references are from Günter Grass, *The Tin Drum*, trans. Breon Mitchell (New York: Houghton Mifflin Harcourt, 2010).
2. Günter Grass, "The Art of Fiction No. 124." Interview by Elizabeth Gaffney. *Paris Review* 119 (Summer 1991); https://www.theparisreview.org/interviews/2191/gunter-grass-the-art-of-fiction-no-124-gunter-grass (accessed August 18, 2015).
3. Stephen Kinzer, "Günter Grass Dies at 87," *New York Times* (April 13, 2015); https://www.nytimes.com/2015/04/14/world/europe/gunter-grass-german-novelist-dies-at-87.html.
4. Adam Tooze, "No Lives Untouched." A review of Nicholas Stargardt's *The German War: A Nation Under Arms, 1939–1945*, *New York Times Book Review* (Nov. 15, 2015), 16.
5. J. P. Bauke, "A Talk with Günter Grass," *New York Times* (May 31, 1964); http://www.nytimes.com/books/99/12/19/specials/grass-talk64.html
6. Janet Malcolm, "Dreams and Anna Karenina," *NYR* 62:11 (June 25, 2015), 10–12; see 10.
7. Keith Miles, *Günter Grass* (London: Vision Press, 1975), 56.
8. Leah Dickerman, ed., *Inventing Abstraction 1910–1925: How a Radical Idea Changed Modern Art* (New York: The Museum of Modern Art, 2012), 14.
9. Karen Rosenberg, "Back in the Blue Saddle, for a Gallop to Abstraction," *New York Times* (Oct. 4, 2013), C28.
10. John Reddick, *The Danzig Trilogy of Günter Grass: A Study of The Tin Drum, Cat and Mouse and Dog Years* (London: Secker & Warburg, 1975), 65.

Chapter 9

Imre Kertész's *Fatelessness* (1975): Rendering the Holocaust as a Present Tense Event

"I regard as kitsch any representation of the Holocaust that is incapable of understanding or unwilling to understand the organic connection between our own deformed mode of life … and the very possibility of the Holocaust."

Imre Kertész, "Who Owns Auschwitz?"[1]

Introduction

Hungary was the last chapter of Hitler's war against the Jews. Hitler marched into Hungary March 19, 1944. Hungary was a member of the Axis and suffered huge losses on the Eastern Front, especially during the Battle of Stalingrad. When Hungary wanted to pull out of the war and began secret negotiations with the USA and UK, Germany installed a puppet regime. Until then Jews had been deprived of their rights and a great many suffered economic losses, but they were protected from the Final Solution. Ghettoization began outside Budapest in April 1944; by mid-May, under the supervision of Adolph Eichmann, deportations began and about 440,000 Jews were deported in 145 trains. By July 1944 only the Budapest Jewish community remained, and under the anti-Semitic Ferenc Szálasi's Arrow Cross regime, a reign of terror was launched against the Jews, culminating in 70,000 people living in an area of 0.1 square miles. Less than a third of the 825,000 Jews survived in Hungary that had been temporarily enlarged, beginning in 1938, by its own aggressive conquests of areas in which Hungarians lived. Before these

Reading the Modern European Novel Since 1900: A Critical Study of Major Fiction from Proust's Swann's Way to Ferrante's Neapolitan Tetralogy, First Edition. Daniel R. Schwarz.
© 2018 John Wiley & Sons Ltd. Published 2018 by John Wiley & Sons Ltd.

conquests, Hungary had shrunk after the defeat of Austria-Hungary in World War I; the ensuing Treaty of Trianon in 1920 left Hungary a land-locked country.

Winner of the 2002 Nobel Prize in Literature (the only Hungarian winner to date, although by 2002 Kertész had long left Hungary for Germany), Imre Kertész (1929–2016) was interned in Auschwitz, Buchenwald, and Zeitz for a period totaling about a year, although he has claimed to have spent the entire year in Auschwitz. He lived in Germany but wrote in Hungarian. He published his first novel, *Fateless* or, more correctly, *Fatelessness* (the Hungarian title *Sorstalanság* translates as "Fatelessness"), in 1975, although it was written between 1960 and 1973. Kertész wrote the screenplay for the 2005 Hungarian film *Fateless* based on his book. Since fatelessness is not an English word, the producers no doubt thought *Fateless* was a more appropriate title.

Before he won the Nobel Prize, Kertész was barely recognized in the United States and the novel sold very modestly. When I was researching my book *Imagining the Holocaust* in the late 1990s and trying to identify the most influential texts and films on the Holocaust – and asking for suggestions from colleagues at my university (Cornell) and elsewhere – no one mentioned *Fatelessness*. When, immediately after Kertész was awarded the Nobel Prize, I called Northwestern University Press to order the 1992 Wilson translation of *Fateless*,[2] I was told sales had been minimal and not many copies were in stock. Fortunately I called early enough to get the copies that I needed for my seminar.

Fatelessness – the title of the now standard Wilkinson translation (2004) – renders a year of the life of a Hungarian adolescent named Georg (György) Koves.[3] Georg is not yet fifteen in 1944 when he is conscripted to work for the Germans; very soon afterwards, he is deported to Auschwitz, then after three days in Auschwitz to Buchenwald, then to Zeitz, and back to Buchenwald.

Since many of my readers may not be familiar with what happened in Hungary, I suggest the Oscar-winning documentary film *The Last Days* (1998; directed by James Moll, produced by June Beallor and Kenneth Lipper with Steven Spielberg as executive producer). Featuring the stories of five Hungarian Jews supplemented by accounts of a few Americans who helped liberate the camps, this film helps us understand *Fatelessness*.

The Relevance of *Fatelessness*

We read for many reasons, and one is to complement the lives we live by learning about life in different times and conditions. In this regard, fiction can be as compelling if not more so than history or biography. Notwithstanding its strong autobiographical sources, Kertész rightly insists that *Fatelessness* is a novel, but it is a novel with strong elements of testimony and witness. Kertész implies his role of witness when he discusses *Fatelessness* thirty-eight years after its publication; he wanted both to show how he received his "moral education [under] totalitarianism and [in] concentration camps" and to give his novel a human face: "I created a work representing the Holocaust as such, but without this being an ugly literature of horrors. … I tried to depict the human face of this history, I wanted to write a book that people would actually want to read" (Imre Kertész, "The Art of Fiction No. 220").[4] He believes that "What was at stake [in his work and the work of others writing after the demise of National Socialism, including Jean Améry and Tadeusz Borowski] was the creation of new values from such immense suffering" (ibid.).

Readers invest in creative works for different reasons, and one reason that *Fatelessness* speaks to us is that it speaks to what it is to be deprived of the ordinary choices we in democracies take for granted. Kertész's novel speaks of how an adolescent is wrenched from his comfortable upper-middle-class world and from expectations for his life's trajectory inculcated by his family and culture. He has to re-evaluate every value and emotion he knows.

Today *Fatelessness* is relevant to ethnic cleansing, genocide, autocracies, kleptocracies, and deprivation of human rights and human hopes, including the issues foregrounded in the hope and disappointment of the 2010–2011 Arab Spring and in the lives of victims of totalitarian regimes and terrorism today.

From a Jewish perspective, it is an admonition that one is Jewish because others define anyone of Jewish heritage as Jewish whether they want to be defined that way or not. Internment, Kertész has said, "obliged me to be Jewish. I accept it, but to a large extent it is also true that it was imposed on me."[5]

Kertész disdains what he feels is the tendency to turn the Holocaust into kitsch: "The drive to survive makes us accustomed to lying as much as possible about the murderous reality in which we are forced to hold our own, while the drive to remember seduces us into sneaking a complacent self-satisfaction into our reminiscences, the balsam of self-pity, the martyr's self-glorification."[6] In a more sustained critique, he writes:

. . . .

It is obvious that [in his 1993 film *Schindler's List*] the American Spielberg, who incidentally wasn't even born until after the war, has and can have no idea of the authentic reality of a Nazi concentration camp. Why, then, does he struggle so hard to make his representation of a world he does not know seem authentic in every detail? ... I regard as kitsch any representation of the Holocaust that is incapable of understanding or unwilling to understand the organic connection between our own deformed mode of life ... and the very possibility of the Holocaust. Here I have in mind those representations that seek to establish the Holocaust once and for all as something foreign to human nature; that seek to drive the Holocaust out of the realm of human experience. I would also use the term kitsch to describe those works where Auschwitz is regarded as simply a matter concerning Germans and Jews, and thereby reduced to something like the fatal incompatibility of two groups; when the political and psychological anatomy of modern totalitarianism more generally is disregarded; when Auschwitz is not seen as a universal experience, but reduced to whatever immediately "hits the eye." Apart from this, of course, I regard anything that is kitsch, as kitsch. (Kertész, "Who Owns Auschwitz?")

....

For Kertész, kitsch – a concept used more often in serious discussions of art in Europe than in the United States – means excessive or exaggerated melodrama that provokes sentimentality and lacks self-awareness, complexity or irony. Kitsch (explored by Walter Benjamin) offers instant gratification without calling upon the intellect of the audience and is thus art that is appealing to the masses.[7]

We cannot be sure, but some of the foregoing critique could apply to Elie Wiesel's *Night* (1960). In his *Paris Review* interview, where he does praise Holocaust writers "who were brave enough to stare down this abyss," Wiesel is ostentatiously omitted. Whether or not Kertész is implying that Wiesel's *Night* has an element of kitsch and self-glorification, he does differentiate *Fatelessness* from *Night* (Kertész, "The Art of Fiction No. 220"). Wiesel's autobiographical memoir focuses on his experience as a Hasidic Jew who is the same age as Georg. Taught about God's goodness, young Elie becomes disillusioned by the inexplicable evil of Auschwitz. But for Kertész, the Holocaust is explicable and his secular, assimilated narrator is seeking to find the explanation. However, despite his detailed narrative of what happens to him, his explanations are partial, and he doesn't fully understand the larger historical ramifications.

Kertész demonstrates dramatically how Jewishness was not something one could choose in 1944 Hungary. As the Jews are about to leave Hungary, a gendarme asks them for their valuables since the Germans will confiscate them anyway: "After all, you're Hungarians too when it comes down to it!" (74). But when, after negotiations for exchanging valuables for water fail, the gendarme excoriates them: "Stinking Jew! ... Die of thirst, then" (74).

The Artistry of *Fatelessness*

Fatelessness is much more than an important history lesson. It is a narrative in which the self-dramatizing teller strikingly fails to move from immersion to full reflection and speaks even at the end from the limited perspective of aporia or undecidability. Kertész explains why he uses a young boy as his narrator:

> I invented the boy precisely because anyone in a dictatorship is kept in a childlike state of ignorance and helplessness. For that reason, I not only had to create a specific style and form, but I had to pay close attention to temporality. ... [I]f you tell the story of a child, you have to conceive of a temporality that is appropriate, for a child has no agency in his own life and is forced to endure all. (Kertész, "The Art of Fiction No. 220")

What is different about Kertész's text from other Holocaust texts? *Fatelessness* is a unique fictional rendering of the Holocaust from the point of view of an adolescent experiencing arrest by being pulled off a bus in Budapest, living in several different concentration camps, falling critically ill, finally being released, and returning home a totally different person. He cannot relate to those who haven't had his experience in the irrational camp universe. What differentiates *Fatelessness* from other Holocaust first person novels and memoirs is the lack of a retrospective adult perspective.

Kertész uses resonances of Kafka – whom he praised in his Nobel Prize speech[8] – in placing a character in uncanny circumstances for which he is unprepared. The eyes of Kertész's adolescent speaker become the readers' eyes. What we see is a dramatization of how Georg stayed alive by means of his adaptability, practicality, resilience, resourcefulness, resolve, and luck. After he is freed, we experience the cost of his experience in dislocation and estrangement.

The novel's nine chapters follow stages in Georg's education and resemble a traditional Bildungsroman, except here the education is into the concentration camp universe. Everything Georg knows is turned upside down. He compares his concentration camp days to the most tedious of his former days and yearns for them. What he has taken for granted about middle-class comforts in terms of food, clothes, sleep, and freedom of movement become part of his camp re-education, a radical transvaluation of everything he has known. He learns to rely on his imagination as his "means of escape" (155) since the other possibilities – failure to meet roll call while sleeping, hiding, or trying to escape the camps – could result in physical punishment or, in the case of attempts to escape, death. Learning that "the confines of prison walls cannot impose boundaries on the flights of one's fantasy" helps him survive (157), although in chapter seven when he is ill he does flirt with giving up and "letting himself go" (172). But, finally, notwithstanding illness and depression, his resilience and tenacity combined with luck enable him to survive.

Kertész creates a narrator who is at first naïve, composed, and relies upon rationality to understand what is happening to him. At times he seems detached, almost anesthetized as if he is describing what happened to a third party, but his ability to cope, to find solace, even happiness, in camp routines, to take one day – even one hour – at a time saves him. As is the case in Primo Levi's *Survival at Auschwitz*, very basic medical care at opportune times also keeps him alive. In part, Kertész wrote *Fatelessness* to understand why he survived and to put that very partial understanding first into words and then, by editing, into narrative form; "I think a man turns into a writer by editing his own texts. Writing changed my life. It has an existential dimension, and that's the same for every writer. Every artist has a moment of awakening, of happening upon an idea that grabs hold of you, regardless of whether you are a painter or a writer" (Kertész, "The Art of Fiction No. 220").

Georg doesn't have a religious tradition or the presence of his father; unlike Levi he is not a worldly and educated adult with such cultural resources as the memory of Dante's *Inferno* and the figure of Ulysses who survives by his wiles and perseverance before succumbing to pride and taking his followers on a fatal second voyage. Unlike Tadeusz Borowski's non-Jewish Polish narrators, Georg is not a kapo or a medical orderly with special privileges. Nor is Georg a political prisoner, like Borowski's narrators in *This Way for the Gas, Ladies and Gentleman*, who, because they are not Jewish, do not have "selection" for the gas chambers hovering constantly over their heads as the ultimate threat and fear.

In the last pages, Georg, still an adolescent, has made an existential commitment to staying alive – but not to either personal or historical values. We as readers sit on the borderland between experiencing Georg's narrowly focalized rendering of the Holocaust and realizing that the mature Kertész is taking a somewhat ironic view of the younger man, a surrogate for the writer's younger self. Kertész wants us to understand that the young Georg is unable to synthesize fully what he has learned, but that he is making progress addressing "our own deformed mode of [human] life" in the camps. A fierce pessimism underlies Kertész's narrator, but also an awareness that surviving is an act of hope and possibility: "I am already feeling a growing and accumulating readiness to continue my uncontinuable life" (262).

How *Fatelessness* Begins: Entering Georg's World

Kertész's novel begins with a powerful and brilliantly crafted opening chapter. As with many Holocaust novels and memoirs, the novel begins with a radical disruption of the comfortable life in which the protagonist has been living and his or her halting and sometimes clumsy efforts to respond to the conditions of a far different new life. We see this in Wiesel's *Night* and Levi's *Survival at Auschwitz*. Georg's very first words take us readers into the seemingly bland and innocuous present: "I didn't go to school today." Only gradually do we realize that we are listening to a monologue of an unnamed adolescent boy who is becoming aware that he is caught in the terrifying grip of the Holocaust (3).

Rereading, we see how the very anonymity of the confused narrator transforms him into a representative figure whose personal freedom is erased by historical fate. He cannot put the past behind him. Thus upon release from the camps he exists in a no-man's land between the grim fate he has encountered and memories of his former freedom.

The speaker, an assimilated Jewish Hungarian who pays little attention to religion, acknowledges that he really is not sure what is going on when his father turns over his business to Mr. Suto, a former bookkeeper and manager – who "does not wear a yellow star" – without the drawing up of a contract (5). Baffled by what he has observed, Georg recalls how "I didn't understand at first what they were talking about" (6). A marginally attentive adolescent mostly worried about the immediate effects of events on himself, he is alternately bored by the process of his father's departure the next day and aware that something cataclysmic is occurring. For example, he realizes that Mr. Suto "has, in a sense, risen to a higher status than us" (5).

Indeed, at first the speaker does not locate himself in a particular place. We learn that his name is Georg Koves and that he is fourteen. Georg doesn't have much affect as he describes his and his extended family's response to his father's plight. While one could attribute some of the anomie Georg is describing to the older teller whose capacity for feeling has been destroyed, Kertész also wants to place us in the very present Georg confronts as his world is turned upside down. Without emotion, Georg offers us an almost clinical description of events that he cannot grasp and does so as if they were happening to people he barely knew. He doesn't quite understand what it means for his father to have been "called up for labor service" (3).

By the second chapter, Georg himself is caught in the maelstrom of a present he cannot understand. With historical foreknowledge of what will probably occur, we modern-day readers look backward with anxiety and compassion. Kertész's point is that Georg survives, as Georg himself says, one step at a time. Because we know the historical events of the 1940s, we know in general terms what is going to happen even as Georg reveals how he and his family are being economically, culturally, and physically marginalized and ostracized by the Nazis.

Georg cannot find the tools to understand fully what is going on personally or politically. He doesn't tell us what is happening in Budapest, only what is happening to him. He can't tell us because he doesn't know. Kertész wants to create that state of not knowing and the gradual discovery of knowing from the focal point of the adolescent boy. At first Georg seems almost anesthetized as if unwilling to face the reality in which he finds himself. Yet he realizes that he needs to display his yellow star at all times. We readers know that "amusement" is not quite the word he is looking for to describe "going around" wearing the yellow star that Jews must wear: "[L]ater on, I no longer took any notice of it" (9–10). But Kertész wants us to see that Georg, confronting the uncanny, is striving to find a comfortable attitude towards his puzzling new experiences as well as the words to describe what is happening to him.

What Kertész does is dramatize the process of discovery when an adolescent's personal life becomes part of a terrible and inevitable historical process. We cannot be sure of an exact correlation between Kertész's life and that of his character, but we can assume that by creating his ingenuous adolescent gradually awakening to what is happening, Kertész finds a surrogate for his own youthful combination of constrained anger, frustration, and cynicism.

While telling his story, Georg has not only the camps in mind but also the entire experience in which his perspective of what life is has permanently changed. Yet at the same time Georg is narrowly focused on his own day-to-day concerns and transforms the extraordinary into the ordinary as a way of coping. His insouciance becomes something of a survival tool as he confronts one inexplicable horror after another. That he responds to his immediate experience along with drawing upon the three R's – resourcefulness, resolve, and resilience – stands him in good stead in his odyssey through the camps. Ironically, his resistance to generalizing what he experiences to the point where he becomes (or perhaps we should say remains) emotionally and morally anesthetized enables him to maintain a strong will and to survive. His epistemological naïveté – what might be called his somewhat underdeveloped categorizing sensibility – is a condition of Georg's life at fourteen, and may be a condition, in Kertész's view, of adolescence. By the novel's end, we realize that because of Georg's intense experience of the Holocaust abyss, combined with his relative inexperience, ingenuousness, and lack of knowledge of so much else, Georg may never emerge from the tentative position of partial and narrow knowing. That is, with a kind of tunnel vision he knows the horror of the Holocaust personally in terms of his own experience, but he does not know much historically. But his tunnel vision allows him to extricate himself enough from the web of history to assert his freedom to continue his life.

With his father's departure, Georg is about to lose his custodial parent and be consigned to his stepmother with whom he feels uncomfortable. Perhaps his deference to adults and the self-control that disguises his emotions are the effects of his being caught in a tense divorce and custody dispute which has left him living with his father and stepmother and feeling guilty about not being with his mother. Of his parents' divorce, he says: "In truth, though, I had never managed to figure out anything more precise" (26), adding in chapter two, "as best I know the court awarded in my father's favour" (30). That he doesn't always understand his own feelings, and is on the whole reticent in the company of adults, is perhaps the result of the awkward position he feels with both his parents and his stepmother.

In 1975, Kertész presents the historical irony of Hungarian Jews in 1944 responding inadequately to what is happening to their fellow Jews. At a family gathering in the evening before Georg's father's departure his stepmother's cousin, Uncle Willie, assures the family that an "absolutely reliable" "confidential source" (17) had informed him that the Germans were using the Budapest Jews "'to wring advantages, at our expense, out of the Allies,' who, of course, would do all they could for us" (18); "shocked" "world opinion" would, according to Uncle Willie, play a role and he was "quite confident" that Georg's father "would soon be back home" (18–19). Uncle Willie has the optimism of those Jews who continued to rationalize what was occurring because of their humanistic faith in a decent orderly world.

By contrast, the religious Uncle Lajos, his stepmother's oldest brother, tells Georg that he needs to understand "today" was the end of "the carefree, happy years of childhood" (19). He is mistakenly assuming that Georg is thinking the same; of course, naïve Georg is not thinking that his childhood has ended. According to Uncle Lajos, the "Jewish fate" was God's punishment "meted out ... for their past sins" (20). While bafflement enters into the boy's response to Uncle Lajos's argument, he is not oblivious to Uncle Lajos's apocalyptic prophecy: "Though I did not quite follow the train of thought that had led up to this ... I still grasped somehow what he was driving at" (20). He is even more puzzled by his sharing a Hebrew prayer with his uncle: "I was a bit put out by not understanding a single word of what we were saying to God" (21).

Georg's self-dramatizing narrative alternates the present with occasional moments of retrospection. For example, he speaks of Uncle Willie's "wishful ponderings" (18). Speaking in the past tense he is "not sure" whether he said goodbye to his father or vice versa: "I don't even clearly remember the circumstances; ... I no longer remember now what I promised Father" (25–26). As he and his father are alone on the evening before he leaves, he doesn't "know if my tears stemmed from that or simply from exhaustion," but he knows his father was pleased (26).

The second chapter begins in the present two weeks after Georg is assigned to "a permanent work-place" at the Shell Petroleum Refinery Works (28). When Uncle Lajos tells him that he must be on his best behavior because he is representing "the entire Jewish community," Kertész expects us to see the irony of Georg's comment: "That would truly have never occurred to me; still, I realized that he might well be right, of course" (29). For Kertész knew, as Georg learns, that individual Jews are perceived in terms of stereotypes and qualities found in a few are assigned generically to all.

Kertész may be thinking of Anne Frank's *Diary of a Young Girl* – another major paradigmatic Holocaust work he does not praise (or mention) in the *Paris Review* interview and which seems to fulfill his definition of kitsch – by using the present tense. He may be offering a gentle critique of Anne's occasional naïveté and ingenuousness as well as of her humanistic conclusions that have received a great deal of world attention: "In spite of everything I still believe that people are really good at heart. I simply can't build up my hopes on a foundation consisting of confusion, misery, and death. … [I]f I look up into the heavens, I think that it will all come right, that this cruelty too will end, and that peace and tranquility will return again."[9] Like Anne, Georg is caught between two parents and is puzzled by the so-called wisdom of adults. Like Anne, Georg has a flirtation, in his case with Annamarie, who is more experienced sexually. Annamarie's sexual precocity, like Anne's, may be related to the pressure of historical circumstances, but we can't be sure that this is true of either young woman.

More substantive is the scene Georg and Annamarie share with two Jewish sisters in which all four discuss the implications of wearing the star of David and of being defined by "differentness" (36). Kertész includes this vital scene to show how the Nazis forced the insouciant adolescents to recognize their difference and how painful was their discovery that Jewishness is not, for those who hate Jews, a religion but a race. Georg feels the same mixture of pride and shame that the elder Jewish sister feels. Kertész emphasizes the naïveté of Georg's thinking, even while recognizing that the reader will feel empathy for his innocent and circular reasoning: "[A] person can't decide for himself on his differentness; in the end, that is precisely what the yellow star is there for, as far as I know" (36). Georg relies on trying to reason when reason doesn't work.

The third chapter two months later is a matter-of-fact, past-tense narration of his capture and deportation as Georg is going to work on the very next day. Kertész uses the bathetic irony of how Georg perceives the events in contrast to what is actually happening. When Jews are ordered off a bus taking him to work, he responds, "Ah well, I thought to myself, no doubt they want to do a spot-check on the papers of everyone going across [the bridge]" (40). It was as if they were going to summer camp. That he and the other Jewish boys can't imagine what is in store for them is a source of painful pathos to the reader; indeed, the boys at first think it is quite hilarious and fun that they are pulled off the bus. They are taken to a Customs House where, as they wait not knowing what is next, "plenty of jokes were cracked," jacks were played, and someone teaches the other boys a song (44).

In elaborate sentences and long paragraphs, as if probing his memory and bringing those days alive, Georg recreates a harrowing present-tense account of what it was like to be in the camps. Rather than have Georg give us historical contexts or philosophic and moral overviews, Kertész renders the adolescent speaker's limited perspective as he responds to his experience. In a sense there is a diary aspect to the way the boy presents immediate events without the full introspective weight of an adult. To be sure, we are on occasion reminded that he is looking back, but his perspective seems to be right after his release and return to Budapest rather than from a later adulthood: "I too recall the first day [in Auschwitz, his first camp] most precisely, and more precisely indeed, when I think about it, than I do the days that followed" (101). Irony gives way to self-pity, but never to the point where he gives up. Moreover, his pride takes a back seat to acceptance of hard conditions and even humiliation, and his poise evaporates in the face of immersion in the grotesque rituals of survival at all costs.

While reading, we do not come to a time when Georg reaches adulthood and looks back. At first, we experience his adolescent perspective; he is absorbed in the seeming importance of the minutiae of a fourteen-year-old's middle-class life. Kertész enacts Georg's confusion, puzzlement, and, in later chapters after his release, his detachment from the world that didn't share his trauma and could not fathom what he has seen and knows. Sometimes Georg seeks refuge in flipness and efforts at humor, as when he critiques his education for not teaching him about Auschwitz: "I ought to have been learning all along exclusively about Auschwitz. Everything would have been explained, openly, honestly, reasonably" (113). If occasionally we think that the narrator lacks affect, isn't this because he is somewhat traumatized by his experience? Even though he may believe that he has freed himself from his historical fate by surviving, we see that he has not; in fact, he suffers from what we now call post-traumatic stress.

Auschwitz, Buchenwald, Zeitz, and Back to Buchenwald

Very much like Joseph K. in Kafka's *The Trial*, Georg, the young adolescent, often describes his experience and reveals his feelings but is not aware of the historical contexts which define those experiences. Like Joseph K. Georg is baffled by the situations in which he finds himself and responds without much foresight, hindsight, or awareness of larger patterns. Georg is treated as a criminal but doesn't feel guilty. He does not have much sense of his Jewishness, yet he is punished for being a Jew or what he terms "on account of … his bloodline" (103). After arriving at Auschwitz, he recalls, in one of his presumably retrospective moments shortly after his release: "I still considered myself to be what I call a sort of guest in captivity … in full accordance with the propensity to delusion that we all share and which is thus, I suppose, ultimately part of human nature" (101–102). Despite the strong effect of Auschwitz on Georg's memory, he spends only three full days there before being put on a train for Buchenwald (120).

We see in the above passage a stylistic idiosyncrasy, which will become more prominent as Georg's narrative proceeds, namely a wordiness ("I suppose") and a tendency to mime thought processes as if he were trying to discover what he means. Why, we ask, doesn't he simply say "in full accordance with human nature"? We begin to understand that his evasions, disclaimers, bleak matter-of-fact descriptions of incomprehensible horrors are part of the way he comes to terms with experience. Yet his fumbling for the right language to share experiences that resist language also enacts his lack of guile.

The purpose of Kertész's having Georg describe these three days in such detail is that it provides a paradigm for the selection experience through the eyes of an ingenuous observer. Long graphic paragraphs gradually trace the process of Georg's discovering what is going on in gruesome detail: "In truth it slowly became clear that the chimney stack over the way … was not actually a tannery but the chimney of a 'crematorium,' a place where corpses are reduced to ashes, as we were told the word meant" (108). We readers see how the sentence dramatizes – "in truth," "actually," "as we were told" – Georg's simultaneous resistance and recognition and the struggle between the two.

The more we read, the more stylistic surprises and incongruities we find. Indeed, rereading we see that what is uncanny is the telling as much as what is told. For example, when Kertész renders Georg's impressionistic response to his physical environment on entering the hospital at Buchenwald, it is as if Georg were an infant discovering his surroundings: "You can take a look around you, inspect things, get your bearings a little. … You may work out that this tint, this impression caressing your eyes, is actually the all-pervasive dark red color of some gleamingly lacquered material of the floorboards" (201). Why does Kertész have Georg switch to the second person plural here? Perhaps to dramatize a different kind of consciousness now that he is ill, the pronoun shift is accompanied by a response to sensory phenomena but little ratiocinative activity.

We realize that Georg is describing the process – perhaps in an intensified version – of his discovery of conditions each time he is moved. It is this ability to take the measure of a new place and adjust to it that is the major reason that he survives.

Kertész uses his narrator, Georg, to present a grim travelogue of concentration camps. This travelogue gives Kertész the opportunity to include the paradigmatic extermination camp, Auschwitz, with its crematorium and foul-smelling smoke; Buchenwald where Georg is put to work; and Zeitz – a satellite camp of Buchenwald and one in which mostly Hungarians were imprisoned – as well as the transport trains.

Kertész keeps his distance from his speaker; he knows – and so do we – what the speaker is learning. The speaker is a kind of Candide, seeing the best of all possible worlds – or perhaps a Don Quixote figure who is deluded about what is happening. He agrees to be transported to a work detail: "What I could look forward to from working, though, was above all orderliness, employment, new impressions, and a bit of fun – all in all, a more sensible lifestyle more to my liking than the one here in Hungary, just as was being promised. ... [I]t also crossed my mind that this might also be a way of getting to see a bit of the world" (64). When Georg is taken off the bus and arrested, he seemed unusually ingenuous and "felt a bit like laughing, in part out of astonishment and confusion," and in part because he imagines his "step-mother's face" when he doesn't turn up "for supper this evening" (57).

Kertész expects the reader to recognize the distinction between what we know about the Holocaust and what little his speaker knows. Auschwitz is where the boy enters a universe totally different from anything he has experienced, but one which we and Kertész know well. Is there gentle irony on Kertész's part in Georg's being in Auschwitz only three and a half days rather than an extended stay and thinking he can take the full measure of a camp where inhabitants were either gassed or, for months or even in some cases for years, were worked to death or near death? The artlessness of the boy is poignant. After seeing for the first time in his life "real convicts, in the striped duds of criminals," he is a puzzled visitor to an incomprehensible world. When he first sees "convicts" and "prisoners," he thinks, "I would have been curious to know what offenses they committed" (82).

Only later does Georg realize that he is judged guilty of a racial crime that he shares with the others, even though he had once thought himself physically different and more attractive than Jews. He had remarked with supercilious disdain upon those Jews who met his transport: "Their faces did not exactly inspire confidence either: jug ears, prominent noses, sunken, beady eyes with a crafty gleam. Quite like Jews in every respect. I found them suspect, and altogether foreign-looking" (78). What we realize – but Georg doesn't – is that these are desperate men deprived of food, sleep, and human dignity. Georg's knowledge of German helps him understand their Yiddish and that saves him; he learns that he must claim to be sixteen to be considered a potential worker. He naïvely trusts the handsome, "cultured" German doctor in charge of selecting workers for the "fit group" without realizing that the gas chambers are the alternative (86).

One of the defenses that serves Georg well is that he domesticates and normalizes what he sees into the ken of his own understanding. Note how often he uses the word "naturally," especially – but no means exclusively – when he encounters Auschwitz and in particular the selection process. It is as if he were resisting the inexplicable and uncanny procedures he is observing, procedures where the fit boys over sixteen become workers and most others are sent for gassing. The proliferation of "naturally" derives from his resistance to the incomprehensible and irrational in what he observes.

That many of his naïve judgments are imperceptive and myopic helps Georg adjust to the circumstances in which he finds himself. He judges from his fourteen- and later fifteen-year-old upper-middle-class perspective. He at first distances himself from Jews, many of whom are religious, speak Yiddish, and are physically unfit, and thinks of the German soldiers he sees when arriving in Auschwitz as "smart and trim, the sole anchors of solidity and calm in the whole tumult" (80). He sides with those who think they should be "cutting questions and goodbyes short, within reason, so as not to give the Germans the impression of such a rabble" (80). We readers of course see the folly of his views.

What Kertész stresses is the banality of evil; he also stresses that Georg survives because of his ingenuous belief that what happens is not catastrophic but a sequence of explicable events. The boy reifies and domesticates his response to Germans to contexts that approach normality. By not thinking of the Germans as other but rather as fellow human beings, they become less frightening. Their "air of scornful composure and invulnerability all at once made the kind of respect with which the Germans were normally spoken of … more clearly comprehensible. … [T]hey did not strike me as the slightest bit intimidating; they were ambling up and down in leisurely fashion, … answering questions, nodding, even cordially patting some of us on the back or shoulder" (83).

Kertész expects us to see how the secular Georg seeks Enlightenment logic to find explanations that fit into the presumption of a rational world – contrary to Wiesel in *Night* who sought religious explanations – in which he had been educated. Georg discovers by trial and error that there is no explanation for the concatenation of events that befall him. The novel's fundamental paradox is the dramatization of Georg's tunnel vision in the context of historical events beyond both his knowledge and comprehension. A second paradox is the apparent simplicity of his response narrated in complicated sentences – no doubt intentionally on Kertész's part – that are so different from Wiesel's trenchant, spare telling. Georg's often circumlocutious sentences speak to the young narrator's confusion and desperate effort to make sense of what is happening and in the final chapter – but elsewhere to a lesser extent – to its significance.

The narrator doesn't fully succumb to the concentration camp universe, but lives at times on the borderline between the inside and outside world.

At times he rebels against his own detachment and exhibits a grim humor about how the camps came to be. But it is a humor deriving from his own limited life experience: "After all, people would have had to meet to discuss [the selection process he encounters at Auschwitz, with the bathhouse and gassing], put their heads together, so to say, even if they were not exactly students, but mature adults, quite possibly – indeed, in all likelihood – gentlemen in imposing suits, decorations on their chests, cigars in their mouths, presumably all in high command, who were not disturbed right then – that is how I imagined it" (111).

Notwithstanding his attempt at irony, Georg presents a reductive cartoon vision of how adult decisions are made. Kertész expects us to see the greater irony in an adolescent – and one with limited experience and historical knowledge – describing how the Nazis operated. Part of the noir humor is that the speaker's language is under-determined as opposed to the over-determined language of, say, Jerzy Kosiński's speaker in *A Painted Bird* where excessive descriptions of sexual violence, xenophobia, and torture undermine the effect. Here we want the boy to respond more vigorously, passionately, angrily, and his failure to do so borders on the uncanny and inexplicable.

Before long Georg is immersed in the world of captivity, especially at his third camp, Zeitz (following three days in Auschwitz and some months in Buchenwald), where his strength and ability to cope begin to unravel. He knows that "[N]owhere is a certain discipline, a certain exemplariness, I might even say virtue, in one's conduct of life as obviously important as it is in captivity" (137). But in the face of hunger and illness, Georg cannot sustain the discipline. He gradually becomes what is called a "Muslim" – those who have completely succumbed – and loses much of his self-respect: "I was alive: even if only guttering and, as it were, turned down to the very lowest mark, a flicker of life nevertheless burned within me as they say, or to put it another way, my body was here, I had precise cognizance of everything about it, it was just that I myself somehow no longer inhabited it" (184). As he spirals downward, he engages in more circumlocutions ("and, as it were," "to put it another way"), hesitations ("as they say," "somehow") that impede the forward progress of his thought and enact how language is resisting his efforts to recall the horrors of the camps and to articulate his feelings.

As Georg drifts into illness, the enervated language of fatigue and inertia mime his depression. When he was transferred to a new hospital, time is again defined by the routines of his illness: "[H]ere too time had started to elapse, and in essentially the same manner as at the previous place, with only minor differences" (180). At this stage, Kertész creates for Georg a detached, evasive, wordy style which mirrors how his mind has lost its precision and lucidity and much of the time exists in a kind of miasma.

Georg becomes more repetitious. At the outset of chapter seven, he recalls, "I too found peace, tranquility and relief" (171), but what he describes is depression and virtually giving up. He ceases to care if he is beaten for such infractions as sitting down at roll call. Some pages later he virtually repeats himself: "[I]t had been a long time since I had felt so easy, tranquil, almost lost in reverie – so comfortable" (185). He is no longer proudly holding himself apart, measuring his time, and using the monotony of routine – such as looking forward to the time after work and the evening soup – to structure his life.

We understand the irony of chapter nine when we recall that the "peace, tranquility and relief" Georg felt in chapter seven was close to his giving up. When he has suffered the worst, something slightly better seems acceptable; thus Buchenwald – his last stop before being freed – plays the role of offering minimum comfort and care. After expecting to die and awaiting death, he concludes chapter seven: "I would like to live a little bit longer in this beautiful concentration camp" (189). No doubt because the Germans knew that the Allies' arrival was imminent, they took better care of their prisoners during the last days of Buchenwald.

Return to Budapest: Fatelessness within History's Fateful Web

In the last chapter Georg returns to Budapest, alienated from the world in which he now finds himself. Because of his year in the camps, his world is far different from the one he has left behind. Georg can never go home because he has been transformed by his internment. He thinks of his older uncles as "old boys" – not men – as if his experience makes him older than everyone who has not shared that experience (256).

With both understanding and irony, Kertész presents Georg's anger and frustration as well as Georg's narrowness of vision when the latter returns to Budapest. What, the novel asks, is the meaning of "freedom" if history overwhelms us? If "we are fate" (260), that is if we are caught in history's maelstrom, is there any existential freedom? The answer in *Fatelessness* is a very tentative and much qualified affirmative because there is a scintilla of freedom in every step Georg took and in every moment in which he survived.

He takes umbrage at whatever is said to him. When questioned by a journalist, he answers with one or two words. He resists having his experience generalized or politicized or historicized. When the journalist gives him his address, he "tossed the slip of paper away" (252).

Georg's experiences in the camps radically pull him from his (and our customary) sense of time – a sense that offers pleasurable moments of fullness when we are not aware of the tick tock of passing time – into a new sense of time where only the next minute matters. Paradoxically, if one conceives time in terms of one forward step following another, it becomes less chronological and more spatial.

Nor does he recover his former sense of perceiving time when he is released and returns to Budapest. Georg uses the metaphor of movement, one existential step at a time, as a mode of survival: "Everyone took steps as long as he was able to take a step; I too took my own steps" (258). For one thing Georg – like his creator – rejects the role of witness and wants to simply take the next step in his life: "[E]verything becomes clear only gradually, sequentially over time, step-by-step. By the time one has passed a given step, put it behind one, the next one is already there" (249). One makes choices of events, and this is how, to echo Sartre, we wrench being from nothingness: "I took the steps, no one else, and I declared that I had been true to my given fate throughout" (259).

Georg does not want to be part of an historical argument or philosophical or moral generalizations; yet he knows he cannot resume his life as if the dreadful events had not happened. He seems to be opting for existential freedom in a world where that is impossible. For he knows that his life was co-opted by events and that the release from historical inevitability is more a wish than a possibility: "I too had lived through a given fate. It had not been my own fate, but I had lived through it. ... I now needed to start doing something with that fate, needed to connect it to somewhere or something; after all, I could no longer be satisfied with the notion that it had all been mistake, blind fortune, some kind of blunder, let alone that it had never happened" (259).

Fatelessness is ironically an impossible yet desired condition of freedom that we can never reach. Fatelessness (or Fateless) also is a term that describes the indeterminate interlude between when Georg is extricated from the inevitable fateful forces of the Holocaust and when he begins to have the opportunity to create a new narrative. But Kertész expects us to understand that no one can fully make his own destiny. He realizes that by the time he wrote *Fatelessness* Hungary and its denizens, despite the 1956 uprising, were firmly shaped by Hungary's place as a satellite in the USSR's orbit.

But there is another important meaning of fatelessness. The concept of fatelessness seems to imply loss of control over one's life, to be cast into the abyss even as it paradoxically means the freedom to escape the inevitability of history. Gradually the speaker loses his ironic detachment and becomes depressed, despairing, and even loses his pride if not his interest in surviving. The loss of control troubles him because it makes us no more than cogs in history's wheel. He rejects the term "came about" to describe events because it takes away the role of human agency in creating what befell him: "[W]e had gone along with it too" (257). By "we" he means Jews and perhaps also Hungarians. But the reader draws a circle of judgment around Georg and realizes that his freedom – and that of the Jews in Hungary and in the rest of Europe – to have taken a different direction was not there. When Georg concludes that his uncles "had known, foreseen, everything beforehand" (260), Uncle Fleischmann objects that Georg is blaming his fellow Jews for what happened to them, and we are as sympathetic to Georg's accusation – implying the naïveté and blindness of the Hungarian Jews in 1944 – as we are to Uncle Fleischmann's objection.

Furthermore, the self-dramatizing telling demonstrates how, whatever Georg intended, he is pulled back to the experience he wants to leave behind. Fate triumphs over fatelessness; put another way, historical determinism shapes our lives. Georg's mind resists finding the words, even as Kertész does find them by writing his novel based on his memories. Although he claims, "I didn't notice any atrocities," he certainly has presented atrocities not only in Auschwitz, but also later when he is ill and hungry in Zeitz. One could argue that once Georg accepts the concentration camp universe, atrocity takes on a new meaning. But we realize that in his view such a large wall separates those who haven't had his experiences from those who have that he simply refuses to let them enter into his world. When his Uncle Fleischmann tells him, "[Y]ou must put the horrors behind you," he asks, "Why should I?" and "made the comment that what had happened had happened and … I couldn't give order to my memory" (256).

In Kertész's view, history is fate, and fate is the river in which we each must swim. After Georg returns to Budapest, starting a new life is impossible: "I would only be able to start a new life, I ventured, if I were reborn or if some affliction, disease, or something of that sort were to affect my mind" (256). Isn't Georg responding, like Sartre, to the shibboleth of Western humanism that "A man's character is his fate," which is attributed to Heraclitus in *On the Universe*? Yet for Kertész fate is actuality and fatelessness a dream, for there is only so much we can do to make our own destiny and choices in the face of history.

Now he argues that our lives are time-defined. When we look back we can see how our lives are "finished, unalterable, finite, so tremendously fast, and so terribly opaque" (257). When experiencing our lives, we are "fateless" moving one step after another through time, sometimes with little control as when transports arrive at Auschwitz; there, each individual moves toward the place where who will live and who will die is decided by the Germans in charge: "Now, all this time the queue is constantly moving, progressing, and everyone is taking steps, bigger or smaller ones, depending on what the speed of the operations demands" (257).

Kertész expects his reader to see the poignant irony of Georg's conclusion that he ought to speak about "the happiness of the concentration camps" (262).

Kertész wants us to understand that in context of the dire concentration camp universe, where death is pervasive, simply breathing itself is a kind of happiness. Perhaps he also wants us to realize that for a fifteen-year-old boy who has lived Georg's life, happiness is simply his awareness of himself as alive.

The narrator's contradictions and paradoxes are part of his adolescent confusion. He has become caught in the fateful web of history where his existential choices narrow to a moment-to-moment commitment to stay alive, and even that resilience and resolve falters in the face of the inevitability of the Nazis' treatment of Jews.

Georg's anger derives from his belief that his uncles don't understand either how he intends to overcome anomie or his desire to make an existential commitment to taking the next step. He desires to salvage his own identity and be "neither winner or loser," because "I was neither the cause nor the effect of anything" (260). Even within the "torments" of his internment, there were "intervals" and "something that resembled happiness," for he was alive (262). And that knowledge sustains him as he seeks to find positional assurance by balancing the possibilities of the future with the awareness that he can't leave the past behind: "I was already feeling a growing and accumulating readiness to continue my uncontinuable life" (262).

Conclusion

Fatelessness depends on keeping the reader off balance and inviting him to both empathize and on occasion question Georg's responses. *Fatelessness* resists an allegorical reading because Kertész's narrator insists on reporting his particular experience without continually giving it a moral dimension. It is his story rather than the story of the Jews in Hungary or in Europe. Kertész does not want this narrator-protagonist to be regarded as a paradigm or an example. Georg has told us how his life changed and how he survived. Some texts – and not just Holocaust texts – want us to see a clearly defined moral lesson but this one does not. *Fatelessness* lives in the particular, the nominalistic, the idiosyncratic, the implausible, the uncanny. Even the lessons Georg learns are *his* lessons; thinking back on the last pages of his conversation with the older sister (of the two he and Annamarie are visiting) two months after his father has been sent away and the day before he himself is interned, he asserts: "I would now be able to tell [the older sister] what it means to be 'Jewish.' … None of it is true, there is no different blood, nothing else, only … and I faltered" (258–250). Perhaps the only explanation for Georg is that there is no explanation for what happened, and perhaps Kertész wants to leave it at that.

Study Questions for *Fatelessness*

1. How would you characterize the character and psyche of the evolving narrative persona?
2. Why did Kertész choose to make the narrator an assimilated fourteen-year-old Hungarian middle-class Jew?
3. What is the meaning of the title?
4. Given that Georg only spent three days in Auschwitz, why is so much space given to describing that camp?
5. What is the significance of the ending? From what vantage point is it told?
6. Why does the speaker in the last chapter claim that he had some happy days in the camps? What has he learned from his experience?
7. Why is this novel so powerful? Does it deserve the recognition – it is no doubt the main reason Kertész won the Noble Prize in Literature in 2002 – that it has received? Why?
8. How would you compare the book with *Fateless*, Lajos Koltai's 2005 film of Kertész's novel, for which Kertész wrote the script?
9. What recurring themes from other texts discussed in this volume do we see here and what recurring ethical issues? In what ways does the novel parallel Müller's *The Hunger Angel* and Kafka's *The Metamorphosis*?
10. If you have had experience with other major Holocaust narratives, how would you compare Kertész's narrative strategies in *Fatelessness* to Wiesel's *Night*, Levi's *Survival at Auschwitz*, and Borowski's stories?
11. To what extent, to understand *Fatelessness*, do we need to know about Hungary's history in the first half of the twentieth century, and especially the World War II years, as well as to know about Kertész's biography? That is, do we need to historicize?

Notes

1. Trans. John MacKay, *Yale Journal of Criticism* 14.1 (2001), 267–272.
2. *Fatelessness* was originally published in the USA as *Fateless*, trans. Christopher C. Wilson and Katharina Wilson (Evanston, IL: Northwestern University Press, 1992; orig. Hungarian ed, 1975).
3. Imre Kertész, *Fatelessness*, trans. Tim Wilkinson (New York: Vintage, 2004). Page numbers are from this edition.
4. Imre Kertész, "The Art of Fiction No. 220." Interview by Luisa Zielinski. *Paris Review* 205 (Summer 2013); https://www.theparisreview.org/interviews/6235/imre-kertesz-the-art-of-fiction-no-220-imre-kertesz
5. Kertész, in a 2001 interview with the Spanish daily newspaper *El País*, quoted in Jonathan Kandell, "Imre Kertész, Nobel Laureate Who Survived Holocaust, Dies at 86," *New York Times* (March 31, 2016); http://www.nytimes.com/2016/04/01/world/europe/imre-kertesz-dies.html

6. Quoted from "Who Owns Auschwitz?" in Adrienne Kertzer, "Reading Imre Kertész in English," in *Imre Kertész and Holocaust Literature*, eds. Louise O. Vasvári and Steven Tötösy de Zepetnek (West Lafayette, IN: Purdue University Press, 2005), 121.
7. See Walter Benjamin, "The Work of Art in the Age of Mechanical Reproduction," in *Illuminations*, ed. Hannah Arendt, trans. Harry Zohn (New York: Harcourt, Brace & World, 1968).
8. Imre Kertész, Nobel Lecture. *Nobel Prize* (2002); https://www.nobelprize.org/nobel_prizes/literature/laureates/2002/kertesz-lecture.html
9. May 3, 1944, 237, in Anne Frank, *The Diary of a Young Girl*, trans. B. M. Mooyaart-Doubleday with an intro. by Eleanor Roosevelt (New York: Doubleday, 1952).

Chapter 10

Milan Kundera's *The Unbearable Lightness of Being* (1984): History as Fate

"A novel examines not life but existence."

Milan Kundera, "On the Art of the Novel"[1]

Introduction

Every time I reread *The Unbearable Lightness of Being* I make new discoveries about its complexity, subtlety, and originality. On first reading, *The Unbearable Lightness of Being* may seem to be overly focused on sex and Russia's – then called the USSR – invasion of Czechoslovakia after the political liberation of the Prague Spring. But upon each rereading, we see that, notwithstanding some faults that I will discuss later, Kundera's novel is an aesthetic and thematic tour de force.

The Unbearable Lightness of Being is a brilliantly innovative but pessimistic, even dark if not cynical and disturbing novel describing – and often protesting against – mediocrity, kitsch, the ordinariness and disappointments of life, the painfulness of love, the quirkiness of desire, the process of aging as well as death's inevitability and ubiquitous presence in all human life. Kundera (1929–) knows that such protest is futile and that life for most is a dwindling of expectations and a diminishment of possibilities. For Kundera's cynical, hard-edged commentator-narrator and the characters the narrator presents, it is the moments of love that are life's poetry and the saving grace, even if death hovers over those moments.

Reading the Modern European Novel Since 1900: A Critical Study of Major Fiction from Proust's Swann's Way to Ferrante's Neapolitan Tetralogy, First Edition. Daniel R. Schwarz.
© 2018 John Wiley & Sons Ltd. Published 2018 by John Wiley & Sons Ltd.

Kundera focuses on his fictional characters during and after the collapse of Alexander Dubcek's liberal leadership (Jan. 5, 1968–Aug. 21, 1968) – known as the Prague Spring – when Dubcek reduced restrictions on free speech, travel, and the media. This reform movement was followed in August 1968 by the ruthless Russian/Warsaw Pact invasion of Czechoslovakia and the persecution of those who supported Dubcek. It took eight months to stifle the non-violent protests – including sporadic suicides – that ensued; many people emigrated as a result of this suppression and subsequent disillusionment, including Kundera.

Kundera is repelled by what he considers kitsch, which to him is homogenized mediocrity and lack of initiative that characterize Communist rule: one example of kitsch is social realism, which he despises. Political kitsch often pretends to offer the lightness of freedom from responsibility, but in fact offers the weight of stifling initiative. Following the Warsaw Pact invasion ending the Prague Spring, the Russian presence is the quintessence of political kitsch. Kitsch is essential to the Communist system, but it exists everywhere. It is a shifting concept which finally, the reader realizes, does not have a fixed meaning in the novel, except what all kitsch has in common, that is mediocrity, lack of imagination, disdain for individuality, and reliance on convention and tradition for its own sake.

Kundera intermixes an examination of individual lives with the historical and political. He stresses how personal lives are in large part shaped by historical forces beyond the control of individuals. Indeed, the role of history in determining the parameters of each life is a major theme of most of the novels in this volume, notably *Metamorphosis*, *The Tin Drum*, *The Hunger Angel*, *Fatelessness*, even *The History of the Siege of Lisbon* and *My Name is Red*.

The Unbearable Lightness of Being, Kundera's fifth novel, was written in 1982 but not published until 1984 in translation with the original Czech version appearing in 1985. Living in France since 1975 and becoming a French citizen in 1981, Kundera thinks of himself as a French writer, especially because all his books since 1983 have been written in French and he himself revised the French translations of his earlier novels. Kundera had been brought up in a world where "the strictest realism had been required" (61), but his novels ostentatiously flout the standards of social realism. Indeed, Kundera thinks of himself as an heir to Cervantes and Kafka, earlier writers who turned from realism to fantasy and nightmare. Or, as he puts it: "A novel examines not life but existence. And existence is not what has occurred, existence is the realm of human possibilities, everything that man can become, everything he's capable of. Novelists draw up *the map of existence* by discovering this or that human possibility" (Salmon, 134; emphasis Kundera).

Kundera writes about the place of beauty, imagination, memory, narrative, love, and sex in a country that tried and failed to overthrow the repressive and arbitrary Soviet puppet regime. Thus, if *The Unbearable Lightness of Being* is a protest novel against the monstrous Russian domination of Czechoslovakia, it is also, as I shall argue, much more. While Kundera's narrator presents the imagination and sexual desire as human qualities that cannot be destroyed by totalitarianism, rereading, we understand that this is also a melancholy novel about exhaustion and mortality as well as about the pathos and bathos of human life. That Kundera eschews interior monologue in *The Unbearable Lightness of Being* supports his claim that he does not write psychological novels: "My novels are not psychological. More precisely, they lie outside the esthetic of the novel normally termed psychological. ... Meditative investigation (investigative meditation) is the basis on which all my novels are constructed" (Salmon, 119, 126).

The Unbearable Lightness of Being – a paradoxical title if ever there was one – describes not only the issues in the novel but also the experience of reading this complicated text that oscillates between narrative and philosophy, often circles back rather than proceeds linearly, and often does not give characters a sufficiently intricate grammar of motives or a history of characters' past. Kundera seems to imply that time is an artificial construct by which we organize narrative and that we need other methods of organizing a narrative. *The Unbearable Lightness of Being* has more in common with collage and dance choreography than with the what-happened-next telling of a traditional story. One could say his 143 chapters that jump from story to philosophy to lexicography to aesthetics are a deformation of traditional narrative and a disfiguration of traditional characterization.

With its multiple short chapters, swift changes of focus, circular and disrupted chronology, philosophic meditations and speculations, and discussions of crucial words, Kundera is challenging the expectations we bring to a traditional novel and presenting a fragmented, even jagged surface for the reader. As he puts it in his *Paris Review* interview: "A novel is a meditation on existence, seen through imaginary characters. The form is unlimited freedom. Throughout its history, the novel has never known how to take advantage of its endless possibilities. It missed its chance" (Milan Kundera, "The Art of Fiction No. 81").[2] By including politics and philosophy as well as referring to other art forms – painting, photography, and notably music – Kundera, like Günter Grass, is aspiring to something like *Gesamtkunstwerk*, or the total artwork, that embraces many art forms.

Kundera taught film in Czechoslovakia and *The Unbearable Lightness of Being* shows the influence of film with its surprise cutaways to new subjects, sometimes not returning to the central narrative for quite some time. The frequent use of flashbacks, as well as surrealistic dream sequences, is perhaps influenced by Luis Buñuel and Federico Fellini. In a sense the chapters are like short films, or even a short series of cinematic frames, tied together by a director's eye.

The Paradoxical Concepts of Lightness and Weight

The Unbearable Lightness of Being begins as a philosophical novel, with the narrator dispensing with the idea of reincarnation and eternal life and suggesting, from an historical perspective, the lightness or insignificance of each of our lives in terms of its importance. Much depends on "Einmal ist keinmal," which is defined as "once doesn't count" or "one occurrence doesn't matter." Tomas, the protagonist, thinks of "Einmal ist keinmal" as "What happens but once … might as well not have happened at all. If we have only one life to live, we might as well as not have lived at all" (8).[3] This view, embraced by Kundera, depends on rejecting purposeful theories of life in the form of reincarnation or of a just God's weighing our life on earth as a preparation for an afterlife and deciding who will go to heaven and who to hell.

One aspect of lightness is the knowledge – one might say cynical knowledge – that history and human behavior don't teach us because important circumstances in our lives don't recur. Kundera's materialistic view that our life lacks metaphysical significance means that life is the here and now and that life is no more than a journey with a definite ending in death. Kundera emphasizes how, even though we may attribute importance to our individual lives or those of others we might know or even to historical figures, from a cosmic perspective each human life is insignificant. By neither providing last names for his major characters nor probing into the depths of his characters' psyches, Kundera is taking an ironic if not cynical view of the importance of each individual human life.

Although interested in his characters, most notably Tomas and his second wife, Tereza, Kundera eschews traditional cause and effect in explaining human behavior. He does not put the onus for Tomas's compulsive philandering on the political climate or suggest it is a form of protest against the regime's heaviness, but rather leaves it to the reader to propose such an hypothesis. Often his explanations for behavior are partial, as when he defines the weight of compassion as a reason for Tomas's return to Prague when the lightness of being beckoned in Switzerland and Czechoslovakia was in the hands of the Russians.

Kundera's complicated weight and lightness opposition informs the entire novel. Much of the novel depends upon a shifting dialectic between the concepts of lightness and weight, concepts which are applicable to personal behavior and historical trends. Lightness is associated with fun, drinking, dancing. Lightness is living in the present, responding to impulse, and freedom from responsibility. Sex outside marriage is lightness because it is pleasurable play; unmarried or adulterous participants in casual sex don't have the weight of marriage or even of a sustained relationship. Lightness of being means living out of time with no responsibilities, commitments, or conscience. It means favoring the pleasure principle over all else and it means narcissism. Indeed, lightness is erasure of memories, absence of guilt, and indifference to personal responsibility. In the English translation, light wards off the darkness of guilt, shame, and burdensome responsibilities.

By contrast, heaviness is duty, seriousness, responsibility, compulsions and fixations, crucial decisions, the force of history, inevitability, and death. Heaviness is commitment in the form of love; having a sense of responsibility for another's happiness and welfare is weight. Heaviness includes the full knowledge that the lightness of being means renouncing love and responsibility. Heaviness means not only the responsibility that comes from love and compassion, but also recognition that the past shapes behavior as well as awareness of the presence of the past and of the consequences of the present on behavior in the future. For most humans some aspects of heaviness are inevitable no matter their desire to avoid it.

Let us turn to the specific implications of lightness and heaviness within Kundera's narrative. Weight includes the dreams that haunt Tereza and the guilt she feels for being entrapped by her one adulterous experience; it includes Tomas's guilt for not taking better care of Tereza when refusing to cooperate with the political authorities. Heaviness means understanding the consequences of personal decisions. Heaviness enters into our lives when we no longer think primarily of our own pleasure as paramount.

Kundera's novel is also about how the demise of a nation adds an oppressive weight to every aspect of human life. In its political and historical dimension heaviness is when we must respond to political situations that disrupt the needs and aspirations of our day-to-day lives. Heaviness is the pervasive and claustrophobic Russian domination after the Warsaw Pact invasion that ended the Prague Spring and the way that the Communist state and apparatus shape individual lives. Upon his return from Zurich, Tomas finds street names changed and private recorded conversations broadcast on the radio. Tomas marvels how "improbable fortuities" – "chance" – had shaped his love for Tereza: "If love is to be unforgettable, fortuities must immediately start fluttering down to it like birds to Francis of Assisi's shoulders" (48–49). He is fired from his position as a surgeon because he won't retract an article he wrote in support of democracy even though the published article has been changed from the words he wrote. After becoming a window washer, he is again asked to retract and again refuses.

But death is the ultimate heaviness, smothering life, and finally all that matters are the simple pleasures of individual lives because ultimately our lives are only significant to ourselves. In addition to following Tomas and Tereza to their deaths, the novel follows Tomas's lover Sabina, who emigrates to America, where she dies, and Sabina's one-time lover Franz, a scholar, who dies after being mugged in Southeast Asia. Best to live fully, Kundera implies, because death comes when least expected. For Franz, the best year of his life was with Sabina, whom he mythicizes as his "unearthly love" as opposed to his student mistress, his "earthly love" (126).

We make of the lives of others what we will, Kundera implies, and so adds another irony to the title. We make the "being" – the very existence in the world – of one person into part of our "being," often in ways that the person we reconfigure in our world would not understand. We can transform another's weight into our lightness, and vice versa. Franz like Tomas finally finds meaning in the person who cares for him, in Franz's case, the unnamed student mistress: "[T]he girl with the glasses was his real life, his only real life!" (274).

Furthermore, we make of the dead what we wish. Indeed, death can be an unbearable weight for those who survive. For Tomas's gravestone, his son Simon has arranged as epitaph: "HE WANTED THE KINGDOM OF GOD ON EARTH," which we know was the furthest thing from Tomas's mind. After Franz is brutally mugged, his wife, Marie-Claude, whom he detests, arranges his funeral at which he is praised for sustained "conjugal love" (276). For Franz's gravestone, Marie-Claude has ordered an ambiguous epitaph: "A RETURN AFTER LONG WANDERINGS," as if to imply not only that Franz found rest in death but also that after his mid-life crises at fifty he had wanted to return to her, which was hardly the case (276). Kundera's narrator ironically asks whether "all heirs had that right from time immemorial" to make sense in their "own vocabulary" of those they have lost (276).

In terms of history, lightness is the Prague Spring, notably its freedom of expression, its release from the daily weight of living under Russian captivity, and the possibility of living in a world without censorship, secret police, and fear of offending authority. Weight is the 1968 Warsaw Pact invasion of Czechoslovakia and the ubiquitous presence of the Russians. Lightness includes the opportunity to enjoy purposeful work: Tomas as a doctor, Sabina as an artist, Tereza as a photographer of the invasion, and Franz as an intellectual.

But, as we have seen, lightness and weight are often inseparable. Lightness can also mean irresponsibility and not fulfilling family and social roles, as in Tomas's casting off his first wife and son. It can mean indifference to others, as when Sabina's narcissistic preference for being a free spirit rather than settling down hurts Franz who as an intellectual and committed political activist is burdened by weight, including the guilt he feels for having an affair with Sabina while he is married. In her one brief adultery, Tereza discovers that "casual sex … is light, weightless," but for her, it is also weight because her betrayal, perhaps with an agent of the secret police, means feelings of guilt (159).

The Unbearable Lightness of Being depends on paradoxes. It offers what seems to be fixed concepts and abstractions, only to test, undermine, and reconfigure them. Lightness finally is meaningless, but paradoxically in the context of mattering historically so is its opposite, heaviness. For example, heaviness is the illusion that we have a moral commitment and responsibility to the concept of the Great March of History, but to the skeptical Kundera there is no such march. Indeed, Kundera would agree with the Russian skeptic Alexander Herzen, whose work he might have known. As Gary Saul Morson explains: "In historical change, as in biological evolution, Herzen came to argue, law and chance interact. Repeat a situation and it might develop differently. … Herzen insisted that there are no definitive solutions, that history has no aim, and that at any moment multiple futures are possible."[4]

Tomas and Tereza

We meet Tomas when he is the quintessence of lightness, a forty-year-old surgeon who is promiscuous. He has sex with countless women but only shares a nighttime bed – and for him this is the beginning of weight – when he takes Tereza, his eventual wife, into his apartment, after she shows up in Prague uninvited. After losing his post as surgeon and becoming a window washer, his major activity seems to be promiscuous sex. Later as a farm worker on a collective, he seems to be more devoted to Tereza.

Tomas seeks lightness in his sexual athleticism – the same lightness his lover Sabina seeks in sex – and in his love of surgery, but Tomas's commitment to Tereza and hers to him are what defines them. They are each other's weight and they limit each other's choices. He loves her and feels responsible for her. Tereza, who desperately needs to escape an unstable mother, is neurotic, but Tomas and she need each other. Tereza always feels weak in relation to Tomas and helpless to change him or herself. After emigrating to Zurich, Tomas returns to Prague – a journey that is perhaps the climax of the plot and an event that takes place in the first ten chapters of the novel. Tereza is partly responsible for his social and economic diminishment because she puts him in danger when she returns to Prague from Zurich, perhaps knowing intuitively that he would follow her.

If there is meaning to life, it is in the personal and most emphatically in whom we love and how we love them. Weight, not lightness, defines the relationship between Tereza and Tomas. Full of fretting, Tereza's life moves from weight to weight; she cannot find lightness because of her personal past and Tomas's philandering. Tereza adores Tomas and responds to his voice: "For it was Tomas's voice that had once coaxed forth her timorous soul from its hiding place in her bowels" (55). She is fixated on him, and he haunts her dreams. Her jealousy becomes a burden, but he loves her and feels responsible for her. Indeed, his obsessive and uncanny commitment to Tereza is his version of love. When she returns to Prague, Tomas, after a few days of relief thinking that he can now return to his former lightness, "was hit by a weight the likes of which he had never known. The tons of steel of the Russian tanks were nothing compared to it. For there is nothing heavier than compassion" (31). He feels compassion, defined by the narrator as "the pain one feels with someone, for someone, a pain intensified by the imagination and prolonged by a hundred echoes" (31). Compassion creates the "weighty resolution" of "Es Muss sein! it must be" as opposed to "the sweet lightness of being" that Tomas felt for the first two days in Zurich after Tereza returns to Prague (31–33). For Tomas, "it must be" includes his compulsive philandering and his love of medicine, but "it must be" after Tereza returns to Prague gives way to a more complex meaning including compassion and empathy for another.

While Tomas reluctantly turns to love and responsibility, Sabina chooses to follow her impulses. Kundera is interested in the balance between freedom and responsibility – Tomas returns from Zurich to Prague and Tereza, Sabina flees from Franz in Geneva – as well as why we respond as we do, but he sees that our lives are shaped by history and politics more than we realize.

Were Tomas and Tereza in a different country and time, their history would have been much different. They are ground down by the weight of the Communist system. Tomas's commitment to his political integrity becomes a weight. He had written a letter comparing those Communists who had ruled before the Prague Spring to Oedipus; in the comparison, Tomas had stressed that Oedipus recognizes guilt and puts out his eyes, while the Communists do not have any sense of guilt or shame. His refusal to recant this provocative letter is the catalyst for his and Tereza's losing their positions. Under the heavy thumb of a totalitarian system, they are intimidated, tricked, and humiliated, and are never sure when and if they are being watched by spies. The novel stresses the waste of talent in Tomas's becoming a window washer and Tereza a barmaid because he excelled as a surgeon, while she took iconic pictures of the Russian invasion.

For Kundera, some aspects of human life paradoxically include lightness and heaviness, notably the human body, but Kundera's insistence on this duality may be off-putting to some readers. Tereza's sexuality is associated with flatulence and her bowel movements. Feces may be the antithesis of lightness – of desire, of fun, of forgetting who we really are – but, for Kundera, feces is part of being human and to deny its existence is to deny life. Like Joyce, Kundera insists on including bodily functions in his anatomy of human life. "Kitsch is," according to the narrator, "the absolute denial of shit, in both the literal and figurative sense of the word; kitsch excludes everything from its purview which is essentially unacceptable in human existence" (248). Or, as Marjorie E. Rhine puts it: "Kundera's portrayals of angst-ridden bodies emphasize how the individual body is a critical pressure point between an oppressive or imposing political system and all that is most private, most in need of being protected if any sense of individual integrity is to be retained" (Rhine, 231).[5]

Analism and, yes, the way the human body works to produce an unsavory waste product fascinate Tomas and especially Sabina, and by implication Kundera. Sabina has an orgasm imagining Tomas watching her defecate (247). Indeed, the resistant reader might ask, isn't there something infantile as well as unpleasant about this interest in the intestines, even as we understand Kundera is not only insisting on the duality of the body and indeed life as well, but also stressing that our bodies are much of what we have left in a repressive, authoritarian regime.

Sabina

A painter whose work subverts the social realism required by Communism, Sabina, Tomas's mistress, is a free spirit who finds her freedom in sex. More than any other character, Sabina chooses and embodies lightness. She is a rolling stone, eschewing commitment, and living in the present. For Sabina, the past is past and only the present matters: "Everything beneath the surface was alien to her" (273). In her will, she chooses cremation as a way of disappearing: "She wanted to die under the sign of lightness. She would be lighter than air" (273).

Sabina's solipsism enables her to escape weight, but she does so at the expense of self-awareness: Sabina thinks of Tomas not as Don Juan but as Tristan, the Cornish knight who fell in love with the Irish princess Iseult after drinking a love potion (124). Sabina prefers to think of herself as Tristan's counterpart, the passionately loved Iseult, rather than one of the many women bedded by Don Juan. Self-delusion, like narcissism, is a kind of lightness, and self-knowledge can be a kind of heaviness.

When Franz wants to domesticate their relationship into something more than sex, she "sensed an expanse of freedom before her, and the boundlessness of it excited her" (116). Sabina cannot come to rest; as the narrator puts it: "[I]n the mind of a woman for whom no place is home the thought of an end to all flight is unbearable" (125). But Kundera lets her become a supernumerary in his imaginary world. By the end of the narrative, the reader is indifferent to her life in California, in part because she won't even open the letters from Tomas's son. That she "took less and less interest in her native land" establishes a parallel with Kundera, who had gone into exile in France, perhaps in part to escape the political heaviness of Russia's domination of Czechoslovakia (272).

Kundera disdains positivism and its logical explanations for behavior, considering them a kind of kitsch. At times he necessarily provides sketchy explanations for behavior. One example is how Tereza is shaped by the weight of her irresponsible mother.

Like her creator, Sabina hates kitsch. But it is the heavy weight of her father as well as the conformity Communism imposes to which her need for lightness is responding. Moreover, while her compulsive betrayals are a form of lightness to her, the reader understands that the weights of both her personal (her rigid and repressive father) and political past (authoritarian art school insisting on social realism) are among the basic causes that define her behavior. As we learn about Sabina's compulsive need to move on, even when staying with Franz might be in her interest, we realize that freedom – lightness of being – has its own weight.

It is possible for one person in a relationship to feel lightness and the other weight. Franz's weight is his marriage and the ideology of the Great March, even as he seeks lightness in his affair with Sabina and later his student. Thus a crucial passage describes the intense passion of the final time Franz and Sabina have sex. He thinks the sexual act is forging a commitment, while she knows she wants no part of the commitment he desires: "Each was riding the other like a horse, and both were galloping off into the distance of their desires, drunk on the betrayals that freed them. Franz was riding Sabina and had betrayed his wife. Sabina was riding Franz and had betrayed Franz" (117).

The Political Theme

Shortly after the Warsaw Pact invasion, Czechoslovakia became a nightmare world. Those who had sympathized with Dubcek's reforms lost their jobs, the secret police taped conversations, and intimidation and humiliation of those who didn't hew to the Communist Party line were the norm. I gave a talk in Prague a few years after the Velvet Revolution of 1989, after the Soviet domination had ended, and found former professors and political dissidents still working as museum guards.

Kundera's palpable rage informs the narrator's presentation of what ensued after the invasion: "The fact that any public undertaking (meeting, petition, street gathering) not organized by the Communist Party was automatically considered illegal and endangered all the participants was common knowledge" (220). Using Tomas and Tereza as examples, the narrator presents the deterioration in the quality of life, the fear and anxiety that inform every aspect of life in a country where the secret police seem to be everywhere and everyone seems to be watched. Tomas refuses to recant his comparison of those Communists who had ruled before the Prague Spring to Oedipus. By rendering Tomas's thoughts, the narrator clearly empathizes with Tomas's refusal to sign a petition asking for political amnesty for those imprisoned after the invasion: "Would amnesty be granted because people jettisoned by the regime (and therefore themselves potential political prisoners) request it of the president?" (215).

The fictional 2006 film *The Lives of Others*, focusing on how in East Germany as late as 1984 the Stasi (Ministry of State Security) spied on citizens and controlled every aspect of political and artistic life, recalls the world Kundera depicts after the Warsaw Pact invasion. We might note that Kundera himself had been accused of being an informer in 1950, which he denied.[6]

The political and historical allegory is an important aspect of the text, although a consistent allegory with a one-to-one relationship between signifier and signified is not sustained. Nevertheless, foregrounding Tomas's striking comparison of the recent history of Czechoslovakia with the Oedipus story is Kundera's way of calling attention to the need for us to read allegorically. Kundera is using the story to emphasize the distinction between the shame and guilt of Oedipus and the lack of self-awareness in members of the Communist Party who had destroyed Czechoslovakia.

. . . .

The story of Oedipus is well known: Abandoned as an infant, he was taken to King Polybus, who raised him. One day, when he had grown into a youth, he came upon a dignitary riding along a mountain path. A quarrel arose, and Oedipus killed the dignitary. Later he became the husband of Queen Jocasta and ruler of Thebes. Little did he know that the man he had killed in the mountains was his father and the woman with whom he slept was his mother. In the meantime, fate visited a plague on his subjects and tortured them with great pestilences. When Oedipus realized that he himself was the cause of their suffering, he put out his own eyes and wandered blind away from Thebes.

Anyone who thinks that the Communist regimes of Central Europe are exclusively the work of criminals is overlooking a basic truth: the criminal regimes were made not by criminals but by enthusiasts convinced they had discovered the only road to paradise. They defended that road so valiantly that they were forced to execute many people. Later it became clear that there was no paradise, that the enthusiasts were therefore murderers.

Then everyone took to shouting at the Communists: You're the ones responsible for our country's misfortunes (it had grown poor and desolate), for its loss of independence (it had fallen into the hands of the Russians), for its judicial murders!

And the accused responded: We didn't know! We were deceived! We were true believers! Deep in our hearts we are innocent! …

Oedipus did not know he was sleeping with his own mother, yet when he realized what had happened, he did not feel innocent. Unable to stand the sight of the misfortunes he had wrought by "not knowing," he put out his eyes and wandered blind away from Thebes. (175–178)

By contrast, the Communists who destroyed the country seem oblivious to what they have done and feel no guilt at all. Interestingly, the image that Tomas has of Tereza as an abandoned child – left like Moses in a "bulrush basket daubed with pitch and sent downstream for Tomas to fetch at the riverbank of his bed" – is the catalyst for his thinking of Oedipus, another abandoned child (6).

Kundera creates suggestive analogies if not homologies between the personal and political. When Dubcek falls, the entire nation falls with him. Tomas's own social devolution from a leading surgeon to a window washer and finally to a rural peasant suggests Dubcek's (and his nation's) humiliating forced submission to the Russians. Perhaps Tomas's promiscuity and focus on pleasure are a comment on how Czechoslovakia's relationship with Russia and the Warsaw Pact is barren of principle and derives from doing what satisfies their immediate security and economic needs rather than the country's best interests. Not every reader notices the same historical nuances and contexts, in part because we bring different degrees of historical knowledge to our reading, but we cannot ignore the strong historical pressure of twentieth-century European history on events in *The Unbearable Lightness of Being* as well as on most of the novels I discuss in this study.

Kundera explicitly identifies Tereza's behavior with Dubcek's humiliation. The narrator highlights the parallel: When Tereza decides to leave Zurich, "She was like Dubcek, who made a thirty-second pause in the middle of a sentence; she was like her country, which stuttered, gasped for breath, could not speak" (75). In Zurich, she frames in similar terms her commitment to her female dog, Karenin, who has taken on a male pronoun: "In periods of despair, she would remind herself she had to hold on because of him, because he was weaker than she, weaker perhaps even than Dubcek and their abandoned homeland" (74). Tereza unconditionally loves the helpless Karenin, an androgynous metaphor for the helpless Czechoslovakia, in part because the dog is completely dependent on her and never betrays her or makes her anxious the way Tomas does.

In his interview with Christian Salmon in *Salmagundi*, Kundera commented on the parallel between Dubcek and Tereza in a way that gives us a clue to how he uses history to create existential situations for his characters that require their making crucial life-defining decisions:

· ·

Not only must historical circumstance create a new existential situation for a character in a novel, but history itself must be understood and analyzed as an existential situation. Example: In *The Unbearable Lightness of Being*, Alexander Dubcek – after being arrested by the Russian Army, kidnapped, jailed, threatened, forced to negotiate with Brezhnev – returns to Prague. He speaks over the radio, but he cannot speak, he loses his breath, in mid-sentence he makes long, awful pauses. ... [This] is weakness. ... Tereza cannot bear the spectacle of that weakness, which repels and humiliates her, and she prefers to emigrate. But faced with Tomas's infidelities, she is like Dubcek faced with Brezhnev: disabled and weak. ... And, intoxicated with weakness, she leaves Tomas and returns to Prague, back to the "city of the weak." Here the historical situation is not a background, a stage set before which human situations unfold; it is itself a human situation, a growing existential situation. (Salmon, 130–131)

· ·

Whether Kundera realizes it or not, within the imagined ontology of *The Unbearable Lightness of Being*, the problem for characters making existential decisions is that historical conditions change, mortality hovers over individual lives, and their decisions drift into passivity and inconsequentiality.

Kundera uses characters to represent aspects of Czechoslovakia, beginning with the irresponsibility of Sabina. What they all have in common is the knowledge that after the invasion by Warsaw Pact countries under Russian auspices, they can change nothing. Both Sabina, bullied by her father, and Tereza, bullied by her mother, suggest Czechoslovakia compensating for allowing itself to be bullied by its powerful neighbors, including Hitler's Germany and the Russia of Stalin and his successors, and, before 1918, the Hapsburgs. Tomas's passive and passive-aggressive response to events epitomizes how Czechoslovakia, in Kundera's eyes, has let itself be intimidated into compromise and submission.

More than any other character, Tereza is Kundera's image and at times metonymy for Czechoslovakia. She is depicted as sentimental in embracing her dog, barely in control of her persistent indigestion, passive-aggressive, and effectual as a photographer during the days of the invasion but, with a certain rigidity, unwilling to define herself professionally in other terms. Yet she is willing to take an anonymous place in the economic system as a bargirl and then a peasant farmer, even though she has the capacity for more productive work. For the most part, she is submissive – comfortable with subjection and doing the will of others – even while she can be consciously and unconsciously manipulative. Kundera suggests some parallels between Tereza's submission to her mother and Czechoslovakia's years of Soviet domination after World War II when Czech lives necessarily turned inward to focus on day-to-day existence.

By having Tereza recall her own past before the Prague Spring and her dependence on Tomas, Kundera suggests a strong parallel between her and Czechoslovakia: "She realized that she belonged among the weak, in the camp of the weak, and that she had to be faithful to them precisely because they were weak and gasped for breath in the middle of sentences" (71). She has in mind Dubcek's speech when he returned from Moscow, a shadow of himself and a Soviet puppet: "If nothing was to remain of Dubcek, then at least those awful pauses when he seemed unable to breathe, when he gasped for air before a whole nation glued to its radios, at least those pauses would remain. Those pauses contained all the horror that had befallen their country" (72). Dubcek's ignominious return mirrors her own return. At this point she believes that the narrow, claustrophobic, stifled life she has led before Tomas entered it will be resumed, especially since she does not know he will follow her. Such a life is filled with small deceptions such as her mother's allowing her stepfather to enter the bathroom to watch her shower or her mother's claiming she had cancer. But as soon as Tomas returns to Prague the process of diminishment, the closing of opportunities, begins.

Karenin, completely dependent on Tereza for happiness and survival, at times also seems to be a metaphor for Czechoslovakia, dependent as it is on Russia. It is as if the dog's death represents the hopeless plight of a country where the air has been let out of its political system. But what Kundera is stressing is a cycle of dependence, where each person is more needy than the next: Tomas cannot resist the supplications of Tereza; Franz is dependent on various women, and so on. Finally everyone is dependent on the state the way the dog Karenin is dependent on Tomas and Tereza.

Death hovers over the entire novel. The sustained description of Karenin's death in the final pages emphasizes the performative and ritualistic aspects of a slow death of the helpless Czech people: "All his life Karenin had waited for answers from Tereza, and he was letting her know (with more urgency than usual, however) that he was still ready to learn the truth from her" (300). Because Tomas had purchased Karenin when there was still hope for the Czechs before the Russians suppressed the Prague Spring, the dog's death becomes an epitaph for Czechoslovakia's promise of freedom.

Kundera's narrator is bitterly ironic about the notion that history is evolving upward. It is not accidental that it is Franz who believes his namesake Kafka would have been the last person to accept this. A play on the Marxist notion of upwardly evolving history, the Grand March is a pathetic – and bathetic – protest against injustice, a fruitless effort to stem the tide of continually terrible events. Seen from the narrator's cynical perspective, the Grand March has no tangible effect and is a liberal delusion: "[F]inally the Grand March is a procession, of rushing, galloping people and the platform is shrinking and shrinking until one day it will be reduced to a mere dimensionless dot" (267). Could, the narrator asks, any Western protest event do anything about "the dying population of Cambodia" during the years of Pol Pot and the Khmer Rouge (277)? Furthermore, Kundera's narrator implicitly asks, what did cheering on the humanistic and democratic Dubcek revolution as part of the Grand March of History do to stop the Warsaw Pact countries from violently destroying that revolution?

It is worth noting how an underlying motif of *The Unbearable Lightness of Being* is diminishment: a lowering of expectations, narrowing of possibilities, acceptance of compromises, exhaustion, and the inevitable movement towards the death of the characters. Cemeteries and gravestones proliferate. As mentioned, Sabina's will specifies her cremation. When he is preparing to put down his and, even more, Tereza's beloved Karenin, Tomas, little knowing how close he is to his own demise, thinks: "Assuming the role of Death is a terrifying thing. … But then he realized that he could grant Karenin a privilege forbidden to humans. Death would come to him in the guise of his loved ones" (299–300).

For Tomas and Tereza, diminishment means becoming part of a farm collective – the quintessence of Communism, a kind of soulless parody in its inclusion of a church and a tavern of what was once village life – and "breaking with all their former friends and acquaintances, cutting their life in two like a ribbon" (282). In fact, Tomas and Tereza's downward trajectory has come to an end, as Tereza, blaming herself unfairly, understands: "Now they were in a place that led nowhere. … They didn't even have a reason to move to another village" (310). In her mind she has turned Tomas into a helpless rabbit dependent, like Karenin, upon her: "[S]he had always wanted him to be old. Again she thought of the rabbit she had pressed to her face in her childhood room" (313).

Kundera stresses the corrupting nature of Communism on country life. Ironically, everyone but Tomas and Tereza wants to leave and move to town. Alluding to how ownership is a source of pride, even as it is a weight that gives life meaning, Kundera's narrator observes: "A farmer who no longer owns his own land and is merely a laborer tilling the soil forms no allegiance to either region or work; he has nothing to lose, nothing to fear for" (283).

The Narrator Wearing the Mask of Author

Kundera wants to raise questions about the traditional components of novels: narrator, plot, character. For example, the narrator identifies himself as author within the text even as he debunks the convention that he is talking about real people: "It would be senseless for the author to try to convince the reader that his characters once actually lived. They were not born of a mother's womb; they were born of a stimulating phrase or two or from a basic situation. Tomas was born of the phrase '*Einmal ist Keinmal*.' Tereza was born of the rumbling of a stomach" (39).

Kundera's narrator oscillates between a distant philosophic view and sympathetic engagement in the travails of Tomas and Tereza, particularly when rendering Tereza's responses to events. He is often a distant presence jumping from subject to subject, even in some cases within his short chapters abandoning the story to take up another subject, shifting points of view, pontificating on an abstruse topic, discussing the applicability of a word or phrase, and sometimes seemingly leaving a point or character in limbo.

Yet to the extent that *The Unbearable Lightness of Being* revolves around the narrator's intimate knowledge of – as well as empathy with – the protagonist Tomas, it is a more traditional novel than perhaps Kundera realizes. In chapter three of Part One, the first person narrator casually introduces himself: "I have been thinking about Tomas for many years" (6). That the narrator understands the quality and depth of Tomas's love for Tereza, what it means for Tomas to share a bed with her and to respond to the pain she experiences in dreams, somewhat undermines the bemused detachment of the author-narrator.

Let me repeat my theorem: The maximum revelation of the author – the moment he reveals the most about himself – becomes the point of reference for understanding him or her as a self-dramatizing character within the imagined ontology of the novel. In *The Unbearable Lightness of Being*, the authorial presence expresses itself in the narrator's continuing interventions, his ironic and noir playfulness, his speculations about the meaning of life, and his erudition manifested in the wide range of references from Nietzsche and Parmenides to Robespierre and Hitler. And the aforementioned references all occur within the first three pages!

Kundera's surrogate, his narrator, asserts that his characters have "crossed borders that I myself have circumvented. It is that crossed border (the border beyond which my own 'I' ends) which attracts me most. For beyond that border begins the secret the novel asks about. The novel is not the author's confession; it is an investigation of human life in the trap the world has become" (221). The word "trap" reveals the narrator's strong sympathy for Tomas who has lost his position as a doctor and is at this point a window washer. Tomas is clinging to Tereza, the one part of his life that still has meaning for him, and refusing to sign a petition because it might lead to unpleasantness for her: "She was all that mattered to him. ... [S]he was the only thing he cared about" (219). That he loves her has been his weight and increasingly the center of his life ever since he took her into his apartment long ago: "[L]ove begins at the point when a woman enters her first word into our poetic memory" (209).

That Tereza is a photographer reminds us not only that a single image can both arrest and crystallize a moment within time into an image out of time, but also that an image may distort the process of time as it moves from the present moment to an unseen future. Put another way, discourse – the reorganization of the temporal events into a non-chronological narrative structure rich with the narrator's commentary – takes precedence over the concatenation of events that comprise the story. Rereading, we have a strong sense of a self-dramatizing narrator speaking to us in his own idiosyncratic way that defies our expectations of convention or tradition. For example, before the novel is a third over, we learn in the form of a letter from Tomas's son to Sabina that Tomas and Tereza have been killed in a road accident (122). Only later do we learn more about their last days on a farm collective and how their once cosmopolitan world – especially Tomas's – has contracted to that of rural peasants. Even earlier than the aforementioned letter, the narrator hints at their forthcoming deaths (51, 56).

The very originality, insight, and verve of *The Unbearable Lightness of Being* become a comment on the narrowness, diminishment, and pathos of Tomas and Tereza's last days. Yes, before their deaths, they achieve a kind of balance, but at what cost?

Kundera's Concept of Form in *The Unbearable Lightness of Being*

Kundera is boldly claiming that the traditional form of the novel needs to be rethought in the face of the political realities and changes in personal values, including the fact that for many people, including most of his characters, God does not exist. Why, he asks, have a linear plot implying an overarching teleology when there is no evidence in religion, philosophy or history that we are moving to a great goal?

The Unbearable Lightness of Being is about both what and how life means, given that we are tied to the basic conditions and limitations of human life, notably aging and mortality. Perhaps the way, Kundera suggests, to understand life is to find alternative structures to the usual chronological approach that answers the question, "What happened next?" The seemingly serendipitous form of *The Unbearable Lightness of Being*, the non-chronological fluidity of plot, and its often cynical commentary, enact the meaninglessness of life, except for the pathos and bathos of shared love.

Like many non-representational modern painters and sculptors, Kundera expects his readers to complete the hermeneutical circle. Indeed, his presence in the text and his juggling realism with abstraction resonate with twentieth-century painters and sculptors and anticipate twenty-first-century video artists.

By undermining linearity as well as spatial and temporal expectations, Kundera is indebted to New Wave cinema – with its evocation of documentary style but with fragmented, discontinuous editing – and Cubism's formal experiments, including collage. The Cubist influence takes the form of Kundera's narrator's presenting multiple perspectives; we see many events from both Tereza's and Tomas's points of view. After Kundera's narrator presents Tereza's arrival in Prague through Tomas's eyes in Part One, we see the same event from Tereza's eyes in Part Two. Nor does the narrator's commentary resolve the discrepancies in their perspective.

If motion is the protagonist, time is the antagonist. Once time is disrupted, novels tend to take on more of a spatial component. Kundera's narrative, with its shifting surfaces from plot to philosophy to lexicography (recalling Jorge Luis Borges's ironic definitions), has much in common with twentieth-century experiments in the visual arts, including the uncanny mixture of subjects and styles in Cubist and Surrealistic paintings as well as Alexander Calder's mobiles.

With seven parts divided into 143 chapters that constantly shift our focus, *The Unbearable Lightness of Being* becomes for the reader an experience of following moving strands of meaning. We see various situations from different perspectives, but we never do see the whole. Our inability to see the whole is one of Kundera's major points. Rapid changes in tone from comic to noir to empathy with the characters are very much part of the novel's dizzying, vertiginous motion, although the philosophic and aesthetic speculations slow down the pace.

The architectonics of *The Unbearable Lightness of Being* deliberately undermine the chronology of story. Parts One and Five (both entitled "Lightness and Weight") focus on Tomas; Parts Two and Four (both entitled "Soul and Body") and Seven (entitled "Karenin's Smile") focus on Tereza and the simple agrarian life she and Tomas lead, a life that is a kind of purposeless lightness. Part Three (entitled "Words Misunderstood") focuses on Sabina and Franz. One could say that Part Six ("The Grand March") is also about Franz and Sabina since it includes the death of both characters. But much of the early chapters of Part Six really concern the narrator's ironical and noir meditations on the incongruity of God and feces – "Either/or: either man was created in God's image – and God has intestines! – or God lacks intestines and man is not like Him" (245) – and ultimately the dismissal of theology as irrelevant to what happens on earth. The reality for Kundera, as *The Unbearable Lightness of Being* illustrates, is that much of life could be imaged by waste, refuse, and defecation.

The foregoing summary understates the extent that discourse undermines story because the continuous, often overbearing narrative voice is frequently the novel's major character. We might say that the form of this anti-novel is an example of lightness because the form purports to be casual, without adhering to a forward-moving chronological narrative, or even a traditional grammar of motives. By contrast, the narrated events about the characters' behavior and outcome are examples of heaviness.

Kundera borrows formal concepts from music, notably in the recurring themes and leitmotifs. As Guy Scarpetta observes:

. . . .

Here are indications of an overt desire to destroy the classical notions of "novel-istic development" (exposition, peripeteia, reboundings, knotting and dcnoue-ment). In fact everything happens as if, for Kundera, a sense of musical composition took on increasing autonomy in the face of plot's traditional neces-sities. In *The Unbearable Lightness of Being* there is no homogeneous, centered plot, but instead a calculated tangle of semi-independent story-lines. (Scarpetta, 184)[7]

. . . .

Johannes Lichtman pursues the musical analogy: "Kundera bases the archi-tecture of his books on musical concepts of variation (in which the composer repeatedly returns to the same bars, with a slightly different approach each time) and polyphony (in which several melodies play off each other simultane-ously)" (Lichtman).[8]

Kundera is very much aware that his short chapters derive from the influence of music:

. . . .

The chapters themselves must also create a little world of their own; they must be relatively independent. … The chapters are like the measures of a musical score! There are parts where the measures (chapters) are long, others where they are short, still others where they are of irregular length. Each part could have a musi-cal tempo indication: moderato, presto, andante, et cetera. … I first thought of *The Unbearable Lightness of Being* in a musical way. I knew that the last part had to be pianissimo and *lento*: it focuses on a rather short, uneventful period, in a single location, and the tone is quiet. I also knew that this part had to be preceded by a prestissimo: that is the part entitled "The Grand March." (Kundera, "The Art of Fiction No. 81")

. . . .

Thus, to better understand *The Unbearable Lightness of Being*, one needs to respond to it as a musical composition with several motifs. Not only do various phrases recur – "kitsch," "*Es Muss sein*: it must be," "*Einmal ist Keinmal*" – but so, too, do major themes: lightness versus weight, sex versus love, betrayal versus commitment, personal freedom versus responsibility, political freedom versus stultifying domination by another country and by a bankrupt ideology. These phrases and themes become as important and perhaps more important than a plot. Nor should we forget the overarching title concept "unbearable" (what can't be endured or accepted because it is too harsh or extreme).

Kundera hates kitsch by which he means not only bad taste but personal and political mediocrity. Soviet Communism encourages both. For Kundera, one kind of kitsch is the traditional plot with its heavy determinism. Kundera wants to stress the unlikely, even gratuitous nature of our lives and believes the heaviness of traditional plots distorts what really happens:

. . . .

Nothing has become as suspect, ridiculous, old-fashioned, trite, and tasteless in a novel as plot and its farcical exaggerations. … My lifetime ambition has been to unite the utmost seriousness of question with the utmost lightness of form. Nor is this purely an artistic ambition. The combination of a frivolous form and a serious subject immediately unmasks the truth about our dramas (those that occur in our beds as well as those that we play out on the great stage of History) and their awful insignificance. We experience the unbearable lightness of being. (Kundera, "The Art of Fiction No. 81")

. . . .

The elegance of Kundera's polyphonic novel – a concept derived, as we have noted, from music – is his antidote to aesthetic kitsch, and allows, he believes, for the imagination to have full sway, for dream narratives, and for the casting aside of a mechanical and heavy plot:

. . . .

[In *The Unbearable Lightness of Being*] I wanted dream, narrative, and reflection to flow together in an indivisible and totally natural stream. But the polyphonic character of the novel is very striking in part six: the story of Stalin's son, theological reflections, a political event in Asia, Franz's death in Bangkok, and Tomas's funeral in Bohemia are all linked by the same everlasting question: "What is kitsch?" This polyphonic passage is the pillar that supports the entire structure of the novel. It is the key to the secret of its architecture. (Kundera, "The Art of Fiction No. 81")

. . . .

Tereza's dreams introduce magic realism. Kundera rejects reductive, positivist explanations of Tereza's dreams: "There is nothing to decipher in Tereza's dreams. They are poems about death. Their meaning lies in their beauty, which hypnotizes Tereza" (Kundera, "The Art of Fiction No. 81"). For Kundera, easy Freudian explanations of her dreams would be kitsch. For novels are a place to explore rather than assert ideas: "The novel, however, is a territory where one does not make assertions; it is a territory of play and of hypotheses" (ibid.).

Kundera stresses how we each live within our own lexicography. Part Three, "Words Misunderstood," with Sabina and Franz as the examples, demonstrates how we are separated from one another by our experiences and histories, particularly as we age. Franz and Sabina understand crucial words differently, and that difference in what words mean separates them, notwithstanding their sexual rapport. In embracing lightness, Sabina turns her back on politics and leaves Franz without explanation. Perhaps her propensity for betrayal is somewhat a reflection of how Czechoslovakia (represented by her father's submission to Communism) has been betrayed and how Czechoslovakia betrayed its citizens. By contrast, Franz, honored for his intellectual career (and whose name recalls Kafka's first name), has never lived in a Communist country and enjoys thinking about "The Grand March of History" which for him is a surrogate for religion. Conflating his view with Sabina's retrospective view, the narrator muses: "Perhaps if they had stayed together longer, Sabina and Franz would have begun to understand the words they used. Gradually, timorously, their vocabularies would have come together, like bashful lovers, and the music of one would have begun to intersect with the music of the other. But it was too late now" (124).

In insisting that we don't allegorize his novels – even while providing ample evidence for doing so – Kundera wants us to think of his work as a site of shifting planes and for us to see moments of unity and coherence as tentative and soon undermined by what follows. His point is that moments of unity and coherence are illusive in life, as illustrated in his narratives of Tomas, Tereza, Sabina, and Franz, and even more so in the political and historical narrative where the promise of Dubcek is summarily squashed and the Grand March of progressive history is an illusion.

The disrupted and scrambled chronology of *The Unbearable Lightness of Being* shapes our response to characters and themes as much as the narrator's telling, which wanders from anecdote to commentary, and sometimes seems to lose the central thread of his characters' history. Often we learn a few details of a character's past after we see how she or he behaved in the present, but we often lack a coherent grammar of motives. Hopping about from short chapter to short chapter, the narrator's seemingly quixotic movement from plot to philosophic and aesthetic reflection is an odyssey that at times takes precedence over the characters' odysseys, especially because we know what happens to them well before the denouement. Often the narrator seems more interested in what the novel teaches us about life than in telling his story.

Let us think about the effects of this innovative mixture of formal ingredients. When we reread, we are especially aware of how Kundera eschews traditional plot and deliberately proposes challenges to the realistic novel as well as the confessional novel. In his *Paris Review* interview he speaks of

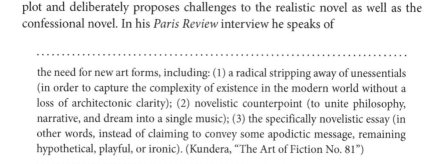

the need for new art forms, including: (1) a radical stripping away of unessentials (in order to capture the complexity of existence in the modern world without a loss of architectonic clarity); (2) novelistic counterpoint (to unite philosophy, narrative, and dream into a single music); (3) the specifically novelistic essay (in other words, instead of claiming to convey some apodictic message, remaining hypothetical, playful, or ironic). (Kundera, "The Art of Fiction No. 81")

Although Kundera says counterpoint is less a factor in *The Unbearable Lightness of Being* than in his other novels, we need to know that counterpoint is a musical term for voices that are interdependent harmonically but independent in rhythm and contour.

We might note the applicability to Kafka of the quotations from Kundera's *Paris Review* interview. *The Unbearable Lightness of Being* takes place in Prague, Kafka's city, and Kafka's imagination and the dysfunctional world he evoked hover over Kundera's novel. Kundera often praises Kafka and cites him as a model:

Kafka's novels are a fusion of dream and reality; that is, they are neither dream nor reality. More than anything, Kafka brought about an aesthetic revolution. An aesthetic miracle. ... My way of doing so is by polyphonic confrontation rather than by a fusion of dream and reality. (Kundera, "The Art of Fiction No. 81")

Kundera has written an experimental novel which is an inquiry into the form of the novel. But rather than the big sprawling novel one might expect from Kundera's ambitious concepts of form and themes, it is only 314 pages in reasonably large print. Kundera notes: "In order to make the novel into a poly-historical illumination of existence, you need to master the technique of ellipsis, the art of condensation. ... The art of ellipsis is absolutely essential. It requires that one always go directly to the heart of things" (Kundera, "The Art of Fiction No. 81"). Yet the very succinctness of some of the chapters and the absence of a fully developed grammar of motives leave much unsaid and leave the reader with a great deal to do in terms of putting together the discrete parts into a comprehensible text. But, yes, it is worth the effort and it is consonant with the difficulty of reading many of the modern novels I discuss in this volume.

Conclusion

I want to conclude by discussing some areas where I am a skeptical or resistant reader.

At times, Kundera suggests comparisons or provides allusions which reveal more about himself than the world he describes. In a weird incident associated with kitsch, Stalin's son – while a prisoner of war held by the Germans – kills himself because he is accused of messing up toilets when he defecates. Are we to understand that Stalin is associated with the heaviness of defecation and kitsch? But is this equation earned by the novel? Isn't this an example of what we might call Kundera's rhetorical irresponsibility?

Another, perhaps even better, example of Kundera's rhetorical carelessness is Tereza's using the term "concentration camp" to describe a dismal personal or political situation as when Tereza recalls her life with her mother in a small apartment: "A concentration camp is a world in which people live crammed together constantly night and day. Brutality and violence are merely secondary (and not in the least indispensible) characteristics" (137; see also 136, 167). Concentration camps in the Holocaust were sites where Jews were starved and arbitrarily killed, and Kundera's insensitivity here is notable.

The premature demise of the major characters – Tomas, Tereza, Franz – and the knowledge that their lives have been wasted, as well as our awareness of the political persecution in Czechoslovakia, weighs upon our reading and make the novel the antithesis of lightness. We know little about what shaped Tomas to behave as he does or what motivates Sabina or Franz or his student lover, in part because Kundera is more interested in his commentaries than on probing his characters' psyches. Rereading, we realize that much of the text comprises the narrator's relatively predictable thoughts revolving around a few simply presented events.

Is *The Unbearable Lightness of Being*, one might ask, a sexist novel where women are reduced to sexual objects for the pleasure of men? Or does Sabina's promiscuous behavior balance that of Tomas? Probably not, for she has far fewer lovers and seems to practice serial monogamy, while by the time Tomas leaves Prague to begin rural life he has had at least two hundred women. Moreover, his imperial command "Strip" to women with whom he intends to have sex reflects a presumptive male privilege. Yet Sabina too has a commanding presence within sexual relationships, including the odd homoerotic scene in which she and Tereza are naked.

I am also somewhat resistant to Kundera's dark vision. If each life is unique, how do we learn from another life? How indeed, we might ask, do we learn from our own life while it is in progress? Do any of Kundera's characters really learn anything of importance? Kundera's cynicism seems to be somewhat modified by the value (and weight) of love and commitment, but only if we take the short view. For do Tomas, Tereza, or Sabina's lives matter? Rereading, we realize that from a cosmic perspective each life may seem irrelevant and minuscule – that is, may seem an instance of lightness – but as humans we cannot afford that perspective and must do the best we can with our own lives.

If nothing recurs, our lives have little significance in the grand scheme and are therefore light, but to know their insignificance is unbearably heavy. In a sense, such a philosophy unwrites the very story we are reading. But Tomas and Tereza do matter – as do Anna, Karenin, and Vronsky in *Anna Karenina*, which Tereza had been reading and brings with her when she arrives in Prague – because as humans we don't take them lightly and we hope we can learn from their experience and the teller's presentation. Were we to believe their stories had no significance, would we read? Is it not fair to say we read great literature for its weight? "It must be" includes our need to make meaning from our experience; paradoxically, that is why we read and why we seek to discover resonances of literary events in our own lives.

Unless we are narcissists, lightness is unbearable because our lives take on weight as we care for others and take on emotional and moral commitments. The opposite of lightness is existential commitment to a set of values. When Tomas follows Tereza to Prague rather than staying in Switzerland to pursue his desires and interests, he is choosing weight over lightness. The same is true when he refuses to renounce his Oedipus parable that critiques Czech Communist leaders. Yet *The Unbearable Lightness of Being*'s terrifying irony is that existential commitment creates meaning in the short term for Tomas, Tereza, and Franz, but in the larger perspective lives come and go, death is inevitable, and finding historical meaning in the Grand March of History is futile.

So, we might ask, why does Kundera write? Citing *Anna Karenina*, Kundera's narrator argues that we create in our real lives narratives with significance:

· ·

Guided by his sense of beauty, an individual transforms a fortuitous occurrence (Beethoven's music, death under a train) into a motif, which then assumes a permanent place in the composition of the individual's life. ... Without realizing it, the individual composes his life according to the laws of beauty, even in times of greatest distress. ... [It] is right to chide man for being blind to coincidences in his daily life. For he thereby deprives his life of a dimension of beauty. (52)

· ·

Are not these moments closely akin to what Joyce would call epiphanies? But how often in our own lives are we aware of these moments of significance when they are recurring? If our moments of clarity are illusions, why are we reading and why is Kundera writing? Presumably Kundera writes and we read in part to discover these aesthetic moments and to understand them as applying to our own world.

Yet for Kundera the ultimate bathos is that these moments of clarity and wholeness only matter to the person experiencing them and have no relationship to a larger pattern. Moreover, these epiphanic moments prove to be illusions. Kundera leaves us with the somber conclusion: Mortality wins, humans lose, and we have neither existential nor cosmological significance. Finally Kundera lives in the borderland between cynicism and nihilism, but, as a resistant humanist reader, I can't join him.

Study Questions for *The Unbearable Lightness of Being*

1. Why is it important that Kundera's narrator speaks dismissively of reincarnation at the outset?
2. Explain the concepts of lightness and heaviness in terms of characters and history. Are these terms sometimes ambiguous and complex?
3. Does Sabina, proponent of lightness, live a satisfactory life? What does the concept of kitsch mean to her? To Kundera? How does Kundera's understanding of kitsch compare with Kertesz's?
4. How do political events – from the Prague Spring to the Warsaw Pact invasion – shape the lives of the characters?
5. Why does Tomas return to Zurich? Why is compassion a weight?
6. How does Kundera regard Tomas's refusal to renounce his letter criticizing the Communists and comparing them unfavorably to Oedipus? Why does Tomas refuse?
7. What is the dog Karenin's role? Why does Tereza love the dog unconditionally?
8. In what ways is *The Unbearable Lightness of Being* an anti-novel? How does *The Unbearable Lightness of Being* function as a political allegory?
9. What is the role of the narrator? How does his commentary at times overwhelm plot? Why does the teller organize the story around themes instead of presenting his story in chronological order?
10. How does the reader respond to Tomas's transformation from surgeon to window washer to farmer tending a small plot of land? What is Kundera's purpose in showing Tomas's diminishment in class and stature?

Notes

1. Christian Salmon, "On the Art of the Novel: A Conversation with Milan Kundera," trans. Linda Asher, *Salmagundi*, No. 73 (Winter 1987), 119–135; here 134 (reprinted No. 185/186 [Winter/Spring 2015], 607–622).

2. Milan Kundera, "The Art of Fiction No. 81." Interview by Christian Salmon. *Paris Review* 92 (Summer 1984); https://www.theparisreview.org/interviews/2977/milan-kundera-the-art-of-fiction-no-81-milan-kundera

3. Page numbers refer to Milan Kundera, *The Unbearable Lightness of Being*, trans. Michael Henry Heim (New York: Harper & Row, 1984).

4. Gary Saul Morson, "Herzen: The Hero of Skeptical Idealism," *NYR* 63:18 (Nov. 24, 2016), 45; http://www.nybooks.com/articles/2016/11/24/alexander-herzen-hero-skeptical-idealism/

5. Marjorie E. Rhine, "A Body of One's Own: The Body as Sanctum of Individual Integrity in Kundera's *The Unbearable Lightness of Being*," in *Critical Essays on Milan Kundera*, ed. Peter Petro (New York: G. K. Hall, 1999), 231–241; see 231.

6. Rob Cameron, "Milan Kundera Denies 'Informer' Allegations," *Radio Praha* (Oct. 14, 2008); http://www.radio.cz/en/section/curraffrs/milan-kundera-denies-informer-allegations-in-first-interview-in-25-years

7. Guy Scarpetta, "Kundera's Quartet [on *The Unbearable Lightness of Being*]," in *Critical Essays on Milan Kundera*, ed. Peter Petro (New York: G. K. Hall, 1999), 184–192; see 184.

8. Johannes Lichtman, "To Forget History," *Los Angeles Review of Books* (July 5, 2015); https://lareviewofbooks.org/essay/to-forget-history

Chapter 11

Saramago's *The History of the Siege of Lisbon* (1989): Rewriting History, Reconfiguring Lives

"Is history truth? Does what we call history retell the whole story? History, really, is a fiction – not because it is made up of invented facts, for the facts are real, but because in the organization of those facts there is much fiction. History is pieced together with certain selected facts that give a coherence, a line, to the story. In order to create that line, many things must be left out. There are always those facts that did not enter history, which if they had might give a different sense to history. History must not be presented as a definitive lesson. No one can say, This is so because I say it happened this way."

José Saramago, "The Art of Fiction"[1]

Introduction

Influenced by Joyce's word play and stylistic experimentation as well as that of other early twentieth-century modernists, the 1999 Nobel Laureate José Saramago's (1922–2010) *The History of the Siege of Lisbon* (1989) is a politically and historically sophisticated novel that draws upon diverse genres. The novel dramatizes how the history of Portugal derives from the conquest of Lisbon – and the Moors – by the Christians. What makes the book fun is that it is simultaneously a novel about a man in his fifties discovering his imagination and awakening to his emotions, including his ability to experience desire and passion; a novel about the act of writing and the process of publishing; a novel about the seminal event in the founding of Portugal that becomes an historical polemic on Eurocentric and Christian-centric imperialism; a love story between a lonely middle-aged man and

Reading the Modern European Novel Since 1900: A Critical Study of Major Fiction from Proust's Swann's Way to Ferrante's Neapolitan Tetralogy, First Edition. Daniel R. Schwarz.
© 2018 John Wiley & Sons Ltd. Published 2018 by John Wiley & Sons Ltd.

woman; a stylistically innovative novel that deviates from standard punctuation and typography; and a comic novel that comments on recurring human foibles that span centuries.

As a narrative, *The History of the Siege of Lisbon* pokes fun at our comfort with one-dimensional interpretations and perspectives, even while showing that great historical events depend on a combination of chance, human needs, and anxieties as well as motives that are dimly understood. Thus Saramago challenges univocal versions of history that focus only on kings and battles. Rather he asks for a pluralistic version which includes not just facts about macrocosmic events but an imaginative recreation of microcosmic matters such as individual motives and desires that shape human behavior and the behavior of various social classes, including simple peasants and soldiers whose day-to-day lives help shape historical events. Such imaginative recreation must also, Saramago believes, take account of the role of chance in shaping history.

The title takes its meaning from (1) the siege of Lisbon conducted by the Europeans to expel the Moors; (2) the siege on Raimundo Silva's routines and emotions carried on by editorial supervisor Maria Sara; (3) the counter-siege on her emotions, eventuating in a humanistic love story; and (4) Silva's siege on the historical text he is editing.

Beginning with a private dialogue between an unnamed historian and proofreader, whom we soon learn is Raimundo Silva, the novel expands outward to include the foundation of Portugal as a state, a metamorphosis of the central character as he falls in love, and musings on religion, historiography, time, and whatever else Saramago wishes to include in his – to borrow a term from Joyce's *Ulysses* – "chaffering allincluding most farraginous chronicle" (*Ulysses* 14.1412). Joyce used this phrase to describe his own work but it also applies to Saramago's novel about the day-to-day life of a middle-aged man in Lisbon within the context of the history and geography of that city. Saramago is indebted to Joyce's focus on Bloom in Dublin within the context of Irish history. Just as Joyce uses various historical periods to give shape and meaning to his novel, so Saramago uses the siege of Lisbon in 1147, but he does not forget the earthquake of November 1, 1755.

With his typical combination of insight and overstated categorizing, Harold Bloom has remarked, "Mark Twain would have admired Saramago; both novelists were anti-Christian savage humanists who depicted the fundamental ferocity of human nature and society" (Bloom, 40).[2] But we should also stress Saramago's combination of humanistic sentimentalism, realpolitik cynicism, and satiric exposure of human fallibility. His protagonist is emotionally stunted until he meets a younger woman who takes the initiative.

224

Saramago's Style: Innovative, Imaginative, Idiosyncratic

Saramago's prose is often a siege on the reader's expectations because he does not use traditional punctuation. Specifically, he does not use question marks, exclamation points, quotation marks, hyphens, semi-colons or colons. His typography is an important part of the reading experience. The first few words of each unnumbered and untitled chapter are all in capitals and the first and third chapters begin with "THE PROOF-READER" as if to stress his importance. Since there are no chapter titles, it follows that there is no table of contents. Saramago's long paragraphs often contain dialogues that lack quotation marks. He indicates a change of speaker by a simple capital letter, but sometimes we don't know if the capital letter indicates a new sentence or a new speaker or both.

Especially but not exclusively in the love scenes, we don't always know who is talking. Saramago's typography suggests that the logic of traditional discourse gives way to the unspoken rhythms of human desire and the human need for companionship and understanding. This technique does make for moments of confusion. Often one needs to reread to discover who is speaking, especially (but not only) in the first chapter. While at first this may be annoying, it is undoubtedly intentional and the reader begins to find the search for the speaker is part of the reading experience and somewhat analogous to the narrator's and Silva's putting together their fictional history.

Saramago's point is that explanations of historical events are often reductive, but so too are, in both life and fiction, the mysteries of why people are attracted to one another. Beyond words are the interstices that can't quite be explained. By recounting the words but blurring who is speaking them, Saramago is emphasizing the unspoken interstices that accompany words. He also stresses (we are in a world before skyping) how telephone conversations when the other party cannot be seen are even more difficult than in-person exchanges. The "not" inserted by Silva in the text he is proofreading becomes a shadow over all unitary explanations, a reminder that there are other ways of processing and understanding information, and that reminder is a siege on historical certainty.

How the Concept of the Siege Functions

The novel begins with an anonymous (and rather second-rate) historian who entrusts the proofing of his book to proofreader Raimundo Silva without asking to see his corrections. Because of the historian's slackness – what author would abandon his text before seeing final revisions? – he has empowered Silva to launch his sneak attack on the text. The attack on the historical text by Silva with one word – an inserted "not" – is the launching of Silva's siege. For that "not" transforms the author's history of the siege of Lisbon in 1147 so that the Crusaders do not help the Portuguese to conquer Lisbon (40).[3] But Silva's siege continues into his fictional rewriting. For if the Crusaders didn't help the Portuguese, Raimundo Silva needs to compose a replacement narrative which explains what conceivably might have happened, and that activity becomes his focus.

Silva's entire life is transformed when he becomes interested in Maria Sara, his boss, who begins a successful siege on his heart and sexuality. His transformation from proofreader to author is stimulated by his burgeoning relationship with Maria Sara, a younger and more educated woman (she has a doctorate). She arouses his interest in her. But Saramago makes clear that for love to succeed, the siege must be mutual. As Silva, a most routinized bachelor, falls in love his range of feelings and his understanding gradually expand. This expansion helps him to create a human history of twelfth-century events that goes beyond simple military deeds. The mutual siege of Maria Sara and Silva on each other's defenses – psychological fortresses to prevent hurt and embarrassment – not only parallels the imagined mutual siege of the twelfth-century lovers, Ouroana and the massive soldier Mogueime, but also releases Silva's powers of feeling and empathy necessary for him to create his version of history.

Maria Sara awakes something dormant within Silva. In their dialogues as their relationship develops, Silva becomes increasingly clever and imaginative and his behavior becomes more proactive. Indeed, as he imagines a fictional revision of history, he creates an alternative history to that of the authors he gently mocks: "You authors live in the clouds, you do not waste your precious wisdom on trifles and non-essentials, letters that are broken, transposed and inverted" (1). Silva's fictional recreation adds the "non-essentials" of human motives and the "trifles" of how individuals live and love. Whereas the historian's "theme is that of battle and siege, and he is writing about the most virile of deeds" (11), Silva's narrative, by contrast, is focused more on the small human stories that compose history. But these microcosmic stories can have macrocosmic implications.

Saramago's narrator reminds us that starvation is a devastating siege upon the body whose defenses weaken as the condition of hunger worsens until death ensues. The famine suffered by the Moors inside the fortress was, in Saramago's narrator's version of history, a principal reason for the victory of the Portuguese. Silva's encounter with a stray dog reminds the reader that the desperate physical hunger of the have-nots, reducing life to no more than an animal's struggle for survival, reaches across eight centuries. The stray dog, "with more than eight centuries of ill-treatment in its blood and genetic legacy, raised its head from afar to give a pitiful howl, a voice of unabashed frustration and despair begging for food" (141). Similarly, Silva's hunger for companionship and love is viewed as essential to a full life, for life without necessary emotional sustenance is limited.

Historical Contexts

Galicia is now an area of Spain on the Portuguese border, but it was an independent state ruling Portugal until 1139 when under the leadership of Dom Afonso Henrigues (1109–1185) Portugal broke away to form an independent state with Afonso as king. (Among the conquering white Europeans within the novel are Galicians.) Because of his seminal role in founding Portugal, Afonso I is called "The Conqueror," "The Great," and "The Founder," terms that Saramago views ironically as reductive, superficial, and inadequate to the complexities of history.

Afonso fought a number of crucial battles with the Moors who had ruled much of Portugal since the eighth century. On July 25, 1139 Afonso defeated the combined forces of the Moors on the plains of Ourique. Crucial to Afonso's victory over the Moors was his capture of the fortress of Santarem on March 15, 1147. He sent Mem Remaries in disguise to case out the city beforehand. (In Saramago's historical novel – or in Silva's humanized version – Afonso clambers over the city wall on the shoulders of the huge Christian soldier named Mogueime.) Subsequently, the Siege of Lisbon lasted from July 1 to October 25, 1147.

European, and in particular Portuguese, historians have considered the Siege of Lisbon a victory for the Christians, because the Pope authorized Crusaders to take part. In fact, some of the Crusaders who landed in Porto on their way to Palestine joined Afonso. In exchange for a chance to pillage the city and get ransom money for expected prisoners, the Crusaders fought with Afonso. Many of them – English, German, and Flemish fighters – settled in Portugal after Afonso captured Lisbon on October 24, 1147. In the papal bull Manifestis Probatum of 1179, Pope Alexander III acknowledged Afonso as King of an independent Portugal and acknowledged the legitimacy of his ruling the lands that he conquered from the Moors.

Reconfiguring History

Saramago undertakes a siege on accepted history with the purpose of showing the predatory nature of colonization. He debunks the Eurocentric view that the more civilized invaders are fighting the primitive Moors by showing, just as Conrad does in *Heart of Darkness*, that the so-called less advanced culture is as humane as, if not more so than, the Europeans. He does this by having his narrator and Silva present a fictional history that takes account of the human responses of the supposedly less civilized non-Christians. Saramago suggests that this invasion and its one-sided history became a model for Portuguese imperialism in subsequent forays into Africa, South America, and Asia as well as for European imperialism in general.

As presented by the historian whose book Silva is proofreading as well as by Silva and the narrator in more human, imaginative terms, the siege of Lisbon is an imperialistic, Eurocentric siege on the black Moors by white Europeans as well as a siege on Islam by Christianity. Dwelling since the eighth century within the walls of Lisbon, the Moors created a relatively tolerant and civil society and religious culture with their Islamic prayers and rituals while building perhaps the largest city in Europe. In the novel, the Moors are presented sympathetically as victims of intolerant Europeans who are less civilized and who hate Muslims and people of a different color and ethnicity.

The fictional rewriting – performed by Silva but summarized by the narrator in such a way that it seems to be taking place under the latter's (and, of course, Saramago's) auspices – also is a trope for the need to rewrite history in view of current attitudes to discredited past behaviors, including imperialistic and racist assumptions applied to the Moors who were both black Africans and Muslims.

Historiography

Saramago suggests that, despite the ravages of history where people kill one another senselessly and indiscriminately, one small act – the proofreader's one-word attack on the historian's text – can transform how we understand history. To that extent, Saramago is a humanist and optimist in believing that one small act by an insignificant man can open the doors and windows to questioning and reconfiguring accepted notions of history. As he puts it in his *Paris Review* interview:

. . . .

The History of the Siege of Lisbon is not a mere exercise in historical writing. It is a meditation on history as truth or history as a supposition, as one of the possibilities, but not as a lie even though it is often deceitful. It is necessary to confront official history with a *no*, which obliges us to look for another *yes*. This has to do with our own lives, with the life of fiction, with the life of ideologies. For example, a revolution is a *no*; that *no* is converted into a *yes*, either quickly or over time; so then it must be presented with another *no*. I sometimes think that *no* is the most necessary word of our times. Even if that *no* is a mistake, the good that could come from it outweighs the negative. *No* to this world as it is today, for example.

> In the case of this book, it is far less ambitious – it is a small *no*, but it is still capable of changing one's life. By inserting a *not* in the sentence – the official history – that stated that the crusaders did assist the king of Portugal to reconquer Lisbon in 1147, Raimundo was not only led to write another history, but he also opened the way to changing his own life. His negation of that sentence is also a negation of his life as he was living it. That negation took him to another level of being; it removed him from his daily routine – from the grayness of his every day, his melancholy. He moves to another level and to the relationship with Maria Sara. (Saramago, "The Art of Fiction No. 155")

. . . .

What Saramago stresses is that we depend far too much on basic received facts without knowing human motives, but he is also implying that the facts themselves may be less knowable than we think. Of course, as resistant readers, aware of Holocaust deniers and of those who defend slavery as a kind of benign paternalism, we know how playing with facts can have invidious repercussions. For that reason we need to be somewhat wary of Saramago's historical hermeneutics, especially the originating one-word siege on facts represented by the insertion of "not."

Saramago lays siege to the concept of univocal history as well as the historian's view that "history was real life" (10). Saramago seeks to undermine the idea of unilateral, sententious, and accepted historical truth by providing alternative possibilities. His implicit view is that history is ever shifting and that there is always a discrepancy between what happened – the actual originating events – and what we think happened, and between what we think happened and how we organize and tell it. Furthermore, by having Silva's own life events shape the telling, Saramago is dramatizing that all history includes an element of disguised autobiography.

Nor should we forget the narrator's siege on the reader's sensibility. The novel begins with a discussion of the *deleatur*, a proofreader's mark for deletion. Rereading, we realize that the *deleatur* becomes an ironic opening anticipating the physical removal of the Moors from their place within the fortified walled city of Lisbon and the deletion of their culture – as well as the human community that lived within that culture – from the history of Portugal.

In a sense, imaginative literature and imaginative behavior are the heroes of Saramago's novel, but the complex subject is what humans live for, and the complex answer includes power, self-expression, love, sex, recognition, companionship, and security. Emerging from the stylistic experimentation are the basic needs that define humankind.

The narrator and Silva are both aspects of Saramago, even if the line between them becomes blurred in the rewriting of history. Using his narrator and Silva, Saramago shows that imaginative, fictional versions of what might have happened can get us closer to what motivated human behavior than hardened clichés and shibboleths that we might have learned in school. He deconstructs the way we put events into patterns and stories, even while understanding that narratives are essential.

Saramago stresses a thick reading of history focusing, on one hand, on a grammar of motives among the participants, and, on the other, on the many unknowable aspects of the past that elude us. For him history is far more than what happens next or simple facts about how one king succeeded another. Because history is more than a chronicle of kings and battles, and must include the lived lives of ordinary people – including proofreaders – history needs to be understood from the bottom up as well as the top down.

With his interest in those marginalized by history such as foot soldiers and prostitutes, as well as his interest in folk legends, Saramago is what we now call a New Historian. For him, history is far more than the history of the nobility. Put another way, he is more interested in the proofreader, whom he compares to a shoemaker, than the self-regarding historian whom he compares to Apelles, a master fourth-century BC Greek painter (6). In fact we learn that the historian for whom Silva is proofreading has written a pedestrian book: "In those four hundred and thirty-seven pages [the proofreader] did not find a single new fact, controversial interpretation, unpublished document, even as much as a fresh reading. Nothing more than yet another regurgitation of those interminable, played-out accounts of the siege" (30). In contrast to the banal history, Saramago counterpoints the fictional story that the proofreader is writing and Saramago's narrator's complementary telling of that story. Saramago's counterpoint to dry history also includes the story of Silva and Maria Sara within the context of the Lisbon they and the narrator inhabit as well as Saramago's own text that we are reading.

Narrative Form

Saramago's ideas about history shape the formal choices he makes to shape his narrative. Under the umbrella of Silva's supposed imagination, the narrator – Saramago's surrogate – has laid siege not only to the original historian's text by taking control of the historical events but also to the imaginary text Silva is writing. Thus what we read is the narrator's text, not the text that Silva is supposedly writing:

. . . .

[E]verything that has been read here in his name, in the final analysis, is nothing more than a free version and adaptation of a text which probably has little in common with this one and that as far as we can foresee, will be kept back until the very last line, and out of reach of the lovers of naïve history. … It is obvious that Raimundo Silva who has none of the characteristics of the writer, neither the vices nor the virtues, could not possibly within thirty-six hours have written so much with so many variations. (138)

....

In the above passage, "this one" refers not to the original historian's text nor to Silva's creation but to a third one written by the narrator.

This playfulness about who wrote what and from what sources the information is derived has deliberate echoes of Cervantes's *Don Quixote*. Saramago may have wanted to place his novel in the Iberian tradition of Cervantes – with strong components of romance and fantasy – rather than the more realistic Western European tradition represented by Tolstoy and Balzac. Like Cervantes, Saramago strongly suggests that fiction can be truer than history because it is multi-dimensional and takes account of human motives.

For Saramago, digression – as with Sterne in *The Life and Opinions of Tristram Shandy, Gentleman* – from the received historical facts and truths is the way we discover the meaning of history. Indeed, the opening conversation between the proofreader and the historian at first seems a digression until we realize upon rereading that the proofreader, while seemingly obsequious, always calling the historian "Sir," takes pride in his craft and is more knowledgeable than the historian.

The narrator and Silva conduct a siege on traditional chronological time – what happens next – by replacing and reorganizing simple chronological time – what we might call story – into complex narrative discourse. Thus, Saramago's discourse moves back and forth across the centuries, focusing one moment on late twentieth-century events, another on twelfth-century events. The narrator is very much a character watching Silva's plight as a putative author with amusement: "The proof-reader Raimundo Silva is going to need someone to help him to explain how, after having written that the crusaders did not stay for the siege, some of them appear to have disembarked, about a hundred men, if we are to believe the calculation made by the Moors, from a distance and at a glance" (158).

Of course, by now we know that the person whom Saramago provides to help Silva weave an alternative history is the narrator. Another joke is that the Moors' perception of about a hundred men is an invention since, according to the received history, virtually all the visiting Crusaders stayed. Indeed, the narrator playfully speaks to their staying in terms which undermine the proofreader's "not": "Now then, so that these people and others may claim their benefices, it was necessary to begin by making them disembark, and so, there they are, prepared to win them with their arms, thus more or less conciliating the decisive

Not with the *Yes,* or *Perhaps* and the *Even so* with which our national history has been written" (159). Thus the narrator qualifies the alternative history by acceding to an extent to the logic of facts.

Among other things, the frame narrator gives us the point of view of the Moors and some insight into how they live. Most importantly, he humanizes them, in particular the muezzin who calls the Muslims to prayers inside the walls of Lisbon fortress and who is not only blind but suffers from vertigo. That the muezzin is a sympathetic figure gives dignity and particularity to those who are the victims of the siege. By contrast, the historian's book provides much less detail about human motives and idiosyncrasies; he focuses on the history of kings and battles and, in this case, the supposed turning point in the creation of Portugal as a nation-state.

When we first meet Silva he does not have a name – we don't learn what it is until chapter three – and is called (in the novel's first three words that begin with capital letters) simply "THE PROOF-READER" as if he had become his function. He is almost overly deferential to the historian, whom he always addresses as "Sir," but as the opening dialogue, comprising the first chapter, continues, we detect a touch of irony in that appellation. We realize that the proofreader's apparent obsequiousness is a mask for disdain. In fact, in this dialogue, the proofreader gets the better of the historian whose book, *The History of the Siege of Lisbon,* he will be proofreading. At every turn in the repartee the proofreader seems to be more knowledgeable, faster on his feet, more witty, and better read than the patronizing and pretentious historian. Challenged by the proofreader about the importance of the historian, the latter facetiously and condescendingly responds rather nastily: "Truly, you are a walking interrogation and disbelief endowed with arms" (8).

On our rereading, the opening dialogue makes much more sense, and we understand better its place in the novel's structure. For the ensuing novel has confirmed the validity of the proofreader's position in the opening dialogue. Saramago has written a novel that shares the proofreader's view that "history is not real life, literature yes, and nothing else" (8). What at first seems playful repartee is the point of the novel. When the historian declares, "history was real life at the time when it could not yet be called history" (8), the proofreader responds, "Sir, are you sure," implying that history distorts and misses the essence of life. Given his own behavior in terms of drastically inserting a word that changes the meaning of the historian's text, it is not surprising that Silva is drawn to the inexplicable side of history, in particular to behavior (such as his own) that defies logic and reason. For example, when Silva or the narrator (the distinction is often not clear) speculates on the Crusader Guillaume's decision not to join Afonso, he claims that the Crusader Guillaume is motivated by visceral dislike of the king: "[F]or no good reason we take a dislike of someone and nothing will change our mind" (135). Similarly, Silva's own insertion of "not" may result from a gut dislike of the self-regarding, condescending, and pompous historian of the first chapter to whom Silva presents himself – probably facetiously, given his abilities and intelligence – as a "simple man ... without training ... [with] no education beyond primary school" (7).

Silva is interested in how and why people behave, including "foibles and mania" (140). Much of what Silva has learned about human behavior comes from his reading literature (140), and that reading has helped form in Silva what the narrator calls "this coherent and contradictory totality we normally refer to as character" (140). The narrator watches the proofreader Silva with amusement, often from a distance, but the distance narrows when he describes Silva's awakening to love, desire, and passion and concomitantly to his imagination and creative potential.

The narrator responds with amusement to received history, including the notion of God's intervention on the side of the Portuguese: "[W]e never cease to importune God with our wise exhortations, but destiny has its own intransigent laws. And so often with the most surprising and dramatic effects" (12). While much of the alternative history is supposedly written by Silva, part of the fun is that we feel the presence of Saramago's more worldly narrator as a second author and, consequently, we don't know who has written what. Thus after presenting the crucial scene where most of the Crusaders under the leadership of Guillaume refuse to stay with King Afonso, the narrator attributes the account that we have just read to a combination of "what was effectively written with what for the moment only exists in [Silva's] imagination" (137).

How we interpret historical events changes as values evolve, so what may seem justified in one era seems more ambiguous or downright unsavory to another. Entire cultures have different attitudes to the way ethnic and racial minorities, gays, and women should be treated. In our era, reductive summaries of the history of kings without reference to their actual complex bundle of motives, obsessions, and desires is unsatisfactory. In that sense, our explanations and discussions become more complex and require digressions from formerly monolithic explanations. Or as the narrator puts it: "Certain authors, perhaps out of conviction or an attitude of mind not much given to patient investigation, hate having to acknowledge that the relationship between what we call cause and what we subsequently describe as the effect is not always linear and explicit" (104). We don't always know exactly why humans behave as they do any more than we can plot a teleology of history. While we can look for multiple causes as to why Silva inserted the "not" and why he and the younger Maria Sara are attracted to one another or why he pours his hair dye down the sink, we cannot find necessary and sufficient explanations.

Unknowability is a theme of the novel. We never even know, Saramago emphasizes, what fully motivates our own contemporary generation to say nothing of past generations to whom we cannot speak. We cannot understand completely what makes individual humans behave as they do; no matter how much we think we know, grey areas remain. Thus not only are we in the dark about what happened in the twelfth century, but even the reasons for Silva's behavior also can elude the narrator "whom the ill-informed believe to know all the facts and to be holding all the keys, were this so, one of the good things the world still possesses would be lost, privacy, the mystery surrounding characters" (106). Here Saramago is admonishing the reader that his narrator is not responsible for knowing everything because he is not fully omniscient, but rather is a knowledgeable voice offering his own perspective.

As with several other novels in this study, including Kundera's *The Unbearable Lightness of Being*, Grass's *The Tin Drum*, and Pamuk's *My Name is Red*, Saramago's novel is making the point that omniscience is a deviation from realism rather than realism. One feature of omniscience is to identify the speakers clearly so we always know immediately who is speaking. But when we remember a conversation, does this clarity occur? The dialogic opening, we realize upon rereading, is an explicit challenge to the convention of omniscience and a deliberate effort to confuse the reader. Flouting expectations, the narrator uses capitals to indicate transitions from one speaker to another, while replacing periods – indicating a stop – with commas. Moreover, the narrator withholds clarifying commentary, leaving the reader to try to figure out who is speaking and to what purpose.

Saramago's style enacts the indeterminacy and uncertainty of knowing that are his themes. One could argue that his muddling and blurring the identity of speakers is a way of showing the generic nature of their conversations as well as suggesting that at times words matter less than the underlying motives. For the most part, while understanding the confusion some readers experience, I see the point of Saramago's formal decision to make identifying the speaker a challenge to readers.

To stress unknowability, Saramago throughout the novel temporarily confuses the reader in what some would call the Fallacy of Imitative Form. That is, he uses confusion to render confusion, including the way that he blurs the identity of a speaker. Furthermore, Saramago plays not only with diachronic resonances – with contemporary characters partially resembling historical ones – but also with synchronic resonances. Thus Maria (with whom Silva has the hint of a flirtatious relationship) is also the name of his housekeeper, while the telephone operator in Maria Sara's office is named Sara.

Unknowability includes looking skeptically at received history. When we accept an historian calling Afonso "The Great," we ignore some of the horrors committed under his auspices, notably killing people of different religions and skin colors to assert the domination of one group over another. Similarly, Saramago implies that Christian historians have oversimplified the conquest of the Moors as a victory for Christianity, favored by God, over the Muslims, whom the historians categorize as pagans. The catalyst for undoing the reductive version of accepted history is Silva's insertion of the word "not" into one sentence. This tiny change in the historian's text by a proofreader sets up a fictional digression from accepted history that uncovers unseen complexities.

Saramago uses Silva to make larger points about a nation's history, values, religion, and art in a way that anticipates Pamuk's *My Name is Red*. By providing an equally plausible history, Saramago shows his skepticism about univocal histories of events eight hundred years old that are dependent on sparse documentation and legends. The accepted "history" depends on miracles including the intervention of the Virgin Mary to restore the Portuguese king's crippled legs to health. Saramago's narrator (and surrogate) has a healthy skepticism about such miracles; that is another reason for the need for an alternate and in-depth version of history that considers not just what happened but the complex causes. For example, in the fictional revisionist history provided by the narrator and Silva, Saramago makes clear that in his view it is likely that the Crusaders who did stay – whether it be the historical larger number or the rump group in the fictional retelling – did so to achieve economic gain rather than for spiritual reasons.

Indeed, Saramago's narrator is much aware of the inextricable relation between the sacred and profane and between the sublime and the bathetic as well as of the complexity of human motives. Although we are dealing with a translation, we cannot help thinking of Joyce's use of "dog" as an inversion of God and how he uses it to emphasize the animality of man. In Silva's telling Knight Heinrich – whose last name is somewhat homophonic with the Portuguese king, Dom Afonso Henriques – is soon elevated to sainthood notwithstanding his having a relationship with the concubine Ouroana.

Raimundo Silva

Just as our ideas and thoughts digress, Saramago implies, so do our private stories. Silva's digression from a man who has lived a most ordinary, uneventful, and routinized life begins with the insertion of "not." That is the moment when he existentially takes hold of his life and begins to create a proactive identity and to become a catalyst for attracting the love that he lacks. He begins to be the cause of his own life.

When we meet the deracinated Silva, he has a strong resemblance to Camus's Meursault in *The Stranger* (in some translations, *The Outsider*). Notwithstanding his sly repartee with the historian in the first chapter, he is timid and passive, and scared of Costa, his supervisor. To emphasize his isolation and his sense of otherness, Saramago uses indirect discourse to render his responses and to emphasize how few words he exchanges with others in between the opening chapters and the awakening of his emotions that takes place when Maria Sara phones him.

Until he inserts his change in the manuscript, Silva had been living a humdrum life composed of very regular routines and not much companionship. He is introduced impersonally as "The Proof-Reader" and is not given a name until the third section (3). He makes a small living as a proofreader but lives a routinized life without much passion or emotion. But the change becomes a catalyst for changes in life. Silva's taking the initiative on the manuscript opens the doors and windows of his imagination and passion.

Saramago's narrator is a somewhat ironic presence bemusedly watching his somewhat poignant character and presenting him as an unlikely candidate to assert himself in any way. Silva seems to lack personal attachments, family history, religious commitment, friends, or even pursuits that matter to him. The narrator calls his lifestyle "sedentary" (29). Economically, he is eking out a living, doing pedestrian freelance editorial work. He eats almost the same food every day, and does not seem to have traveled at all. Basically he lives an abstemious life with few pleasures, but even on his modest salary he can afford a housekeeper twice a week to help keep his apartment in order and cook the same soup for him. The proofreader is a kind of housekeeper to texts; just as Silva leaves menial tasks to Maria, his housekeeper, the historian and other authors leave the housekeeping of their texts to Silva.

The narrator provides ironic and comic allusions. Rereading we understand the comic anticipation and fun of calling Silva a "Romeo gazing upon Juliet for the first time, innocent and transfixed by love" (30). For, dying his hair and reaching middle age without ever having had a sustained love relationship, Silva is a somewhat bathetic older version of a putative Romeo. Yet this most unlikely character does find his Juliet in a younger woman who is attracted to him.

We are not told Silva's exact age but we do know that he is in his "fifties" (25). He thinks of himself as rather elderly, and we hear a hint of regret that age has toned him down: "Age brings us one good thing which is bad, it calms us down, and quells our temptations, and even when they are overpowering, they become less urgent" (6). He is a confirmed bachelor or thinks he is: "[W]ho is going to love me at my age, or who am I going to love, although, as everyone knows, it is easier to love than be loved" (25). Indeed, the narrator tells us: "So there is no woman in the house, nor has there ever been" (25). Silva's only sexual experience with women seems to have been with prostitutes: "[He] has always had to pay, no other solution, even when he did not get any satisfaction" (25).

Silva lives a narrow, insulated, even claustrophobic life defined in large part by his work as a proofreader. Reserved in the extreme, he is a loner whose only interaction seems to be a superficial acquaintance with the person who cleans his house. We learn nothing about his past, his parentage, or what made him the way he is. He lacks self-esteem, initiative, and creativity and seems to be emotionally anesthetized. Indeed, his routinized life has a parallel in the blind muezzin who ascends the minaret to assemble the faithful to prayer. The narrator laughs at Silva's odd appearance, particularly his hair, which he has been dying and which "has a uniform color which nears a striking resemblance to a dowdy moth-eaten wig, long forgotten and then rediscovered in some attic" (90).

The word "not" strikingly represents who Silva is, namely a negation of a fully committed and involved adult with meaningful human relationships and avocations. By subtracting himself from much of life, he has in effect used the *deleatur* on himself; he has deleted himself from much of life and sought refuge in his apartment where he carries on the basic functions of eating, sleeping, and keeping warm. Indeed, the *deleatur* is a version of the inserted "not," for both are substantive negations, negations which are metonymies for a figure that the narrator regards as pathetic in his ostrich-like relationship to life. Silva's use of "not" sets off a concatenation of events that moves him from saying "no" to much of life to embracing it.

Silva's inexplicable addition of "not" changes his life. We might think of such impulsive life-changing moments as Meursault's shooting an Arab in Camus's *The Stranger* or Aschenbach's decision to go to Venice in *Death in Venice*, but the difference is that Silva's existential action leads not to death – as in the case of Meursault and Aschenbach – but to affirmation and expansion of his life. Here the change is for the better. When the narrator, thinking of whether Silva's home is within or without the walls under siege, ominously remarks, "we cannot be sure whether Raimundo Silva is one of the besieged or an assailant, a future conqueror or hopeless loser" (65), we realize that he is describing a man whose life hangs in the balance. We recall Meursault's behavior before the fatal shooting when Silva awaits a response from the publisher to his changing the text. The narrator speaks of Silva's thinking as "inert" and "detached": "[T]here comes a moment in which the vagueness of one's thinking becomes an obsession" (82).

What is ironic is that Silva himself does not understand why he committed his existential act of negation. Nor, apparently, does the somewhat ingenuous narrator who seems bemused by Silva's behavior but also has a limited perspective and sometimes expresses wonderment at what is taking place. We might

define the narrator as a character who has access to the contemporary characters' private conversations – most notably those between Silva and the historian
and between Silva and Maria Sara – but not to the author who invents them. In
other words, the narrator provides an incomplete perspective around which
Saramago draws a circumference of judgment or, put another way, Saramago
inserts another frame so that the narrator becomes a dramatized presence to
which the audience must attend.

The Mutual Siege on Affections: How and Why Maria Sara and Silva Find One Another

The concept of siege also applies to the mutual effort of Maria Sara and Silva to
break through personal fortresses comprised of various defenses (more pro-
nounced in Silva than in Maria Sara) to win the heart of a beloved and fulfill
romantic and sexual desires. In fact, Silva has little experience of the world as
far as we can tell notwithstanding his comically defensive contention that
"proof-readers have had wide experience of both literature and life, giving to
understand that what they did know or wish to learn about life, literature more
or less taught them" (140). Both lonely, Maria Sara and Silva actively lay siege to
each other's emotional defenses.

In a playful wink at the comedy of manners, Saramago equates siege with
seduction. By means of mutual seduction, Silva and Maria Sara remove "not"
from their personal relationship. Maria Sara has ended an affair three months
ago and she is the more proactive of the two: "[A] woman … who is capable of
taking decisive action," she attacks his fortress of privacy and set routines (163).
He is "timid by nature or temperament, averse to crowds" (163) and at first
seems hardly the right man for a love affair. The narrator smilingly intrudes,
calling attention to his own role as puppeteer and enabler of fictions: "So let us
leave in peace this man who is not quite ready to look, even though he spends
his life revising proofs, and who only occasionally, because of some psychological disturbance, notices things, and let us find someone else who, not so much
for his own merits, ever questionable … may take his place in the narrative
quite naturally, so that people will come to say … that they were made for each
other" (163). By rapidly reverting to the twelfth century, the narrator reminds
us that he is both telling the contemporary story and retelling and reimaging
the twelfth-century history and that there are important parallels between the
two narratives. Thus Silva responds to Maria Sara's puzzling but proactive
phone call. As a result of her siege on his heart, he continues to emerge from his
cocoon; in a sweet yet telling gesture, Silva puts the white rose associated with
her on top of the historian's book, *The History of the Siege of Lisbon*.

"Siege" is also used to describe not only the gypsy girl Ouroana's continuing hunger for life's necessities but ours, the readers', as well. As Maria Sara puts it eloquently (if not with romantic idealism) in the penultimate chapter: "Of course we're at war, and it's a war of siege, each of us besieges the other and is besieged in turn, we want to break down the other's walls while defending our own, love means getting rid of all barriers, love is the end of all sieges" (295–296). Maria Sara's siege began when Silva said "no" by putting a "not" to "an incontrovertible historical fact" (296). His "not" becomes an identifying mark of assertion, independence, and humanity. By implication, he becomes one who has the courage to separate himself from the herd. As she puts it, perhaps hyperbolically exalting her lover: "[B]lessed are those who say no. … [T]he kingdom on earth belongs to those who have the wit to put a *no* at the service of a *yes*, having been the perpetrators of a *no*, they rapidly erase it to restore a *yes*" (296). His "no" to love has become a "yes." Silva says "yes" after all his "no's"; these "no's" were not to specific women but to taking the risks of rejection, disappointment, frustration, and misunderstanding.

To stress his awareness that he has understood Maria Sara's saying human needs for love don't change, Silva responds, referencing the lovers in his imaginative recreation of the twelfth century, "Well said, dear Ouroana," to which she responds, "Thank You, dear Moguieme" (296). We understand that Silva *seizes* history and reductively remakes it to parallel the plot lines of his own life. He stresses that the romance between Mogueme and Ouroana parallels his own relationship with Maria Sara.

But, again, a resistant reader understands that there is a huge difference between changing one's mind in personal relationships and rewriting history so as to deny incontrovertible facts, such as how women, like Ouroana, were once treated as chattels, or that the Europeans overthrew the Moors and their culture in the twelfth century, or that the United States tolerated slavery until the Civil War or that Hitler presided over the killing of millions of Jews.

The distinction between Silva and the narrator blurs as if Silva were himself telling a story where he is described in the third person. But in fact we realize that the narrator, in one of his frequent intrusions, has taken over the telling and is summarizing Silva's thinking processes. It is the narrator as much as Silva who reminds us that Maria Sara, unlike Ouroana, is "nobody's concubine, if you'll pardon that indelicate word which is no longer relevant in describing sexual mores. … [W]e can assume all they have in common is desire, felt as deeply by Mogueime at that time as by Raimundo now, such differences as exist, are purely cultural, yes, Sir" (227). But the "Sir," taking us back to the opening dialogue when Silva addressed the historian as "Sir," reminds us that we can not always separate interior monologues from narrative summaries and therefore calls attention to how difficult it is to locate exactly what happens even in the present – indeed even in fiction. We are reminded, too, of the thin line between a homodiegetic narrator, who takes part in the plot, and a hetero-diegetic narrator who does not.

The Crucial Telephone Conversation

Saramago's novel calls attention to parallels and differences between the different customs and means of communication in the twelfth-century world and the contemporary one. Yet, over the centuries, how we understand one another's subjective feelings by listening, observing, and responding does not change much. One of the novel's highlights is the telephone conversation when Maria Sara thanks Silva for calling to ask about her health. Saramago catches the right pitch of the to-and-fro of seduction banter, the evasions, the interruptions, the search for positional assurance as Silva and Maria Sara advance and retreat. At first, although she takes the lead, they both move from formality to politeness to intimacy, even while pretending that his call was just something one ordinarily does when one's boss isn't at work.

Maria Sara reminds him that she had asked that he call her: "Therefore I can assume you couldn't help calling me once I had taken the initiative" (210). She is the more aggressive one, and he is always ready to retreat behind his masque of detachment: "It's you who are evading the question, you're hiding from yourself and want me to tell you what you already know" (211). She actualizes the potential within him: "I telephoned you because I was feeling lonely, because I was curious to know if you were working, because I wanted you to take an interest in my health" (211). Her acknowledgment that she is interested in him causes him to advance in his siege; or, put another way, they are both laying a siege on loneliness and are allies without knowing it. At this point, he reveals his feelings rather bluntly: "I like you" (211). While she claims to be direct, her response shows that she knows the subtleties of flirtation and seduction much better and in more nuanced ways than he does: "You took your sweet time before telling me" (211).

Thinking she is married or engaged, he retreats to his own fortress of shyness: "[M]y biggest mistake right now is to have confessed that I like you, … Because I know nothing of your private life" (212). Assuring him that she is a free spirit and would be interested in him were she married or engaged even while telling him she is not, she asserts: "I am fond of you" (212). Showing an emotional range well beyond Silva's cautious, self-protective fastidiousness, she confides her past and her hopes before demurring: "[P]ay no attention to this wild outburst, it's just that I'm brimming over with joy" (212).

Saramago's narrator is presenting a gentle modern comedy of manners. In a swift change of positions, Silva becomes the aggressor and she the more reticent. When Silva excitedly exclaims, "Can I confide that I love you," she responds, using her own term "fond": "No, simply say you are fond of me. … Then keep the rest for the day you truly love me, should that day ever come" (212). When he says, "Let me leave you a kiss," she responds: "The time will come for kisses" (213). Rhetorically, they have changed places; he is hyperbole, she litotes.

Silva's newly awakened passion and energy find an outlet in a later telephone conversation which is kind of coda to the crucial one I have been discussing. In that later dialogue, he signs off with a direct allusion to the parallel between his writing a fictional account of the siege of Lisbon and his taking a risk with Maria Sara by continuing this counter-siege on her affections: "I haven't come all this way to die before the walls of Lisbon" (219). With a smile, we recall the actual walls are right above his apartment.

Study Questions for *The History of the Siege of Lisbon*

1. What does Saramago find troubling about traditional history with its focus on kings and battles?
2. What does the fictional version add to the historical version of the Europeans' triumph over the Muslims?
3. Why does the proofreader Silva insert the "not" into the historian's text?
4. Why does Saramago use parallels between the twentieth and twelfth centuries?
5. What is the significance of the twelfth-century characters Ouroana and Mogueime?
6. What is the function of the opening chapter? Why are beginnings of fictions so important?
7. How does Maria Sara launch her siege on Silva's routinized life and how does Silva respond with a siege of his own?
8. What is distinctive about Saramago's style? Does the absence of quotation marks create problems for the reader and if so, are they justified?
9. What is the role of the narrator? In what ways is he a character?
10. What similarities and contrasts do you see with other texts in this study?

Notes

1. José Saramago, "The Art of Fiction No. 155." Interview by Donzalina Barroso. *Paris Review* 149 (Winter 1998); https://www.theparisreview.org/interviews/1032/jose-saramago-the-art-of-fiction-no-155-jose-saramago
2. Harold Bloom, "The Grand Comedian Visits the Bible," *NYR* 59:3 (Feb. 23, 2012), 40–43; see 40.
3. Page references are from José Saramago, *The History of the Siege of Lisbon*, trans. Giovanni Pontiero (Orlando: Harcourt, 1998).

Chapter 12

Orhan Pamuk's *My Name is Red* (1998): Cultural Conflict in Sixteenth-Century Istanbul and its Modern Implications

"Space: What you damn well have to see."

Joyce, *Ulysses* (IX.86)

"[P]ainting is the act of seeking out Allah's memories and seeing the world as He sees the world."

Pamuk, *My Name is Red*, 79[1]

Introduction

Part of the pleasure of reading is entering into another time, another place, and another culture. Reading Orhan Pamuk's *My Name is Red* (1998; trans. 2001), we can imagine ourselves in sixteenth-century Istanbul at a time when arbitrary law, including torture, coexists with lawlessness and near anarchy in a civilization marked by a great gulf between wealth and poverty. Pamuk (1952–), Turkey's first Nobel laureate in literature, sets his fictional plot over nine days in the winter of 1591 during the reign of the Ottoman Sultan Murat III. *My Name is Red* not only offers us a window into the Ottoman Empire of 1591, but also brilliantly captures wide swathes of the Ottoman culture that dominated Turkey for several centuries and peaked in the sixteenth and seventeenth centuries. We need to remember that at the height of its power under Suleiman the Magnificent, the Ottoman Empire was the world's dominant political and cultural power.

Pamuk, who before and after writing *My Name is Red* spent a great deal of time in New York, has deep roots in Istanbul which he regards as home. He considers

Reading the Modern European Novel Since 1900: A Critical Study of Major Fiction from Proust's Swann's Way to Ferrante's Neapolitan Tetralogy, First Edition. Daniel R. Schwarz.
© 2018 John Wiley & Sons Ltd. Published 2018 by John Wiley & Sons Ltd.

himself a cultural Muslim but does not believe in God. While *My Name is Red* is very much in keeping with the novel's twentieth-century thematic and formal innovations, it also pays homage to earlier influences that comprise the unique Turkish culture. Pamuk recalls that "[O]nce I was in the United States, … I had to begin by making a strong distinction between the religious and literary connotations of Islamic literature, so that I could easily appropriate its wealth of games, gimmicks, and parables" (Orhan Pamuk, "The Art of Fiction No. 187").[2]

Pamuk explores the difference between Ottoman and European aesthetic conventions in the visual arts, specifically the difference between the decorative and ornamental tradition of the Ottoman aesthetic and the representative European tradition. While Pamuk's focus is on how Ottoman artistic conventions – specifically those of miniaturist painters – were challenged by new ways of conceptualizing what art is, he also shows how these artistic differences are indications of ways of thinking about larger cultural and political issues. Moreover, by implication, he casts a wide net to show that jealousy, violence, and greed motivate human behavior then and now. Indeed Pamuk's *My Name is Red* – with its mixture of satire, social criticism, detective story, historical novel, and noir comedy – has a kind of miniaturist (read: microcosmic) focus on a tiny segment of culture, even while describing macrocosmic conditions, conflicts, issues, and passions that occur in contemporary Turkey and many other, if not virtually all, countries.

Pamuk's novel opens doors to a world different from our other texts. Yet, influenced by Joyce, Kafka, Borges, Nabokov, Calvino, Woolf, Mann, Eco, and especially Faulkner, Pamuk emerges as a modernist in the Western tradition even while paying homage to the Turkish Ottoman heritage, one which combined Arab and Persian influences (Pamuk, "The Art of Fiction No. 187").

The events of the novel take place during the reign of the Ottoman Murat III who was interested in miniaturists and under whose auspices were produced *The Book of Skills*, *The Book of Festivities*, and *The Book of Victories*. In fact, Nakkaş (which means miniaturist) Osman is the model for Pamuk's sixteenth-century fictional Master Osman, and those working with Nakkaş contributed to these books (Fig. 4). Since Osman Gazi is regarded as the founder in the early fourteenth century of the Turkish Empire, Pamuk has another reason for making Osman the leading miniaturist of his fictional world.

In the novel, the fictional Master Osman and Enishte Effendi ("Effendi" is an appellation of respect and courtesy meaning "Honored Sir" or just "Sir") are in a struggle to gain the Sultan's approval and to control the miniature industry. The Sultan commissions Enishte to contract with some miniaturists to secretly compile and edit a book for him in the European representative style, a book that represents "Our Sultan's entire world" (25). Ironically, the Ottoman miniaturists

Fig. 4 *The Siege of Vienna* as illustrated by Nakkaş Osman (last quarter of sixteenth century). http://kilyos.ee.bilkent.edu.tr/~history/ottoman2.html.

trained by Master Osman are already deviating from the pure style of decoration and ornamentation. Even while illustrating traditional stories, they are moving closer than they publicly acknowledge to using individualizing details in the European style. In other words, the Sultan wants a book in which idealization and decorative embellishment are replaced by what the painter actually sees.

While European painters identify themselves by name rather than, as in the world of the miniaturists, efface their individual identity, each of the supposedly anonymous miniaturists has, to the eye of an expert, his own unique stylistic idiosyncrasies. The miniaturists collaborate under a master; each contributes a specialty in which he excels. In part, this is to efface individual differences in style, but in fact, a skilled senior artist such as Master Osman can tell which of his disciples has painted what. Solving the murder mystery involves discovering the nuanced differences in the miniaturists' styles.

Pamuk's challenge was to find a plot that weaves together his ambitious project. His lynchpin is the character Black, a former miniaturist and Enishte's nephew whom Enishte called back from a twelve-year exile to help Enishte with the book he is compiling for the Sultan. It was Enishte who had banished Black for wooing his daughter Sheruke. Black takes on the role of detective in discovering the murderer of one of Master Osman's miniaturists. Specifically, Black tries to figure out which of the three other miniaturists working on the Sultan's book killed a fourth one and, after Black's arrival, also killed Enishte. As in many detective stories, Black successfully pursues a beautiful woman, in this case, Sheruke.

Pamuk's second challenge was to find a way of telling his detective story without an intrusive omniscient narrator and at the same time take his readers into a culture foreign to most of them. In masterful acts of ventriloquy, Pamuk solves this by eschewing a traditional narrator entirely and creating diverse voices – including some inanimate ones – that defy realistic expectations. What is special about Pamuk's *My Name is Red* is his imaginative use of multiple viewpoints.

The first person narratives take the form of dramatic monologues in which the reader is put in the place of a listener who must balance sympathy and judgment. In *My Name is Red* the monologists are self-conscious about the presence, sympathy, and judgment of their audience. Their monologues are not only invitations into the world of the speaker but also self-justifying rhetorical efforts to engage readers on the side of the speaker. Basically, the speakers are all self-dramatizing performative storytellers making their case as if before a jury rather than presenting themselves as entertainers.

Thus we readers are asked to judge the speakers' behavior as if we were within the text and had some kind of authority. Pamuk invites his readers to become part of the novel, sifting evidence, noticing contradictions, making judgments, and closing the hermeneutical circle. The very first speaker, the corpse of Elegant, asks us to "[L]isten to me" and to attend to "underlying truths and voices from beyond" (6). The murderer opens chapter 28 entitled "I Will Be Called a Murderer" by observing, "Doubtless, you too have experienced what I'm about to describe" as if the imagined listener were living within the imagined world of 1591 rather than in Pamuk's end of the twentieth century world (154).

Underlining why he chose multiple perspectives, Pamuk observed in his *Paris Review* interview: "Most of the time I feel better when I'm impersonating someone else rather than writing in the third person" (Pamuk, "The Art of Fiction No. 187"). Twelve narrators speak in fifty-nine separate chapters; no narrator speaks in two chapters in a row. Some of the narrators are entities that we do not expect to be speaking, namely Death, a dog, a tree, a gold coin, a horse, and the color red as well as Satan. To be sure, their voices might be attributed to the ventriloquist storyteller, who functions at times as a kind of surrogate for Pamuk. Red speaks not only as the color of blood and passion – evoking two main themes of the plot – but also to make the point that the miniaturists have one ideal red in mind as opposed to the Venetians, who use a variety of red tones in the same painting.

Pamuk writes as if he were a scholar of this period, and especially of miniaturist art. Although we know that Pamuk as a young man wanted to be a painter and is intensely interested in the visual arts, we do not know how much this display of learning is factually correct. Certainly the inclusion of the chronology at the back of the book gives us some confidence, but in reality this is only a small set of notes. To follow the details, we need to Google Pamuk's abstruse references, but English readers – and my guess is Turkish readers, too – could use more detailed annotations. For example, Enishte is reading *The Book of the Soul* by Ibn Qayyim Al-Jawziyya, who was in fact a Sunni commentator on the Qur'an (Koran); he argued that the souls of the dead remain on earth and can hear the living, which is what the murdered Elegant Effendi is doing. But other claims within *My Name is Red* about great miniaturists and their role in essential decisions made by rulers may be fictional since I could find little confirming evidence to support these claims. Pamuk, like many of the authors in this study, enjoys mixing realism, history, meta-fiction, and fantasy in a mélange of genres that challenge traditional ideas about what the novel should be.

Pamuk would have expected his Turkish readers to know that Murat III presided ruthlessly over Turkey during a period of economic stagnation and that Istanbul, like the entire country, was involved in endless wars. Like other despots, Pamuk's fictional Sultan governs by fear; he uses methods of torture to extract secrets from those whom he distrusts or who challenge his authority. Pamuk may also be alluding to contemporary Turkish history in the 1990s, including political instability, violence, and a covert coup. Pamuk wants us to smile at Enishte's referring to Murat III as "His Excellency, Our Sultan, the Foundation of the World," as if such a ludicrous appellation were necessary for Enishte to keep his position as a privileged figure (25).

Thematic Issues: Ottoman Miniatures versus European Art

For the miniaturist, perfect art approaches eternity by approaching the ideal form. In contrast to the realism of the Venetians and Franks (a term used in the novel for Western Europeans, although the Franks were originally a group of Germanic tribes) whose portraiture presents the uniqueness of each human being, the Ottoman miniaturist does not copy what he sees in this world (137). Olive, who turns out to be the murderer and whose views are inconsistent, expresses – without fully adhering to it – the orthodoxy of the kind of non-mimetic art favored by the Ottoman culture: "[P]ainting is the act of seeking out Allah's memories and seeing the world as He sees the world" (79). If we were to use classical Western concepts, these miniaturists follow the Platonic models that focus on transcendent reality and reject mimesis. They seek to paint the ideal forms of things rather than individual examples in contrast to the Europeans, who are Aristotelians focused on the "ineluctable modality of the visible" and paint, to recall Stephen Dedalus's redefinition of Aristotle's words in Joyce's *Ulysses*, "What you damn well have to see" (III.1; IX.86).

Pamuk draws upon a reading (often favored by Sunnis) of the Qur'an called aniconism in which images not only of God, Muhammad, and the prophets but of all sentient beings – not only humans but animals – are forbidden. Some of this is derived from the Hadith, which describe Muhammad's words and behavior. The miniaturists' paintings reflect the view that Allah is eternal and that individual humans come and go even if human behavior remains more or less a constant.

Aniconism is responsible for the decorative tradition, including calligraphy, geometric patterns, and the rhythmic patterns of the arabesque in Muslim art. Thus the miniaturist paintings are two dimensional, somewhat abstract and stylized and indifferent to variations in human physiognomy. If humans are depicted in Muslim art, they are not individualized but are representative much like trees or mountains. Indeed, the paintings are often done not by one person but in a workshop in part because the art itself is the product of collective respect for Allah rather than the result of individual expression.

Generic humans often illustrate a traditional tale such as Sohrab and Rustum – taken from the Persian epic *Shahnameh: The Book of Kings* – where Rustum slays his long-lost son. While the narrative of such legends is stressed, there is little emphasis on a grammar of motives which would explain human behavior.

Referring to prior myths and legends as a bridge to understanding contemporary events, whether in painting or literature, is a way of saying the present is a version of the past. In *My Name is Red*, literary and visual references are to myths or mythicized versions of the accomplishments of kings rather than to actual events in the contemporary culture of the 1590s. Implicit in this approach is that events of the 1590s replicate what happened in the past and that we need not differentiate between recurring themes and current particularities.

Let us consider the episode when Butterfly turns the tables on Black; the latter had come with a dagger to search Butterfly's home but Butterfly is now physically on top of him with his sword at Black's throat. In his narration of the event, Butterfly transforms moral issues into aesthetic ones: "[O]ne can sense the difficulty of elegantly drawing two men who despise each other yet whose bodies, like ours, have become as one" (362). At this point, Butterfly references tales of prior beheadings – one from *The Book of Kings* (Tur beheading his brother Iraj), another from Persian legend of Geruy beheading Siyavush – and their visual renderings. Yet Pamuk does note the irony of Butterfly's also expressing his own individual feelings – including feeling "excitement" when he imagines his wife watching the struggle – in the tradition of Western realism (362).

Pamuk stresses throughout that what is not said is often as important as what is said. In this case he is showing us that Butterfly's epistemology and semiotics as well as those of the other major characters are shaped by the subcultural world in which they find themselves. While we may resist the practices of the Ottoman world of 1591, our resistance to the world of any culture is often on the narrow grounds prescribed by our own culture. But at times, Pamuk implies, we need to transcend that parochialism, and he may be thinking of his Turkish audience in the 1990s who are still struggling with how to resolve their Ottoman heritage with European values.

When referencing European art, what does Pamuk have in mind? By the end of the sixteenth century Venetian painting meant Titian, Tintoretto, and Veronese, but "Venetian" and "Frankish" masters are also metonymies for European painting. What Pamuk has in mind is the movement, beginning with Cimabue, Duccio, and Giotto, from medieval iconography to a world where even traditional biblical scenes included human models with human expressions of feeling. Giovanni Bellini's *St. Francis in the Desert* (1476–1478) in the New York Frick Collection depicts a quite human St. Francis receiving the stigmata. In the penultimate chapter of *My Name is Red* Olive, when referencing the Venetian school, refers to the Venetian artist Sebastiano del Piombo (1485–1547), who trained with the Venetians Giovanni Bellini and Giorgione and later Raphael in Rome, and combined the Venetian emphasis on elaborate colors with the formal control of the Roman artists.

Pamuk's Aesthetic

In *My Name is Red*, Pamuk's reconciliation of the allegories of Muslim art with the realism of European art evokes Eric Auerbach's *Mimesis*. Written in Istanbul, as Pamuk surely knows, *Mimesis* traces how the novel combines the realistic humanism of the Greeks with the allegorical tradition of the Bible.

Osman, the Head Illuminator, defines an important aesthetic principle of the miniaturists: "Meaning precedes form in the world of our art. As we begin to paint in imitation of the Frankish and Venetian masters ... the domain of meaning ends and the domain of form begins" (318). Pamuk writes about the Ottoman culture from something of an outsider's perspective. As he tells us in his *Paris Review* interview, he considers himself more as belonging to the Western world than to the Eastern world, and he regards the novel as a Western form and himself as an outsider looking at the Turkish past and present:

· ·

The modern novel, dissociated from the epic form, is essentially a non-Oriental thing. Because the novelist is a person who does not belong to a community, who does not share the basic instincts of community, and who is thinking and judging with a different culture than the one he is experiencing. Once his consciousness is different from that of the community he belongs to, he is an outsider, a loner. And the richness of his text comes from that outsider's voyeuristic vision.

Once you develop the habit of looking at the world like that and writing about it in this fashion, you have the desire to disassociate from the community. (Pamuk, "The Art of Fiction No. 187")

· ·

While the non-realistic miniaturist art of the 1590s avoided the here and now, Pamuk's focus is on day-to-day life in the Istanbul of the 1590s, including the poverty and misery to which the Sultan paid little attention. Pamuk uses the descriptive specificity of Western realism to render Butterfly's atelier as well as Stork's and Olive's home as if to show what is missing from the decorative and replicating tradition of their art. It is all very well to depict the world as Allah might see it, but, Pamuk asks, doesn't art also have the purpose of awakening the consciousness of its viewers? While all three miniaturist suspects provide basic representative drawings for the storyteller at the café they visit, what they don't do is render the near chaos going on in Istanbul where murder and marauding seem to be ubiquitous. Implicitly, as I have mentioned, Pamuk may be alluding to chaos in contemporary Turkey in the late 1990s, especially the 1993 covert military coup.

The café's subversive storyteller provides an outlet for the miniaturists' imaginative forays into realism and even magic realism. The storyteller uses their drawings as props for performances that reference the here and now. In the tradition of European realists, the storyteller creates sentient creatures. Their speaking in human voices by means of the storyteller's ventriloquism is a violation of aniconism. In a covert way, the miniaturists have arrogantly taken the act of creation on themselves and given support to the realist tradition they supposedly abhor. The drawings of Death, Satan, and a tree enable the storyteller to introduce mortality and evil as presences within the novel's imagined world and to speak about the aesthetic and moral issues within the novel.

It is fitting that Death is drawn by Olive, the murderer. The rereader knows Olive's identity because Death tells us that his creator "now roams the streets endlessly each night ... [and] he believes he's become what he has drawn"; we know it is Olive who roams the streets at night (129).

Given his preoccupation with Satan, we can also infer that Olive drew him. In the crucial 47th chapter, "I, Satan," Satan prides himself for not bowing down to man and sides with those who refuse to depict humans as they are or place them at the center of pictures. Indeed, Satan offers perhaps the fullest critique of European painting: "[T]hey're not satisfied with merely depicting and displaying every single detail down to the eye color, complexion, curvy lips, forehead wrinkles, rings and disgusting ear hair of gentlemen, priests, wealthy merchants and even women – including the lovely shadows that fall between their breasts. These artists also dare to situate their subjects in the center of the page, as if man were meant to be worshipped" (290).

In fact Satan's position is more complicated than his above critique, for Satan begins his monologue by embracing nominalistic features of this world and thus aligning himself with the very European tradition that he seems to dismiss: "I am fond of the smell of red peppers frying in olive oil, rain falling into a calm sea at dawn, the unexpected appearance of a woman at an open window, silences, thought, and patience" (287). Satan's enthusiasm for the shadows between women's breasts not only has a mischievous wink, but also shows him fascinated with the play of light and shadows which is a major component of European painting, particularly in the late 1590s when Caravaggio came to prominence. But most notable in the above passage is that in praising "silences, thought, and patience," Satan aligns himself with qualities almost all cultures value.

Moreover Satan's monologue is audience-centered as if he needed his listener's approval of his argument – "[Y]ou're astute enough to take an interest in my words" (288) – and as if he were sure the audience (including us readers) will as fellow relativists not only understand but also empathize with him: "[W]e arrive at the heart of the matter: figurative painting" (289). While complaining about European painters focusing on what they see rather than following accepted cultural paradigms, Satan objects to being depicted not as an individual but in stereotypical terms as "a misshapen, horned, long-tailed and gruesome creature with a face covered with protruding moles" (289). Satan makes clear that he has nothing to do with much human evil, and in that regard aligns with what Pamuk demonstrates in his narrative, namely that humans have choices to make: "Many people sin out of their own blind ambition, lust, lack of willpower, baseness, and most often, out of their own idiocy without any instigation, deception, or temptation on my part" (289). In many ways, Satan foregrounds specific human behavior and is thus in the European humanistic tradition that he seemingly denounces. Perhaps Pamuk expects us to see that while paying some homage to the miniaturists' tradition, he like Satan and the storyteller who creates Satan's characterization opts for rendering day-to-day life and individual behavior.

Pamuk is fully aware that Turkey has for centuries sat on the political fault lines between Europe and Asia, between Muslim and Christian world views, even between looking back to medieval times and taking part in the Enlightenment and progress. The Venetians and Franks represent European humanism's challenge to Ottoman values. The movement toward description in miniaturist artistry is a movement to Modernism and away from formulaic art, where human faces are not given individual characteristics and where the psychological and cultural causes of how a particular person behaves are not foregrounded.

Pamuk is wary of historical inevitability, the idea that forces rather than humans shape history. While Pamuk understands the role of historical forces in shaping how humans behave, the inventiveness and originality of his own novel speak to the importance of individuality. The miniaturists live by one big idea; the Europeans want to explore the idiosyncrasies of human life.

But Pamuk, cultural relativist that he is, must know that by the late nineteenth century painting what the artist sees is no longer the only Western paradigm. For example, Degas contended: "[A] painting is first and foremost a product of the artist's imagination, it should never be a copy. … It is all very well to copy what one sees, it's much better to draw what one can see only in one's memory. … [Y]our memories and your imagination are freed of the tyranny of nature."[3] Such early twentieth-century modernist movements as Cubism and Fauvism moved away from representation. Abstract Impressionism accelerated that movement to rendering something within the mind of the painter – not unlike the miniaturists – rather than something in the external world.

Such knowledge enables us to join Pamuk in appreciating that the miniaturists' traditional artistry has its own elegance and perfection. In *My Name is Red*, Pamuk's complex historical vision stresses cultural relativity rather than cultural hegemony, but he also emphasizes the continuity of human motives. While Pamuk's novel dramatizes individual grammars of motives – albeit strongly shaped by their culture – he pays homage to the miniaturists' work by his detailed descriptions of their accomplishments.

At the same time, Pamuk is also aware of cultural discontinuity, the most striking example of which is miniaturists' bizarre valuing of blindness. Because traditional miniaturist painters depict the ideal world as Allah might see it, blindness is not merely a desirable condition but a blessed state brought on by working in difficult conditions without adequate light. The blind miniaturist sees forms with the mind's eye and is not distracted by what is actually in this world. As Olive puts it, "Blindness is a realm of bliss from which the Devil and guilt are barred" (81). If, according to this ideology, the painter is blind, there is no danger that he will paint what he sees but only the repeated idealized images that he remembers. Thus Osman blinds himself to follow in the tradition of the great miniaturist Bizhad who lived in the early sixteenth century and was, according to Pamuk, blind, although I can find no evidence of this and indeed little is known of Bizhad. If Pamuk expects us to understand that to desire blindness is a kind of cultural and individual psychosis, he wants us, I believe, to be aware that such fanaticism is also part of our recent contemporary world. The Turks need look no further than their massacre of Armenians in 1915 and the continuing killing of Kurds.

By contrast, depicting the world as it actually is requires sight. At the very outset Black's inability during his twelve years of exile to remember what his beloved Sheruke looked like becomes an argument for the European way of painting: "With growing panic, I tried desperately to remember her, only to realize that despite love, a face long not seen finally fades" (6). That Pamuk emphasizes what things look like in Istanbul during nine days of the novel puts him squarely on the side of European humanism.

Pamuk's Originality: Transgressive Form in *My Name is Red*

Taking his lead from such diverse authors as Borges, Joyce, Proust, and Kafka, Pamuk plays with narrative conventions that are associated with the realistic novel and innovative alternatives. Part of the novel's formal transgressiveness is having a dog speak in one of the first chapters and the dog's monologue is soon followed by one by a tree, a gold coin, and the color red ("I Am Red") from which the book takes its title.

Like Kundera in *The Unbearable Lightness of Being*, Pamuk does not adhere to the accepted tradition of the European masterpieces of Dostoevsky and Flaubert where an evolving plot reveals characters' psyches, while every aspect of a novel, ideally, is functional in terms of the novel's organic form. If at first *My Name is Red* seems to balance the Ottoman decorative tradition with the "Venetian" realistic tradition of individualizing character, emphasizing details of specific settings, playing with light and shadows to indicate time of day, and using multiple points of view, we gradually realize that while acknowledging the Asian and European aspects of Turkish culture, *My Name is Red* sides mostly with the European aspect.

Let us consider the effects of Pamuk's multiple narrators. Because each of the fifty-nine chapters has a different first person narrator, the reader needs to get his bearings each time the narrator changes. In a sense, these chapters are miniatures or, to switch metaphors, like pieces of glass or stones in a mosaic. While on a first reading, *My Name is Red* seems a slow read with much repetition, upon rereading we do have a better sense of how everything fits into the evolving pattern.

Like John Updike who reviewed *My Name is Red* in *The New Yorker* and about whom Pamuk wrote a laudatory 2014 piece in the *New York Times*, Pamuk wants to be both a bestselling author and one appreciated for his subtlety and craft.[4] Put another way, Pamuk wants to be both a modern version of the storyteller or meddah, captivating his audience as the storyteller does in the café, and a boldly experimental novelist. The storyteller or meddah is a traditional café entertainer in Ottoman culture who uses sketches and props as points of departure for his stories. The meddah often changes characters and voices, much as Pamuk does. As an innovative novelist, Pamuk creates a formal collage – history, realism, satire, and fantasy – in which multiple perspectives are presented for the audience to resolve.

With its self-conscious awareness of its fictionality, its satiric relevance to contemporary Turkey, and use of his own family names, *My Name is Red* has a modern metafictional component that calls attention to the novel's uneasy relationship between fiction and reality. Among its other genres, *My Name is Red* is a noir comedy with a strong satiric component. Pamuk is amused by the hypocrisy of the Muslim world, including its denial of the pleasures of this world. As he puts it, "Islamists are always suspicious of me because I don't come from their culture, and because I have the language, attitude, and even gestures of a more Westernized and privileged person" (Pamuk, "The Art of Fiction No. 187"). As a storyteller who is satirizing aspects of Turkish culture, Pamuk identifies with his novel's inventive storyteller, perhaps including that the storyteller is a victim of fanatics.

As an artist whose home is in Istanbul, Pamuk was well aware that within the volatile maelstrom of Turkish politics, he had to be circumspect about his liberal political views. It turns out he was prescient because in 2005 he was charged with insulting Turkey after he spoke out against the Armenian genocide of 1915; he was eventually convicted and fined. More recently Pamuk opposed the April 15, 2017 referendum which gave Turkish President Erdoğan sweeping executive powers, and as a result a leading newspaper refused to publish an interview that it had done with him.

While the miniaturists under Enishte's auspices move toward realism and away from their Ottoman cultural traditions, Pamuk somewhat breaks from the realistic tradition of the European novel and moves toward fantasy by including the voice of the murdered miniaturist and the voices of inanimate objects, among other metafictional surprises. As in Kafka's "The Hunter Gracchus," the dead souls remain on earth and hear the living. *The Book of the Soul* by Ibn Qayyim Al-Jawziyya – which, as I mentioned, Enishte is reading – similarly argues that the souls of the dead remain on earth and can hear the living.

Pamuk was also influenced by Umberto Eco's historical and philosophic novel *The Name of the Rose*, which takes place in the medieval world in 1327 and satirizes narrow-minded formulaic thinking, in Eco's case that of Catholic monks living in a Benedictine monastery in Italy where murders have taken place. Note Pamuk's play on Eco's title with the iteration of "Name" and the use of the color red. Both novels use a microcosmic perspective to examine macrocosmic issues, and both take place over a handful of days: While Eco's detective story takes place over seven days, Pamuk's takes nine days.

From the outset, *My Name is Red* invites the reader into a world in flux that is emphasized by the rapidly shifting points of view and the inclusion of the perspectives of different social classes, including the Jewish peddler Esther. Istanbul, Black tells us, used to be "a poorer, smaller, and happier city" (7). Black's complaints about change, with his examples of decline, devolution, and decadence, resonate with many readers who have heard such complaints about cultural decline from a better past to present cultural decadence. Whether true or not, such complaints – *Ubi sunt* ("Where are the better times that came before us?") – are made by some people in every era.

Black, the principal character, narrates twelve chapters and is most responsible for moving the love story and detective story forward. The next most prominent is Olive, who narrates three times under that name and six times under "I will be called a Murderer" for a total of nine chapters. Sheruke, Black's love interest and the novel's liveliest presence, narrates seven chapters. Esther, a Jewish peddler, marriage broker and busybody, and a person who carries crucial love letters, narrates four chapters. Butterfly and Stork narrate three chapters each and Enishte and the Head Illuminator Master Osman – who has trained Stork, Butterfly, and Olive – two. If we attribute to the storyteller the anthropomorphized voices of objects, animals, Death, and Satan – all of which are drawn by the miniaturists – and add these chapters to those in which the storyteller speaks as a woman, he narrates eight chapters.

Finally, in the last chapter, Sheruke, who became Black's wife, reveals that the narrator of the entire novel is her younger son Orhan, who shares Pamuk's chosen first name (although actually Pamuk's name is Ferit Orhan Pamuk). She warns readers that Orhan is writing in the realistic European tradition but is not constrained by what actually happened: "For the sake of a delightful and convincing story, there isn't a lie Orhan wouldn't deign to tell" (413). Thus the rereader knows that the nominal author, the grown-up Orhan living in the early seventeenth century, has invented all the monologists, using the material – letters from Black and Hasan – that Sheruke has given him. But the dating at the end of the novel, "1990–92, 1994–98," provides another frame and takes us into the world in which another Orhan – Pamuk himself – has written the novel.

We might recall that often European painting in the Renaissance included more than one source of light and more than one perspective; indeed the best way to look at such paintings is to move around the room in which they are placed. An excellent example of this is Holbein's *The Ambassadors* (1533) where a puzzling object from one perspective becomes a skull from another. *My Name is Red* follows that tradition of inviting multiple perspectives, one begun in fiction by Cervantes's *Don Quixote*, with its complex narration – including both fictional editing and translating – in which we as readers need to think about exactly what we are reading. With his use of multiple frame devices and ambiguity about how the narrative was put together, Pamuk's work evokes Cervantes's novel (which I discussed in my *Reading the European Novel to 1900*).

My Name is Red is also a Swiftian satire of how politics and human nature work. Pamuk uses the miniaturists allegorically to indicate a larger world. Their importance within the Ottoman world seems to be comically exaggerated. Pamuk places their activities, marginal at best in terms of the politics and culture of the vast Ottoman Empire at the end of the sixteenth century, close to the center of the Sultan's focus as if the entire empire depended on this industry. But Pamuk uses parables and myths to create parallels and analogies to the larger human drama as well as to call attention to the parabolic and allegorical nature of the book we are reading.

In the pedantic and arcane discussions about miniaturists' distinctions accounting for small differences, Pamuk presents abstruse arguments, contradictions, and inconsistencies which mirror Talmudic and medieval scholastic discussions about microcosmic matters. Of course, he is also alluding to present discussion of small matters, especially in Turkey, with an eye on intolerance of religious practices. These passages are meant to satirize humorless scholars but can also become a joke at the expense of those readers who would try to parse the very kinds of distinctions that concern the miniaturists. To an extent that has not been noticed, *My Name is Red* is a *jeu d'esprit*. Doesn't Pamuk at times know that our eyes will glaze over when reading these repetitious discussions and recondite references to painters and paintings as well as when reading the practices and beliefs of strange sects? While one could indict him for the fallacy of imitative form, where an author creates the effect of tediousness by writing tedious passages, one could also argue that this over-determinism is part of the transgressive fun of *My Name is Red*.

Shekure

Let us return to the principal characters in Pamuk's narrative. Shekure (the name of Pamuk's mother) is the most fully drawn and interesting character, even though Black takes center stage as speaker more often than she. Sensitive, sensuous, and smart, Shekure has a complex grammar of motives. Her husband has not returned from battle after four years and is presumed to be lost. She is now deciding between her husband's younger brother Hasan, who attempted to rape her, and Black, the nephew of her father, Enishte Effendi. Driven by vanity, sexual desire, economic self-interest, responsibility to her father, and, most notably, motherly love for her two children, she is a bundle of contradictions.

In contrast to the abstruse world of the miniaturists, Shekure lives in the present and adjusts to changing circumstances. After her father is murdered and she is frightened, she becomes even more practical, shrewd, smart, proactive, and manipulative. A master of intrigue, she suspects that Esther, the Jewish peddler and matchmaker, is showing Hasan Black's letters to her; she spies on Black and her father through a peephole; she is alert to the probability that her slave, Hayriye, who sleeps with her father, is watching her. In her love of plotting, Shekure has something in common with Pamuk himself.

While Black, Hasan, and Olive are all in love with her, she takes charge in getting herself married to Black. She tells Black exactly what to do to obtain her hand in marriage, specifically how to bribe the necessary people to get a divorce from her missing husband. At this point, she puts sex on the back burner. For her: "[T]he highest goal in life … is contentment. Love and marriage are but a means of obtaining it" (191).

Often she has a Western Aristotelian perspective: "[I]t seemed to me that the entire world was like a palace with countless rooms whose doors opened into one another. We were able to pass from one room to the next only by exercising our memories and imaginations, but most of us, in our laziness, rarely exercised these capacities, and forever remained in the same room" (407). She responds to the world as it is and makes the best of opportunities to walk through doors to new rooms. Pamuk is showing us that she has much in common with middle-class women today. On balance, she chooses, like Pamuk, a Western humanistic perspective that focuses on life in the present. Pamuk would for the most part agree with her observation that painters "substitute the joy of seeing for the joy of life" (413).

Her children – Shevket and Orhan – are paramount in her life. Even when she performs fellatio on Black when he is brought back to their house wounded after having been stabbed by Olive in the action-packed denouement, she says: "What delighted me then, lying there with the entire world throbbing between my lips, was the happy twittering of my sons cursing and roughhousing with each other in the courtyard" (408). Even while appreciating her enthusiasm, we are expected to smile at Shekure's microcosmic metonymy of Black's penis as "the entire world," and to remember that the term "entire world" was used to describe the Sultan's vast domain.

After her marriage, she prefers sleeping with her children to sleeping with her husband Black, although she has sex with him every afternoon: "All sensible women know how it's much nicer to sleep curled up with one's children than with a melancholy husband who's been beaten down by life" (409). We don't know if Shekure would have been more enthused if Black had not survived "crippled" – the word she uses – but we suspect that his defeatist melancholy is a factor in her wanting to sleep separately (409). Looking back on her twenty-six years of marriage, Shekure mentions that Black sometimes joined other miniaturists "chasing after pretty boys" (409–410). Black's bisexuality might have been offputting to her as a woman, even if it is part of the sixteenth-century Ottoman culture. Yet she speaks of him as "my beloved husband Black" (409) after remarking that "Love … must be understood, not through the logic of a woman like me who continually racks her brain to protect herself, but through its illogic" (408).

Isn't Pamuk reminding us of fifteenth- and sixteenth-century Holy Family pictures (Raphael, Leonardo, Del Sarto) in both Western humanistic terms and in the idealized terms of the miniaturists when Shekure confides to the reader that her ideal would be "the picture of a mother with her two children, the younger one, whom she cradles in her arms, nursing him as she smiles, suckles happily at her bountiful breast, smiling as well. The eyes of the slightly jealous older brother and those of the mother should be locked. I'd like to be the mother in that picture" (413). The older brother is not only Shekure's elder son Shevket (whose name he shares with Pamuk's elder brother) but also in Pamuk's Holy Family allusion a comic version of John the Baptist. Is part of Pamuk's fun that Shekure has never seen the Italian painters and almost certainly does not know anything about the Holy Family? Affirming her ties to the miniaturists, she also would like "the bird in the sky to be depicted as flying, and at the same time, happily and eternally suspended there, in the style of the old masters of Herat who were able to stop time" (412).

The Murder Suspects

The suspects in the murder of Elegant and Enishte, whose aforementioned nicknames Olive, Stork, and Butterfly have been given to them by Master Osman, are fiercely competitive and jealous of one another. As I have mentioned, along with Elegant they were all part of the project under the auspices of Enishte to make a European-style book to celebrate the Sultan's reign, a book featuring a picture of how the Sultan looks along with other realistic portraits and using Western ideas of perspective.

Let us turn to the individuality of the three suspects. Stork has thin legs like a stork and is married. Of the four raised in Osman's workshop, including Elegant, Stork comes closest to the European style. Something of a scoundrel, Stork likes money, cheats in competition, and gives counterfeit money as bribes (78). As his mentor Osman tells us, Stork signs his name with a "victorious flourish" and likes to paint dramatic scenes "of war and gruesome depictions of death" (261, 263). Adapting Western concepts, Stork is something of a transitional figure. When Black and Butterfly visit Stork in their desperate search for the murderer, Stork proudly declares: "From now on, the battle scenes made in the workshops of the Ottomans will be drawn the way I've seen them and drawn them: a tumult of armies, horses, armor-clad warriors and bloodied bodies!" (370).

Master Osman regards Stork as a deserving candidate to succeed him as Head Illuminator in terms of merit, but a poor choice in terms of character: "[H]e's so ambitious and conceited, and so condescending toward the other illustrators that he could never manage so many men, and would end up losing them all" (262). Osman also resents Stork's disrespect for him and for the Ottoman tradition of painting. Osman could be describing Pamuk – who enjoys the metafictional playing with his audience – when he observes: "He had enough self-confidence to mock whatever illustration he made, its subject and himself" (263). In the final retrospective monologue which concludes the novel, Shekure tells us that Stork does succeed Osman two years after the main events of the novel, and the miniaturists return – at least for a time – to the decorative tradition.

Another major suspect in the killing of Elegant is Butterfly, who, among other things, seems to have a homosexual relationship with Osman and is Osman's favorite to succeed him. The latter describes Butterfly as "handsome" and speaks of "the beauty of his boyhood" (258); he acknowledges that he loved Butterfly "more than a son" (259). We think of Butterfly's interest in boys and his relationship as a boy with Osman when he asks Black as they fight after Black comes to interrogate him: "Do you feel the balance of my weight on your back and buttocks?" (362). Aware of Butterfly's past, Black asks Butterfly about his relationship with Osman (a query which is preposterous given the circumstances, namely that Black is still in great danger of being beheaded by Butterfly); Butterfly responds: "[He] would mount me then the way I have mounted you" (363).

Master Osman praises Butterfly as a master colorist whose art is "a festival for the eyes" (258). But he regards Butterfly as having serious character flaws. Butterfly lacks profundity and an awareness that life is more than "jubilation" (259). Moreover, he is "flighty, aimless, and indecisive" (258) and "a slave to praise" in his need to please others (260). Later Butterfly confirms Osman's view when he brags about his skills: "O, the talent of which I am possessed!" (276). He likes money and, although he is married and enjoys having sex with his "beautiful wife," he is a pederast (358). Recalling how he drew the rear end of a horse, Butterfly imagines with pleasure what seems to be rape: "How gentle and curvaceous I made the rear end, lovingly wishing to cup it in my hands like the gentle butt of a boy I was about to violate" (276).

Finally, Osman regards Olive as the miniaturist with the greatest ability but paradoxically as having less of the "God-given gifts" of Stork or Butterfly (257). Of his miniaturists – and there were many that are not named – he regards Olive as "the most quiet and sensitive, but also the most guilty and traitorous, and by far the most devious" (257).

We do need to keep in mind that Master Osman makes the foregoing observations about the miniaturists to Black who faces the prospect of being the first one tortured if the murderer is not discovered. Black is accompanying Osman in his examination of the legendary masterpieces in the Treasury as they search for clues as to which of the suspects painted what; their goal is finding the murderer of Elegant and Enishte.

Religious Fanaticism

One of Pamuk's targets and one relevant to the 1990s and indeed much of Turkish history revolves around religious fanaticism in Turkey, including the slaughter of Armenian Christians in 1915.

Olive, Master Osman mistakenly observes, "didn't believe in anything," which we learn is not true since he belonged – or says he does – to the Kalendris sect which hold dervishes in high esteem because they beg not for themselves but to learn humility and give what they collect to the poor (257). Olive lives in a "deserted dervish lodge" where he prays and has painted for the storyteller the two dervishes as well as Satan (374). In his mind, he killed Elegant to protect the miniaturists from charges of blasphemy. Of course, there is little doubt that Olive is a borderline psychotic; hence that we need to be skeptical of his testimony. No matter how Olive explains it, Olive's reasons for murdering Elegant are pathological: "In actuality it pleased me to show him I was a free-thinking Kalendri throwback or, worse yet, that I aspired to be a Kalendri. When Elegant understood I was the last of the followers of a dervish order based on pederasty, hashish consumption, vagrancy and all manner of aberrant behavior, I thought he'd fear and respect me ever more, and in turn, be intimidated into silence" (394). Pamuk is very much aware that it is not always easy to follow Olive's twisted logic. Enishte became to Olive "a new father to me in this new life" in which borrowing aspects of "Frankish methods" was permitted (394–395).

In justifying his murdering Elegant, Olive claims that Elegant would "tell all to the preacher's dull congregation, exaggerating Enishte's absurdities, the anxieties about affronts to the religion and rendering the Devil in a favorable light, and they'd naturally believe every slanderous word" (394). In other words, the monomaniacal Olive, who is hardly consistent, thinks he is protecting the eclectic method of Enishte, the person he later murders.

One reason Olive kills Elegant is that the latter speaks to Olive's own fears that Enishte is on a sacrilegious path. Indeed, Olive reminds Enishte in the fatal scene that originality itself is a transgression: "Let it not be forgotten that in the Glorious Koran, 'creator' is one of the attributes of Allah. It is Allah who is creative, who brings that which is not into existence, who gives life to the lifeless. No one ought to compete with Him. The greatest of sins is committed by painters who presume to do what He does, who claim to be as creative as He" (160). Olive believed Elegant had broken with his three colleagues – Stork, Butterfly, and himself – and would expose Enishte's project, carried out at the Sultan's behest, as blasphemy and that would encourage the fanatically conservative Erzurumis. The latter are led by Nusret Hoja, who came from the city of Ezurum.

Nusret Hoja believes that the current human suffering within the Ottoman world derives from deviations from the Qur'an's teachings, including blasphemous entertainment and serving coffee. His followers are the fanatics who attack the coffee house where the miniaturists congregate and kill the cross-dressing storyteller.

By including the storyteller's inventive monologues, Pamuk gives voice to the same words to which Nusret and his followers objected. Implicitly, this inclusion of monologues that fanatics would censor puts Pamuk himself at odds with censorship of contemporary Turkish rulers who have their own list of forbidden topics.

The Murderer's Psychology

After knowing that Olive is the double murderer, we reread his monologues – "I Will Be Called a Murderer" and "I Am Called 'Olive'" – for clues that we might have missed. Olive stresses his psychological misery: "Every night a sorrow overwhelms me, a misery descends upon me" (280). Depressed, he wanders around lower-class neighborhoods, dreaming of Elegant's coming back to haunt him. He believes he is under the Devil's influence. Olive's thinking is inconsistent, erratic, and eludes explanation, as befits his religious fanaticism as well as paranoia and other symptoms of psychosis.

The footprints of Pamuk's literary ancestors are often present. Olive's weird rationalizations owe something to Poe's psychotic in "The Tell Tale Heart" and to Raskolnikov in *Crime and Punishment*. The scene in which Olive visits and then kills Enishte owes a great deal to Dostoevsky.

Olive is pleased that Enishte suspects him: "I could see that Enishte Effendi was growing suspicious of me and this pleased and fortified me" (163). Olive thinks that a frightened Enishte is more likely to show him the finished painting. But Enishte, like Dostoevsky's detective Porfiry Petrovich, elicits a confession from Olive. Olive fell to his knees and kissed Enishte's hands and let him stroke his hair "like a father" (162). Enishte seems to have guessed that Olive is Elegant's murderer when he asks Olive: "Who was this miniaturist who fell into a panic like you ...? ... Who killed him?" (163). Olive, somewhat schizoid, sees himself as Other as if he were someone else. "I remember how suddenly my thoughts spiraled out of control and I was stupidly listening to what I thought as if somebody else was thinking" (159).

After murdering Elegant, Olive has his doubts about his justifications for killing Elegant and wants to see the composite painting that Enishte is preparing for the Sultan. Enishte had each of the four miniaturists contribute but had never shown them the whole painting. When Enishte refuses, Olive kills him and takes the painting. Given that he oscillates between loving and hating Enishte, Olive needs to think that he has succumbed to the power of the Devil when he kills Enishte. Another reason that Olive offers for his killing Enishte is that Enishte had betrayed Master Osman into "aping the Venetian artist, Sebastiano," although we don't see evidence of this unless Olive means that Enishte's using the miniaturists to paint in the Frankish manner was a betrayal (396). Olive's even more obscure reason for killing Enishte is that, as he explains, "I lowered myself to ask him whether I had a style of my own ... I considered style to be a variety of rootlessness and dishonor, but doubt was eating me. I wanted nothing to do with style, but the Devil was tempting me and I was, furthermore, curious" (396).

Paradoxically, Olive understands that when a miniaturist graduates from mediocrity, he has an individualized and original style that takes him some steps toward the European style. Indeed, when confessing to his crime, he not only recognizes that the European style may have God's approval, but he also makes a prediction: "God willing, one day, we'll fearlessly tell the story of our own lives the way we actually live them. ... [A]s the methods of the Europeans spread, everyone will consider it a special talent to tell other men's stories as if they were one's own" (397). Doesn't Pamuk expect his reader to see that *My Name is Red* is in the European tradition? Isn't he fulfilling Olive's prediction by inventing his innovative form to capture the fabric of life in 1591 Istanbul?

Historical Implications

My Name is Red is about both the clash of cultural values and challenges to accepted rules. With an eye to twentieth-century Turkey, Pamuk not only stresses that the Ottoman Empire straddles two worlds, the Asian and the European, but also that when one looks closely at the art each culture produced, pure distinctions blur and generalizations about historical dichotomies are often less certain than we think. When we look back over the centuries, the artistic differences are of little consequence and what is being debated to some extent is no different than Swift's Big Enders and Little Enders debating how to crack eggs in *Gulliver's Travels*. Far more important in 1591 was the rising power of Europe, which was challenging Ottoman hegemony.

Put another way, what is a macrocosmic matter from the perspective of the participants in 1591 may be a microcosmic matter to later observers. Within the culture of the miniaturists of 1591, tiny disagreements or departures from accepted norms can lead to events with unimaginable consequences: two murders; three if we count the café storyteller who is murdered by the Erzurumis; four if we count Olive, who is beheaded by Hasan. But aren't small disagreements about religious and political principles sometimes how the seeds of wars are planted?

While not without historical vision, Pamuk focuses on human behavior. What finally motivates the miniaturists are the same things that motivate humans today: jealousy, greed, wrath, vanity, and ambition. Isn't Pamuk suggesting that human nature doesn't change much and that sex, love, fame, pride, and envy are what drive human behavior in every generation? In fact Pamuk may be suggesting that human behavior is often small or miniature, no matter how holy people think their lives are, including their belief that their work is serving Allah or God.

Pamuk's sixteenth-century characters are as complex as modern ones, but he oscillates between seeing them, on one hand, as two-dimensional characters repeating past patterns and, on the other, fully realized figures with complex modern psyches. He often emphasizes the self-awareness of characters, even while asking us to understand that they, like all of us, are myopic about themselves. Aware of their own complexity, they see themselves as individuals not types. Their concepts of themselves – their own self-portraiture – place them, paradoxically, among the Venetians immersed in the complex modern world. Black observes, "How expressing one's reality in words, as truthful as they might be, goads one to insincerity. … [T]he sincerity of the miniaturist … doesn't emerge in moments of talent and perfection; on the contrary, it emerges through slips of the tongue, mistakes, fatigue and frustration" (152–153). In other words, just as the miniaturists reveal something of their own style when they deviate from their models – often without meaning to do so – we are who we are when we unintentionally deviate from how we are supposed to present ourselves.

Part of the fun of reading *My Name is Red* is its comedy and bathos. The idea that the blind artist sees better is an example of how embracing convention and tradition can become a psychosis. Invoking the "Persian poets" as describing the penis as a "reed pen" and women's mouths as "inkwells" is comic and erotic (408). What both metaphors show is how a culture creates its own epistemology and semiotics, and that is also a major point of Pamuk's.

Conclusion: Notes toward a Resistant Reading

My Name is Red could have been shorter. On a first reading, the novel is a slow read with much repetition. To be sure, each of the fifty-nine sections is itself a miniature, but sometimes we may say, "Are they all necessary?" Do we always need every event from multiple perspectives, what I call the Rashomon syndrome after Kurosawa's 1950 film of that name with its multiple views of the same event? Is the distinction between the miniaturists' traditional painting of the ideal world – imagining what Allah envisioned – and Venetian realism overdone? Or as Master Osman puts it, Pamuk at times may be "trying to depict reality itself rather than its representation, in all its detail" (260). Does the novel at times tend towards over-determinism with too much description? I am thinking of Pamuk's cataloguing of the Topkapi treasury or describing in elaborate detail specific miniatures found in various books in the treasury (299–300, 302). Finally, despite its length and detail, could the novel reveal more about characters' psyches and background? Does Pamuk stereotype Sheruke as a manipulative woman who uses her sexuality and wiles to get what she wants, while stereotyping Esther as a conniving Jew? But notwithstanding my reservations, I regard *My Name is Red* as an audacious, innovative novel that takes us into a fascinating world quite different from our own.

Study Questions for *My Name is Red*

1. Why does Pamuk use multiple narration?
2. In what ways is Pamuk writing in *My Name is Red* not only about customs and conventions in 1591 but also about issues relevant to contemporary life?
3. How do Venetian and Ottoman art differ? In twentieth- and twenty-first-century painting and sculpture, do we see parallels to the difference between representing actual reality and suggesting idealized forms?
4. Why does Olive kill Elegant? Why does he kill Black's uncle, Enishte? What more could Pamuk do to provide a full grammar of motives to explain the murders?
5. What motivates Sheruke? In what ways is she a sympathetic character? In what ways does she use her sexuality to manipulate Black? How could you make a case that Pamuk is stereotyping her as well as Esther, the Jewish peddler?
6. Why focus on Black in so many chapters? What is his role in the novel's mosaic of meaning?
7. How is Istanbul a city in transition? What are the parallels to the modern city?
8. What are the differences among Olive, Stork, and Butterfly?
9. In what ways is *My Name is Red* a noir comic novel? Or does the gruesome violence undermine comedy? Explain.

10. In what ways is *My Name is Red* a satiric novel? What are Pamuk's values? Can you provide historical evidence that he is making a statement about political and religious fanaticism throughout history, notably in Turkey?

Notes

1. Page references refer to Orhan Pamuk, *My Name is Red*, trans. Erdağ M. Göknar (New York: Vintage, 2002).
2. Orhan Pamuk, "The Art of Fiction No. 187." Interview by Ángel Gurría-Quintana. *Paris Review* 175 (Fall/Winter 2005); https://www.theparisreview.org/interviews/5587/orhan-pamuk-the-art-of-fiction-no-187-orhan-pamuk
3. Quoted in Anka Muhlstein, "Degas Invents a New World," *NYR* 53:8 (May 12, 2016), 14–16; http://www.nybooks.com/articles/2016/05/12/degas-invents-a-new-world/
4. Orhan Pamuk, "Updike at Rest: Adam Begley's 'Updike,'" *New York Times Sunday Book Review*, April 17, 2014; https://www.nytimes.com/2014/04/20/books/review/adam-begleys-updike.html

Chapter 13

Herta Müller's *The Hunger Angel* (2009): A Hunger for Life, A Hunger for Words

"Books about bad times are often read as testimonies. My own books are also about bad times – I had little other choice."

Herta Müller, *When We Don't Speak, We Become Unbearable, and When We Do, We Make Fools of Ourselves. Can Literature Bear Witness?*[1]

Introduction

Herta Müller (1953–), who received the Nobel Prize for Literature in 2009, chooses a self-dramatizing gay male narrator to present the horrors of five years in a Soviet labor camp. Leo Auberg, her fictional protagonist, was a German living in Transylvania when he was deported as a seventeen-year-old by the Soviets to a labor camp (Nowo-Gorlowks, an actual labor camp in the Ukraine) in January 1945 and stayed there for five years. Told from Leo Auberg's perspective as a survivor, this often poetic novel dramatizes Leo's deportation, the harsh, at times sadistic, treatment of prisoners within the labor camp, the physical ravages of hunger, and the current and lifelong traumatic effects of that experience on Leo. *The Hunger Angel* is a dramatization of Leo's evolving and often erratic consciousness. Leo's telling at a sixty-year retrospective vantage point is a therapeutic effort to liberate himself from terrible memories by giving an artistic shape to his experience. Implicitly, Leo's story is that of all those who suffered innocently after Germany's defeat and all those living anywhere who are mistreated by arbitrary political decisions.

Reading the Modern European Novel Since 1900: A Critical Study of Major Fiction from Proust's Swann's Way to Ferrante's Neapolitan Tetralogy, First Edition. Daniel R. Schwarz.
© 2018 John Wiley & Sons Ltd. Published 2018 by John Wiley & Sons Ltd.

Historical Background

Müller is a Romanian of German ancestry who left for Germany in 1987 before Nicolae Ceauşescu fell in 1989. Writing about German suffering during World War II was not permitted in the claustrophobic atmosphere of Ceauşescu's communistic autocracy. Because Müller lived under surveillance as a member of the German minority and refused to work for the state as an informer and subsequently lost her job, she could identify in some ways with Leo's plight and his position as an outsider. There is much of Müller herself in Leo's pain.

Born in 1953, Müller uses Leo not only to give voice to what she knew from others of life under Nazism, but also to render testimony about living, as she did, in Romania for all but the very end of the Ceauşescu years. As she writes in her essay *When We Don't Speak, We Become Unbearable, and When We Do, We Make Fools of Ourselves. Can Literature Bear Witness?*:

....

Books about bad times are often read as testimonies. My own books are also about bad times – I had little other choice. They deal with the stunted life under the dictatorship, the everyday existence of a German minority that, in giving way to outside intimidation, responded with an internal despotism all its own, and the eventual disappearance of these people as they left for Germany. Many consider my books testimonies. As I write them, however, I don't think of myself as bearing witness. This is because of how I learned to write: not from speaking, but from silence and concealment. That's how it began. Later I had to relearn how to keep silent, since few wanted to hear the whole, exact truth. (Müller, *When We Don't Speak*)

....

The Hunger Angel depends on an historical context of which most Americans are only vaguely aware if at all, namely that Germans in countries occupied by Russia after the war were presumed to be sympathetic to Nazis and considered Fascists, and thus were deported in Eastern Europe to work in Soviet labor camps.

After defeating the Nazis in Romania in August 1944 but while World War II was still going on, the Russians in January 1945 began the deportation of Romanian Germans between seventeen and forty-five, and that event is the historical catalyst for *The Hunger Angel*. In the novel Leo's parents were pro-Nazi but it is not clear why Leo was the family member deported, although we assume that it is because his father was over forty-five.

More broadly, *The Hunger Angel* is a powerful anti-war novel that shows the dehumanizing effects of conquest on the victors as well as the victims.

Müller dramatizes how war brutalizes human relationships and how ethnic rivalry pollutes human relationships. As Müller puts it in her 2009 Nobel Prize address:

My grandfather had been a soldier in the First World War. He knew what he was talking about when he said, often and embittered, in reference to his son Matz [who was Müller's uncle]: *When the flags start to flutter, common sense slides right into the trumpet.* ... Matz was a passionate Nazi. ... He barked out anti-Semitic slogans, and was as unreachable as an imbecile. My grandfather rebuked him several times: he owed his entire fortune to the credit advanced by Jewish business friends. And when that didn't help, he boxed Matz on the ears several times. But the young man's faculty of reason had been erased. (Herta Müller, "Every Word Knows Something of a Vicious Circle")[2]

Müller's own village was Nitchidorf in the Banat region of Romania, an area in which many Germans settled as far back as the eighteenth century. Her grandfather was a wealthy grain merchant but, according to Müller, everything was taken away from him in 1945. (We cannot help thinking how fortunate he was to hold on to his possessions during the war when his Jewish compatriots lost not only their property but in most cases their lives.) That Müller's father volunteered for the Waffen SS during World War II made the family suspect. In fact, Müller's mother was deported to a Soviet labor camp after World War II. As Müller recalls in a 2012 interview: "My father was on the side of the murderers, and my mother had to pay for that. ... It was a really big dilemma for me that I came from the side of the murderers, and that everyone was still singing these Nazi songs in the village. It really tore me to pieces" (Rohter).[3]

Her mother's experience – and that of other deportees from Nitchidorf whom she interviewed – was an important source for *The Hunger Angel*. Müller recalls that when her mother, who had spent five years in the Gulag, "combed my hair, she would tell me how her own head had been shaved, and without telling me she had learned it in the camp, showed me how to peel a potato so that the skin was very very thin, and nothing was wasted" (quoted in Rohter, "Naming her World"). Müller's first name, Herta, honors a friend of her mother's who died in the camp.

The major source of Müller's novel is the experience of the German-Romanian poet Oskar Pastior who, like Leo, was deported from Sibu in Transylvania and who coined the word "hungerengel" or "Hunger Angel." Originally, he was to be co-author but he died in 2006. After *The Hunger Angel* was published Müller learned Pastior had been an informer for the Securitate, the Romanian secret police, perhaps because he was blackmailed after the discovery of his homosexuality. Müller presumably didn't know about his ties to the Securitate when she modeled Leo on Pastior. Indeed, she might have been falsely told by Pastior – and believed – that he had avoided compromising himself by hiding his homosexuality.

Müller herself had been harassed by the Securitate, which wanted her to become an informer. Interestingly, aware from her own experience of how the Securitate manipulated its citizens, Müller has not condemned Pastior but rather expressed understanding: "[T]he longer I turn the details over in my head, the more this has turned to grief" (Porter, 492).[4] Yet two months later Müller did say: "[T]here are two Oskar Pastiors. I am only now getting to know the second one. And that makes me bitter" (ibid., 495).

Because Müller had been often visited by members of the Securitate, her fellow workers thought she had succumbed to their threats. At one point she lost her office and came to work but was given no responsibilities. It was then that she began to write. Writing became not only a release from frustration but also her way of defining herself within a nightmarish situation created by an autocratic regime: "I wasn't trying to write literature, I just put it down on paper to gain a foothold, to get a grip on my life" (Herta Müller, "The Art of Fiction No. 225").[5]

The Title

Originally written in German, the German title *Atemschaukel* means "Breath Swing," that is, the awareness of breathing essential to staying alive and the place the hunger angel chooses to settle on Leo: "He staggers around in small circles and balances on my breath-swing" (133).[6] "Breath-swing" reduces life simply to the very act of breathing breath to breath, but it is also the biological antidote to hunger in that breathing keeps Leo alive. Leo imagines a competition, a dialectic between the air angel and the hunger angel:

. . . .

The hunger angel leans to one side as he walks with open eyes. He staggers around in small circles and balances on my breath-swing. He knows the homesickness in the brain and the blind alleys in the air.

The air angel leans to the other side as he walks with open hunger. (133)

. . . .

Leo's Narration as Bildungsroman Manqué

The effects of Leo's five years in camp – from the age of seventeen to twenty-two – linger six decades later. Underlying a text organized by themes mostly related to hunger is a skeletal narrative that moves forward from deportation to return and is told from a perspective sixty years after his release when Leo is eighty-two. The theme-based narrative is shaped by the self-dramatizing narrator's memories as well as by dreams and hallucinations rooted in those memories.

Leo's telling moves among three temporal perspectives: the immediacy of the period when Leo is in the labor camp, his retrospective thinking with mixed emotions about memories of home while in the camp, and his looking back sixty years after his release from the camp. Narrating sixty years later, Leo is anesthetized to the morality of his past behavior; he reports it as if he were detachedly describing the experience of another. Perhaps this is what *The Hunger Angel* has most in common with Kertész's *Fatelessness*.

Müller challenges the expectations we bring to a novel. At the outset of *The Hunger Angel*, the reader notices important differences from traditional novels. We see that the novel does not adhere to the traditions of a teleological narrative but rather finds its meaning in the interstices and disruptions. Müller's arrangement of chapters and, specifically, of Leo's somewhat circular and spiral telling suggest that the novel's structure depends more on recurring metaphoric and thematic meaning.

The Hunger Angel might be called a Bildungsroman manqué. Keeping the reader off balance, Müller's novel is a mosaic of Leo's impressions, circling back upon themselves rather than a progressive life narrative. The chapters follow the movement – and often the digressive propensity – of Leo's mind, although his narration of five years in the camp does at times provide a spasmodic forward movement through the months and years that he was a captive.

As Leo grows older, we do not see a continuing evolution towards a fully realized and coherent self. The chapter titles deliberately deviate from the usual expectations of a Bildungsroman and/or a Künstlerroman with its narrative moving forward and fulfilling, as the narrator looks back, a teleology or at least a coherent pattern of meaning in which the narrator learns from specific incidents.

Leo is less witty and ironic when speaking in the seeming present of his years in camp, especially when describing his suffering from hunger, than he is when looking back on his earlier years: His parents "believed in the beauty of blond braids and white knee-stockings. They believed in the black square of Hitler's moustache and in the Aryan heritage of us Transylvanian Saxons" (4). At first his parents eagerly follow Hitler's triumphs, but as the war progresses and defeats occur, they are less engaged in the military campaigns.

Leo survives the reality of the labor camp because of the surreal world of his perception, a world in contrast to both the one he has left behind and the one he lives in for five years. At times his mind does revert to the apparent normalcy of his home, a normalcy that he seeks for the sake of stability to reclaim even though the home was fraught with tension. One reason for the tension is that his family – and other Romanians of German descent – are marginalized for their support of Nazism; another is his covert homosexual life.

Within the crucial formative years between seventeen and twenty-two, years when contemporary young people in many countries are often at college or serving in the military, Leo is being punished for crimes he hasn't committed. He is living in a Kafkaesque universe where there is little relationship between cause and effect, and hence where his only goal is to survive one day, one hour, one minute, and one breath at a time. Given that we have no evidence of Leo's Nazi sympathies, we conclude that he is being punished for his heritage and his parents' admiration of Hitler.

Because Leo is speaking about events sixty years ago, the reader needs to wonder about the accuracy of his memory and to realize that there is a distinction between what happened in 1945–1949 and his memory of those events, and a further distinction between what he remembers and the shape his telling takes. Leo's fragmented, often non-linear narrative is an ironic comment on what we might call, after reading Müller's novel, the linear, claustrophobic, illogic logic of the totalitarian Soviet regime and of the former Romanian one. As an imaginative alternative to the one-dimensional half-truths, distortions, and outright lies on which the totalitarian Soviet labor camp and propaganda depend, Leo invents an alternative word world in which neologisms and portmanteau words play an important role. It is ironic that the social realism favored by the USSR and its satellites, including Romania, rejected the very flights of imagination and the intuitive, introspective knowledge on which Leo builds his memories and the metaphors he uses to convey those memories.

Parallels to Holocaust Narratives

Similar to the narrators in many Holocaust novels and memoirs, the narrator in *The Hunger Angel* is relating a traumatic experience that has reshaped his life. We need to think of Kertész's *Fatelessness* where the young teenage narrator-protagonist is arrested and sent to a concentration camp. Within the logic of the Gulag (actually an acronym for the agency that ran the camps) things seem normal that in other situations would be outrageous, disgusting, and immoral. Indeed, abuse and hunger turn the world upside down, although certain behavior, like stealing another's bread, is considered immoral.

What happens in the desperate situation imposed by deprivation of food and human rights, by arbitrary imprisonment that undermines human dignity, is that victims lose their sense of decency and their morality. Bettina Bannasch argues for a deliberate parallel to Imre Kertész's *Fatelessness:* "Alluding to Kertész in this way, Müller's *Atemschaukel* describes the dilemma that results on the one hand from the necessity of accommodating to the normality of the everyday life of the camp, i.e. to the continued existence of the state of emergency, in order to survive, and on the other hand from the associated abandonment of moral and ethical values" (Bannasch, 136).[7]

Müller's use of recurring characters in various anecdotes recalls Primo Levi's *Survival at Auschwitz* and even more, with its similar lack of a clear forward moving narrative, Levi's *The Periodic Table.* Often Müller has Leo's memory take the form of particular incidents displaying individualized characters. This enables the reader to feel distance or sympathy with Leo's fellow camp occupants in a way that his more personalized and lyrical dreamscapes do not.

Just as in Levi's *The Periodic Table* chemical elements become metaphors for behavior, in *The Hunger Angel,* various materials – cement, coal, a handkerchief – take on representative meaning. The oblique nature of the sixty-four chapter headings and the lack of a linear chronology or traditional narrative development further parallel *The Periodic Table.*

Müller wants to remind us that the horror of Hitler's policies did not end with the German defeat or the Holocaust. In presenting the Soviet labor camp, she emphasizes the similarities to Holocaust atrocities and procedures, including death by starvation, the soup line which yields better soup near the bottom where the best ingredients rest, endless line-ups, fear of being shot, arbitrary rules, kapos running day-to-day camp life at the behest of the Camp Commandant with whom they curry favor, and ambiguous deaths that may or may not be suicides, as when Irma Pfeifer falls or jumps into the mortar pit where she drowns. To be sure, some readers will object to Mueller's equating what happened to Romanians of German ancestry who sympathized with Hitler to Jewish Holocaust victims on the grounds that the former were not gassed and cremated or shot by the hundreds of thousands.

Words

Müller is fascinated if not obsessed with how language transmutes experience: "The author takes what is lived and casts it in another form. It is no longer day or night, town or country; the new world is ruled by nouns and verbs, main and dependent clauses, meter and sound" (Parr).[8] Costica Bradatan has written:

> It is Müller's great achievement ... to depict the individual's confrontation with the totalitarian system as a fight over words, discourses (official or dissident), life stories (big or small), historical accounts, grand narratives, history textbooks, and archives. ... If the system's power comes from its ability to affect people's minds through language, any resistance should come from language as well. (Bradatan, "Herta Müller's Language of Resistance")[9]

The title of Müller's Nobel lecture, "Every Word Knows Something of a Vicious Circle," underlines the way that she thinks about words as living and dynamic aspects of life that not only reflect but also create reality. When she was suspected of being a spy and basically a non-person, she discovered her hunger for words:

> I reacted to the deathly fear with a thirst for life. A hunger for words. Nothing but the whirl of words could grasp my condition. It spelled out what the mouth could not pronounce. I chased after the events, caught up in the words and their devilish circling, until something emerged I had never known before. Parallel to the reality, the pantomime of words stepped into action, without respect for any real dimensions, shrinking what was most important and stretching the minor matters. (Müller, "Every Word Knows Something")

That hunger for words also motivates her narrator-protagonist Leo.

Words for Müller have their own life, indeed their own hunger to be what they need to be. It is almost as in the *Paris Review* interview that took place some years later, she is anthropomorphizing words: "It's the words that are hungry. I'm not hungry for words, but they have a hunger of their own. They want to consume what I have experienced, and I have to make sure that they do that" (Müller, "The Art of Fiction No. 225"). Hunger for Müller means an instinctive and intuitive need for something that is necessary for survival.

By anthropomorphizing words – an example is transforming "hunger" into "the hunger angel" – she shows how words can become the concepts they represent and how they can become weapons or defenses or a mixture of both. For Müller, inanimate objects have a life: "Every object becomes steeped with meaning. But the meanings change with the experience of the viewer" (Müller, "The Art of Fiction No. 225"). But Müller is also aware of the limitations of language: "[W]ords have their own truth, and that comes from how they sound.

But they aren't the same as the things themselves, there's never a perfect match. … Even language doesn't reach the deepest places we have inside us" (ibid.). Nevertheless, the writer must keep trying: "Language is so different from life. How am I supposed to fit the one into the other? How can I bring them together? There's no such thing as one-to-one correspondence" (ibid.).

Even in translation from the original German, we are well aware that Müller is challenging convention in both typography and orthography. The short chapters are unnumbered. Except for the first letter of the first word, the chapter titles are in lower case ("On packing suitcases," "The lime women"). More importantly, Müller eschews quotation marks and question marks, capitalizes whole words and even sentences, and strings together two or more words to make a new word; thus to signify Leo's ironic response to death, Müller invents the neologism "Onedroptoomuchhappiness" (59). To signify how, because of Leo's hunger, objects merge in his mind as "a monster," she coins, "toothcomb-needlescissormirrorbrush" (26). My guess is that she has been directly or indirectly influenced by James Joyce who used all these techniques.

Müller's narrator Leo loves the sound, sight, and texture of words as when he plays with three homophonic words at the end of the chapter entitled "Latin secrets," in which he lists medical issues suffered by prisoners. As Leo recalls struggling with the hunger angel in the camps amidst "people too weak to go dancing," word play is foregrounded within his stream of consciousness, beginning with a childhood memory of his "cuddle toy" but soon overwhelmed by his memory of hunger: "KUSCHELTIER – what a soft name for a dog stuffed with sawdust. But here in the camp there's only KUSCHEN – knuckling under – because what else would you call the silence that comes from fear. And KUSHAT' which means eat, in Russian" (142).

Given Leo's metaphoric and metonymic sensibility, we realize that he, like the poet Oskar Pastior on whom Müller modeled him, is an artist. Leo grounds his narrative in material objects even as he creates images of magic realism, most notably the anthropomorphized hunger angel. Thus when he gets a pass and goes into town, he recalls, "I set off, that is to say we set off, my hunger and I" (128). That other self, the ravenous hunger angel, causes him – after finding ten rubles – to gorge himself and become ill.

Müller gives Leo other memorable metaphors that etch the excruciating experience of hunger in the reader's mind: "Before someone dies of hunger, a hare appears on his face. You think: Bread is wasted on that one, it doesn't pay to nourish him any more since the white hare is already on the way. That's why we call the bread from someone with the white hare cheek-bread" (111). The white hare is an imaginative construct, punning in the Boehm translation on white hairs that appear on the face of men no longer shaving or taking care of themselves and thus representing the approach of death: "[H]unger-fur is growing, if the fine white hairs are long enough and thick enough" (111).

Note how Müller has Leo use the present tense to render the immediacy of this recurring phenomenon and thus put the reader in the harrowing present.

How *The Hunger Angel* Begins

Openings take us into a novel's imagined world – its unique ontology – and begin to establish its moral and social codes and stylistic signature. The more we feel ourselves in a created world that has its own individuality, the more compelling our read. While some novels do invent a physical world, the fictional world does not require either invented laws, customs, history, or streets and buildings that never existed. Indeed verisimilitude – evoking in fiction a plausible, credible realistic parallel to a world that exists or existed – is an important component of Müller's world. But the fictional world of a major work usually requires a unique word world – a way of telling – and/or a vision that is little different from other novels, and that is where Müller excels in *The Hunger Angel*.

The first chapter, "On packing suitcases," is the longest and perhaps the most narrative driven. Müller takes us abruptly and unexpectedly into the forbidden world of anonymous homosexual liaisons. Leo's secret is that he is a homosexual who risked imprisonment with every sexual rendezvous until he left Romania in 1968. To an extent, because of his homosexual life before deportation, he had experienced fear and anxiety – as well as a sense of his otherness and marginalization – in a way that Elie Wiesel in *Night* or Georg in *Fatelessness* before their arrests had not. Had he been discovered he might have been blackmailed, like the aforementioned Oskar Pastior, a homosexual apparently induced by pressure into becoming an informant for the Securitate.

Leo's deportation mirrors that of Jews because, as we have noted, Müller is stressing that Romanian Germans, too, were often victims. At first Leo welcomes his deportation because he had a secret homosexual life with men. He is terrified that his secret homosexual life will be revealed to his mother. Had he been discovered by the police, he would have been imprisoned for a minimum of five years for the crime of homosexuality: "I simply wanted to go to a place that didn't know who I was" (2). Thus Leo's main and deeply troubling psychological baggage is his silence on the subject of his sexual behavior and his fear of shaming his family: "Before, during, and after my time in the camp, for twenty-five years, I lived in fear – of my family, and of the state. Fear of a double disgrace: that the state would lock me away as a criminal and that my family would disown me out of shame. … I wanted to escape from my family. … I was also happy I wasn't being sent off to war, into the snow at the front" (4–5).

His hunger for sexual experience becomes a dominant motif even before he is sent to the Gulag. Notwithstanding the risk, he is unable to stop himself from returning to the park where he has anonymous sex with a number of men. We need to remember that even in cultures where homosexuality is legal, to have sex with an older man when one is an adolescent boy would be an offense on the part of the older man. Homosexuality was a crime during Hitler's Nazi era, and a boy having promiscuous sex with men would have been imprisoned, too. After the 1917 Bolshevik revolution homosexuality was permitted in Russia, but after 1934 under Stalin's leadership, it was considered a criminal deviation from normalcy. That would have been the case in the labor camp.

Before Leo left home, everything reminds him of his sexual activities. When his mother chastises him for his table manners, he thinks: "Why is she saying meat when she is talking about forks and potatoes. What kind of meat does she mean. I was my own thief, the words came out of nowhere and caught me" (4). The translation which is simultaneously crude and unclear – presumably true to the original German – does not quite convey the relationship between food as a metaphor for sex in Leo's mind. Perhaps it is supposed to anticipate his later desperate desire for food or, perhaps in the retrospective narration, to link these two basic needs.

His mother can be insensitive and crass. For example, when she is packing his clothes for his imminent departure and he is late coming upstairs from the courtyard, she upbraids him: "Why don't you just pack your satchel and go out in the world and do whatever you want" (6). We wonder if she knows that he is gay and has guessed something about his covert life. He poignantly responds: "But I'm your child, where am I supposed to go" (6). But he is also dealing with a mother who is emotionally disturbed and suffers pathological insecurity. In a bizarre moment in which she acts like a small child, she once played dead to test how much he cared about her. On that occasion she jumped up and exclaimed: "So, do you love me. See, I'm still alive" (7).

That he very much fears his mother's rejection and harshness explains his response upon his return to the brother born while he is away. Viewing his younger brother as a rival, Leo is extremely jealous of him and calls him his mother's "ersatz-child" (252): "I'm as little as Robert, and Robert is as big as I am. … Everything Robert did made me uneasy" (256, 263). He sees Robert as a replacement for him in the absence caused by his deportation as well as for his family a new post-war beginning that puts aside the family's Nazi past. Robert is favored by his mother, Leo implicitly suggests, because Robert does not carry the suspicion of being a homosexual and because he is not, like Leo upon his return, burdened if not traumatized by the camp experience.

The Labor Camp

The second chapter, "Orach," takes us abruptly into the world of the camps. Leo, Müller's self-dramatizing narrator, strikingly organizes his narrative around the edible quality of the Orach, known as mountain spinach. By doing so, he takes us into a word world where experiences are organized by a diverse set of metaphors, objects, and fantasies, sometimes in combination; thus the titles of Müller's sixty-four short chapters include "The lime women," "Handkerchief and mice," "On the heart-shovel," "On the phantom pain of the cuckoo clock," and "White hare."

Why is "Cement" the third chapter? Seemingly omnipresent at the labor camp, cement is the basic substance with which the inmates work, carrying bags to construction sites, mixing mortar, and watching it harden into a grim windowless building. Fluid until it hardens, cement becomes for Leo a metonymy for what cannot be controlled, namely the inevitable conditions of the camp: "Stalin's cheekbones and voice may have been made of steel, but his mustache was pure cement" (32). Stalin is evoked because the authoritarian rules of the Gulag forced labor camp – including the relentless, daily work with cement – are a direct result of his leadership. Cement is a forbidding substance under the control of the camp officials; it is seemingly malleable, yet resistant to the prisoners' will: "And apart from hunger, the only thing in our minds that's as quick as cement is homesickness. It steals from you the same way cement does, and you can drown in it as well" (32). The rereader understands that this is exactly what happens to Irma Pfeifer seven chapters later when she either falls into or jumps into the mortar pit: "Perhaps HELPHELP or ICAN'TTAKEANYMORE – we couldn't make out the exact words" (59).

In these first chapters set in the camps, we realize that Leo's reality is grim, but his poetic imagination – often a function of anger and desperation – reshapes that experience and gives life to it. What is striking is that the poetic world of Leo's imagination, a world fed paradoxically by desperation, gives the reader a richer experience than the one Leo is experiencing. The words that give shape to Leo's experience simultaneously render the experience and create something of a lyrical alternative. Even after his release, he relies on his poetic imagination to feed the humdrum existence he leads and the traumatic memories of the camp.

Close to starvation in the labor camp, hunger is Leo's dominant need. Had Leo not introduced his homosexuality so blatantly, we would not be so conscious of how little he discusses it in his narrative of the labor camp. Sex becomes something of the repressed subject even if we realize his responses to various males – Karli Harman, the Kapo Tur Prikulitsch – may have a sexual component.

Hunger

Given the English title, *The Hunger Angel*, it is not surprising that in the camps everything reminds Leo of food. Hunger – the absence of sufficient food – is a dominant motif: "No words are adequate for the suffering caused by hunger. ...

For sixty years, ever since I came back from the camp, I have been eating against starvation" (18). In the Gulag forced labor camp, hunger and deprivation shape behavior and reduce human life to the survival of the fittest. For many prisoners the result of hunger is reversion to brutishness; thus Paul Gast, a lawyer, eats his wife's food until she starves to death. In a grim parasitic demonstration of how the living use the dead as hosts when someone dies, their bread and clothing become available: "We undress them before they turn stiff. We need their clothes so we won't freeze to death. And we eat their saved bread. Their death is our gain" (112).

The hunger motif in its basic form as food deprivation not only hovers over the camp but plays a role in the arrest of Trudi Pelikan in Leo's hometown, the arrest that brought her to the same camp as Leo. She had tried to evade the Russians by hiding in a hole in a neighbor's yard until the snow gave away her mother's footprints when her mother brought her food. Hunger is first and foremost a horrifying physical condition. As a physical condition, "Hunger pulls open your pores and crawls in. Once it's inside, the cement seals them back shut and there you are, cemented in" (31).

Hunger is also a metaphor for basic human needs. Whenever the basic need for food is met, cravings remain in the form of hunger for satisfactory shelter and clothing to protect against the elements, meaningful work, family and home (homesickness), companionship, communication with others, sex, human dignity, memories of the past, and plans for the future. That memories and fantasies of the world left behind persistently intrude on Leo's consciousness is an expression of these other kinds of unfilled hunger. In Leo's case, hunger includes his desire for fulfilling his sexual needs, needs which others fulfill with women within the promiscuous culture of camp life. For Leo, who likes to watch the young Russians on duty taking a shower, "the hunger angel" has a sexual dimension because he cannot fulfill his desire for male liaisons (107). If he had been caught in a homosexual act in the labor camp, he might have been "dead," that is, killed on the spot. Finally – and here Müller is alluding not only to Leo's immediate problem, but to life in Romania under Ceauşescu – hunger also means hunger for relief from oppression, for freedom, and for hope.

Leo's Imagination

Müller draws on the traditions of magic realism and surrealism to present Leo's reality. While he does not identify himself as a creative writer, his powerful imagination is an essential part of how he, as a self-dramatizing narrator, presents himself. The uncanny and fantastic are as much a part of his narrative as his eye for details. Recurring dreams both haunt and sustain Leo, including the surrealistic one in which he was "riding home through the clouds on a white pig" (179). While he has a strong interest in the physical things he observes and experiences – cement, coals, sand – these physical objects are often points of departure for more imaginative thoughts, often taking the forms of metaphors and metonyms. After reflecting on various kinds of coal, he asserts, "my head has deposits of its own" (115). We understand that those deposits are memories of the world he has left behind. And now sixty years after he has left the camps those deposits shape his telling.

Leo not only has a lively imagination and an eye for metaphors, but he also loves the sound and texture of words. An example is how the handkerchief given to him by a Russian mother whose son has been sent to Siberia becomes a talisman – and a metonymy – for his grandmother's strong belief in his return. That he anthropomorphizes the handkerchief shows us the poetic power of his imagination: "I was convinced that my grandmother's parting sentence I KNOW YOU'LL COME BACK had turned into a handkerchief. I am not ashamed to say that the handkerchief was the only person who looked after me in the camp. I'm certain of that even today" (70). This passage becomes even more interesting in light of Müller's Nobel address:

· ·

DO YOU HAVE A HANDKERCHIEF was the question my mother asked me every morning, standing by the gate to our house, before I went out onto the street. I didn't have a handkerchief. And because I didn't, I would go back inside and get one. I never had a handkerchief because I would always wait for her question. The handkerchief was proof that my mother was looking after me in the morning. For the rest of the day I was on my own. The question DO YOU HAVE A HANDKERCHIEF was an indirect display of affection. Anything more direct would have been embarrassing and not something the farmers practiced. Love disguised itself as a question. … Can it be that the question about the handkerchief was never about the handkerchief at all, but rather about the acute solitude of a human being? (Müller, "Every Word Knows Something")

· ·

Müller believes that a good part of our sense-making depends on our seeing life within a constellation of objects: "Can we say that it is precisely the smallest objects – be they trumpets, accordions, or handkerchiefs – which connect the most disparate things in life? That the objects are in orbit and that their deviations reveal a pattern of repetition – a vicious circle" (ibid.) What she means is that objects can elicit associations with experience – especially traumatic experiences and those that touch deeply seated fixations and compulsions – and vice versa, namely that experiences can elicit memories of particular objects.

Leo fears the poisonous substances in the cellar where he works. In Leo's lively imagination these substances have metaphoric implications, as does the cellar itself with its underground location. Leo takes solace in the half liter of fresh milk he is given once a month as if the liter were enough to protect him against the poisons. Writing in the present tense even though he is thinking retrospectively, he poignantly asserts: "I believe the milk. I believe that it helps my lungs. That every sip destroys the poison, that the milk is like the snow, whose purity surpasses all expectations" (178). We need to note how, in the foregoing passage, his imagination increases the stakes with each sentence and how wish – in the face of desperate circumstances – fathers the thought. He seems to be aware that he is building hope on the flimsy foundation of a desire to believe: "I don't dare say it but I say it nevertheless: I hope the fresh milk is the unknown sister of my white handkerchief. And the flowing version of my grandmother's wish. I know you'll come back" (178). It is almost as if he were building a religion out of talismans that sustain him.

The Parabolic Function of Characters

While Leo is a fully realized character, Müller objectifies people in the camp as functions of his fight for survival. Thus within Leo's consciousness and memory, many of the other camp occupants play parabolic roles. They are used by Leo as moral barometers to show how deportation orders and the claustrophobic rules of the camp are in tension with the desperate human need to survive.

Fenya is a Russian woman who meticulously and fastidiously distributes the daily portion of bread, and for that reason she is never far from Leo's consciousness. Indeed, in one of countless examples of how Leo's obsession with hunger shapes his perception and contracts his imagination to the claustrophobic world of the labor camp, she becomes a metonymy for the bread: "She was like the rationed loaves we coveted – appallingly wet, sticky, and disgracefully nourishing" (100).

Notwithstanding the dehumanizing effects of hunger, Müller shows that some people – even when reduced by hunger to the basic animalistic need for survival – maintain a scintilla of civility and morality in their sense of fairness. The prisoners maintain a remnant of their humanity to protect the feeble-minded and/or emotionally disturbed Kati Sentry. Kati is depicted in hauntingly beautiful terms as an insouciant innocent who has probably been deported to the labor camp by mistake and is barely aware of what is going on. A primitive version of fairness is the unspoken acceptance of a bread code. Karli Halman was beaten by fellow prisoners and pissed on for stealing bread from Albert Gion and thus violating the bread code. Leo, who had been uncharacteristically a leader in this vigilante "bread court" action against Karli, recalls: "My bloodlust had swallowed my reason" (103).

To see Leo transformed into a violent man who beats Karli Halman and urinates in his face is one of the text's most troubling moments for the reader, no matter our awareness of how deprivation may bring out the potential for reductive and animalistic behavior. We understand how violence begets violence, just as on a larger scale the Nazis' wartime behavior towards the Russians begets the Soviet labor camps for Germans who supposedly sympathized with the Nazis. The narrator's paratactic prose emphasizes the arbitrariness of the bread court and mirrors the simple and reductive logic of the tit for tat punishment meted out for a deviation from the norms established within the inmates' subculture:

· ·

We didn't hold the theft against Karli Halman. And he never held his punishment against us. He knew he had earned it. The bread court does not deliberate, it punishes. It knows no mitigation, it needs no legal code. It is a law unto itself because the hunger angel is also a thief who steals the brain. Bread justice has no prologue or epilogue, it is only here and now. ... You cannot approach the bread court with conventional morality. (103–104)

· ·

After Karli's punishment, it is Karli who restores bread to the aforementioned Kati Sentry after Conrad Fenn tricks her out of it by exchanging a piece of wood for her bread.

Yet, not everyone accepts Leo's justification about the bread court. The reader understands from a later incident that the perpetuation of prisoner violence within the closed and lawless world of the camps derived from each person's having their own ideas about what is fair. Two months after this incident the barber Oswald Enyeter deliberately cuts Leo, while shaving him after shaving Karli (now lacking two teeth due to the violence inflicted by the bread court) as if to rebuke Leo for his leadership role in the reversion to barbarism that has taken place.

A major villain during Leo's five years in the Gulag camp is the Kapo Tur – once called Artur Prikulitsch – who, because he could translate Russian into German and therefore was indispensible to the Russian Commander, became an adjutant to the camp administration and lorded over his fellow prisoners whose assignments he determined. Tur is conniving, sadistic, erratic, and often adds his own orders to those of the Russians. Tur insists that the barber Oswald Enyeter keep Tur's fingernails and nose hairs trimmed, even though that was not the custom where both men came from. In this anecdote, we again see how the abuser – in this case, the barber who had deliberately cut Leo – is also the abused and we see how bullying begets bullying. After the interned Germans were released, Tur was found brutally murdered in Vienna, no doubt by one or more of his fellow prisoners who despised him.

Leo's Return: Dissonance and Homosexuality

Leo has a sexual hunger for men that continues even after he returns home and marries. Just as the camps destroy his expectations of young adulthood and frustrate his sexual desires, his return home five years later fails to fulfill his hopes, some of which are related to his homosexuality. Even after leaving Romania for Austria, he is a melancholy, restless figure, haunted by his memories and by his sexual needs.

After his return, Leo experiences disorientation and post-traumatic stress symptoms. The camp experience accompanies him everywhere and informs his every perception and experience. We might recall what George Eliot said of Bulstrode in *Middlemarch*: "With memory set smarting like a reopened wound, a man's past is not simply a dead history, an outworn preparation of the present: It is not a repented error shaken loose from the life: it is a still quivering part of himself, bringing shudders and bitter flavors and the tinglings of a merited shame."[10] Even back at home, the hunger angel is never far away, and the hunger angel includes Leo's desire for men.

Once home, the counterpart to the anthropomorphized hunger angel is the anthropomorphized disabler, who represents awkwardness and fear and thus prevents normal relations with his family: "The disabler at home was like the hunger angel in the camp. It was never clear whether there was one for all of us or if each of us had his own" (256). The disabler not only shapes Leo's behavior towards his family and theirs towards him, but also plays a role in other situations. Leo is disabled, in part because of his continuing secret. However, from his point of view, his entire family has also become disabled, although the reader recalls that his mother was unstable before he was deported to the Soviet camp. He upbraids himself for not knowing how to interact with his family now that he is home: "I needed to be patient with them because I loved them. Except how could I say that if I couldn't even think it to myself" (256). But we understand that he is troubled less by the attention heaped upon his brother than by the experiences of the last five years that haunt him. At home the clock ticking on the wall was "my breath-swing, in my breast it was my heart-shovel, which I missed very much" (253).

Leo marries Emma and he stays with her for eleven years during which he continues his homosexual dalliances. Fearing arrest and using the excuse that he is going to visit his Aunt, he heartlessly abandons Emma and goes to Austria where he has lived for thirty years at the time of his narrating. He seems devoid of feeling, sending Emma a heartless two-sentence postcard to announce that he has abandoned her:

. . . .

Dear Emma,
    Fear is Merciless.
    I am not coming back. (278)

. . . .

Does his cruelty to her remind us of his behavior to Karli Harman? Does it suggest that the hardness necessary to survive the labor camps cannot be cast aside? Has he been traumatized by that experience or even by the earlier necessity of living a secret life as an adolescent in his hometown park when he let himself "be passed from one man to the next" in what he calls "a wild animal crossing" (2)? Had he been caught, he would have gone to a penal colony from which few returned and those that did were "walking corpses" (3).

One might hope that upon his return from the camp world, Leo might grow beyond sex in dark places. But, perhaps because of his youthful escapades in the park and his camp experience, he is a pitiable figure who can't connect emotionally with those with whom he has sex. Leo has a need for anonymous couplings that seem devoid of intimacy. In the camps Leo observed anonymous heterosexual sex with an understanding based on his own anonymous sexual experience. That he does not develop a capacity to love his male sexual partners could be a result of living in a culture where homosexuality is illegal and unacknowledged by the community as a legitimate way of loving others. But Leo's inability to grow into a mature adult capable of loving also shows how the camp experience with its traumatic hunger deprivation and suffering has deformed Leo.

My Resistant Reading

One aspect of a resistant reading would ask whether Müller's depiction of the shallowness, permissiveness, and irresponsibility of gay sexuality reflects her own prejudice. Her presentation of Leo makes a disapproving statement about homosexuality. Leo uses the very term "wild animal crossings" – this time in the plural – to define his later anonymous sexual liaisons that he had used to describe his adolescent adventures in his home town where homosexuals met in the park as if he were describing a compulsion if not an incurable illness (279). Because Müller does not take a different perspective of Leo's view of his homosexual behavior as obsessive if not disgusting, there may be a homophobic aspect to *The Hunger Angel.*

Müller equates homosexuality with insatiable desire and one night stands rather than with love. While suggesting that Leo's hardness and cynicism derive from the camps and that his adolescent and adult promiscuity relates to living in cultures that consider his behavior deviant and criminal, Müller does not seem as sympathetic to Leo's problems as we might expect. Homosexuality, as presented in this novel, is secretive, impersonal, anonymous, and has only to do with gratification of lustful needs: "The urgency of lust and the fickleness of luck are now long past, even if my brain still lets itself be seduced at every turn" (279). That Leo – admittedly based on Oskar Pastior, but still Müller's creation – does not seem to have ever had a male partner or companion, or indeed ever wanted one, tells us something about Müller's narrow if not benighted view of homosexuality.

I want to take up another even more compelling reason for a resistant reading, namely the suggestion of a parallel between sufferings described in *The Hunger Angel* and the systematic slaughter of Jews in the Holocaust.

Ernest Wichner, a German-Romanian writer who left Romania in 1975 for Germany and who knew Müller and Oskar Pastior personally, has observed: "[P]robably the book tells more because it depicts people in extreme situations, presents basic survival strategies, scenes of comfort and hate, affections and indifferences, and gives you an idea of the whole spectrum of human behavior in all its variations. And this level of experience applies to many different terrible places in many countries" ("Interview with Ernest Wichner," 49–50).[11]

Let us consider Wichner's observation about "different terrible places in many countries" by pointing out that, however terrible, what happened to Romanian Germans after World War II was different not only in degree but also in kind to what happened to European Jews during the war. It may be unfair and reflect my own teaching and writing about Holocaust texts, but I am uncomfortable with what I take to be Müller's deliberate parallels – beginning with lists and roundups and deporting people in cattle cars – to Holocaust fiction. As Brigid Haines notes: "Unlike the Nazi extermination camps, the main purpose of the Gulags was economic: people were sent there not to die (though many did) but to work" (Haines, 123).[12] It is worth remembering, as Haines reminds us, that eventually the prisoners were paid, that Leo never gives up hope of returning home, and is in fact transported home. While the prisoners are desperately hungry and mistreated, and some die, they do not face arbitrary selection or killing en masse. Nor, I should add, were children deported and gassed.

Müller is evoking these parallels to make a special plea that Romanians of German ancestry also suffered because of their ethnicity. Leo's deportation mirrors that of Jews. Müller is explicitly saying that Germans too were often victims. With some justification she seems to be insisting on the arbitrariness and unfairness of who among the German Romanians are deported. But are we to have amnesia about the support these Germans gave Hitler and the probability that they knew what was happening to Jews in Romania?

There is a difference between a labor camp for political prisoners of a certain ethnicity – no matter how horrible – and a death camp where residents are brought to be gassed by Zyklon B or shot and then cremated. As traumatic as the Soviet labor camps may have been in requiring the inmates to develop survival strategies for responding to hunger, a resistant reader must insist that although Leo was imprisoned in a grim and gruesome labor camp, he was not transported to an extermination camp. Unlike Jews, some of whom were sent not to concentration camps but to death camps, the inmates do not confront daily selection.

Study Questions for *The Hunger Angel*

1. How important is Leo's homosexuality in shaping his telling? In what ways does it define his behavior in the camp?
2. What are the striking features of deprivation in the labor camp to which Leo is deported?
3. To what, besides food, does the concept of "hunger" refer?
4. What are the most innovative features of both Müller's narrative presentation and style?
5. How does Müller balance realism and surrealism?
6. In what ways does *The Hunger Angel* deviate from the traditions of a forward-moving narrative? How does Müller create meaning in the temporal interstices and disruptions?
7. How does the way that Leo leaves his wife – namely with a terse two-sentence letter – reveal not only selfishness but also cruelty? How does it recall his cruelty to Karli Harman?
8. In reading *The Hunger Angel*, what does one need to know about the historical contexts and Müller's own life?
9. How does Primo Levi's epigraph to his *The Periodic Table* – "Troubles overcome are good to tell" – apply to Leo's telling and Müller's authorship? In what way is Leo's telling a kind of self-therapy?
10. Rather than presenting fully realized characters, why and how does Mueller have his narrator, Leo, evoke secondary characters – Karli Harman, Kati Sentry, Tur Prikulitsch – to make thematic points?
11. If we know the differences between what happened to those of German ancestry at Soviet labor camps and the Nazi concentration and death camps during the Holocaust, why and how do we resist Müller's efforts to create parallels between the two?

Notes

1. Herta Müller, *When We Don't Speak, We Become Unbearable, and When We Do, We Make Fools of Ourselves. Can Literature Bear Witness?* Trans. Philip Boehm; http://www.bu.edu/european/2012/05/20/can-literature-bear-witness-a-conversation-with-herta-muller/

2. Herta Müller, "Every Word Knows Something of a Vicious Circle." Lecture, Nobel Peace Prize (Dec. 7, 2009); https://www.nobelprize.org/nobel_prizes/literature/laureates/2009/muller-lecture_en.html

3. Larry Rohter, "Naming her World, Part by Part," *New York Times* (May 18, 2012); http://www.nytimes.com/2012/05/19/books/herta-mullers-literature-born-of-isolation.html

4. Anna Porter, "The Lonely Passion of Herta Müller," *Queen's Quarterly* 117.4 (201–), 488–495; see 492.

5. Herta Müller, "The Art of Fiction No. 225." Interview by Philip Boehm. *Paris Review* 210 (Fall 2014); https://www.theparisreview.org/interviews/6328/herta-muller-the-art-of-fiction-no-225-herta-muller

6. Page references are from Herta Müller, *The Hunger Angel*, trans. Philip Boehm (New York: Henry Holt and Co., 2012).

7. Bettina Bannasch, "Zero – A Gaping Mouth: The Discourse of the Camps in Herta Müller's *Atemschaukel* between Literary Theory and Political Philosophy," in *Cultural History and Literary Imagination, Vol. 18: Other People's Pain: Narratives of Trauma and the Question of Ethics*, eds. Martin Modlinger and Philipp Sonntag (Oxford: Peter Lang, 2011), 115–144; see 136.

8. Bud Parr, "Can Literature Bear Witness," *Words Without Borders* (May 22, 2012); http://www.wordswithoutborders.org/dispatches/article/can-literature-bear-witness

9. Costica Bradatan, "Herta Müller's Language of Resistance," *Boston Review* (March 14, 2014); http://bostonreview.net/books-ideas/costica-bradatan-herta-muller-cristina-double

10. George Eliot, *Middlemarch: A Study in Provincial Life* (New York: Collier Books, 1962 [orig. ed. 1871–1872]), 569.

11. Ernest Wichner, "Interview with Ernest Wichner," in *Herta Müller: Politics and Aesthetics*, eds. Bettina Brant and Valentina Glajar (Lincoln and London: University of Nebraska Press, 2013), 36–53; see 49–50.

12. Brigid Haines, "Return from the Archipelago," in *Herta Müller*, eds. Brigid B. Haines and Lyn L. Marven (Oxford: Oxford University Press, 2013), 117–134; see 123.

Chapter 14

Elena Ferrante's Neapolitan Quartet: Women Discovering Their Voices in a Violent and Sexist Male Society

"To you I am neither man nor woman. I come before you as an author only. It is the sole standard by which you have a right to judge me – the sole ground on which I accept your judgment."

Charlotte Brontë[1]

Introduction

In her compelling and psychologically deft Neapolitan quartet or tetralogy the pseudonymous Italian author Elena Ferrante has written one of the most important series of novels of the twenty-first century, novels that I would guess – given the originality, power, and wide appeal of her voice – may earn her consideration for a Nobel Prize in Literature. In order of their tracing the lives of two women from childhood to old age, their titles are: *My Brilliant Friend* (2012; subtitled *Childhood, Adolescence*), *The Story of a New Name* (2013; subtitled *Youth*), *Those Who Leave and Those Who Stay* (2014; subtitled *Middle Time*), and *The Story of the Lost Child* (2015; subtitled *Maturity, Old Age*).[2] While rendering poverty, class differences, and violence in Naples from 1950 to 2010, the four novels take place against the backdrop of Italian and world politics. The Neapolitans live in a world of strong emotions; anger, rage, hatred, jealousy, ambition (and the hope to move into a better economic and social class), and sexual desire pulsate on every page.

How many novels change the way the reader sees the world and ultimately himself? For me these do, in large part because as a man I understand better

Reading the Modern European Novel Since 1900: A Critical Study of Major Fiction from Proust's Swann's Way to Ferrante's Neapolitan Tetralogy, First Edition. Daniel R. Schwarz.
© 2018 John Wiley & Sons Ltd. Published 2018 by John Wiley & Sons Ltd.

what it meant, as the second half of the twentieth century developed, to be a woman striving to find her own voice in a male-dominated society and the emotional responses women may have to motherhood, sex, and cultural expectations.

What follows are the reasons why these novels make such an impact, including the ambitious nature of the project of writing an epic novel that includes macrocosmic views of world politics and social change and microcosmic views of the ebbs and flows in individual lives. What I admire, too, is the deep analysis, with a strong focus on women, of such basic emotions as jealousy, desire, anger, and various kinds of love – with tensions and betrayals – including love between parents and children, husbands and wives (or unmarried but intimate partners), and between friends. Ferrante understands the complexity and fluidity of these emotions as well as the mysterious nature of emotional life and how it undermines reason.

The foundation of the tetralogy depends on two women – the narrator, Elena Greco, who is called Lenuccia or Lenù, and Raffaella Cerullo, called Lina by everyone except by Elena, who calls her Lila. They are both born in 1944 to poor parents in a lower-class Naples neighborhood in which corruption is rampant. They become friends during childhood and their lives are so intertwined that it is not too much to think of them as secret sharers or doublegangers, as their resonant names also suggest. The name Lina is close to Lenù as well as close to Lena, a shortened version of Elena. While Elena thinks of Lila as the title character of *My Brilliant Friend* in Book One, it is Lila who before her wedding, with which *My Brilliant Friend* concludes, says to Elena: "you're my brilliant friend, you have to be the best of all, boys and girls" (I.57).

The four volumes consist of the first person narrator, Elena Greco, writing an intensely personal narrative – what purports to be a memoir – of her entire life from early childhood to international success as an author. The novels draw upon multiple genres, including Bildungsroman, Künstlerroman, family chronicle stretching over sixty years, and historical docu-fiction. Ferrante's powerful rendering of Elena's perspective as a child, adolescent, and still later as an adult experiencing marriage, motherhood, divorce, and betrayal by a lover in whom she invests great hope is the essence of these remarkable inquiries into a woman's psyche. Rendering not only Elena's awakening to sexuality but Lila's quite different experience is one of the tetralogy's strengths. The final section of Book Four focusing on old age is particularly compelling in part because major canonical fiction rarely focuses on such a period in a woman's life; even Mrs. Dalloway is only in her early fifties.

The tetralogy is not only a story of two women finding their voices and of the lives of their families, friends, enemies, and acquaintances, but it is also social and political history. In the course of the tetralogy, which covers the period between World War II through the first decade of the twenty-first century, the narrative alludes to the Vietnam War and other international developments, but its real historical focus is the ever-shifting political landscape in Italy, with a special focus on the history of the Left. Such crucial events as the kidnapping by the Red Brigade of the prominent Christian Democracy Party President and former Prime Minister Aldo Moro on March 16, 1978, and his murder fifty-five days later when the demands of his kidnappers were not met, are given considerable attention.

Ferrante may be quite consciously implying that for her to write, the Apollonian aspect of herself represented by Elena, whose qualities of control and reason often dominate, requires Lila with her Dionysian forces of disarray, impulse, and the uncontrollable. Indeed, we see this conflict within the narrative, and we see both Elena and Lila on occasion cross-dress as the other.

Using her fictional surrogate, Elena, Ferrante zeroes in on politically revolutionary characters such as Pasquale Peluso, who participates in extreme Leftist violence and whose revolutionary sentiments originated in his Communist father, Alfredo Peluso; the latter dies in prison after being – perhaps unjustly – convicted of murdering the loan shark Don Achille Carracci, who stole Alfredo's business. By focusing on individual characters with whom she grew up and whose families are intermarried with hers, Elena brings to life both the insidious and invidious effects on ordinary families of the Camorra (the Neapolitan version of the Mafia) and its ties to the political establishment as well as extreme political behavior and its causes.

Rereading, even more than on a first reading, I am torn between, on one hand, empathy and sympathy for both the complex narrator and her friend, and, on the other, repulsion by the violence in their lives. I alternate between caring a great deal about the lead women, Elena and Lila – who is always a function of Elena's perspective – and being repelled by recurrent child abuse and neglect, wife beating, financial chicanery, and political posturing even on the part of the Left, which is presented far more sympathetically than the Right. In the repellent category, I should add males beating one another in recurring street violence and even murdering one another for political reasons or as a result of gangster feuds and personal grudges.

I am also saddened by the absence of psychiatric help for Lila – a symptom of the era and the culture – who seems to have bipolar disorder. It is clear that Lila has major shifts in mood from depression to exhilaration, something akin to manic depression. When Elena goes to Lila to learn more about her "unreliable," manipulative, and egotistical lover, Nino, who continues to betray her, Elena observes that Lila "knew everything out of pure and simple fear of all that is living and dead," that is, Elena believes Lila "knew" – or Lila thought she knew – as a way of controlling her demons (IV.I.54).

What Kind of Fiction is Ferrante Writing?

One striking feature of the Neapolitan novels – and of epic novels such as *Ulysses, War and Peace,* and *Bleak House* – is their inclusiveness. By moving her characters around – especially Lila – Ferrante can explore various aspects of the social structure, including the onset of the computer age, the increasing mobility of the well-to-do and privileged due to air travel, urban development and its failures, predatory capitalism, and the Camorra's involvement in every aspect of Neapolitan life, including the burgeoning drug epidemic. Ferrante's scope includes not only social illnesses like heroin addiction, but related economic issues such as rampant unemployment and urban squalor. Taking account of changes in sexual attitudes, including awareness if not consistent acceptance of homosexuality, as well as the AIDS and heroin epidemics plus recreational drug use by the elite classes, her modern epic refers not only to Naples but to all of Italy. Ferrante also uses Lena's experience and perspective to explore the customs and hypocrisies of the academic and publishing world as well as of the supposed leadership class of the political world.

When an editor calls Elena's second novel "A sort of autobiography, an arrangement in novel form of [her] experience of the poorest and most violent Naples," we realize, yes, that is, in a sense, what Ferrante has us reading, but we understand that the tetralogy is so much more (IV.I.81). A major theme is women finding their voices in the 1960s within a patriarchal culture in Italy and especially in Naples where not only sexism but also violence towards women (and men, too) is accepted. Among other things, these novels tell a searing story of women's place in a male society where women, including accomplished intellectuals and successful writers, are subservient, have little voice, and are repressed and suppressed. Such is often the case for Elena, who writes about women's liberation while allowing her husband and even more so her lover Nino to make her a second-class citizen in her relationships with them.

Yet we have a sense of an impressively dialogic tetralogy, because, with Elena and Lila, we have not only two often opposing voices but also two characters with multiple voices whose fluidity is very much part of the tetralogy's originality and focus. By fluidity, I mean both Lila's and Elena's changeableness in the face of evolving circumstances and the way they are impelled by needs, desires, fears, and fixations they barely understand. Ferrante stresses that in a rapidly evolving world, we are many selves. Furthermore, our emotional lives are often on a roller-coaster or even in the eye of a hurricane that we cannot control. Verbal excess is pervasive; scenes conclude with strident accusations and name-calling, especially those scenes involving the tempestuous and highly volatile Lila. Elena's feels a great range of emotions but rarely overflows verbally with the intensity of Lila or Elena's own mother.

We also have in Ferrante an author who, not without cynicism, is aware of Elena's limitations – some of which Elena is not fully aware of in her self-dramatizing narrative – and expects the reader to notice them. In other words, Elena is not always a self-critical, perceptive narrator, and recognizing this is an important part of our reading experience. Elena has a tendency to turn sexual relationships into commercial transactions. At the University in Pisa, Franco Mari, a well-to-do fellow student, is her boyfriend. While he fails as a student, he is a ticket to travel and a source of personal gifts that would have not been possible for someone of Elena's means. Part of why Elena is originally attracted to her husband Pietro is his offering her entry into a far different social world. Marrying Pietro – she is certain he was on "the side of truth and justice" – seems for a time to be a bridge for Elena to another, more ordered and civilized world than the dysfunctional world of Naples where violence, Catholic religious rituals, and obsolete patriarchal customs still hold sway (III.7). Later, she is attracted to Nino because she sees him as upwardly bound as well as having the sexual magnetism that Pietro lacks. Ironically, he uses her more than she uses him.

Moreover, we have the cacophonous voices of many secondary characters and they too can be inconsistent, angry, frustrated, obsessive, temperamental, and confused. A great many of the characters in Naples' downtrodden working-class neighborhood often live on the emotional edge where shouting and screaming and outbursts of temper and frustration take the place of rational conversation and normal restraints. Which is to say that characterization takes its cue from the author's strong realistic impulse and her stress on how we are shaped by our lineage, social class, and language spoken by our family and by those in our neighborhood, as well as by our physical environment. Ferrante's gritty, crowded cityscape – populated by a great many people trying to survive in an economy that has passed them by – takes its cue from Dickens, Balzac, Dostoevsky, and Joyce.

Even nature seems to be on the side of violence and disruption. The lurking presence of the active volcano Mount Vesuvius, which erupted on August 24 in the year 79 CE to destroy much of the surrounding area, including Pompeii and Herculaneum, is an apt metaphor for the characters' tempestuous emotional lives. More specifically, while Elena is dealing with "jealousy and envy" due to Nino's presence in the building she shares with Lila, she hears "thunder," which she thinks of as a truck running into "our foundations, crashing and shattering everything" (IV.I.48). What she hears is the November 23, 1980 earthquake which destroyed a good deal of Naples and set off a panic in the city.

In one of the tetralogy's most striking episodes, Lila's daughter Tina mysteriously disappears; one theory is that she was hit by a truck (IV.II.11). We realize that if the earthquake is an apocalyptic event for Naples and Elena the disappearance is a personal apocalypse for Lila, "crashing and shattering everything" and killing all hope in her bipolar personality (IV.I.48). Even if on first reading the aforementioned thread, depending on the word "truck" in translation, is tenuous, on a rereading we see how Ferrante – perhaps influenced by the epic tradition within which she wants to place her tetralogy – is trying to link the violence of setting with the violence and turbulence that inform the emotional lives of her characters.

Ferrante's epic scope includes the political and social milieu of Naples. She is sympathetic to have-nots and sensitive to the exploitation of the working class, including those who have mindless, demeaning jobs such as Lila's in Bruno Soccavo's sausage factory where women face the continuous threat of sexual exploitation and sexual violence. Yet Ferrante is suspicious of fixed views, whether in politics or personal relations. While sympathetic to the political awakening in Italy inspired by the Left and understanding of its motives, Ferrante is skeptical about the political purity of radical Leftists, especially those who come from comfortable backgrounds. She also stresses the strong relationship between the personal and political.

Not only in Naples, but throughout Italy, the lives of Ferrante's characters, even those in the university world, turn out to be enmeshed in the intersection of politics, business, and criminality that underlies Italy. Within the tetralogy, characters who seem to hold themselves aloof from the fiery political wars and seem to be part of the establishment, like Guido and Nino, are eventually implicated in Italy's web of intrigue and corruption. In one of Elena's interior monologues early in *The Story of the Lost Child*, she reminds us of what will be – and perhaps has been – demonstrated: "[A]uthority is a patina and at times it doesn't take much to crack it" (IV.I.16).

In the second book, *The Story of a New Name* (2013), Ferrante renders Elena's observations in a more elaborate style to represent her more complex and confused perceptions. With each succeeding book of the tetralogy, the style becomes somewhat more convoluted as Elena's interior experiences become more complex. Thus the focus of the second book is more on the self-dramatizing Elena than on Lila. Elena uses her education, notably her writing ability, to expand her horizons beyond her poor neighborhood and that of her friend and rival Lila, who, although equally bright, never gets beyond the fifth grade or ever leaves the neighborhood.

In contrast to the prevailing Catholicism in Italy, Ferrante makes clear that she does not believe in a transcendent God watching over us and to whom we account for our actions. Indeed, as the tetralogy works its way through the post-World War II decades, Catholicism becomes a religion less of intensely held spiritual beliefs and more of just lip service to obsolete forms of devotion. Ferrante believes that we live in terms of how we develop our potential. But that potential is shaped by environment – the social customs of the neighborhood in which we grow up, and our personal relationships with others, notably family and close friends. The problem is that there are infinite roadblocks to developing our potential, including not only our impulses, obsessions, sexual desires, and bad judgments, but also the presence of the dead who have shaped our parents and parents' parents. As Ferrante puts it in an interview in *The New Yorker*:

The idea that every "I" is largely made up of others and by the others wasn't theoretical; it was a reality. To be alive meant to collide continually with the existence of others and to be collided with, the results being at times good-natured, at others aggressive, then again good-natured. The dead were brought into quarrels; people weren't content to attack and insult the living – they naturally abused aunts, cousins, grandparents, and great-grandparents who were no longer in the world. … Our entire body, like it or not, enacts a stunning resurrection of the dead just as we advance toward our own death. We are, as you say, interconnected. And we should teach ourselves to look deeply at this interconnection – I call it a tangle, or, rather, *frantumaglia* – to give ourselves adequate tools to describe it. (Lagioia)[3]

Radical Disruption: Ferrante's *The Days of Abandonment* (2002)

Let us turn to Ferrante's second novel, *The Days of Abandonment*, which in many crucial ways anticipates the themes of the tetralogy. Ferrante's focus is already on radical disruptions in life narratives, moments when our essential assumptions are challenged: "I enjoy breaking through my character's armor of good education and good manners. I enjoy upsetting her self-image, her will, and revealing another, rougher soul underneath, someone raucous, maybe even crude" (Ferrante, "Art of Fiction No. 228").[4] Such is the case when marriages disintegrate as in *The Days of Abandonment*; here Olga's husband's announcement that their marriage is over leads to a complete behavioral transformation. In the Neapolitan tetralogy the two lead characters realize that their husbands or lovers are not fulfilling their needs and/or that their choices are illusions. Such is the case for Lila with Stefano and Nino, and Elena with Pietro and Nino.

In the case of Olga, the self-dramatizing narrator-protagonist of *The Days of Abandonment*, the breakup leads to a nervous breakdown, a complete descent into a personal hell. When we first meet Olga she has much more in common with Elena than with the often raging Lila, who lives on the emotional edge if not, after the loss of Tina, in the abyss to which Olga descends. Olga is, like Elena, a writer although not as successful, and like Elena she has been brought up in a poor Naples neighborhood. Now living in Turin, she prides herself on self-control. Like Elena with Nino, she has put her self-interest on the back burner to please a man, a successful engineer who has used her to get where he is professionally and socially. She has known and encouraged him since his boyhood. Only after he departs does Olga learn that he is regarded by others as an opportunist.

Gradually Olga – an odd name for an Italian, although it was used more frequently in Italy early in the twentieth century – looses her moorings and begins to return to what she regarded as the primitive world of her family which she thought she had put behind her: "I hated raised voices, movements that were too brusque. My own family was full of noisy emotions" (10).[5] This is the family culture that repels Elena in the tetralogy. The past returns in Olga's memory in the form of her childhood awareness in Naples that a woman who loses her man is cursed: "Women without love lose the light in their eyes, women without love die while they are still alive" (9.44). She identifies with a woman from her childhood who had fallen apart when her husband left and whom her neighborhood knew as the *poverella* – that poor woman – because she had poisoned herself in a desperate effort to regain her husband by getting his attention.

Olga's upper-middle-class armor is revealed as the emperor's new clothes, and as she falls apart, she casts aside all the polite niceties of a comfortable life, begins to punctuate her talk with obscenities, no longer observes amenities in personal relationships, and barely sustains her role as mother of two children. She oscillates between paralyzing depression and rage that blinds her to her basic responsibilities. At one point when she accidentally meets her husband and his younger lover, she physically attacks him. The absence of psychiatric help is striking in *The Days of Abandonment* as it will be in the tetralogy. Olga never thinks of that resource even though she is of the social class which does so in the United States and some European countries.

Social Class and Class Satire

Class distinctions and class aspirations are an important part of the Neapolitan tetralogy. Ferrante is conscious of social class and in the world of these novels, socio-economic distinctions matter a great deal. Within Elena's Naples neighborhood, money and power matter more than lineage, and the Solaras replace Don Achille as the dominant force.

Elena and Lila know what their neighborhood is and how hard it is to depart from the expected life narrative when one is born and raised there. Education is one vessel to improve one's station, but poor parents with several children need and expect financial help from their children to eke out a living. Elena abhors her mother until they reach some reconciliation when her mother is dying of cancer (III.41–42), and she is ashamed of her father who is a porter. Yet unlike Lila's parents, they have grudgingly let her continue her education in secondary school and university, although Elena's mother frequently asks her to contribute to the family's support, which is part of the tradition in the neighborhood.

Thus Lila's parents don't encourage education and she is working for her father and brother when, according to middle-class values, she should be in middle school. For some women and fewer men, marriage is another way to advance socially and economically. Even with her education and success as an author, Elena doubts whether she can cast off her neighborhood origins and be part of the elite cosmopolitan world of her husband Pietro and his family.

Lila believes as a sixteen-year-old bride that marriage is the road to class transformation when she becomes Signora Raffaella Carracci. But she is soon disillusioned with her choice of a husband, Stefano Carracci. In an ugly scene he rapes Lila when she refuses him. After her affair with Nino, she refuses to acknowledge that Rino is Stefano's son rather than Nino's; we don't know if she is in doubt or wants to punish Stefano. It turns out that Stefano is probably the father (although without a DNA test we can't be certain).

In the last chapter of *My Brilliant Friend*, while at Lila and Stefano's wedding reception, Elena realizes that she now knows the answer to her teacher Maestra Oliviero's once asking her if she knew who the plebs were:

. . . .

At that moment I knew what the plebs were, much more clearly than when, years earlier, she had asked me. The plebs were us. The plebs were that fight for food and wine, that quarrel over who should be served first and better, that dirty floor on which the waiters clattered back and forth, those increasingly vulgar toasts. The plebs were my mother, who had drunk wine and now was leaning against my father's shoulder, while he, serious, laughed, his mouth gaping, at the sexual allusions of the metal dealer. They were all laughing, even Lila, with the expression of one who has a role and will play it to the utmost. (I.62)

. . . .

But, and this is part of Ferrante's irony, Elena is somewhat defined at this point by her social class. Not yet exposed to a different set of manners, Elena does not behave well at the wedding, ignoring her neighborhood boyfriend Antonio and flirting with Nino. In sexual matters she can be as impulsive and fluid in her feelings and in her affections as Lila, although Lila's instability carries over into all aspects of her life.

As part of her effort to give her novel an epic dimension, Ferrante interweaves the personal stories of Elena and Lila with the political, social, and intellectual movements in Italy. Yet she is aware how personal life often dominates; no matter the historical sweep of events, people live in their own narrow worlds. To be sure, Ferrante reminds us that the historical backdrop of a dramatic shift in Elena's personal life is the 1978 kidnapping and subsequent murder of former Prime Minister Aldo Moro. But this does not seem to much affect the lovers, Nino and Elena. After leaving Pietro for Nino, the compulsive womanizer, liar, and narcissist, Elena recalls her "true life" began one and a half years ago when she went to his room in Florence and speaks of the "miraculous splendor ... [W]e took refuge in us. ... We wanted only to hold each other, cling to each other" (IV.I.20). Elena feels guilty for thinking more of herself than her children, but Ferrante expects us to notice that her guilt does not change her behavior.

In Book Three of the tetralogy, *Those Who Leave and Those Who Stay*, we see an example of how family history and social class shape the present. Pietro's father is Guido Airota, a distinguished Greek professor, and his mother Adele has stature in the publishing world as a powerful literary agent. Elena realizes how Pietro has a "protective family, a sort of well-fortified castle" that gives him and his sister advantages and that those advantages allow Pietro to pursue his dreams. Pietro's father, Professor Airota, "had given his children magical weapons before the battle" (II.108). They have something Elena doesn't have, "the armor to advance serenely" (II.108).

But even as class differences matter, they are challenged by social change. In the 1970s and 1980s troubles come even to those who have class advantages, and even elite families are not protected. To an extent, Ferrante archly challenges some of what Elena has naively observed in the seemingly impervious privileged classes and shows ways in which they are wanting and not so different from other classes. It turns out that Guido has indiscreetly distributed political funds of doubtful origins and Adele has had her share of affairs.

Ferrante is not only an observer of cultural pretension, but also a scathing satirist. Thus I assume from Elena's cosmopolitan view of extreme political rants that Ferrante doesn't believe the macrocosmic Marxist gibberish spoken by the well-to-do (including by Franco, Elena's former boyfriend), which I take to be a satire of radical chic or how the socially prominent and/or economically comfortable adapt the words of the radical Left without taking the same risks as they do. For example, Nadia, the daughter of Professor Galiani – a Naples teacher who encourages Elena to pursue her education – has been brought up in a privileged environment compared to Lila and Elena. Yet she is attracted to Pasquale, the angry revolutionary firebrand from Elena's violent Naples neighborhood.

While there is little in Ferrante that makes us laugh, what humor we do find is often grim noir humor of incongruity based on inappropriate behavior or speech. For example, when Elena wants approval of her writing from her former lover Franco, he says, "objectively, it is not the moment for writing novels" (III.17). We realize this ostentatiously pretentious statement is to be taken by the reader as an example of political foolishness. But it also expresses the nastiness of Franco – who has not finished his degree or accomplished much of anything – to someone who has surpassed him. That Franco calls her book "a story of petty love affairs" bothers Elena because his dismissive view expresses Elena's self-doubt and secret fear that her work doesn't matter (III.18).

Elena is caught up in the rush of cultural change and is a vehicle for Ferrante's explorations of those changes. When Elena visits the Airotas's daughter Mariarosa in her own home, Elena's perspective is shaped by what she sees as liberation from traditional norms. Mariarosa's home is as much the center of sexual experimentation – she sleeps with men and women – and drugs as it is a place for female consciousness raising and intellectual dialogue. In another instance of radical chic, the upper class bohemians not only appear to be sympathetic to the have-nots, but also take on the manners of the class that they hope to appeal to and in some ways emulate, even while maintaining some of the economic advantages of their privileged position. Thus Mariarosa speaks the lower-class language that Elena thought she herself had left behind.

Seeing this version of freedom, Elena, who is not having much sex with Pietro, and what sex she is having is not satisfactory, wants to pursue her own path. In particular, she has not only become bored and dissatisfied with being Pietro's wife and the mother of their children, but resents sacrificing her career. She wants the freedom to experiment with her sexuality that she sees developing for women of a certain social class. For her at this point, "marriage was a prison" and she wants to join the circus of "breaking the rules" (III.69). She is jealous of the freedom she has not experienced and becomes flirtatious. In contrast to the lower-class customs and mores with which she grew up in Naples, she sees "a game of freedom where female shyness was considered a sign of hypocritical foolishness," and she wants to take part in this new life (III.68). She announces her "availability" by showing her legs, unbuttoning the top of her blouse, and engaging in what she calls the "game of seduction" (III.68).

With some irony, Ferrante foregrounds the changing role of women and of sexual relationships. Thinking of her own life, with many lovers which she mentions casually, as well as her handful of primary relationships, Elena concludes, "[T]he time of faithfulness and permanent relationships was over for men and for women" (IV.II.21). In contrast to Elena's parents' generation where even dysfunctional and violent marriages continue, virtually all the marriages of Elena's generation dissolve.

Naples

Naples is a major character. Using her narrator Elena, Ferrante presents a microcosmic view of how life is lived among the poor. Elena calls Naples a "place of disorder and danger" and this does not change over the tetralogy's sixty years (III.1). While she appreciates some of the views, particularly of the sea and Vesuvius, for her Naples remains ugly, violent, and aggressive as well as unresponsive to people's economic needs. Students physically fight at the University in Naples. In Ferrante's Naples, men grope women in public areas, obscenities are pervasive, and people live on the economic edge in a gruesome competition for survival of the fittest. Rumor, gossip, envy, fear, superstition, and Catholicism all play a role in shaping behavior.

What is most striking about life in Naples is the pervasive violence which hovers over the entire tetralogy. Parents beat their children, husbands beat their wives, men fight one another, and people are murdered with some regularity, whether gangsters or radical politicians of the Left or Right. At one point when Lila is a child her father throws her out the window. When women in the neighborhood are beaten by their husbands (as Stefano beats Lila on her honeymoon for refusing his sexual advance), the neighbors pretend not to notice.

In this neighborhood, people speak to one another in an aggressive, even at times threatening, way and name-calling is ubiquitous. Parents take an abrasive tone with their children and we see few words of encouragement or gentleness, gentleness; neighbors berate neighbors, teachers intimidate young students, and business dealings are accompanied by threats. Ferrante has remarked: "Violence has, at least in Italian, a meaningful language of its own – smash your face, bash your face in. You see? These are expressions that refer to the forced manipulation of identity, to its cancellation" (Ferrante, "Art of Fiction No. 228"). Although sexual customs evolve during the sixty years during which the tetralogy takes place, it is still quite usual to hear a woman called a whore if she flirts with a man whom the speaker disapproves of or if she sleeps with a person outside marriage. Even family members, including mothers speaking to their own daughters, use the appellation "whore" to upbraid women in their own family.

Beginning with *My Brilliant Friend*, Naples is beset by violence. From an early age, children in the neighborhood learn violence and the first volume has multiple examples. They are shaped by this milieu where violence is always close to the surface and ready to erupt. Early on, Elena and Lila learn that Don Achille, reputed to be a Nazi spy as well as an important neighborhood gangster, is killed by Alfredo Peluso whose grocery store he took over. The boys bully the girls and later on rape them. When Enzi, bested by Lila in math, throws rocks at her and Elena, Lila throws them back. She behaves as if she is afraid of nothing, but we realize her seeming courage disguises fear. When Marcello gets fresh with Elena, Lila pulls a knife and draws blood from his throat. When the Solaras are outdone in fireworks they begin to maliciously shoot fireworks at those they consider their adversaries.

For American readers the world of the Solaras, which grows with each volume until the brothers are murdered, is reminiscent of that of the Godfather films and the *Sopranos*, except that some of the characters in those films engage our sympathies more. The Solaras control a great deal of business in the neighborhood. They are engaged in loansharking, receiving stolen goods, and later drugs. Their families intermingle with other families in business and personal relationships. The Solaras spread their tentacles throughout the neighborhood and beyond and, like a social cancer, devour everything in Naples: young women, families, and small businesses, including the shoe business begun by Lila's father and brother based on a shoe of her design. Marcello Solara marries Elena's sister, and the Solaras employ two of her brothers as well as Elena's forrmer boyfriend to do whatever dirty work the Solaras want done. The Solaras brothers' mother, Manuela, keeps the ruinous loan book which keeps many in the neighborhood in economic bondage. Later she is murdered, as are her two sons, who have become major criminals if not sociopaths with a propensity for violence.

Among the discouraging aspects of Naples is the absence of psychiatric care or indeed any medical resources for emotional illness. The most notable character in need of psychiatric intervention is Lila herself who, as she reaches adulthood, is increasingly on the edge of a nervous breakdown even before her daughter's disappearance. Lila is intermittently schizoid, paranoid, bipolar, and out of control. Indeed, in depicting not only Lila's mental and emotional demons but also those of several others, Ferrante is saying something about life in working-class neighborhoods, for no one in Elena's and Lila's Naples neighborhood seeks the psychiatric help they need.

Olga's collapse in *The Days of Abandonment* looks forward to the psychotic behavior of the widow Melina Cappucci in *My Brilliant Friend*; she is badly in need of psychiatric help when her lover, Donato Sarratore, breaks with her and leaves the neighborhood. Another deeply troubled character in the Neapolitan tetralogy is Alfonso, who is struggling with gender issues and, in his last days, is a victim of sadistic beatings. Pasquale's mother, Giuseppina Peluso, is clearly depressed after her husband's arrest for killing Don Achille and eventually commits suicide. Franco, after being beaten and maimed by Fascists, is clearly suffering emotionally before his suicide, and he, like Olga, could afford therapy.

Form and Style: The Shape of the Narrative

The Neapolitan novels are driven by plot and characterization and in that way take their place in the tradition of the European novel. With a respectful nod to Cervantes as the founder of the European novel, Ferrante uses the narrative trick of the discovered manuscript at the outset of the tetralogy's second volume, *The Story of a New Name*, to explain how Elena knew so much about Lila. Elena's memory is complemented by a box of writing – eight notebooks – that Lila, fearful that her husband, Stefano, would read them, gave her in 1966. After studying them, Elena discards them by tossing them into the Arno, although she claims to have learned "by heart the passages I liked" (II.1).

Rereading, we are aware that by beginning with Lila's disappearance as a prologue, Ferrante, before turning to the section "Childhood: The Story of Don Achille," is calling attention to the difference between chronological story – the telling of events from beginning to end – and discourse – the arrangement of the story into a structured narrative form with disrupted chronology, commentary, short chapters with epiphanic endings, and nuanced imagery.

Ferrante's searing urban realism (with attention to the role of the underworld) resonates with the grim cityscapes of Dickens's London, Balzac's Paris, and Dostoevsky's St. Petersburg. Ferrante is also very much aware of how the contemporary city is depicted in words and images, notably in Italy, including *Arte Povera* in painting and sculpture, Italian films, and TV soap operas. At times the short chapters resemble diary entries; at other times, these chapters suggest a sequence of very short stories – really anecdotes – or even, in their colorful visuals, a series of narrative paintings. More frequently, the chapters read like newspaper articles and – with their strong images – articles accompanied by pictures. We might think of the newsreels and sometimes short documentaries that accompanied features in movie theaters, especially at the time the earlier volumes of the tetralogy took place.

Surely there is a cinematic quality to the view of Naples that recalls Roberto Rossellini's neorealism and Michelangelo Antonioni's *Red Desert* (1964) with its depiction of Ravenna, and there is much in the tetralogy's account of decadent behavior of the well-to-do that recalls Fellini's *8½* (1963). At times the chapters resemble a montage in their series of short shots that are edited and arranged into a narrative sequence as a way of condensing space, time, and information. The quick cutaways, sometimes in the form of dramatic and epiphanic shifts at the end of chapters, owe much to cinema. Yet the ensuing chapter may begin with picking up the action prior to the cutaway. Another cinematic technique is the alternation between, on one hand, long views in the form of summaries of events that have taken place offstage over a period of time in the lives of minor characters and, on the other hand, close-ups, especially intense scenes that take place within small spaces.

Although Ferrante uses some strikingly brilliant metaphors, she is not a stylist – at least not in the translations by Ann Goldstein – in the tradition of Proust, Borges, Joyce, and Woolf where every word is nuanced and even the phonics matter. Her basic structural concept is not the elegant sentence but the short chapter, in which a small amount of material takes its form and meaning from the final sentence or two or even the final word. Ferrante observes: "A page is well written when the labour and pleasure of truthful narration supplant any other concern, including a concern with formal elegance. I belong to the category of writers who throw out the final and keep the rough when this practice ensures a higher degree of authenticity" (Jobey).[6] This authenticity is at the heart of Ferrante's writing, whether she is rendering the complex psyches of Elena and Lila, the cityscape of Naples with a focus on the poor outskirts, or the political and social maelstrom of post-World War II Italy. This is the same authenticity that Elena, Ferrante's dramatized narrator and at times surrogate, seeks within the narrative she is telling.

While some chapters simply provide essential information, often about characters that have been offstage for a while, the short chapters fit together like mosaics in a larger whole. We don't know how many of the intricacies and nuances of the sweeping tetralogy Ferrante had in mind when she began writing or even when she published *My Brilliant Friend*. But given that the Prologue of *My Brilliant Friend* contains the ending of the tetralogy – Lila's disappearance – we can be sure she had the basic plot details in mind from the first even if, as is inevitable, she not only did some fine-tuning but also made some important imaginative additions and transformations while writing.

Ferrante's tetralogy owes something to the computer age. Elena learns to use a computer to write, and Lila develops a successful computer business. Indeed, at times the tetralogy's short chapters read like long Facebook posts or sustained emails. But they are carefully structured, often focusing on one central episode or scene and concluding with surprises and transformative insights. Some of these surprises and insights are no longer than the (until recently) 140-character Twitter limit.

Often the chapters' conclusions are vital to Ferrante's artistry. In these cases, Elena shares with the reader a moment of awareness and enlightenment, although that moment may concern Lila. It is almost as if Ferrante decided on the apocalyptic endings of chapters with their revelatory moments – sometimes unexpected plot twists and turns, but often moments of intense insight – before she wrote the beginnings and middles. Yet Elena's epiphanies are often different and less perceptive than what Ferrante shares with her reader from whom she expects greater understanding than Elena's. The use of ironic epiphanies where the reader's awareness is different from and richer than the characters' perception owes much to Joyce, but Ferrante uses this technique less frequently than Joyce.

One key to understanding the tetralogy that has been overlooked by readers immersed in Elena's struggles to find her own voice as a woman and a writer is that there is an oscillating distance between Ferrante and her self-dramatizing first person narrator. One of Ferrante's central techniques is the frequent use of Elena's reflective interior monologues, which are often but by no means always insightful. At times these monologues reveal Elena as an imperceptive if not myopic narrator. We need to keep the possibility of distortion and forget-fulness in mind because what we know – or think we know – of Lila is mostly filtered through Elena's consciousness; even dialogue is dependent on Elena's memory.

That Ferrante wants us to think of the novel in the Western literary tradition is underlined by naming her narrator Elena Greco (Greek). By giving her the name Greco, Ferrante suggests El Greco, the Greek painter known by that Spanish appellation. He depicted events first in Italy and later in Spain. Elena, living in Turin (where Anita Raja also know as Elena Ferrante her creator lives), writes about the world she left, but perhaps even more to the point, Ferrante hasn't lived in Naples since she was three and gives her narrator the identity of an insider when she is in fact an outsider, like El Greco was in Spain.

Elena's experiential journey, including its frequent digressive episodes, takes the form of a physical and figurative odyssey that begins and ends in Naples. Like that of Leopold Bloom in *Ulysses*, Elena's odyssey always has an interior psychological aspect. The allusions to Dante's *Inferno* add to the odyssey motif since Dante's accompanying Virgil through hell is an odyssey, and we readers are joining Elena on her journey through Naples, a secular hell. The Dante references take on even more meaning if we recall that Ulysses is consigned deep in the eighth circle of Dante's hell (canto xxvi) for betraying his cohorts after returning to Ithaca; stirred by restlessness and ambition, Ulysses leads them on a disastrous second voyage. We can see Elena's abandoning her children – or at least consigning them to a subsidiary position – when she leaves Pietro for Nino as a parallel undertaking of a second voyage.

Ferrante explicitly evokes Joyce's epic novel *Ulysses* not through the educated Elena but through Lila. The latter, while walking with her son, meets her for-mer teacher, Maestra Oliviero, who, very much aware of Lila's potential, has been extremely unhappy with the decision of Lila's parents to take Lila out of school. When the teacher notices that Lila is carrying Joyce's *Ulysses*, she asks, "Is it about the Odyssey?" Lila responds: "No, it's about how prosaic life is today." Maestra Oliviero: "And so?" Lila: "That's all. It says that our heads are full of nonsense. That we are flesh, blood, and bone. That one person has the same value as another. That we want only to eat, drink, fuck." When Maestra Oliviero asserts, "Don't read books that you can't understand, it's bad for you," Lila responds: "A lot of things are bad for you" (II.98).

Lila's growth continues outside the educational system and she refuses to be intimidated. Ferrante's larger point is to puncture various shibboleths about what is good for people raised in a subculture dominated by poverty and violence and defined by limited opportunities. But she is also reminding us that Joyce taught successor authors to emphasize the day-to-day challenges of human life as well as its basic animal components of eating, drinking, and fucking.

What gives the tetralogy its epic ballast is the inclusion of historical contexts stretching over the sixty years as well as a wide range of literary and philosophical references. The author presents a widely read narrator, Elena, who is immersed in the contemporary European feminist intellectual movement as well as in the street life of a downtrodden neighborhood of Naples. For Elena – and for her creator – Naples becomes a metaphor for the violence, cynicism, and rapacity of most human beings even while it remains the site of a microcosmic analysis of its corruption. Both Elena and her creator see Naples as metaphor for the world in which "the dream of unlimited progress is in reality a nightmare of savagery and death" (IV.II.1).

Form: Opening

The opening of an important novel resembles Genesis in that we enter into an imagined world created by the author, and that world has its own particular artistic rules as well as both a physical geography and a grammar of motives. Put another way, openings of novels seal off the world we live in and take us into an ontology created *ex nihilo* by an author.

Ferrante's openings are often quite special. For example, the first sentence of Ferrante's *The Days of Abandonment* is almost Kafkaesque in its matter-of-factness: "One April afternoon, right after lunch, my husband announced that he wanted to leave me" (1.9). Olga's first responses are relatively reasonable, recalling Gregor Samsa's response to his awakening as a giant beetle.

Let us turn to the beginning of the remarkable Neapolitan tetralogy. With a Prologue entitled "Eliminating all the Traces" that describes Lila's disappearance, *My Brilliant Friend* begins with events very close to the end of the story that the tetralogy is telling. Its very first sentences are matter-of-fact understatements: "This morning Rino telephoned" (I.Prologue.1). Living in Turin, Elena gets a call from Lila's son, Rino (Gennaro), who tells her that his mother and Elena's close friend has disappeared. Elena describes the son as "a small-time crook" with "no brain" whom we later learn has had a drug problem (I.Prologue.1).

Responding to Lila's effort to read herself out of the text of her own life, Elena's telling reverses that erasure and establishes the major themes of the novels, including the pervasive violence and the omnipresence of fear in a neighborhood where criminals are in control. Lila has not only disappeared, but she has also taken all her belongings and even cut her own picture out of photographs that she has left behind. "Angry" at how Lila has tried to erase herself from Elena's memory, Elena, the aging self-dramatizing narrator, now in her sixties, will use her writing to erase Lila's disappearance and give her meaning and definition (I.Prologue.3). We are aware from the Prologue that Elena's memories are filtered through the distorting lens of memories that go back sixty years. Because she and Lila are inextricably bound in her memory and imagination, Elena will try to give her own life renewed clarity, meaning, and definition. In other words, Elena is not going to let Lila disappear or let her own borders between self and world dissolve the way Lila thinks hers do.

By introducing the friendship between Lila and Elena as well as their contrasting personalities and their tacit competition, the opening chapters of *My Brilliant Friend* set the table for the entire series. What marks Elena's early impressions of Lila is her fearfulness, boldness, determination, ruthlessness "on occasions of violence" (I.5), and her insolence at school. By contrast, Elena "always felt slightly detached from my own actions" (I.3). She "liked pleasing everyone" (I.7), and as rereaders we see this is often true.

"Disheveled, dirty," and "fragile in appearance" (I.8, I.13), as Elena describes her, Lila is also exceptionally intellectually gifted; she has precociously learned to read and write and is the best student in the elementary school. When asked who taught her, she replies in one of Ferrante's abrupt and powerful chapter climaxes, "Me" (I.6). That is, she is self-taught at six, and we learn that she has been reading since the age of three (I.7). She also does "complicated calculations in her head" (I.8) and makes "beautifully colored drawings" (I.13). She displaces Elena as the teacher's favorite and Elena, accepting "Lila's superiority" (I.8), determines to "model myself" on her (I.7); she thinks of Lila as "that terrible, dazzling girl" who is "prettier than I am" (I.8, I.9).

Mostly, Elena presents the past as a living present, but we are very much aware that she is looking back. Elena wonders if Lila, who often lacks self-knowledge and speaks and acts impulsively, understands the consequences of her words and actions. But Elena also questions her own judgment and behavior, although perhaps not as often as she should.

Ferrante captures the tunnel vision and capacity for fantasy of childhood. Rereading, we see how Elena's childhood perception that "[W]e were always going toward something terrible that had existed before us yet had always been there waiting for us, just for us" informs the entire tetralogy (I.2). Such a dark and uncanny foreboding hovering over childhood, a time when Elena stresses that we are entirely focused on our own existence, is particularly ominous. Yet it is part of Ferrante's larger vision – somewhat in contrast to the existentialism that prevailed in post World War II Europe – that we become part of a pre-existent world that shapes us; no matter what we do, Ferrante insists, we cannot fully escape that world.

Thus, it is probable that some of the continuing sexual tension between Nino and Elena has its roots in childhood. We learn very early that as a child Elena "loves" Nino whom she finds "handsome" (I.9), "so meek, so quiet" (I.8), but also "so languid" (I.9), a quality she dislikes and notices when he "collapse[s]" in an elementary school competition. Rereading, we realize that this collapse foreshadows his later revealing his lack of character – his narcissism, untruthfulness, inconsistency – in many ways. As a young boy he announces to Elena in somewhat bullying fashion when she is eight: "When I grow up I want to marry you" (I.11), and she rejects him.

In keeping with the mysterious disappearance in the Prologue, the first chapter introduces a dark magical aspect into the tetralogy that doesn't ever disappear. At the age of eight, almost nine, Elena and Lila climb the stairs to Don Achille's top floor apartment, but at this point we don't know why. Don Achille is the most feared and hated figure – "the ogre of fairy tales" with a capacity for unimaginable evil – in the neighborhood, and a figure Elena is warned to avoid by her father: "I was absolutely forbidden to go near him, speak to him, look at him, spy on him" (I.1). Appropriate to a child's imagination, Elena worries that "Maria, Don Achille's wife, would put me in the pan of boiling oil, the children would eat me, he would suck my head the way my father did with mullets" (I.1).

This very first chapter introduces how Elena's perceptions are heightened and transformed by her imagination. Characteristically, Ferrante uses the chapter's epiphanic ending to foreground the human implications of the chapter in terms of Elena's life. Lila takes the lead as they climb the stairs, but when Elena reaches her: "[S]he gave me her hand. This gesture changed everything between us forever" (I.1). For Elena, this is a crystallizing moment in her life, giving her a bond amidst the confusion of childhood exacerbated by fear of violence.

Note how Ferrante brilliantly rearranges the chronology. We only learn in subsequent chapters that Elena and Lila are climbing these stairs to demand that the dolls – which they deliberately pushed through the grate into the basement floor below – be returned. After descending into the basement and not finding them there (I.10), Lila is certain Don Achille took them, but we are not sure if her version of events is a figment of her imagination. When they finally confront Don Achille and ask for the dolls, they see that he is human: "No minerals, no sparkle of glass. His long face was of flesh, and the hair bristled only around his ears. … [H]e was an ordinary person" (I.14). Never acknowledging that he has taken the dolls, he gives them money to buy new dolls, but instead they buy Louisa May Alcott's nineteenth-century novel *Little Women*. As young children Elena and Lila find inspiration in *Little Women*, a novel in which the March sisters move from child-hood to adulthood and respond to – and, especially in the case of Jo, escape – the nineteenth-century expectations and constraints of gender roles.

Elena's and Lina's reduction of Don Achille from a seemingly larger-than-life male figure in terms of power or great prowess to relative ordinariness is a recurring pattern within the tetralogy. What gives the tetralogy its feminist inflection is this process of disconfirmation and diminishment of males and the corresponding – albeit finally limited – empowerment of females.

Violence is introduced into Elena's world at a very early age: "I feel no nostal-gia for our childhood; it was full of violence" (I.5). The fourth chapter begins with the word "Blood," as if it were a metonymy for the world of the Naples neighborhood. Elena lives in a world where "adults were often wounded, blood flowed from the wounds, they festered, and sometimes people died" (I.3). She catalogues the deaths and wounds of people she knew, and of course that cata-logue intensifies her fear of Don Achille, who is a dreaded presence to her father and the entire neighborhood: "With these words and those years I bring back the many fears that accompanied me all my life" (I.3). In her imagination, Don Achille is associated with blood, especially after he attacked Alfredo Peluso, a man who accused him of taking his carpentry shop: "Don Achille had showed himself to everyone for what he was: an evil being of uncertain animal-mineral physiognomy who – it seemed – sucked blood from others while never losing any himself" (I.4).

Violence is part of domestic life, too. Elena's father beats her mother and threatens Elena (I.7). Her mother is unhappy with her household tasks and lack of money; she abuses Elena and makes Elena feel "superfluous in her life" by the time she is six (I.7). Nor is the violence restricted to men: "The women fought among themselves more than the men, they pulled each other's hair, they hurt each other" (I.5). While the men, who "were always getting furious," eventually calm down, the women "flew into a rage that had no end" (I.5). An example is the rivalry between Donato Sarratore's wife, Lidia, and his lover, Melina. When the Sarratores leave the neighborhood, Melina has a fit and throws her kitchenware out the window and finally her iron, which could have killed Nino had it, hit him, as it almost did (I.12). Domestic turmoil will play a big role in the tetralogy; Nino's affairs with both Lila and Elena are the focus of some of the turmoil.

Violence and fright underpin everything in the neighborhood. Elena describes how a simple elementary school contest leads to a series of fights and an apology from Lila's fearful father to Don Achille "without ever saying what he was apologizing for" (I.9), the reason being that Lila had bested Don Achille's son Alfonso in a math competition. At first, Lila defers to Alfonso in the school contest – although she finally decides to win – because she is aware of the "fear-rancor-hatred-meekness that our parents displayed toward the Carraccis and transmitted to us" (I.9).

From the example of adults, children learn to respond to frustration with violence. We learn that the rock throwing begins with Enzo Scanno taking the lead soon after Lila bests Enzo in the school math contest. The non-verbal Enzo is recognizing her as a rival and equal in the only way he knows, namely violence; this pattern of expressing rage and frustration informs the entire tetralogy. Lila responds in kind, with the result that he hits her on the head with a rock that draws blood and leaves him in tears. When later she and Enzo will live together and launch a successful computer business, Ferrante is making the point that childhood ties inexplicably shape the future, often in uncanny ways. Put another way: In the tetralogy, the past is always present as an *is* not a *was*.

Rereading *My Brilliant Friend*, we see how the tetralogy is a unified whole. From childhood, Lila's credo is to intimidate those who want to intimidate you (III.38). In *Those Who Leave and Those Who Stay*, when Michele Solara tries to intimidate Lila and talks about training women to obey and how he taught women to whistle in two hours, Lila concludes the chapter: "I've known how to whistle since I was five years old" (III.44). This is an example of how Ferrante presents a chapter that simultaneously takes its meaning both from its epiphanic conclusion – whistling since she was five – and from what precedes, for the ending of the chapter informs far more than the chapter. Here we see that Lila is demonstrating her fierce independence, which we have seen from the outset of *My Brilliant Friend*. Later, she carries that edge into setting up a computer business and challenging the Solara dominance in the neighborhood. But when she loses her daughter, she is no longer interested and, to use her Neapolitan neighborhood metaphor, loses most of her whistle.

Let us think of another example of how we experience resonance on a rereading. In 1969, when Elena is about to get married to Pietro, Lila and Elena converse most of the night. We think of Lila's wedding night at the conclusion of *My Brilliant Friend*. Lila confides that she doesn't get much out of sex, while Elena affirms that she herself does: "[F]or me it's not like that" (III.46). Sensing her own vulnerability, Lila asks that Elena watch her fall asleep and "Watch me always" (III.46), and Elena does so intermittently. Later we see that there is a mutuality to their intervention in each other's lives and that Lila has Elena's interest in mind on crucial occasions. While helping Elena raise her children when they live in the same building, Lila watches out for Elena. Without telling Elena, Lila has Antonio, who is Elena's former boyfriend and an employee of the Solara mobsters, spy on Nino. She learns enough from Antonio to realize that Nino is a scoundrel who uses women to advance himself and that, like Nino's father, he has no control over his sexual impulses. Elena even catches him having sex with the nanny she has hired for her children.

Rereading the first two volumes, we see that Nino is more of a rascal than we realize on first reading because we see how he uses people. He maliciously fails to submit Elena's first attempt at publication because he fears that she might outdo him. Both women married men who don't regard them as equals, and both women at first see Nino as a sexually exciting, handsome, highly intelligent, and sympathetic alternative. But Elena comes to realize that Nino is only perfunctorily interested in her writing; that like her husband Pietro, Nino patronizes her and does not care about her opinions. The cynical and manipulative Nino believes, as he tells Elena's daughter Dede in front of her mother, that Elena doesn't know "how the world we live in functions" (IV.I.71).

Form: Epilogue

Because the last novel of the tetralogy, *The Story of the Lost Child*, ends in irresolution, what we might call an open ending, so does the entire tetralogy. Lila is still missing and we see the pentimento of Lila as a child as well as her lost daughter peeking through the title. Not only do we not know what happens to Lila, but we don't know whether the Solara brothers kidnapped Tina in revenge for Lila's antipathy; nor do we know who murdered the Solara brothers.

That the tetralogy has a circular structure, coming back to the beginning, emphasizes how in terms of basics, nothing has changed in Naples, Italy, and perhaps the world, even while human lives have proceeded from beginning to end. When we finish the last volume we in fact need to go back and reread the first volume and see how Ferrante has brilliantly set up the entire structure from the beginning. On rereading, sentences like Elena's recalling that "she [Lila] never left Naples in her life" take on a new resonance (I.Prologue.1). We now know why Lila wants "to disappear without leaving a trace" (I.Prologue.2) because we know of her daughter Tina's disappearance and Lila's subsequent gradual falling apart. We also know of Lila's pathological symptom expressed by her feeling that on occasion everything is dissolving into one substance, what she calls "disappearing boundaries."

Let us turn to the Epilogue of *The Story of the Lost Child*, where Elena settles some accounts and leaves others open. Lila's disappearance at sixty-six becomes the catalyst for the tetralogy we are now reading, the sequence of four fictional autobiographical memoirs. In a characteristically self-doubting meditation on the efficacy of her writing, Elena frets that she "will die without knowing if I succeeded" in capturing who Lila was (IV.Epilogue.1).

Elena returns to the Naples apartment in which Lila lived as a child, "a space darker, more run-down than it had been" (IV.Epilogue.1). When someone is murdered on the library steps, she thinks of "the thread of seductive chatter, promises, deceptions, of blood of the story" that she has been telling and "that prevents any true improvement in my city or in the world" (IV.Epilogue.1). Elena is dismissive of Nino, once slim and handsome and now "bloated" and "constantly celebrating himself" (IV.Epilogue.1). By contrast, she praises Pasquale's "generous ideas" even though he has spent years in prison for his politically inspired crimes against those he regarded as oppressors (IV.Epilogue.1).

I am skeptical of Elena's – and, by implication, Ferrante's – using Naples as a metonymy for the world because there is not enough dramatized evidence in the narrative to sustain this signification. For example, does the Cambridge, Massachusetts area where Elena's children live with her ex-husband deserve the ominous description as a place immune to "true improvement" unless we accept a cynical perspective of unmitigated pessimism (IV.Epilogue.1)?

In the second and final chapter of the Epilogue, a package with Elena's and Lila's childhood dolls arrives. While at first this might imply that Lila is alive and might turn up, we remember that the dolls had never been recovered since they disappeared down the grate. While it is possible that Lila, unbeknownst to Elena, managed to locate the dolls and sent them to Elena, their arrival after almost sixty years is a mysterious and uncanny event reminding us about the arbitrariness of fiction under the auspices of authorial control, although the characters in the the the fictional works have lives that matter to us.

Elena concludes: "Unlike stories, real life, when it has passed, inclines toward obscurity, not clarity" (IV.Epilogue.2). Ferrante's point is that it is impossible to really know others, to know what shapes the psyches of individuals no matter how well we think we understand their personal histories and the cultural and historical contexts that shape them. Ferrante also emphasizes that it is difficult if not impossible to find the terms to describe what we think we know. Ferrante's odyssey – dramatized through Elena's writing – is a quest to know and to put that knowledge into words, even as she is learning the impossibility of fulfilling that quest. But perhaps a final point is to call attention to the necessary legerdemain that makes fiction, fiction compelling, or perhaps that is the penultimate point, and the final point is that stories, like real life, always have an element of obscurity.

Elena and Lila's Relationship and Their Struggle for Freedom in a Patriarchal Society

By examining the various chronological phases of womanhood from childhood, adolescence, young adulthood, motherhood, maturity, and old age, Ferrante shows how hard it is for women to define themselves in a patriarchal culture where women are shaped by male cultural expectations.

Ferrante wants to stress the different kinds of accommodations that Elena and Lila make to respond to cultural and social expectations, even while allowing for their very different personalities. Looking back from the vantage point of Book Three, *Those Who Leave and Those Who Stay*, Elena thinks that she had to make "her own head masculine so that it would be accepted by the culture of men" (III.77). We realize that Elena lies to herself about her relationships with Franco, Pietro, and Nino because her desire to please men conflicts with her theoretical feminism. Nor does she fully understand how each of her major relationships with males is a somewhat crass transaction in which she trades something for something else: in Franco's case, access to experiences, money, and social position in exchange for providing sex, intellect, and companionship; in Pietro's case, social position and stability in exchange for holding the position of a wife and mother and being intellectually respectable; in Nino's case, desire, sexual excitement, and temporary relief from responsibility in exchange for taking the role of mistress. As Lila puts it to Elena: "Lies are better than tranquilizers" (IV.I.57). Of course, all relationships have a transactional component, but Elena's problem at times is a myopic lack of awareness.

On the other hand, Elena does choose with whom she sleeps, even if she is obsessed for decades with Nino. Interestingly, for all her liberal views about the fluidity of sexual identity and the homoeroticism that underlies several scenes, including Elena's preparing Lila for her wedding day, she and Lila never experiment with touching each other.

Let us further examine the source of Elena's and Lila's sexual rivalry. Both Elena and Lila leave their husbands for the same man, Nino, and in both cases they fail to understand that Nino is an adventurer without sexual ethics. Elena deeply resents that Lila as a teenager had taken Nino away from her, all the more so since Lila already had a husband. Years later, when she is having her affair with Nino, Elena still fears Lina's putative appeal to Nino. She worries when Lila is in the same room with Nino, even after Elena realizes that Nino has manipulated her and has no integrity or decency.

Elena's infatuation with Nino began as a child when he precociously announced he would marry her and she declined. Nino's allure for Elena is that he seems to combine both Apollonian and Dionysian aspects of behavior and appeals to Elena's dominant Apollonian side and her repressed but percolating Dionysian side. But in fact Nino is a predator in both his sexual and romantic needs, wanting – indeed, needing – to control the women in his life. While Elena argues for new ways of living, she becomes a traditional mistress for Nino. Contrary to her theoretical book on women and her claim that "everything is changing, we are inventing new forms of living together," she allows herself to be used by a man who keeps her in a separate apartment because he lacks the nerve or will to leave his wealthy wife (IV.I.30).

One of the attractions of Nino is that he is from her Naples neighborhood and is part of the social class to which she feels she will always belong. When Nino is staying with Elena and her husband Pietro, he becomes aggressive to Pietro in the way of the neighborhood and makes "an extremely well-educated Airota [lose] ground" (III.108). Nino's behavior stems from sexual rivalry, rivalry intensified by his frustration with the patronizing superiority and privilege that Pietro wears as armor. Sharing Nino's class resentment, Elena understands what is going on, but asks herself, why did Nino need to "hurt" and "humiliate" Pietro (III.110)? Allegedly to talk to him about how he is treating Pietro, Elena goes to Nino's bedroom; after he says (with his manipulative sense of how to get what he wants), "You've decided," she takes off her nightgown (III.110).

Rereading, it is clear that first and foremost in Elena's narrative is the love–hate relationship between Elena and Lila and how they shape one another even while infuriating one another. Even though Lila's experience is limited to Naples, and mostly to their neighborhood, Elena takes seriously Lila's visceral responses to events and her strong opinions of people. An example of Lila's raw emotions is her angry response to Marcello Solara's wearing the first shoes that she both designed and gave to her husband Stefano. Yet while feeling Lila's rage, Elena realizes that she is, by contrast, "incapable of violent reactions" (II.2).

For significant periods of time, one or the other breaks off the relationship and they do not speak to each other. We realize that even though Elena may live elsewhere she, too, is among those who stay – recalling the title of Book Three, *Those Who Leave and Those Who Stay* – because she cannot extricate herself from the customs and thinking of the poor neighborhood on the outskirts of Naples in which she was born. When she thinks that "Maybe Lila is right to want to go back," we realize that she will do the same and in fact lives for quite a few years in the apartment above Lila's while they raise their children together (III.53).

Elena often thinks of Lila as her "shadow" self. In fact, Lila is often the mirror in which Elena sees her own reflection. Not only is Elena influenced by Lila – as when she slaps a fellow university student who accuses her of theft or hits Nino when she is furious with him (I.I.23) – but she measures herself by Lila (II.84). While Enzo is proud of Lila, Pietro, Elena thinks, "appeared willing to love me only provided I continually demonstrate my nothingness" (III.83). In one interior monologue, Elena imagines Lila as a revolutionary – perhaps participating in killing Fascists – after Lila becomes a Communist firebrand; thinking of herself as accomplice, Elena worries that they have become "abstract entities" to each other, perhaps losing their former intimacy (III.87). Yet Lila and she always take each other seriously, certainly something the men in their lives rarely do. If Enzo does take Lila seriously, he doesn't understand her.

Elena fears loss of control, and Lila always carries the potential for the intrusion of the unexpected, the unknown, and the uncontrollable. Only when Elena at the age of thirty-six feels "more mature" than Lila can she "welcome her back into my life, acknowledging her fascination without suffering from it" (IV.I.44). By now, even the first-time reader knows that any intimacy that Elena has with Lila will cause pain, and living together is a recipe both for being loved in Lila's unique and sometimes peculiar, even harsh, way. When they are pregnant – Elena with Nino's child, Lila with Enzo's – Elena takes Lila to her doctor; "[W]e became girls again. ... I calm, she anxious, I likeable, she malicious" (IV.I.44).

The on and off intimate relationship between Elena and Lila is fraught with love, jealousy, anger, even hatred; sometimes they share lives, but at other times, as their lives evolve and take different turns, they withdraw. Flush with success as a journalist, Elena is angry with Lila (to whom she tells nothing about her marital difficulties): "She can't tolerate my good fortune" (III.65). Lila can deliberately wound Elena with her sometimes harsh honesty if not pure and unnecessary nastiness.

But Elena can be jealous of Lila's success. The two women are fiercely competitive. From childhood on, Lila is larger than life for Elena. In her teenage years, Lila is the center of Elena's attention. Marrying Stefano, Don Achille's son, at sixteen, Lila chooses to elevate her stature in the neighborhood and to live in economic comfort, but soon she despises her choices and her husband who has sold out to the Solaras. Lila is passionately drawn to the perpetually womanizing Nino – who never leaves Elena's sexual desire radar – with whom she has a relatively brief affair. Perhaps in part because of their competitive relationship, Elena becomes even more obsessed with Nino.

How Elena and Lila respond to the 1980 earthquake is a telling comment on their differences in adulthood. While Elena copes and is now, unlike in childhood, the more courageous, Lila has a panic/anxiety attack and feels "dissolving boundaries" (IV.I.51). Lila describes, perhaps for the only time to Elena, "the disquiet of my mind," attributing her belief that "with me love doesn't last" to this emotional turbulence. She begs Elena not to "leave me, or I'll fall in" (IV.I.52). Elena feels "stable," while Lila "perceived herself as a liquid" and "erased herself and, terrified, became nothing" (IV.I.53). Rereading we realize that Lila has major psychological problems even before her daughter disappears. As she oscillates between depression and mania, we realize that she has what might now be called bipolar psychosis.

Elena as Author

Elena's major act is telling, that is, putting an order on the disorder of life. Lila reminds Elena: "each of us narrates our life as it suits us" (III.63). Rather oddly using the male pronoun, Elena later echoes Lila: "[E]ach of us organizes memory as it suits him" (IV.II.8). Elena controls shape and boundaries – gives form to inchoate emotions and incipient disorder – by imposing order within her writing.

Elena tossed Lila's notebooks into the Arno because the notebooks challenged Elena's boundaries, her sense of security, and her belief that her life had more amplitude and depth than Lila's. More to the point, she fears Lila may be the smarter and more fully alive (II.105). But while Lila often responds emotionally and impulsively without drawing upon reason – at times behaving erratically and self-destructively – and Elena uses reason to make decisions and plot her narrative, it is soon clear that there are often reversals in this dichotomy. When raising children before Tina's disappearance, Lila often has the more mature judgment.

Using her writing in part as self-therapy, Elena tries to know herself but is only partially successful; perhaps Ferrante is implying that in terms of self-knowledge, this is the best we can do. Describing her success at the University in Pisa, Elena calls herself a "very brilliant student" (II.103); yet a few chapters later she feels "ignorant" and "inexperienced" (II.106). This ebb and flow in Elena's self-esteem and self-evaluation – although far less intense than Lila's mood swings – is very much part of Elena's psychological complexity throughout the tetralogy. Elena oscillates between self-doubt and a strong sense of self, between rational decisions in personal relations to blindly and obsessively loving a man who is a congenital womanizer and liar. She also oscillates between writing feminist theory and living as an appendage to the men in her life, and between relying on Lila to lead her and provide intellectual stimulation and submitting to an abusive relationship with her.

Elena desperately wants to leave the unrestrained emotions, verbal excess, and violence of her Naples neighborhood, but in fact even when she is away from Naples, it is part of who she is. Triggered by her intellectual and emotional curiosity, she undertakes an odyssey of experience "to learn everything about the world" that she has not known (III.9). But isn't Ferrante presenting Elena's desire to conquer knowledge ironically, as if knowing could take place without imagination and feeling and as if it were possible to fully take control of our lives? Elena feels a great range of emotions but rarely overflows verbally with the intensity of Lila or Elena's mother. At the same time, she rejects the controlled world of Pietro for the seemingly larger-than-life passions of Nino.

Lila both wants and resents Elena's success. Elena comes to believe that Lila's childhood story *The Blue Fairy* is the source of Elena's first novel: "Lila's childish pages were the secret heart of my book" (II.122). When Elena gives Lila a copy of *The Blue Fairy* at the sausage factory – where Lila is working in economically and sexually exploitive conditions – Lila throws it into the fire as if to say neither her own past nor Elena's triumphant publication matter in the hardscrabble world in which she is living (II.124).

Later, in Book Three, *Those Who Leave and Those Who Stay*, when her marriage is falling apart, Elena can't tolerate Lila's situation since Lila and Enzo are having sex, seemingly managing their lives better than she is, and finding economic success in their computer business. In addition to her failing marriage, Elena is having other difficulties. Her articles are rejected, she has post-partum depression after the 1970 birth of her first child, and is not taking care of her baby as well as she might. Furthermore, she is not keeping up her appearance. Finally, Elena is limping – fulfilling her obsessive fear that she will inherit her mother's limp – from sciatica (III.65).

Notwithstanding the device of Lila's missing notebooks, we need to remember that we see Lila through Elena's eyes and that Elena is frequently less perceptive than she thinks she is. Yet in *Those Who Leave and Those Who Stay* Ferrante makes sure we hear Lila's angry point of view. Lila tells Elena, "In the fairy tales one does as one wants, and in reality one does what one can" (III.95). What Lila is reminding Elena and the reader is that she has had a much tougher life than Elena because she stayed in Naples. Even when living outside the neighborhood in which they grew up, she never left its constraining world. By contrast, Elena, from the time she continued her education and certainly from the time she went to university, always has had one foot in another world, even if she can't completely leave behind the world in which she grew up.

Elena discovers that Lila, despite her limited education, writes well. Yet when Lila speaks, sometimes she "seemed unable to bear the order she had imposed on herself. Everything became breathless, the sentences took on an overexcited rhythm, the punctuation disappeared" (II.1). Interestingly, we realize that what Elena says about Lila's writing applies to her own narrative: "She had fixed moments that were decisive for her without worrying about anything or anyone" (II.1). Elena accuses Lila of having "appropriated me, as she did every person or thing or event or thought that touched her" (II.1). Yet perhaps the reverse is also true and it is Elena who, as she herself fears, appropriates Lila.

Isn't appropriation what Lila accuses Elena of doing to her when Elena publishes *A Friendship* and before that when Lila read what became Elena's second novel? Indeed, doesn't Elena, like many non-fiction writers, do that to all the people she puts in her books when she selects and arranges her characters and incidents, imposes her views of their significance, and gives them a shape within the form of her writing? Hasn't Elena made her reputation with an autobiographical first novel featuring her first sexual experiences with Nino's father, Donato? Elena's abusive mother feels Elena's writing about sex has disgraced the family. Isn't there a narcissism to Elena's telling about her experience and an ingenuousness about the effects of her work on those living persons she evokes? If Ferrante is implying that all first person memoirs have an element of exploitation, she may be self-consciously raising issues about the ethics of her own non-fiction.

Family relations are a crucial part of these novels. While we see a strong emphasis on Lila's relation to her parents and her brother and some attention is given to Elena's family, the major focus in the later two books is on Lila and Elena as mothers. Elena stresses the mother–child relation as seen not only through her and Lila's eyes in their roles as mothers but also to some extent through her three children – two of whom with her husband Pietro and one with Nino. Elena feels guilty when her career takes precedence over her mothering two and later three children. When she returns to Naples after leaving Pietro, she lives in the same building as Lila and they often share child-rearing. Elena's comparison of Imma, her child with Nino, with Lila's Tina when the children are both close in age – and her fear that her less precocious daughter may be retarded – is at times unpleasantly competitive but rings true. The event that sends Lila into a downward spiral from which she never recovers is Tina's disappearance.

Elena often doubts her efficacy – and indeed questions whether anyone can get at the ultimate truth – even while knowing that writing is how she makes sense of life. Elena is wary of her tendency to rely too much on realism fed by her own experience. Lila tells Elena, "[T]he disgusting face of things alone was not enough for writing a novel; without imagination it would seem not a true face but a mask" (III.75).

When Lila discovers that Stefano's mistress, Ada (the aforementioned Melina Cappuccio's daughter), is pregnant, she finally leaves him for good. She lives in very modest circumstances with Enzo, son of the fruit and vegetable man, who values her as more than a sexual toy. She works in a sausage factory where she becomes a Marxist after working in terrible conditions at a dismal salary and being sexually harassed by the owner (who has ties to the mobster family, the Solaras). Later, Enzo with her encouragement learns about computers and they develop a thriving business that challenges the Solaras's prominence in the neighborhood. Lila's metamorphosis from Marxist to capitalist strains credibility unless we see her rapid political changes as resulting from her instability, that is, as a symptom of "dissolving boundaries" when everything becomes shapeless. It is not unreasonable to see Lila's political behavior as simultaneously sincere and a function of her battling undiagnosed depression and psychosis.

Before Lila's disappearance, Elena regrets that their friendship has been cut off when in old age "we are in need of closeness and solidarity" (IV.II.53). After Elena, by now in her sixties, publishes in 2007 the successful short book entitled *A Friendship*, which includes the mysterious disappearance of Lila's child Tina, Lila, feeling betrayed by Elena's using a friend as source material, will no longer speak to her. Elena had wanted to give Lila "a form whose boundaries won't dissolve, and defeat her, and calm her, and so in turn calm myself" (IV.II.53). Ferrante makes clear that *A Friendship* also fulfills Elena's need to give herself boundaries and definition and defeat the Lila shadow within herself.

The Author in the Text, The Author as the Text

It is just as foolish to discount what we know about the author as to pretend that we can establish a one-to-one correlation between the author's life and work. Even at this late date, we need to discover a way to talk about authors (and visual artists from Picasso and Rodin to Hitchcock and Truffaut) within texts and differentiate important resonances of authors' lives from bald facts. Of course that differentiation will be a dotted line and at times a matter of degree not kind. Modern authors often self-consciously create a persona through letters, reviews of other writers, and in the last several decades interviews in the *Paris Review* and similar outlets, as well as, for the fortunate handful, their Nobel Prize addresses. Each interview, letter, or authorial intervention outside the imaginative texts becomes part of an author's textual mosaic. That mosaic creates a persona – what we might call the biographical or authorial textuality – that may inform our reading as much as an author's other works.

We cannot and should not treat authorial interviews any more than the author's letters as absolute truth. One basic rule is that letters and interviews are selections and arrangements of experience as much as fiction is. But they do become part of the biographical textuality that shadows and is shadowed by the author's creative work. That shadow text – I use that word deliberately since Elena considers Lila a shadow – has all the nuances and contradictions that we find in good biographies and in collections of an author's letters. In letters and interviews there is always a discrepancy between what happened and what the author remembers happened. The longer time passes, the further away the author gets from accurately recalling and describing events. Furthermore, there is also discrepancy between what the author remembers and what takes place in the transformative process in which the author discovers the language that he or she will use to present that memory. What I am arguing is that the textuality created by the author is as open to interpretation as the fictional texts.

Notwithstanding Ferrante's supposed anonymity, which to an extent keeps us from conflating Elena Greco with the author, the very name Elena is a textual expression suggesting parallels. Ferrante's many written interviews invite parallels between Elena Greco's narrative and Elena Ferrante's texts, whether Ferrante is a pseudonym or not. Indeed, we need to realize that the interviews create a controlled autobiographical document, a point of reference for readers, not so different from actual facts, and this biographical textuality comprised of Ferrante's own words shapes our reading once we are aware of it. If we haven't read her entire canon or most of it, the following is clarifying. "The 'I' who narrates my stories is never a voice giving a monologue. It's always a woman writing, and this writer always struggles to organize, in a text, what she knows but doesn't have clear in her mind" (Ferrante, "Art of Fiction No. 228").

We need to consider the above statement when we consider how Ferrante has dismissed the reader's wish to know about her and restricted herself to interviews and letters: "I believe that books, once they are written, have no need of their authors. If they have something to say, they will sooner or later find readers; if not, they won't."[7] Ferrante is calling attention to the biographical fallacy, namely that we equate a text with an author's life or at least use that author's life as a way of understanding her fictional texts. But as I shall argue, she herself violates her own credo by presenting a persona in her interviews and statements.

That Ferrante's narrator shares the author's pseudonymous first name pushes the reader into thinking about a seemingly narrow distance between author and narrator. Because the tetralogy often feels as if it has a strong autobiographical component, we can't be faulted if we wonder whose personal life we are reading, or if we feel at times like a voyeur peeking through a keyhole or eavesdropping on private conversation. This is the case even though Ferrante's narrator, Elena, insists that she is turning her own life experiences into fiction. Yet notwithstanding this claim, Elena's strong realistic presence and her drawing her characters from her life as well as her depiction of a recognizable Naples place the novel in the realistic novel genre and push the reader to reflect on the parallels between Elena and her creator.

Ferrante deliberately eschews the consistency that we might expect in a sustained four-volume enterprise. Contradictions and paradoxes, perhaps deriving as much from her art as from her temperament, are part of the reading experience. To be sure, novels – and especially long novels – often deconstruct their own premises by offering not only multiple perspectives on events and on characters but also on the evolving personality and character of the author. The author's reflections are often not consistent – especially in a series of novels written over a period of years – and they are not consistent in Ferrante's tetralogy.

To be sure, Ferrante steers us away from locating the author in the text:

. . . .

The four volumes of the Neapolitan novels are my story, sure, but only in the sense that I am the one who has given it the form of a novel and to have used my life experiences to inject truth into literary invention.

> If I had wanted to recount my own business, I would have established a differ-
> ent pact with the reader, I would have signaled I was writing an autobiography.
> (Jobey)
>
> ....

But we need to read with skepticism such ambiguous biographical textuality from an interview. We understand that the writer is creating her own narrative, just as her surrogate Elena creates hers, as well as realize that, in many respects, Ferrante's narrative is very close to Elena's.

Ferrante has made much of her anonymity and has taken an arch view of those requiring biographical information.

> ....
>
> Evidently, in a world where philological education has almost completely disap-
> peared, where critics are no longer attentive to style, the decision not to be present
> as an author generates ill will and this type of fantasy [that we need to know the
> extent to which the author is revealed in the text]. The experts stare at the empty
> frame where the image of the author is supposed to be and they don't have the
> technical tools, or, more simply, the true passion and sensitivity as readers, to fill
> that space with the works. So they forget that every individual work has its own
> story. Only the label of the name or a rigorous philological examination allows us
> to take for granted that the author of *Dubliners* is the same person who wrote
> *Ulysses* and *Finnegans Wake*. (Ferrante, "Art of Fiction No. 228")
>
> ....

We cannot prevent what we know about an author from becoming in our minds not merely simple facts, but a presence, a shadow text to which we as readers respond as we seek to understand the text we are reading. What Ferrante writes in letters and in transcribed interviews provides a text for what she calls a "philological examination." We ask ourselves how these so-called non-fictional words inform her fictional texts, whether they are consistent with what we are reading and whether they deflect us from conclusions or intensify our understanding.

To return to Ferrante's example, knowing something about the Ireland Joyce grew up in – although nominally part of the United Kingdom, but basically an Irish colony dominated by British control as well as Catholicism – helps us understand his work. Moreover, knowing Joyce's early fiction is helpful; *Dubliners* anticipates *Ulysses* in many ways: the cityscape, the epiphanies, the recurring characters and themes, the critique of Catholicism and British impe-rialism. We read *Ulysses* more perceptively by having in mind *Dubliners* and *A Portrait of an Artist* as well as knowing about Joyce's life. What I know of Joyce's life and bring to my reading of his fiction is biographical textuality gleaned from his letters and essays and my reading and rereading of Richard Ellmann's biography and, more recently, Kevin Birmingham's 2014 *The Most Dangerous Book: The Battle for James Joyce's Ulysses*.

Part of the authenticity of the Neapolitan novels is that Ferrante not only seems to know Naples intimately but in interviews writes as if she were claiming knowledge based on her personal experience: "Some of the poor Neapolitan neighborhoods were crowded, yes, and rowdy. To gather oneself, so to speak, was physically impossible. One learned very early to have the greatest concentration amid the greatest disruption" (Lagioia). And yet it turns out that we now learn that Ferrante did not live there after the age of three. Our knowing this makes us recognize that her fiction is more inventive and less autobiographical, but it still means that her presence is woven into the texture of every page of her work.

Ferrante has told us she is a mother, is not married, has a degree in classics, teaches and translates. Because of many similarities with Elena, we suspect that the novels are personal when they deal with the narrator's responding to rejection, motherhood, sexuality, desire, and depression, as well as with ambivalent feelings about her body; these feelings range from enjoyment of sexuality to disgust and include fear of aging and fear of replicating her mother's limp. Even without knowing all the actual biographical facts, we recognize that the author must share much of Elena's experiences. Ferrante's probing into women's experience has a depth and authenticity that would, we assume, need some basis in experience, either her own or that of someone very close to her. What she has revealed or invented about her life hovers over and informs the text we are reading.

The Concept of Authorial Textuality

I am arguing that theoretical concepts such as "exit author" or "author-function" become a canard for a contemporary writer who gives interviews and creates the text – which I have been deliberately quoting – of her own life.

But what matter for the reader as much as or more than biography, is the textuality created by an author's writings other than those of hers or his that we are reading, and that textuality includes other imagined works. Unlike the imagined world of the text which we are reading and which is limited by the words on the pages, the textuality of the author has no finite borders. With new creative texts, new letters, and new interviews, living authors can add to the text, but what matters will vary with each author and to an extent with each reader.

What is included in an author's textuality? Certainly an author's polemics such as D. H. Lawrence's *Study of Thomas Hardy*, which helps us understand *The Rainbow* and *Women in Love*, or *Studies in Classic American Literature*, which helps us understand *Sons and Lovers*. Ferrante has published a book entitled *Frantumaglia: A Writer's Journey* (2016) that includes letters, interviews, and reflections and apparently reveals some biographical details. As Ferrante puts it in her *Paris Review* interview, *frantumaglia* is a Neapolitan dialect word meaning "bits and pieces of uncertain origin which rattle around in your head not always comfortably" (Ferrante, "Art of Fiction No. 228"). Translated into English, *Frantumaglia* is the act of falling apart, a term that describes one of Ferrante's essential themes and focal points in her Neapolitan tetralogy and in *The Days of Abandonment*.

Textuality varies for each reader, but includes what we know about the period in which an author writes. To return to Ferrante, what we know about Italian post-war political and social history and the theoretical issues in European feminist thought affects our reading. Textuality may include our familiarity with the places about which an author writes. That I know Naples and can recall my own experiences there – including a day when a strike was called, every purveyor shut down out of fear of violent repercussions, and a lecture I was to give was cancelled – enables me to understand what Ferrante is describing in terms of incipient violence and the grip of the Camorra on every aspect of Neapolitan life.

Ferrante as Authorial Presence?

I want to pursue how Ferrante has in fact inserted herself within the tetralogy while pretending anonymity. On one hand, Ferrante insists that she tells us nothing about her life, even though she does present herself in interviews. But, on the other hand, she offers rather strong interpretive guides which could be understood as strictures. Let me quote again from Ferrante's 2015 *Paris Review* interview:

. . . .

Much of the story depends on the differences between Elena and Lila. These can all be traced back to the changing condition of women. Take reading and studying, for instance. Elena is extremely disciplined. She diligently takes up the tools she needs, she recounts her journey as an intellectual with a certain pride, she shows an intense engagement with the world. She also likes to emphasize that Lila has remained behind. Elena is always insisting that she has outdistanced Lila. But every so often her story breaks down and Lila appears much more active, above all more ferociously – I would say also, more viscerally – involved. But then she truly withdraws, leaving the field to her friend. What you called a difference is an oscillation innate in the relationship between the two characters and in the very structure of Elena's story. That's why women readers – men, too, I think – can identify with both women. If this oscillation were not there, the two friends would be doubles of each other, by turns they would appear as a secret voice, an image in the mirror, or something else. But it's not that way. When Lila's pace becomes unsustainable, the reader grabs onto Elena. But if Elena falls apart, then the reader relies on Lila. (Ferrante, "Art of Fiction No. 228")

. . . .

With the purpose of showing that the authorial reading provided by an author is not – to pun – necessarily an authoritative reading but one of many possible readings, I want to deconstruct her statement by providing possible alternatives to Ferrante's discussion of her own work.

(1) The differences between Elena and Lila owe much more to the differences in their psyches than to "the changing condition of women." The latter phrase has validity but has an ingredient of reductive essentialism because it does not do justice to Ferrante's complexity of characterization. My own reading experience responds to Lila's serious psychological problems; in contemporary terms, she is bipolar and has symptoms of both severe paranoia and schizophrenia.

(2) In fact, Elena and Lila do exist as secret sharers, mirroring one another, and Elena, calling Lila her "shadow," is very much aware of this. They are not exactly "doubles of each other," but they are certainly in the literary tradition of doubles (*Doppelgänger*) dating back to Dostoevsky and including *The Strange Case of Dr. Jekyll and Mr. Hyde*. Yes, we are sympathetic to both characters, but more so to Elena because it is her voice we hear, her words we read, her quest to control what she learns and how she feels, and her organization and selection to which we respond.

As I have discussed, Elena has an obsessive fascination with Lila that includes Elena's competitive relationship with Lila. Despite her superior education and recognition as an author, Elena worries that somehow Lila knows more than she does about a great many things. She admires Lila's boldness and courage in following her own feelings. She also believes that Lila's intellect and imagination are catalysts and inspirations for her own writing. While there is no sex between them, her bathing Lila on her wedding morning is suffused with eroticism.

(3) Because we respond to Elena's reading of Lila, despite Lila's "visceral" eruptions, our attention does not "oscillate." Notwithstanding the notebook device, we are focused on Elena's response to Lila much more than on Lila herself. Thus my reading experience does not conform to Ferrante's comment: "[I]f Elena falls apart, then the reader relies on Lila." I don't rely on Lila, in part because she is unreliable and unstable, but more so because Lila is not the teller. What we know, even the dialogue Elena purports to remember, is filtered

through Elena's eyes and mind. To be sure, we are aware that Elena's judgment can be myopic, foolish, and inappropriate, but usually it takes more than Lila's perspective to give us the knowledge to understand when Elena is imperceptive. To draw a circumference of judgment around Elena's limited perspective, we draw upon Elena's words – she tells us when she is depressed and when she behaves badly – as well as our sense of when she goes off the rails. (I call this the "Tell-Tale Heart Syndrome" because we know without any prompting that Poe's narrator is psychotic as soon as he begins to tell us how he killed and buried an older man under the floor boards.)

Anita Raja aka Elena Ferrante

In October 2016, Elena Ferrante's identity was revealed as Anita Raja: daughter of Golda Frieda Petzenbaum, was born in Worms, Germany into a Polish Jewish family and a Neapolitan father. As Rachel Donadio summarized in the *New York Times*:

. . . .

But as it turns out, Ms. Raja's history is very different from those of her heroines, Elena Greco and Lina Cerullo. Ms. Raja was born in Naples, but she moved to Rome at the age of 3 and grew up there. Her father was Neapolitan, but not poor – he was a magistrate. Her mother was a German Jew who fled to Italy in the 1930s to escape Nazism, and who lost most of her family to the Holocaust. ... In recent years, Ms. Raja's name and that of her husband, the novelist Domenico Starnone, have been most often mentioned as possibly being responsible for Ms. Ferrante's books because of stylistic echoes in Ms. Ferrante's work, in Mr. Starnone's novels and in Ms. Raja's translations of German novels [by Christa Wolf] whose self-aware female narrators recall those in Ms. Ferrante's books. (Donadio)[8]

. . . .

Domenico Starnone's more personal knowledge of Naples may be an important source for the Neapolitan novels.

Some are angered that we know something more about Ferrante, but we already knew a good deal even if she has told us not to take everything she says about herself seriously. (Indeed, even that statement is part of the textuality she has created.) Alexandra Schwartz has objected:

. . . .

To fall in love with a book, in that way that I and so many others have fallen in love with Ferrante's, is to feel a special kinship with its author, a profound sort of mutual receptivity and comprehension. The author knows nothing about you, and yet you feel that your most intimate self has been understood. The fact that Ferrante has chosen to be anonymous has become part of this contract, and has put readers and writer on a rare, equal plane. Ferrante doesn't know the details of our lives, and doesn't care to. We don't know those of hers. We meet on an imaginative neutral ground, open to all. (Schwartz)[9]

. . . .

We already have a Ferrante-text, one she invented for us, and this and subsequent revelations will make us better readers of her novels.

Now that Ferrante's identity has been revealed as Anita Raja, we can begin to see if what we now know about her – and we will undoubtedly learn more in the future – will further shape our understanding of her fiction and even nonfiction. We need to seriously consider why Ferrante is so defensive about revealing who she is and why she never returns to the history of her mother's family.

Through emails, interviews, and essays Ferrante has created a biographical text that is based on her thoughts and opinions more than on the actual facts of her life. Because the *Paris Review* interview was conducted by Sandro and Sandra Ferri, the husband and wife who own Edizioni E/O, Ferrante's publisher, and they obviously know her identity, we can say that they contribute to the Ferrante-textuality. Or put another way, they have abetted Ferrante's creating the persona of her author. Is this creation so different from Ferrante's creating Elena, her narrator-protagonist?

With this new information about Ferrante's identity, the textuality of Ferrante's life changes. Now we need to ask whether it matters that Raja's mother was someone who avoided the Holocaust by escaping to Italy but lost family members in the Holocaust, and whether Ferrante's rage at poverty, abuse, bullying, and violence in Naples has to do with stories of the Holocaust that she heard from her mother.[10] While it is surely impossible to claim that there are no traces of Anita Raja's personal history in Elena Ferrante's fiction, nonetheless we can only speculate about how much her mother's life informs her fiction without having further information. That Ferrante tells of the Neapolitan poor, of post-war Italy, and of social, political, and male oppression reveals a great deal about her own concerns.

Moreover, one of the major points within her novels is how we are shaped by our parents and the world in which they grew up. Thus we cannot ignore her mother's past any more than we should ignore Ferrante's marriage to a man who knows Naples. The mindless violence and senseless murders in Raja's Naples which might also reflect stories that Raja's mother told her about foreign Jews – her mother had arrived from Germany in 1937 – placed by Mussolini's regime in internment camps as helpless victims of Fascism. After the war her mother lived in Naples for eleven years, but at the age of three the family left for Rome.

Rereading, we realize that Elena has intermittently tried to eliminate traces of her past by relocating to Pisa, Florence, and now Turin, and leaving the dialect and often the customs and manners of her Naples neighborhood behind. And so, we have learned, has Anita Raja, the creator of the pseudonymous Elena Ferrante and Raja's surrogate, left much behind in the public persona she has presented as Ferrante in her interviews and correspondence. Like her created character Lila, does not Raja want "to eliminate the entire life that she had left behind" (I.Prologue.3)?

Thus, the revelation of Ferrante's identity and her prior insistence on anonymity open the door to a larger discussion about the meaning of "Exit author," that is, the belief that we should study the text created by the author and not the author. My mantra has been, "Always the text; always historicize," and historicizing means knowing as much about the author and the culture in which she wrote as possible. As with all historicizing, we need to make judgments about which contexts are most relevant.

Let me return not to Anita Raja's family but to a prominent literary scholar who lived through World War II and knew that Jews were being deported from Belgium at that time. Does it matter that Paul de Man, who argued for the irrelevance of authors, had disguised his Nazi or at least collaborationist past after arriving in the United States? Do we read him differently because of that and is it wrong to do so? Here we have an example where an author assiduously creates a biographical textuality – in this case a new identity and a theory of literature which renders authors' lives irrelevant – to replace the original textuality of his life and writings. But perhaps his original texts are a kind of pentimento that peeks through his text when we know about his life. And maybe we should be looking at what peeks through in the Ferrante texts when we know that had her mother not moved to Italy, she would have probably been among the Nazis's victims.

Rather ironically, in view of the de Man narrative, authenticity is a value in Holocaust texts and most of us feel dismay when someone appropriates the identity of survivor and victim, as was the case of Bruno Dossekker who, under the name Benjamin Wilkomirski, in 1995 published *Fragments: Memories of a Wartime Childhood*, which turned out to be a fraud.

I might conclude this discussion with a whimsical joke to stress how Ferrante's persona has become part of the text. Think for a minute how discovery of the Shakespeare interviews with a noted dramaturge of the early seventeenth century have modified our understanding of *Hamlet*, *Macbeth*, and *King Lear*. Oops, there are no such documents to add to and modify how we read Shakespeare. But we can be relatively sure future revelations and interviews, including those about the life Ferrante has suppressed, will modify the textuality of Ferrante's life. Undoubtedly, new evidence will further discussion of the relationship between her life and work and illuminate her fiction.

My Reservations

While I have some reservations, I do not believe that these seriously undermine Ferrante's achievement.

In the tradition of Zola's naturalism, Ferrante sometimes seems to believe in a positivistic grammar of motives, in which children inevitably inherit qualities of their parents. Like his father Donato Sarratore, who molests Elena and later is her first lover, Nino is a compulsive womanizer without sexual ethics. The other strand of positivism, recalling Zola's naturalism, is that social environment plays a very large part in determining who the characters are, whether they be Lila or Pietro.

Ferrante frequently calls attention to the characters speaking in Neapolitan dialect rather than standard Italian but the translation does not make the distinction and, according to Ann Goldstein, neither does Ferrante:

> The obvious reason Ferrante doesn't use dialect is because many Italians wouldn't understand it. But a second reason may be that, as an Italian professor at CUNY was saying, Neapolitan dialect is very much a spoken language, and if she [Ferrante] were writing it, there would be no point, in a way. It would lose the character that it has as a spoken language. (Dotson, "The Face of Ferrante")[11]

But, in response to Goldstein, we might recall that Mark Twain successfully renders Huck Finn's character by means of his speaking in dialect.

Another problem is the convoluted plot whose frenzy of coincidences challenges plausibility and sometimes reminds us of soap operas. At times, the changing of partners among principal and secondary neighborhood characters seems to be sexual musical chairs or sexual roulette.

I am also on occasion puzzled as to why Elena includes direct quotes sometimes and not others – see, for example, IV.I.4–7 – since the narrator would have been hard-pressed to remember the exact words spoken in sustained conversation in what purports to be her own memoir. Either Elena should wear the mantle of uber-memory or not.

Finally, the exhaustive references and the allusions do not create a consistent pattern of meaning that gives breadth to our understanding of characters, unlike the way that the *Odyssey* gives shape, form, meaning, and significance to Joyce's *Ulysses*. Moreover, at times I feel a disconnect between the attempt at theorizing and the narrative. Do we really learn how feminist theory informs Elena's feminist tract?

But notwithstanding my reservations, I still consider the Neapolitan tetralogy an extraordinary achievement that presents in depth an entire subculture, while being attentive to major developments in cultural, political, and intellectual history in Italy over a sixty-year period.

Study Questions for Ferrante's Neapolitan Tetralogy

1. Who is "My Brilliant Friend?" Does the title apply to Nino and, if so, is that inclusion ironic?
2. How are Lila and Elena doubles? Is Lila bipolar?
3. How is Naples a central character rather than merely the setting? In what ways is the culture of Naples under powerful and angry indictment?
4. How does Elena find her own voice and how does she on occasion lose it?
5. Is your response to Elena and Lila's struggles diluted by the tetralogy's violence? What forms does that violence take?
6. How is Elena justified in seeing Naples as a metaphor for Italy and the world? Or is her perspective on occasion both reductive and hyperbolic?
7. How does the rhetoric of sequels shape our response to the novels? In other words, does the reading of each subsequent novel invite us to reinterpret (and reread) the preceding ones in the sequence?
8. How do Elena and Lila respond to the strong patriarchal culture of Naples?
9. Should we be troubled to learn that Ferrante apparently only lived in Naples when she was a very small child? Is this cultural appropriation? Should authors only write about their own experience?
10. In what way does the tetralogy fulfill its epic aspirations? In what ways does it not?

Notes

1. Letter, Aug. 16, 1849, in Elizabeth Gaskell, *The Life of Charlotte Brontë* (New York: Penguin, 1998 [orig. ed. 1857]), 396.
2. Numbers in the text refer to the the tetralogy volume (I–IV) and chapter numbers. (As my numbering makes clear Vol. IV has two parts): Elena Ferrante, *My Brilliant Friend*, trans. Ann Goldstein (New York: Europa Editions, 2012); *The Story of a New Name*, trans. Ann Goldstein (New York: Europa Editions, 2013); *Those Who Leave and Those Who Stay*, trans. Ann Goldstein (New York: Europa Editions, 2014); *The Story of the Lost Child*, trans. Ann Goldstein (New York: Europa Editions, 2015).
3. Nicola Lagioia, "'Writing is An Act of Pride': A Conversation with Elena Ferrante," *The New Yorker* (May 19, 2016); https://www.newyorker.com/books/page-turner/writing-is-an-act-of-pride-a-conversation-with-elena-ferrante
4. Elena Ferrante, "Art of Fiction No. 228." Interview by Sandro and Sandra Ferri. *Paris Review* 212 (Spring 2015); https://www.theparisreview.org/interviews/6370/elena-ferrante-art-of-fiction-no-228-elena-ferrante
5. Page references are from Elena Ferrante, *The Days of Abandonment*, trans. Ann Goldstein (New York: Europa Editions, 2005).
6. Liz Jobey, "Women of 2015: Elena Ferrante, Writer." Interview. Trans. Daniela Petracco. *Financial Times* (Dec. 11, 2015); https://www.ft.com/content/1f019b5c-9d18-11e5-b45d-4812f209f861?mhq5j=e2

7. Quoted in James Wood, "Women on the Verge: The Fiction of Elena Ferrante," *The New Yorker* (Jan. 21, 2013); http://www.newyorker.com/magazine/2013/01/21/ women-on-the-verge

8. Rachel Donadio, "Who Is the Real Elena Ferrante? Italian Journalist Reveals His Answer," *New York Times* (Oct. 2, 2016); http://www.nytimes.com/2016/10/03/ books/elena-ferrante-anita-raja-domenico-starnone.html

9. Alexandra Schwartz, "The 'Unmasking' of Elena Ferrante," *The New Yorker* (Oct. 3, 2016); http://www.newyorker.com/culture/cultural-comment/the-unmasking-of-elena-ferrante

10. Claudio Gatti, "The Story Behind a Name," *NYR Daily* (Oct. 10, 2016); http://www. nybooks.com/daily/2016/10/02/story-behind-a-name-elena-ferrante/

11. Katrina Dotson, "The Face of Ferrante." Interview with Ann Goldstein. *Guernica* (Jan. 15, 2016); https://www.guernicamag.com/interviews/the-face-of-ferrante/

Index

Note: Page numbers in **bold** refer to illustrations.

Reading the Modern European Novel Since 1900: A Critical Study of Major Fiction from Proust's
Swann's Way *to Ferrante's Neapolitan Tetralogy*, First Edition. Daniel R. Schwarz.
© 2018 John Wiley & Sons Ltd. Published 2018 by John Wiley & Sons Ltd.